£20.99

Contested Landscapes

D1388787

Contested Landscapes:

Movement, Exile and Place

Edited by
Barbara Bender and Margot Winer

Oxford • New York

First published in 2001 by
Berg
Editorial offices:
150 Cowley Road, Oxford, OX4 1JJ, UK
838 Broadway, Third Floor, New York, NY 10003-4812, USA

Berg is an imprint of Oxford International Publishers Ltd.

Library of Congress Cataloging-in-Publication Data
A catalogue record for this book is available from the Library of Congress.

British Library Cataloguing-in-Publication Data
A catalogue record for this book is available from the British Library.

ISBN 1 85973 462 6 (Cloth)
1 85973 467 7 (Paper)

Typeset by JS Typesetting, Wellingborough, Northants
Printed in the United Kingdom by Biddles Ltd, Guildford and King's Lynn

We dedicate this volume to
people-on-the-move
for whom landscapes are never
a taken-for-granted and are
often a source of pain . . .

Contents

Acknowledgements   xi

List of Contributors   xiii

List of Illustrations   xv

Introduction
Barbara Bender   1

Part I Contested Landscapes

1   The Shadow of the Sacred Rock: Contrasting Discourses of Place
under the Acropolis
Roxane Caftanzoglou   21

2   Matter and Memory in the Landscapes of Conflict: The Western
Front 1914–1999
Nicholas J. Saunders   37

3   Contested Landscapes in Inner Mongolia: Walls and Cairns
Caroline Humphrey   55

4   Negotiating the River: Cultural Tributaries in Far North Queensland
Veronica Strang   69

5   Crannogs: Places of Resistance in the Contested Landscapes of
Early Modern Ireland
Aidan O'Sullivan   87

6   Landscapes of Punishment and Resistance: A Female Convict
Settlement in Tasmania, Australia
Eleanor Conlin Casella   103

Contents

7   Cultural Keepers, Cultural Brokers: The Landscape of Women and Children – A Case Study of the Town Dahab in South Sinai
Heba Aziz   121

8   Whose New Forest? Making Place on the Urban/Rural Fringe
Andrew Garner   133

9   The Political Economy of Landscape: Conflict and Value in a Prehistoric Landscape in the Republic of Ireland – Ways of Telling
Maggie Ronayne   149

10   Bringing Contemporary Baggage to Neolithic Landscapes
Gabriel Cooney   165

Comments on Part I: Intersecting Landscapes   181
Julian Thomas

Responses to Julian Thomas's Comments
Veronica Strang Replies   189
Eleanor Conlin Casella Replies   190
Roxane Caftanzoglou Replies   191
Maggie Ronayne Replies   192

Part II Landscapes of Movement and Exile

11   Landscape and Commerce: Creating Contexts for the Exercise of Power
Penelope Harvey   197

12   Pilgrimage and Politics in the Desert of Rajasthan
Marzia Balzani   211

13   Landscapes of Separation: Reflections on the Symbolism of By-pass Roads in Palestine
Tom Selwyn   225

14   Rites of Passage: Travel and the Materiality of Vision at the Cape of Good Hope
Jessica Dubow   241

Contents

15   Landscapes, Fear and Land Loss on the Nineteenth-Century South
African Colonial Frontier
Margot Winer   257

16   Places of Longing and Belonging: Memories of the Group Area
Proclamation of a South African Fishing Village
Anna Bohlin   273

17   Homes and Exiles: Owambo Women's Literature
Margie Orford and *Heike Becker*   289

18   Egypt: Constructed Exiles of the Imagination
Beverley Butler   303

19   Migration, Exile and Landscapes of the Imagination
Andrew Dawson and *Mark Johnson*   319

20   Hunting Down Home: Reflections on Homeland and the Search for
Identity in the Scottish Diaspora
Paul Basu   333

Comments on Part II: Far From Home
Nick Shepherd   349

Responses to Nick Shepherd's Comments   359
Anna Bohlin Replies   359
Beverley Butler Replies   359
Jessica Dubow Replies   360
Marzia Balzani Replies   361
Mark Johnson Replies   362

Index   363

Acknowledgements

We would like to thank the organizers of the World Archaeological Congress held in Cape Town, South Africa, for bringing us all together and for creating a social and political ambience totally conducive to meeting many very different people, and to talking through the day and long into the night.

We would like to thank all the contributors to this volume. They were enthusiastic about the project, patient with our editorial requests, and tolerant of our procrastinations.

We would like to thank our two commentators, Julian Thomas and Nick Shepherd, for allowing the discussion to move out from the chapters, for asking questions, and for making it obvious that what we do is always, just like landscape, 'on the move'.

And, finally, we would like to thank Kathryn Earle of Berg Publishers for having – right from the beginning – great faith in us, and for knowing when it was right to lean on us, and when it was right to hold back.

List of Contributors

Heba Aziz, Researcher and Lecturer, University of Alexandria, Egypt, and University of Surrey Roehampton, UK

Marzia Balzani, Senior Lecturer in Social Anthropology, University of Surrey Roehampton, UK

Paul Basu, PhD candidate, Department of Anthropology, University College London, UK

Barbara Bender, Professor of Heritage Anthropology, Department of Anthropology, University College London, UK

Anna Bohlin, PhD candidate, Department of Social Anthropology, Göteborg University, Sweden

Beverley Butler, Lecturer in Cultural Heritage and Museum Studies, Institute of Archaeology, University College London, UK

Roxane Caftanzoglou, Social Anthropologist and Researcher at the Institute of Urban and Rural Sociology of the National Centre for Social Research, Athens, Greece

Eleanor Conlin Casella, Lecturer in Colonial Archaeology, School of Art History and Archaeology, University of Manchester, UK

Gabriel Cooney, Professor of Archaeology, Department of Archaeology, University College Dublin, Republic of Ireland

Jessica Dubow, Cultural Geographer, Department of Geography, Royal Holloway College, University of London, UK

Andrew Garner, PhD candidate, Department of Anthropology, University College London, UK

List of Contributors

Penelope Harvey, Professor of Social Anthropology, Department of Social Anthropology, Manchester, UK

Caroline Humphrey, Professor of Asian Anthropology, Department of Social Anthropology, University of Cambridge, UK

Andrew Dawson and Mark Johnson, lecturers in Social Anthropology, Department of Social Anthropology, University of Hull, UK

Margie Orford, Independent Scholar, Namibia, and Fulbright Scholar, Department of Comparative Literature, Graduate Centre, City University of New York, USA

Aidan O'Sullivan, Lecturer, Department of Archaeology, University College Dublin, Republic of Ireland

Maggie Ronayne, Lecturer in Archaeology, Department of Archaeology, National University of Ireland, Galway, Republic of Ireland

Nicholas Saunders, British Academy Institutional Fellow, Department of Anthropology, University College London, UK

Tom Selwyn, Professor of the Anthropology of Tourism, University of North London, UK

Nick Shepherd, Postgraduate Programme Convenor, Centre for African Studies, University of Cape Town, SA

Veronica Strang, Senior Lecturer, Department of Anthropology, University of Wales, Lampeter, UK

Julian Thomas, Professor of Archaeology, School of Art History and Archaeology, Manchester University, UK

Guy Tillim, Independent photographer, Cape Town, SA

Margot Winer, Associate Professor, Department of Anthropology and Sociology, Saint Mary's College of California, USA, and Honorary Research Associate, Department of Archaeology, University of Cape Town, SA

List of Illustrations and Tables

1.1   Traces of houses built against the rock (photo: R. Caftanzoglou)   26

1.2   The Anafiotika 1999 (photo: R. Čaftanzoglou)   28

2.1   Cratered devastation in the Ypres Salient, 7 June 1917 (photo courtesy of the Imperial War Museum, London, No. Q64641)   41

2.2   The Cloth Hill at Ypres (Ieper), Belgium, August 1998 (photo: N.J. Saunders)   43

2.3   The Menin Gate Memorial to the Missing at Ypres (Ieper), Belgium, August 1998 (photo N.J. Saunders)   44

2.4   Excavations at Beecham Farm, near Passchendaele in the Ypres Salient, Belgium, August 1999 (photo Johan Vandewalle, copyright Association for Battlefield Archaeology in Flanders, Zonnebeke)   48

3.1   Sketch map of the environs of Mergen Monastery, Inner Mongolia   56

3.2   A temple inside Mergen Monastery (photo: B. Zhimbier)   57

4.1   Fishing for yabbies near the Mitchell River (photo: V. Strang)   72

4.2   Negotiating the Mitchell River (photo: V. Strang)   73

4.3   Bull catching at Rutland Plains Station (photo: V. Strang)   74

4.4   Red Dome Gold Mine (photo: V. Strang)   79

5.1   Richard Bartlett's map 'attack on a crannog' (National Library of Ireland   92

5.2   Richard Bartlett's map 'Monaghan' (National Library of Ireland)   93

5.3   Richard Bartlett's map 'attack on a crannog, Dungannon and Tullahoge' (National Library of Ireland)   94

6.1   Site surface plan of the Ross Female Factory, Van Diemen's Land.   105

6.2   Table of button typology   112

6.3   Table of distribution and frequency of button assemblage   114

6.4   Table of distribution of illicit objects   116

7.1   Sketch map showing the movement of Bedouin men, women, children and tourists across the landscape   122

7.2   Bedouin children weaving friendship bracelets on the Beach   128

8.1   'New Forest Pony': cover of the Ordnance Survey map, Outdoor Leisure 22, 1996   137

8.2   'Bucklers Hard': cover of the Ordnance Survey map, Outdoor Leisure 22, 1992   138

9.1   Traces of the Neolithic at the Bend of the Boyne (after Shee Twohig 1981, permission of Ordnance Survey Ireland; and after Stout 1993, permission of the Geographical Society of Ireland)   150

9.2   *Brú na Bóinne*/Newgrange: The making of a timeless archaeological landscape (bottom right insert copyright Brady, Shipman and Martin 1996)   151

9.3   *Brú na Bóinne* or Newgrange?   155

11.1   Chewing coca beside the clay miniatures of two-storey houses, a record player with loud speaker and a motor bike   201

11.2   Market day in the main square of Ocongate   208

13.1   Slicing through hills in the West Bank   227

13.2   Road building through farmland   228

14.1   Thomas Baines: 1847 *Southeaster in Table Bay*   244

14.2   Thomas Baines: 1847 *The Curlew off Cape Point*   247

14.3   Thomas Baines: 1852 *Klaas Smit's Drift – Waggon broke down, crossing the drift*   251

15.1   Four phases of colonial domestic architecture in Salem   262

16.1   Map of the Cape Peninsula. (after Delport 1991)   277

16.2   The fisherman's flats overlooking Kalk Bay   279

18.1   'Plato's Obelisk', 'Old' Heliopolis, Cairo   309

19.1   Hein and Tuan pose in the 'traditional' Hue restaurant which Hein runs.   326

20.1   'I was very moved during our visit to Culloden. . .'   339

20.2   'I certainly saw my visit to the now empty Isle of Pabbay as returning to my native land. . .'   341

20.3   Relics   345

Cuito: An Angolan Town

In November this year Angola celebrated its 26th year of independence from Portugal. But the date also marked a less auspicious, unacknowledged milestone – it was the 26th year of the Angolan civil war.

This is in a country that produces more barrels of crude oil a day than Kuwait, in fact, only six countries in the world produce more. But the wells may as well be dry for all the good they do most of the country's 12 million people. The civil war sops up most of the windfall, and corruption eats away at much of what remains, leaving the population with nothing. No where is this more evident than in Cuito.

The city of Cuito, the provincial capital of the central province of Bie, has suffered appallingly during this war. It was devastated by a nine month siege by UNITA rebel forces (fighting the MPLA government), and it is estimated that 15,000 people died during that time, either from the direct effects of the war or indirectly through starvation and related diseases. For six months the frontline ran through the centre of town.

For four months, at the end of 1998 and beginning of 1999, UNITA again shelled the town daily before they were pushed back. Not a single dwelling or building remains unscathed by the war, and for the moment, in relative calm the residents are moving back into their houses. Refugees from fighting in the surrounding countryside have moved into other buildings such as former Ministry of Education, Ministry of Finance and the Central Bank.

1. UNITA leader Jonas Savimbi's former residence in Cuito. His headquarters were in Kuito until 1993, when fighting in the town after the 1992 election forced him to move south. Now inhabited by residents of the town whose houses were destroyed. © Guy Tillim.

2. Duststorm. © Guy Tillim.

3. An MPLA government army helicopter flies over Cuito. Fighting in the surrounds has resulted in a 150,000 refugee population that is sustained and fed by the World Food programme. © Guy Tillim.

4. Former Bishop of Cuito's residence in central Kuito, now inhabited by refugees. © Guy Tillim.

5. The former Ministry of Education, inhabited by refugees from the countryside. A boy climbs through a hole in roof made by artillery shells. The town was shelled for four months in 1999. © Guy Tillim.

6. Refugees live in the former Ministry of Finance. The walls were reclad in the period 1994–98, but refurbishments were abandoned in 1999 when UNITA shelled the town. © Guy Tillim.

7. Residents employed by the MPLA government administration clip bushes at Liberation Square, in the centre of town, in front of the former Central Bank.

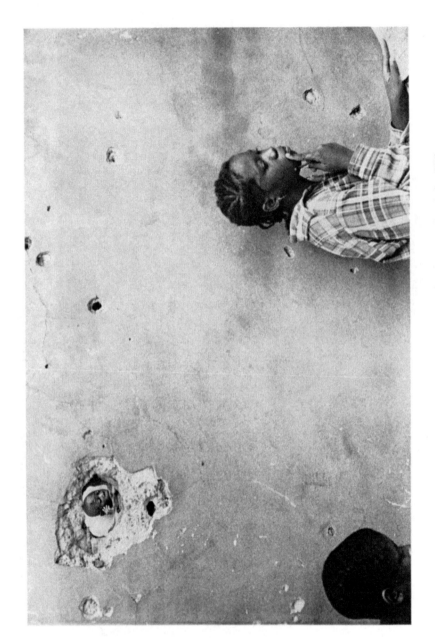

8. A high school in central Cuito. Roofless, and shattered by gunfire. © Guy Tillim.

9. An amputee's grave. © Guy Tillim.

10. Avenida Joaquim Kapanga, the main street in Cuito. Young boys plays with trucks they have made out of scrap tin. © Guy Tillim.

Introduction

Barbara Bender

Many of the chapters in this volume were first presented in a Landscape session at the World Archaeological Congress held in Cape Town, South Africa, in early 1999. This was no ordinary conference, for in some sense the World Archaeological Congress was 'coming home'. WAC's turbulent biography began in 1986 when it split from the IUPPS[1]. The main issue was the banning – at the request of the African National Congress – of all South African delegates to the international conference held in Southampton, England. The decision was not an easy one. There were fierce divisions between those (mainly North American) who felt that knowledge should be made available to all, that scholars and scholarship must be allowed to move freely, and who said – with some justification – 'If South Africa, then why not all the other countries with repressive regimes?' and those who felt that intellectual endeavours were always politically situated, always reflexive, and that there were times and places when academics had to take a stand (Ucko 1987). WAC had been one of the few academic organizations to respond to the ANC and now, in 1999, WAC was being welcomed to Cape Town. There was a great sense of celebration and, for those of us who had never been to South Africa, of wonderment.

When Margot Winer and I decided to put together a Landscape session it seemed obvious that it had to resonate to the time and place – had to be responsive to the urgency of contemporary developments – not just in South Africa, but worldwide. It seemed important to grapple with the politics of landscape, to try to understand how people in a turbulent world create a sense of place and belonging, loss or negation. It seemed right to ask people to talk about contested landscapes, and about landscapes of movement, migration, exile and home-coming.

What we had not expected was the way in which the chapters presented and the vivid discussions that ensued were, over and over again, drawn into or pitted against our sense of the place we were at, the landscapes that we glimpsed. The classical façade of the university, perched high on the hillside 'looking over' the landscape, with the long, grand flight of steps that funnelled the delegates up to the great hall, and the wide promenade for the sauntering scholar, held within its bricks and mortar the story of the production and consumption of particular kinds

---

1. International Union of Pre- and Protohistoric Sciences.

of knowledge during the colonial period, under apartheid, and now in the 'new dispensation'. What, within this space of legitimation, with its architectural references back to classical learning, could/can be said – or not said? Who was/is allowed to hear it and partake? Where in time and space was/is the heartache of those rejected? And where were/are the times and places of silences, abstentions, acts of cowardice or resistance? Where, too, were/are the other 'silent' landscapes, the places and spaces – the paths and back-doors – of those who serviced (still service) the university community? How do their daily routines circumnavigate those of the formally acknowledged 'inhabitants' of this place? And how should one infer the invisible lines that link this place of high learning to other intellectual centres, and to places of governance and commerce?

Up on the hillside we were the 'intellectual community'. Down on the seafront or the upper (grander) slopes of the town, we were the tourists. We fed into and sustained new social and spatial divisions that were visibly tensioned. The hotels we lived in, with their fine swimming pools, bougainvillea and palm trees, were grilled and portcullised against 'the intruder'. During our stay the bustle of the sanitized seafront was disrupted by bombs. And as we took our 'guilt-tours' around the city to District 6, the Black townships, or Robben Island, the complexity of landscape, the commoditization of a brutal heritage, the ambiguity of our own placement, created a strong sense of dis-ease. But also, sometimes, of exhilaration and hope. District 6, once an impoverished but mixed and vibrant community, is now a wasteland. It was destroyed in the 1960s under the Group Area Act (Hall in press). The streets were torn up as part of an erasure of memory – although, sometimes, in the heat of summer, their outlines surface as shadows on aerial photographs. But the authorities dared not destroy the churches and they remain, empty perhaps but still markers for those who remember. And they dared not, in the bitter aftermath of the destruction, rebuild, and so the desolation serves to commemorate. And in the small museum – in the church opposite the police station in which people were tortured – are the old street signs, almost miraculously preserved by the man on the bulldozer who, feeling some unease at the destruction, stashed them away for decades. They are there, and they trigger the memories of the people who come back from the townships to mark their place on the map that covers the floor, lovingly adding their names to a house-lot or filling in a missing alleyway or street corner. More concretely, they play their part in recent demands for restoral of property or restitution.

I could go on, but this is thin history, thin understanding, just enough to shake any lingering complacency and to make all of us feel, as we filed back into the seminar room, that the study of landscape is much more than an academic exercise – it *is* about the complexity of people's lives, historical contingency, contestation, motion and change.

There are still those who would like to reserve the word 'landscape' for a particular, elitist way of seeing, an imposing/imposed 'viewpoint' that emerged alongside, and as part of, the development of mercantile capital in Western Europe. But this is just one sort of landscape which, even for those who enjoyed 'a fine prospect', was partaken of in very different ways depending on finely graded and gendered subtleties of class (Williams 1973; Daniels and Cosgrove 1993). Moreover, this class-driven 'view-point' suppresses the landscapes of those 'being viewed' or 'out of sight'. It ignores the labour that has gone into landscape and obscures the relationships *between* landscapes – the connections, for example, between factory or plantation landscapes and secluded English country houses and landscaped gardens (Said 1989). If, instead of this narrow definition, we broaden the idea of landscape and understand it to be the way in which people – all people – understand and engage with the material world around them, and if we recognize that people's being-in-the-world is always historically and spatially contingent, it becomes clear that landscapes are always in process, potentially conflicted, untidy and uneasy (Bender 1993; 1998: 25-38).

The Western-elitist-notion of landscape also creates a sense of things being 'in place'. The emphasis is on a visual 'scape in which the observer *stands back* from the thing observed. But, even within this limited understanding of landscape, stasis is an illusion. Whether painting or view, movement is required before the correct vantage point is achieved. And even when the body is stationary, the eye moves from foreground to background and back again. More importantly, as we have just seen, these 'static' landscapes are the precipitate of movement – of people, labour and capital – between town and country, between colony or factory and home county. Even in these formal landscapes, we can recognize the density and complexity of landscapes-in-movement.

The chapters presented at the WAC session, and those commissioned after the event,[2] are very varied, but they have in common this notion of landscape as tensioned, always in movement, always in the making. The division we have made in this volume between Contested Landscapes and Landscapes of Movement and Exile is a matter of emphasis rather than of sharp distinction. We have asked Julian Thomas (England) to comment on the chapters in the Contested section, and Nick Shepherd (South Africa) to comment on those in the Landscapes of Movement and Exile. We asked them to pose questions to which the people who wrote the chapters could respond. We wanted the book, like the landscapes we talk about, to be both open-ended and untidy.

Because we have the Commentaries, I have not spend time on the individual chapters but have instead elaborated some ideas about contested landscapes and landscapes-on-the-move.

2. Fourteen of the chapters were written for the Landscape session, six after the event.

Barbara Bender

Contested Landscapes: Landscapes of Movement and Exile

It is through our experience and understanding that we engage with the materiality of the world. These encounters are subjective, predicated on our *being in* and learning *how to go on* in the world. The process by which we make landscapes is never pre-ordained because our perceptions and reactions, though they are spatially and historically specific, are unpredictable, contradictory, full of small resistances and renegotiations. We make time and place, just as we are made by them.

Depending on who we are (gender, status, ethnicity and so on) and the biographical moment, we understand and engage with the world (real and imagined) in different ways. Which bit of ourselves we bring to the encounter also depends upon the context. And as neither place nor context nor self stays put, things are always in movement, always becoming. So there are bound to be frictions and these are mediated in ways that range from well-worn daily practices and rituals that contain the friction, to covert or violent coercion in which certain 'viewpoints' are legitimated, while others are marginalized or criminalized. The political and economic playing fields are rarely level, and the goalposts move.

Attempts to enforce a particular viewpoint and to 'other' – and thereby contain – the other take many forms and deploy many different technologies. There will be laws that frame difference and exclusion (Stewart 1995; Bohlin in Chapter Sixteen of this volume); maps whose seeming neutrality mask the work of suppression and suggestion (Harley 1992; O'Sullivan in Chapter Five); transport systems that spearhead colonization and policing, slicing through and bisecting the landscape (Selwyn in Chapter Thirteen); architecture that creates a hierarchy of places and strives to control (Casella in Chapter Six); signposts that change direction, or renamings that usher in forgetfulness of earlier meanings and ways of doing things (Ronayne in Chapter Nine).

Landscapes contain the traces of past activities, and people select the stories they tell, the memories and histories they evoke, the interpretative narratives that they weave, to further their activities in the present-future (Cooney in Chapter Ten; Garner in Chapter Eight).

> . . . Memory is not the true record of past events but a kind of text which is worked upon in the creation of meaning. Identities are continually crafted and recrafted out of memory, rather than being fixed by the 'real' course of past events . . . (Thomas 1996).

Some pasts are more audible than others:

> . . . the names of propertied men overwrite the presence of unnamed others – not-male, not-white, or simply 'not-us' – in the landscape of memory (Steedly 1993: 28).

Within nation states, history and heritage tell powerful stories, often ones that stress stability, roots, boundaries and belonging. We need to be alert to whose stories are being told, and to be aware that they naturalize particular sorts of social relations (Caftanzoglou in Chapter One; Strang in Chapter Four; Bender in press).

Silent voices can become more audible (Saunders in Chapter Two; Caftanzoglou in Chapter One).[3] But again, we need to be wary of romanticizing these voices – of turning them into victims, dissenters, purveyors of radical alternatives (Massey 2000). There is as much variety, as much potential for good and evil, for suppression and omission, among those 'without history' as among those whose history is trumpeted (Bohlin Chapter Sixteen).

Tensioned landscapes-in-movement occur at every scale, from the global to the most personal. From macro to micro and vice versa the different scales are indissolubly linked (Giddens 1985).

In this Introduction, I want to approach these landscapes-in-movement from two directions.[4] On the one hand, thinking about close-grained phenomenological studies of people in place and emphasizing the importance of movement; and, on the other, looking at the more sweeping studies of contemporary movement and emphasizing the importance of landscape. The first moves from micro to macro, the second reverses the order.

From Micro to Macro

Recent phenomenological approaches focus on a being-in-the-world attachment to place and landscape (Tilley 1994; Gow 1995; Ingold 1993). By moving along familiar paths, winding memories and stories around places, people create a sense of self and belonging. Sight, sound, smell and touch are all involved, mind and body inseparable. Often, in these studies, experience is conceived of as a sort of 'stock-taking' at points along the way, but it would be more accurate to think in terms of what Ingold (2000, citing Gibson) calls 'ambulatory vision' or, better still, 'ambulatory encounters'. As people go about their business, things unfold along the way, come in and out of focus, change shape and take on new meanings. 'Horizons, since they are relative to place and move as people move, do not cut the land into pieces. Hence they mark the limits of perception, but they do not enclose . . .' (Ingold 1997).

3. In the 'great house' at Strokestown, Co. Roscommon, for example, the story of the assassination of the Anglo-Irish landowner during the Irish famine is told from seven different 'viewpoints' (Johnson 1996).

4. It will be clear by now that this text is littered with landscape and landscape-in-movement metaphors. Metaphors are an essential part of language; they are part of the way in which particular understandings of the world are naturalized and empowered (Salmond 1982). For this reason, they require close attention (Tilley 1999).

These phenomenological accounts often focus on familiar places (Feld and Basso 1996). But even for people who live in the same place for generations and work 'within their knowledge', there are always other places (real, or encountered through hearsay, story and imagination). The familiar topography gives way to the unfamiliar, one landscape nests within another like Chinese boxes – except that the boxes are permeable. How do people deal with the part-familiar or the unknown? Walking along seasonal pathways, a person part-knows the way, part-knows that each time of return there will be change and unfamiliarity; part-fears, part-revels in the chance encounter, the possible adventure. Arriving is important but so are the stories woven around the travelling (Edmonds 1999). The Papua New Guineans embarking on sea-borne exchanges (Battaglia 1990); or prehistoric people from Stonehenge traversing unfamiliar landscapes as they search for and bring back the sacred stones from South Wales or North Wiltshire; or pilgrims walking – recreating – the Nazca lines: how do they deal with unfamiliar places and people? What real or fictive kinscapes and clanscapes are created to ease the journeys? What song-lines or sacred topographies woven to embrace the unknown? What webs of exchange (of people, things, information and ideas) spun? Who does the travelling? Who is left behind? Who encountered? Who tells the stories? Who gets to hear the tale?

People's sense of place and landscape thus extends out from the locale and from the present encounter and is contingent upon a larger temporal and spatial field of relationships. The explanation of what is happening moves backwards and forwards between the detail of everyday existence and these larger forces (Pred 1990; Sontag 1983: 385–401; Edholm 1993).

Take bell hooks walking to her grandmother's house:

It was a movement away from the segregated blackness of our community into a white neighborhood. I remember the fear, being scared to walk to Baba's, our grandmother's house, because we would have to pass that terrifying whiteness – those white faces on the porches staring us down with hate . . .

Oh! That feeling of safety, of arrival, of homecoming, when we finally reached the edges of her yard, when we could see the soot black face of our grandfather, Daddy Gus, sitting in his chair on the porch, smell his cigar, and rest on his lap (hooks 1992).

Or Jamaica Kincaid's Lucy, an Antiguan au pair in North America:

Along the paths and underneath the trees were many, many yellow flowers, the shape of play teacups, or fairy skirts. . . . I did not know what these flowers were, and so it was a mystery to me why I wanted to kill them. Just like that. I wanted to kill them (Kincaid 1994: 29).

The daffodils, for that is what they were, triggered memories of the poem by Wordsworth that she had had to recite as a child. She had never seen daffodils, they were just part of her colonial education. Part of the larger, gendered structure of endlessly unequal relations. For hooks, a trajectory of fear, for Kincaid one of oppression and anger, for both a present moment hung within a long coercive past.

By and large, there has been a tendency to assume that a rooted, familiar sense of place requires staying put. But as Humphrey (1995; also Chapter Three in this volume) has shown, for some nomadic communities in Mongolia it is quite possible to create an ego-centred world in which the 'centre' moves and the *axis mundi* – the joining of earth to sky – is recreated through the smoke that rises from the campfire at each resting point along the way.[5] For many contemporary Roma the landscape is ego-centred in a different way. Although the seasonal landscape may be familiar, the temporary campsite – grudgingly 'given' by authorities or claimed without permission – is treated as alien and polluted space. Whether on the move or within this alien space, 'home' and the centre of the world is the caravan.

There is also a tendency to create an opposition between a rooted sense of belonging and the alienating forces of modernity. Often it may be so, but sometimes, just as settled landscape can be both familiar *and* unfamiliar,[6] it may also be both rooted and undergoing rapid change. The forces of modernity may rework a landscape, but also be reworked in response to a local sense of place, a particular way of being-in-the-world. Harvey (Chapter Eleven) suggests how, in Peru, a burgeoning transport system is responsive to a sacred topography; Balzani (Chapter Twelve) discusses how a 'traditional' Rajasthan pilgrimage is tailored to contemporary political agendas.

So already the notion of small-scale, familiar, rooted landscapes needs to be questioned, and the phenomenological approach opened towards a stronger sense of movement within enlarged worlds.

On the other end of the scale, the contemporary anthropological focus on 'migration', 'diaspora', 'nomadology', and 'borderlands' needs not only to be set within longer histories of movement and displacement (Ghosh 1992; Eco 1980) but also to be grounded, to take on board an embodied, phenomenological approach.

5. Humphrey also points out that for other Mongolian nomads a sense of belonging is created through a narrative of landscapes in which place names commemorate the mythical adventures of the shamanistic ancestors.

6. A familiar world may also become suddenly 'unfamiliar'. Thus a white Australian landscape and an unthinking sense of control may suddenly, with the MABO agreement and the (remote) possibility of successful Aboriginal claims to the land, feel threatened. The ground slips (Gelder and Jacobs 1995).

From Macro to Micro

The current emphasis on global movement is about the reality of compressed time and space; of people 'being in touch' at first, third, tenth hand; of a global inequality which works to generate a leisured travelling world for some, a world of desperate economic deprivation for others, a thin wash of entrepreneurs travelling globally, and a wave of underpaid labour making its way from the 'peripheries' to (grudging) 'centres'; of civil wars and dispossession.[7] All of which interlock and work off each other and all of which have to be understood in terms of what went before:

[A Third World poster:] WE ARE HERE BECAUSE YOU WERE THERE (Rich cited in Smith and Katz 1993)

The focus on global movements is also a repudiation of a Western reading of 'core'/'periphery', of victor and victim. Deleuze and Guattari react against rooted histories for good reason: 'We're tired of trees. We should stop believing in trees, roots and radicles. They've made us suffer too much' (Deleuze and Guattari 1981: 15). They offer instead the metaphor of rhizomes and the trope of Nomadology. But such tropes threaten to flatten out important differences. They make it seem as if '"We" [are] all in fundamentally similar ways always-already travellers in the same postmodern universe' (Ang 1994 cited in Cresswell 1997).

But even writers who eschew such generalizations assume that movement creates a *dis*-location between people and landscape. Clifford, for example, offers a finely nuanced and gendered approach to the 'specific, discrepant histories' involved in diasporic experiences, but emphasizes the historical and social, at the expense of spatial (Clifford 1997: 244; Smith and Katz 1993). Dislocation is also relocation. People are always in some relationship to the landscape they move through – they are never nowhere: 'Every movement between here and there bears with it a movement within here and within there' (Minh-ha 1994).

Augé (1995: 86) suggests that 'The traveller's space may . . . be the archetype of *non-place*'. He talks of transit lounges, motels, airports. But are they non-places or are they just particular sorts of places? Are they not invested with many and fluctuating sorts of meaning dependent on experience? Thus, for example:

Migrant workers, already living in the metropolis, have the habit of visiting the main railway station. To talk in groups there, to watch the trains come in, to receive first-hand news from their country, to anticipate the day when they will make the return journey (Berger and Mohr 1975: 64).

7. A recent estimate suggests that 25 million people have been forced to leave their country; 25 million people have been internally displaced; and another 75 million are on the move because of economic or environmental circumstances (Vidal 1999).

Introduction

Or:

> I like it here [in the airport]. I am a human maggot. I will build my nest here, in a place that belongs to nobody . . . I will live in the artificial light of the airport as an example of the postmodern species, in a transit phase, in an ideal shelter, in purgatory, in an emotionally sterile room (Ugresic, a 'Yugoslavian' woman who, under the new dispensation, feels 'homeless', cited in Jansen 1998).

This latter is, of course, a very 'knowing' account, but see how it creates, out of 'neutral' airport space, a sense of 'nest', 'transit', 'shelter', 'purgatory'. It is not a 'non-place', it is a place around which imagination weaves itself, a place that is pitched against other meaningful places in the author's biography.

Phenomenological approaches do not replace socio-political-economic analyses, they form part of them. Sometimes, they cut against the grain. There have, for example, been numerous attempts – by academics and by bureaucrats – to 'categorize' different types of movement. Clifford (1997), in his discussion of diasporic movement,[8] admits the categories blur. Experiential accounts demonstrate more forcibly the inadequacies of many of the designations, as well as the power of legal niceties to affect the attitudes and actions of reluctant host and desperate 'guest'.

These are male African 'economic migrants':

> [They] no longer recalled the stages or the place-names on the next leg of the journey . . . So far as they know, and they were delirious for long periods, they crossed the Algerian Sahara in two months . . . . [Williams' companion] explained they had eaten leaves, sucked up the water from pools of sandy mud and drunk their own urine . . . He spoke of 'trekking' to the point of death, of seeming to die on his feet, falling into an abyss of exhaustion, only to be resurrected by the furnace of the late afternoon (Harding 2000).

These 'political refugees':

> They arrive at the huts [in the harbour of Otranto, Italy] drenched and chilled to the marrow. They are shivering, terrified, nearly ecstatic – a state induced by the journey and the fact of having survived it. . . . After an hour or so, the men begin milling about, while the women sit with their heads bowed and the children sleep (Harding 2000 – note the different gendered experience).

---

8. Clifford defines diaspora as: 'A history of dispersal, myths/memories of the homeland, alienation in the host (bad host?) country, desire for eventual return, ongoing support of the homeland, and a collective identity importantly defined by this relationship' (Clifford 1997: 247).

This the experience of being categorized:

> The migrants shuffle down the line with their hands extended. The abrupt introduction of the illegal alien to the grudging host state begins. In this parody of greeting, gloved hands reach out to bare hands, seize them, flatten them down on an ink block, lift them across the table-top and flatten them again onto a square of paper (Harding 2000).

We need to think about the experiences of place and landscape for those on the move, experiences that are always polysemic (they work at many different levels), contextual (the particularities of time and place matter) and biographical (different for different people and always in process, happening). How do people (variably) relate to unfamiliar and often hostile worlds? How create bridges between what is and what has gone before?

We need to work with the particular, and from the particular to the general. Take, for example, John Berger's account of (primarily) Turkish *gast-arbeiter* (Berger and Mohr 1975). A little out-of-date perhaps, but combining in rare measure empathy and trenchant analysis. The fearful journey gives way to the alienation of arrival:

> One of the walls of the corner where his bed is, leads to a door, the door opens onto a passage, at the end of the passage are the taps to wash under and the place he can shit in, the wet floor of this place leads to the way out, down the stairs into the street, along the walls of the buildings on one side and the wall of the traffic on the other, past the railing, under the glass and the artificial light to the work he does . . .

> But after work and on Sundays it is hellish . . . (Berger and Mohr 1975: 87).

And yet a sort of 'dwelling' is created:

> By turning in circles the displaced preserve their identity and improvise a shelter. Built of what? Of habits . . . the raw material of repetition turned into shelter . . . words, jokes, opinions, objects and places . . . photos, trophies, souvenirs . . . The roof and four walls . . . are invisible, intangible, and biographical (Berger 1984: 63).

From the old life, what gets brought, what left behind? What remembered, what erased? How does the old get eased into new and hostile landscapes?

> In certain barracks the authorities have tried to forbid migrant workers keeping their suitcases in their sleeping rooms on the grounds that they make the room untidy. The workers have strongly resisted this . . . In these suitcases they keep personal possessions, not the clothes put in the wardrobes, not the photographs they pin to the wall, but articles which, for one reason or another, are their talismans. Each suitcase, locked or tied around

with cord, is like a man's memory. They defend their right to keep the suitcases (Berger and Mohr 1975: 179).

Reminiscing, silently remembering, touched by the physicality of 'things' that matter, the migrant 'gets by'. John Berger talks us through the migrant worker's complex landscapes, and reiterates:

> To see the experience of another, one must do more than dismantle and reassemble the world with him at its centre. One must interrogate his situation to learn about that part of his experience which derives from the historical moment. What is being done to him, even with his won complicity, under the cover of normalcy? (Berger and Mohr 1975: 104).

Which is what Parkin does when he 'interrogates' how and why, in the worst of circumstances, when people are forced to flee their homes, they seize upon certain things:

> Personal mementoes provide the material markers . . . , inscribed with narrative and sentiment, which may later re-articulate the shifting boundaries of a socio-cultural identity . . . But the objects are also . . . archetypal possibilities for the commemoration of the death of those in flight and even of a community (Parkin 1999).

Berger's account circles round a particular nexus of male migrant workers and tends to homogenize their experience. A recent account of Indian migrant workers employed in the Persian Gulf states suggests that, under different circumstances, they are 'less deracinated from the web of social relations' and more able to create 'a home away from home'. The authors stress, too, the variability of migrant experience and the effect of this on their status and identity on their return home (Osella and Osella 2000).

Most ethnographies on migrant workers focus on male migrant workers, as though women always stayed home. But this is often not the case,[9] and as Clifford suggests:

> Life for women in diasporic situations may be doubly painful – struggling with the material and spiritual insecurities of exile, with the demands of family and work, and with the claims of the old and new patriarchies (Clifford 1997: 259).

Orford in Chapter Seventeen talks of Namibian women on-the-move, in exile, and, too, of the problems of return.[10]

---

9. As Brah points out, women form the majority of Cape Verdian workers migrating to Italy, Filipinos to the Middle East, or Thais to Japan (Brah 1996: 179).

10. Nixon (1996) notes that: 'There is an inextricable link between South African literature's amnesia towards rural space and its amnesia towards the experience of women.'

Under different conditions, the relationships between 'here' and 'there' sometimes cast similar shadows, sometimes seem remarkably different . . . A small Jewish boy flees Germany:

> . . . In the customs hall in Dover . . . they looked on with horror as Grandfather's pair of budgerigars, which had so far survived the journey unharmed, were impounded. It was the loss of the two pet birds . . . and having to stand by powerless and see them vanish for ever behind some sort of screen, that brought [them] up against the whole monstrosity of changing countries under such inauspicious circumstances (Hamberger cited in Sebald 1998: 176).

A Polish Jew 'settled' in London, returns 'home' in memory:

> . . . What would be left of me if by some ungodly edict I were to be stripped of all that is Polish in me [?] First of the language, which . . . remains part of the furniture without which the inner space would be empty; of the poems and verses with which I lull myself to sleep; of the recollection of landscape, its singular sights and smells . . . Were one to lose the link with that language and landscape . . . one would feel bereft, impoverished, incomplete (Felek Scharf cited in Lichtenstein and Sinclair 2000).

Another Jew refuses any such nostalgia and celebrates his 'rootlessness':

> Some-one in a Cambridge common room [pestered] the self-designated 'non-Jewish Jew' and Marxist historian Isaac Deutscher . . . about his roots. 'Trees have roots,' he shot back, scornfully, 'Jews have legs.' (Schama 1995: 29 cited in Olsen in press)

But did Deutscher (and indeed the others) always feel the same sentiment, or just sometimes? Was it the context of interrogation that brought the sharp response?

The historical conditions matter, and the moment in time and place. Wardle (1999, citing Mintz) suggests that Caribbean people, transported into an alien geography, empty of indigenes, and individuated by the socio-economics of colonialism, were modern even before the Europeans. He suggests that for the migrant (male) Jamaican worker neither the 'here' nor 'there' take precedence, but rather the telling of an ego-centred 'adventure'. While this may be so in certain contexts – in the story-telling to an enraptured audience 'at home' – it is almost certainly less true for other moments along the way, as V.S. Naipaul's sharp insight, on his first journey from Trinidad to England, as the aeroplane stops down in North America, makes clear:

> At home, among his fellows, just a few hours before, he was a man to be envied, his journey indescribably glamorous; now he was a Negro, in a straw-coloured jacket obviously not his own, too tight across his weight-lifter's shoulders . . . Now, in that

jacket (at home, the badge of the traveller to the temperate North), he was bluffing it out, insisting on his respectability, on not being an American Negro, on not being fazed by the aeroplane and by the white people (Naipaul 1987: 101).

Naipaul himself rejects Trinidad as 'home', and turns rather to India, from where an earlier generation of indentured labour had come, or to England as promised and portrayed in his colonial education. And yet the landscapes of his 'non-home' haunt his English landscapes (Bender 1993).

Or take Gilroy (1991), memorably summarizing the landscapes of young Blacks in Britain: 'It's not where you're from, it's where you're at.' It says something about being both British and something else (Clifford 1997: 251), but doesn't necessarily say everything. Sometimes 'where you're from' does matter, and – depending on context – matters in different ways.[11]

Landscapes on the Move: Landscapes at Home

So far, the focus is on the landscapes of those on the move. But that's not the end of it. Those on the move affect the landscapes of those being moved through. And they affect the landscapes of those being left behind.

Pheng Cheah recently took Homi Bhabha and Clifford to task, suggesting that they focus too much upon a metropolitan scenario of migrancy and mobility. Clifford's 'chronotope of travelling culture does not give equal time to the tenacity of national dwelling' (Cheah 1998). Some truth perhaps in this criticism, but 'the tenacity of national dwelling' is shaken up by, and to some extent created out of the knowledge that somewhere – close at hand or at a distance – people are on the move, or by what Clifford (1992) describes as the 'forces that pass powerfully *through* – television, radio, tourists, commodities, armies'. Avtar Brah (1996: 242) uses the term 'diaspora space' to embrace *"the entanglement of the genealogies of dispersal"* with those of *"staying put"*. Aziz in Chapter Seven works with such a 'space' but in landscapes tensioned by the socio-economics of tourism rather than diasporic movement; while, in rather different ways, Dawson and Johnson in Chapter Nineteen and Basu in Twenty touch on being both 'at home' and in exile.

Landscapes of Colonization

Recent anthropological literature on diaspora or migration has recognized the link to Empire and colonization.

---

11. The tensions and ambivalences are clear in several recent novels by young black women writers (Melville 1990; Levy 1999).

. . . It is one of the unhappiest characteristics of the age to have produced more refugees, migrants, displaced persons, and exiles than ever before in history, most of them as an accompaniment to, and ironically enough, as afterthoughts of great post-colonial and imperial conflicts (Said 1994: 402).

But the process of colonization has tended to be analysed in terms of landscapes of power: the technology of control and the power of the Western Gaze to distance, objectify, attempt to control 'the other' – whether people or land (Pratt 1992; Mitchell 1989). Without dismissing the reality of this power, it is important to recognize that at the back of the unequal colonial encounter lurked the unequal encounter 'at home': the economic conditions, punitive laws, and downward social mobility that sent the young conscripts on their way. There is a terrible irony and:

. . . a strange fate. The unemployed man from the slums of the cities, the superfluous landless worker, the dispossessed peasant: each of these found employment in killing and disciplining the rural poor of the subordinated countries (Williams 1973: 283).

And it was not just conscripts, but felons (see Casella in Chapter Six) and settlers. And not just men, but women and children.

We need to understand the experiences of the colonizing agents: the bitterness and misery – and, often, hope – of the leave-taking, the drear conditions of travel, and the fearfulness of arrival (see Dubow in Chapter Fourteen; and Goldsworthy 1996). Even for those better placed, the administrator or military man, (just as for the transcontinental entrepreneur today), the experiences of 'being in' and 'presiding over' work off each other and forge tensioned relationships with place and people (Blunt and Rose 1994; Foster 1998; Ong 1998).

To Return to the Beginning

And so to return to the beginning. Most of us at the WAC conference were tourists. We were tourists in a country that had been colonized and brutally segregated. Tourism is another form of colonization. I have skirted the question of tourist landscapes-on-the-move (but see Chapters Seven to Nine and Twenty). Nor have I mentioned landscapes-on-the-move where 'freedom' of the road is a cause for celebration (Cresswell 1992), partly for want of space, but more out of embarrassment at the non-equivalence of the seemingly slight experience of tourism alongside the pain of many landscapes-in-movement (see Butler in Chapter Eighteen). But, of course, tourism is only 'seemingly slight'. Its effect on those it passes through is powerful. And for the tourists – for us – the experiences shadow some of those already touched on: departures, arrivals, unfamiliarity, gendered fear, settling/ unsettling, different perceptions surfacing in different contexts, small things standing in for huge events and historical reckonings, emotional and intellectual baggage reworked in new social and geographical spaces. We affect and are affected by the landscapes we move through. We return home, but not to the same place.

References

Ang, I. 1994. On not speaking Chinese: postmodern ethnicity and the politics of diaspora. *New Formations* **24** 4.

Augé, M. 1995. *Non-Places: Introduction to an Anthropology of Supermodernity.* London: Verso.

Battaglia, D. 1990. *On the Bones of the Serpent: Person, Memory and Mortality in Sabarl Island Society.* Chicago: University of Chicago Press.

Bender, B. 1993. Introduction: landscape – meaning and action, in B. Bender (ed.) *Landscape: Politics and Perspectives.* Oxford: Berg.

— 1998. *Stonehenge: Making Space.* Oxford: Berg.

— In press. The politics of the past: Emain Macha (Navan) Northern Ireland, in R. Layton, P. Stone and J. Thomas (eds) *The Destruction and Conservation of Cultural Property.* London: Routledge.

Berger, J. 1984. *And Our Faces, My Heart, Brief as Photos.* London: Granta.

Berger, J. and Mohr, J. 1975. *A Seventh Man.* Harmondsworth: Penguin Books Ltd.

Blunt, A. and Rose, G. 1994. *Writing Women and Space. Colonial and Postcolonial Geographies.* London: The Guildford Press.

Brah, A. 1996. *Cartographies of Diaspora.* London: Routledge.

Cheah, P. 1998. Given culture: rethinking cosmopolitical freedom in trans-nationalism, in P. Cheah and B. Robbins (eds) *Cosmopolitic: Thinking and Feeling beyond the Nation.* Minneapolis: University of Minnesota Press.

Clifford, J. 1992. Traveling cultures, in L. Grossberg, C. Nelson and P. Treichler (eds) *Cultural Studies.* New York: Routledge. 99–116.

—— 1997. *Routes. Travel and Translation in the Late Twentieth Century.* Cambridge, Mass.: Harvard University Press.

Cresswell, T. 1992. Mobility as resistance: a geographical reading of Kerouac's *On the Road. Transaction of the Institute of British Geography* **18** 249–62.

—— 1997. Imagining the nomad: mobility and the postmodern primitive, in G. Benko and U. Strohmayer (eds) *Space and Social Theory.* Oxford: Blackwell.

Daniels, S. and Cosgrove, D. 1993. Spectacle and text, in J. Duncan and D. Ley (eds) *Place/Culture/Representation.* London: Routledge.

Deleuze, G. and Guattari, F. 1987. *A Thousand Plateaus: Capitalism and Schizophrenia*. Minneapolis: University of Minnesota Press.

Eco, U. 1980. *The Name of the Rose*. London: Secker and Warburg.

Edholm, F. 1993. The view from below: Paris in the 1880s, in B. Bender (ed.) *Landscape: Politics and Perspectives*. Oxford: Berg.

Edmonds, M. 1999. *Ancestral Geographies of the Neolithic: Landscapes, Monuments and Memory*. London: Routledge.

Feld, S. and Basso, K. 1996. *Senses of Place*. Santa Fe: School of American Research Press.

Foster, J. 1998. John Buchan's *Hesperides:* landscape rhetoric and the aesthetics of bodily experience of the South African highveld, 1901–1903. *Ecumene* **5**(3) 323–47.

Gelder, K. and Jacobs, J. 1995. Uncanny Australia. *Ecumene* **2**(2) 171–83.

Ghosh, A. 1992. *In an Antique Land*. London: Granta Books.

Giddens, A. 1985. Time, space and regionalisation, in D. Gregory and J. Urry (eds) *Social Relations and Spatial Structures*. London: Macmillan.

Gilroy, P. 1991. 'It ain't where you're from it's where you're at', the dialectics of diasporic identification. *Third Text* **13** 3–16.

Goldsworthy, K. 1996. The voyage south: writing immigration, in K. Darian-Smith, L. Gunner and S. Nuttall (eds) *Text, Theory and Space: Land, Literature and History in Southern Africa and Australia*. London and New York: Routledge.

Gow, P. 1995. Land, people, and paper in Western Amazonia, in E. Hirsch and M. O'Hanlon (eds) *The Anthropology of Landscape: Perspectives on Place and Space*. Oxford: Clarendon Press.

Hall, M. in press. Memory as cultural property: Cape Town's District Six, in R. Layton, P. Stone and J.S. Thomas (eds) *The Conservation and Destruction of Cultural Property*. London: Routledge.

Harding, J. 2000. The uninvited. *London Review of Books* February 3.

Harley, J. B. 1992. Deconstructing the map, in T. Barnes and J. Duncan (eds) *Discourse, Text and Metaphor in the Representation of Landscape*. London: Routledge.

Hirsch, E. and O'Hanlon, M. (eds) 1995. *The Anthropology of Landscape: Perspectives on Place and Space*. Oxford: Oxford University Press.

hooks, bell 1992. Representing whiteness in the Black imagination, in L. Grossberg et al. (eds) *Cultural Studies*. London: Routledge.

Humphrey, C. 1995. Chiefly and shamanist landscapes in Mongolia, in E. Hirsch and M. O'Hanlon (eds) *The Anthropology of Landscape: Perspectives on Place and Space*. Oxford: Clarendon Press.

Ingold, T. 1993. The temporality of the landscape. *World Archaeology* **25**(2) 152–74.

—— 1997. The picture is not the terrain: Maps, paintings, and the dwelt-in world. *Archaeological Dialogues* **1** 29–31.

—— 2000. *The Perception of the Environment: Essays on Livelihood, Dwelling and Skill*. London: Routledge.

Jansen, S. 1998. Homeless at home: narrations of post-Yugoslav identities, in N. Rapport and A. Dawson (eds) *Migrants of Identity*. Oxford: Berg.

Johnson, N. 1996. Where geography and history meet: heritage tourism and the big house in Ireland. *Annales of the Association of American Geographers* **86**(3) 551–66.

Keith, M. and Pile, S. 1993. Introduction part 1: the politics of place, in M. Keith and S. Pile (eds) *Place and the Politics of Identity*. London: Routledge.

Kincaid, J. 1994. *Lucy*. London: Picador.

Levy, A. 1999. *Fruit of the Lemon*. London: Review.

Lichtenstein, R. and Sinclair, I. 2000. *Rodinsky's Room*. London: Granta Books.

Massey, D. 2000. Living in Wythenshawe, in I. Borden, J. Kerr, A. Pivaro and J. Rendell (eds) *The Unknown City*. London: Wiley.

Melville, P. 2000. *Shape-shifter*. London: Bloomsbury.

Minh-ha, T. 1994. Other than myself/my other self, in G. Robertson, M. Mash, L. Tickner, J. Bird, B. Curtis and T. Putnam (eds) *Travellers' Tales*. London: Routledge.

Mitchell, T. 1989. The World as Exhibition. *Comparative Studies in Society and History* **31** 217–36.

Naipaul, V.S. 1987. *The Enigma of Arrival*. London: Penguin.

Nixon, R. 1996. Rural transnationalism: Bessie Head's southern spaces, in K. Darian-Smith, L. Gunner and S. Nuttall (eds) *Text, Theory and Space*, London: Routledge.

Olsen, B. In press. The end of what? History and identity in a post-modern world, in R. Layton, P. Stone and J. Thomas (eds) *The Destruction and Conservation of Cultural Property*. London: Routledge.

Ong, A. 1998. Flexible citizenship among Chinese cosmopolitans, in P. Cheah and B. Robbins (eds) *Cosmopolitics. Thinking and Feeling beyond the Nation*. Minneapolis: University of Minnesota Press.

Osella, P. and Osella, C. 2000. Migration, money and masculinity in Kerala. *Journal of the Royal Anthropological Institute* **6** 117–33.

Parkin, D. 1999. Mementos, reality and human displacement. *Journal of Material Culture* **4**(3) 303–20.

Pratt, M. 1992. *Imperial Eyes: Travel Writing and Transculturation*. London: Routledge.

Pred, A. 1990. *Making Histories and Constructing Human Geographies*. Boulder, San Francisco: Westview Press.

Rapport, N. and Dawson, A. (eds) 1998. Home and movement: a polemic, in N. Rapport and A. Dawson (eds) *Migrants of Identity*. Oxford: Berg.

Said, E. 1989. Jane Austen and empire, in T. Eagleton (ed.) *Raymond Williams: Critical Perspectives*. Oxford: Polity Press.

—— 1994. *Culture and Imperialism*. London: Vintage.

Salmond, A. 1982. Theoretical landscapes. On cross-cultural conceptions of knowledge, in D. Parkin (ed.) *Semantic Anthropology*. London: Academic Press.

Schama, S. 1996. *Landscape and Memory*. London: HarperCollins.

Sebalt, W. 1998. *The Rings of Saturn*. London: the Harvill Press.

Smith, N. and Katz, C. 1993. Grounding metaphor, in M. Keith and S. Pile (eds) *Place and the Politics of Identity*. London: Routledge.

Sontag, S. 1983. *A Susan Sontag Reader*. Harmondsworth: Penguin.

Steedley, M. 1993. *Hanging Without a Rope*. Princeton: Princeton University Press.

Stewart, L. 1995. Louisiana subjects: power, space and the slave body. *Ecumene* 2(3) 227–45.

Thomas, J. 1996. A precis of *Time, Culture and Identity*. *Archaeological Dialogues* 1 6–21.

Tilley, C. 1994. *A Phenomenology of Landscape: Places, Paths and Monuments*. Oxford: Berg.

—— 1999. *Metaphor and Material Culture*. Oxford: Blackwell.

Ucko, P. 1987. *Academic Freedom and Apartheid*. London: Duckworth.

Vidal, J. 1999. The endless diaspora. *Guardian* April 2.

Wardle, H. 1999. Jamaican adventures: Simmel, subjectivity and extraterritoriality in the Caribbean. *The Journal of the Royal Anthropological Institute* 5(4) 523–39.

Williams, R. 1973. *The Country and the City*. London: Chatto & Windus.

Part I
Contested Landscapes

The Shadow of the Sacred Rock: Contrasting Discourses of Place under the Acropolis

Roxane Caftanzoglou

Of People and Place

Late twentieth-century processes of migration, displacement and deterritorialization call the fixed association between identity, culture, and place into question, confronting cultural and anthropological studies that focus on people's relationship to place with an increasingly complex situation (Gupta and Ferguson 1997: 1–6; Lovell 1998: 1–24; Maalki 1997). Yet, as Hastrup and Olwig (1997: 11) have recently observed, there is a certain irony in the fact that while social scientists have been actively 'liberating' the concept of culture and identity from previously assumed bonds to location in place, social groups are actively involved in constructing and defending all the things under re-examination: rootedness and belonging, ways of life, realities and senses of place, boundaries that certify and maintain distinctiveness. Whatever the problems of the analytical concept of 'the local' (as developed by Asad 1993: 7–10) location and place ' – chosen or fated – still govern the lives of most humans' (Durham-Peters 1997: 91–2). What seems called for is an approach that allows us to 'neither drain the concept of culture of its ties to place and matter nor freeze it into absolute identity' (ibid.). Approaching place as socially constructed, 'meaningfully constituted in relation to human agency and activity' (Tilley 1994: 10), may offer a way of overcoming the methodological and conceptual tensions between totally 'unhooking' identity and culture from place and constructing them as place-bound.

This chapter explores the encounter and interaction of contrasting representations and uses of place in an area beneath the Acropolis of Athens, articulated by unequally empowered discourses produced on one side by the managers of the archaeological site and on the other by a small community that has been living under the Acropolis since the 1860s.[1] By approaching this community as a site of

---

1. Following Cohen's (1985) proposition to seek 'not the lexical meaning of the word (community) but its use', the term community is used here in the sense of a group of people who share a sense of

production of social memory I hope to show how a hegemonic vision of time and space that accords priority to antiquity and the monumental has produced a counter-discourse, in the form of 'small' narratives that emphasize the local and the vernacular, and how the landscape under question here emerges as 'tensioned and multivocal' (Bender 1992: 735) by these conflicting discourses.

Some caveats must precede this presentation: as embedded in the same overarching national culture, the hegemonic discourse and the subordinate 'counter-discourse' while playing off each other, actually share many values and assumptions, though they may ascribe different meanings to such categories, strategically using them to further their claims, as Herzfeld (1991) has demonstrated in his study of the Cretan town of Rethemnos. Studies that focus on the encounter of opposed discourses tend to present them as seamless and self-containing while in fact both are full of internal contradictions, ambivalence, and 'grey zones'; such approaches may also overlook the presence of essentializing features in the 'subordinate', 'hidden' discourses.

The Community of Anafiotika

The settlement of Anafiotika, a small cluster of roughly fifty houses, was built in the 1860s by immigrant workers from the Cyclades specialized in construction, in an area already marked off as archaeological ground. Its houses and inhabitants were from the start considered illegal squatters and as a consequence have always lived under the threat of demolition and relocation, threats that actually materialized in the 1930s and the 1970s. The settlement is inhabited by forty-five people, mostly middle-aged to elderly retired manual workers and petty employees. Most of them are descendants of people who settled there in the early 1900s or earlier; about ten are newcomers, younger people without previous ties to the community.

National Cultural Identity, National Scholars, Hellenism and Modern Greece

It is my proposition that the interpretation of the conflictual relationship between this settlement and the surrounding society in terms of an encroachment on archaeological grounds can only serve as a starting point for reflection that opens up on to wider issues: the construction of a viable national cultural identity, the hegemonic ways of hierarchizing and allocating time and space by 'national scholars' involved in this process, the interaction between the 'global', the 'national'

---

togetherness, common origins and deep ties to a specific inhabited territory, features that distinguish them in a significant way from the members of other putative groups.

and the 'local', as expressed in unequally empowered, often conflicting discourses. The 'case study' presented here thus offers material that 'is good to think with', for it leads to a critical questioning of taken-for-granted statements about the 'character' of a site and its 'appropriate' uses.

A number of scholars have described and analysed the process of a national identity formation following the creation of the Modern Greek nation state and the opposed visions of Hellas and Greece in Greek discourse (Kyriakidou-Nestoros 1978; Herzfeld 1982, 1989; Just 1989). As Herzfeld (1982, 1989) has pointed out, this opposition echoes the tension between an outward-directed conformity to western powers' expectations about what Modern Greece was to be, and an inward-looking, self-critical collective appraisal. Both visions emerged in response to the regulating discourse formulated by Western political and intellectual powers, a body of representations accumulated from the Renaissance onwards, strongly oriented toward classical antiquity. As central agents in the construction of national cultural identity and the management of Greece's archaeological remains, national scholars took on the additional task of 'convincing' sceptical Western onlookers that the new state could fulfil its role as guardian of the heritage of the glorious past, thus claiming indigenous control over the idea of Greece and its identity.

The management and landscapings of monumental sites provide striking instances of interventions by the apparatuses of modernity that work on the multiple layers of meaning inscribed onto landscapes through time, striving to rearrange these living palimpsests in ways that are deemed appropriate to the national project. And the Hellenic-centred 'purist' vision (Greece as Hellas) held a key position in the discourses of the agents involved in such interventions.

When Athens was chosen as the site for the modern capital of the new nation, and its (re)construction was planned along lines of Hellenic purity, the unsettling evidence of Greece's Ottoman heritage along with local vernacular forms had to be confronted, all the more so when situated in the immediate vicinity of remains of classical antiquity. Early nineteenth-century Athens was viewed as a 'disgraceful sight' (Boyer 1996: 163) full of imperfections, ranging from the city's physical aspect to the spoken language,[2] that called for 'filtering-out' interventions.

In the midst of this process, a group of rural immigrants employed – and this is one of the ironies of this story – in the neoclassical-inspired reconstruction of the capital proceeded from the 1860s onwards to build themselves a cluster of small houses just under the Acropolis of Athens. By the end of the nineteenth century their settlement, the Anafiotika, formed a permanent presence on the northeast slope of the sacred Rock.

---

2. Herzfeld (1989: 101–22) explicitly links the 'language question' to other forms such as architecture, music, dress, gesture, moral values, seeing them as domains where the issue of the double image of Greek cultural origins is played out.

Scholarly texts of the last two decades of the nineteenth century construct the Anafiotika as an undesirable and illegal 'matter out of place' (Douglas 1966) defiling the sacredness of the monumental site. This attitude is rooted in the special place the Acropolis occupies in the Western imaginary, described by Loukakis (1997) as 'a free-floating signifier', disconnected from its social environment, as well as in a related and well-documented tradition of selective readings of the Greek countryside by Western travellers to Greece since the eighteenth century that bear evidence to their disregard of, or frank annoyance with the local populations they encountered (Loukakis 1997; Angelomatis-Tsougarakis 1990; Augustinos 1990; Buck-Sutton 1995, 1997; Leontis 1995).

Considering space as a resource in national-identity construction is also essential to understanding how the settlement was viewed. As Alonso (1994) has observed, 'enclosing, measuring, commodifying space are key for the production of the modern notion of national territory bounded by frontiers that sharply distinguish inside from outside'. Yet it is just as necessary to pay attention to the internally oriented, symbolic production of space: I refer to the carving up of national territory into discrete spheres or zones that are assigned different values, meanings, and functions and the creation of internal boundaries that demarcate and uphold the differences between discrete kinds of 'inside', disciplining space and especially local populations that do not necessarily comply with hegemonic constructions of space and the meanings assigned it. Crossing such boundaries, as Douglas (1966) and Zerubavel (1993: 29–30) have shown, is a dangerous venture, met with sanctions.

This is central to understanding the predicament of the Anafiotika, for the settlement was, and for some still is, seen as a disorderly and polluting irruption of social time in the midst of the isolated and well guarded 'buffer zone' designed to surround and isolate the Acropolis from the disturbing presence of contemporary Greek society, an intrusion in the perimeter of the 'noninhabitable, nonutilitarian and enclosed space' of the monumental site, constructed by 'aesthetics and archaeology combined with legal, economic, political and other institutional considerations' (Leontis 1995: 56–9), a space from which local populations were ideally removed, despite the fact that local people had always been living around and under the Acropolis. Simply by being where they were, this settlement of immigrants challenged the hegemonic hierarchizing of space and time. As trangressors of imposed symbolic and material boundaries, they had to be dealt with and were dealt with, through various means that allow us to see national cultural identity building as a process of exclusion as much as of inclusion.

Dispossession and Exclusion: Texts, Pictures and Demolitions

Textual Constructions of the Community

In 1883, the secretary of the Greek archaeological society Stephanos Koumanoudis petitioned the government asking for the evacuation of the settlement and the removal of the 'unhappy residents' in the interest of 'their security and health and the aims of archaeology'. The wording of his petition evokes a long tradition of constructing a targeted social group as suffering and unhealthy, as pathological; to encounter such a 'medicalizing' rhetoric, often called upon in histories of dispossession and space reallocation in the interests of dominant groups[3] in such a different context is, to say the least, striking.

Demetrius Vikelas, a cosmopolitan writer educated in England wrote an article in 1897 describing the surroundings of the Acropolis:

> On the other side of the rock the remnant of the old Turkish town and more recent hovels rise with defacing effect to the very base of the Acropolis. These are condemned and will have to be pulled down sooner or later . . . The plans are ready . . . the steep base of the rock will then be cleared of the accumulated rubbish and of the unsightly dwellings and more relics of antiquity will it is hoped be brought to light.

This text betrays an anxious desire of convincing the sceptical Western powers that national institutions were capable of caring for their classical heritage and of erasing traces of the local and vernacular situated at an uncomfortably small distance from their foremost monument. The 'unsightly' and the 'rubbish' are telling terms.

Yet it was not only scholars primarily interested in antiquity who saw the Anafiotika as an unwelcome and intruding 'matter out of place': in describing the old neighbourhoods under the Acropolis, the Athenian writer Demetrius Kambouroglou (1920), a passionate defender of the city's recent history against the excesses of archaeologists, even while paying lip service to their 'picturesqueness', portrayed the Anafiotika as: 'intruders who have nothing to do with historic Athens, a very new and temporary settlement'.

Half a century later, we encounter an architect's proposal for the rehabilitation of the historic district of Plaka whose rhetoric is practically identical to Vikelas's and brings together both aspects of the settlement's exclusion from the city's historical identity: the Anafiotika (to be demolished in his proposal) are described as

---

3. See for instance Edholm (1993) on Hausmann's redrawing and restructuring of Paris, Nzegwu (1996) on the racializing of neighbourhoods in colonial Nigeria, Sciorra (1996) on the dispossession of Puertoricans in New York City.

Figure 1.1 Traces of houses built against the rock (photo: R. Caftanzoglou)

hovels *that have nothing to do with the old town,* **and** apart from being ugly and misshapen, are *an insult to the surroundings of the Acropolis* that must be free from whatever angle one views it (Papageorgiou 1965, my emphasis).

Visual Representations of the Settlement

Interestingly, the exclusion of the Anafiotika is replicated in visual representations of the city. It is a commonplace that visual information about a place in the form of maps, photographs, drawings, etc. is to be taken just as seriously as the written text favoured by the logocentric view. The faith in visual representations of space as instruments of 'objective', 'scientific', 'rigorous' quality rests upon the primacy accorded to vision by Western culture; 'visualism' as Fabian (1983) has called it confers upon such representations immense power as a means of disciplining space and populations.[4] Maps, for instance, have been termed, 'preeminently a language of power' whose 'silences' exert social influence (Harley 1988: 277–312).

A look at maps, city plans and travel guides of Athens shows a shadowed or coloured strip extending below the Acropolis between the rock and the neighbour-

4. See Foucault (1980); Anderson (1991: 163–85).

hood of the Plaka bearing a name: Anafiotika. Thus represented, the settlement is relegated to a non-place; the existence of a neighbourhood with its houses, paths, and above all, its living component, citizens of the Greek State, is obscured. If, as Shields (1996: 231) has suggested, the city can be treated as a representation of the society which constructed it, if the spatial divisions of the city indicate the faultlines of social relations, surely we can read the visual representation of a city as indicating social discrimination. Thus, what is overlooked – excluded – from the map becomes equally significant and worthy of attention as what is included in it and therefore visible. As such, the map, the city plan, or even the 'innocent' travelogue bear evidence to symbolic violence against the settlement by magicking it into a non-place.

Mediatic Appropriations of the Settlement: 'Looking without Seeing'

In its 'picturesqueness', the settlement is constructed as an object of urban nostalgia by the media, a 'countersite' of salvaged traditionality in the context of changes brought about since the explosion of building activity in the 1970s destroyed many of Athens' historic landmarks; an 1996 issue of the lifestyle magazine *Metro* (interestingly entitled 'Escape') offered the prospect of a walk through the Anafiotika as an escape fantasy to its public, somewhere to go in order to 'get away from it all'. Television films, coffee-table books with photographs of the Anafiotika, and 'glossies' all cater to the need of contemporary mass culture industry for new arenas to colonize, for enclaves of 'traditionality' to offer to mass cultural consumption, encouraging what Bauman (1997: 132–5) calls 'looking/ versus seeing': a surface reading of the neighbourhood, that refuses any form of engagement with the people who live there. It is indeed striking and paradoxical that in most representations of the Anafiotika, the people who created and live in the settlement are as if invisible.

Physical Interventions in the Settlement

The account of physical interventions in the settlement by state authorities tells the story of how restrictions placed on lived space may succeed in curtailing the social reproduction of an entire community. Between 1936 and 1939, the American School of Classical Studies (ASCS) in Athens acquired eleven houses in the Anafiotika for archaeological purposes, most of which were demolished. In the late 1960s during the dictatorship, legal arrangements for the expropriation of the settlement's houses by the Ministry of Culture and the freeing of the grounds for excavations began. In 1977, the inhabitants of the row of houses nearest to the rock were notified by the Director of the Ephorate of the Acropolis that they had to vacate their homes. He was, however, only interested in reconstituting the ancient

Figure 1.2 The Anafiotika 1999 (photo: R. Caftanzoglou)

peripatos, a circular path around the base of the rock, and repeatedly pointed out that he wished the rest of the settlement to remain as it was, since it provided a 'bridge' between the contemporary city and the monument. Despite strong protests from architectural students who mounted an exhibition (Margaret Kenna, personal communication), questions asked in parliament and critical articles in the press, the houses were pulled down. Today, an iron fence separates the settlement from the Rock but the circular walk is still not reconstituted. During the first two mandates of the Pasok government, the Anafiotika were more or less left in peace, most probably owing to Minister of Culture Melina Mercouri. However, everyday surveillance of the settlement continued, in connection with the severe restrictions imposed on any restoring activity. To this day, the Anafiots who wish to restore their homes have to ask for permission from what they call 'The Archaeology'; such permission is not always granted, and when it is, it includes strict rules and is carried out under close supervision. Often, the 'Archaeology's' reply is accompanied by a letter pointing out that the houses are expropriated and that their eviction and demolition is pending.[5] The residents complain that they cannot even repair leaking roofs without having 'the Archaeology' nosing around them, and enjoy telling the story of how a particularly agile man who used to repair their homes had become expert at escaping surveillance.

These restrictions have preserved the vernacular architectural form of the settlement, allowing another prospect of dispossession to emerge: an 'empty shell' project, whereby its homes would house services of the Ministry of Culture, entailing the annihilation of the community's social fabric. Yet ironically, these measures have also provided the residents with an asset they often invoke, pointing to the traditional aesthetic aspect of their neighbourhood as compared to the rest of the city.

Anafiot Narratives, or How 'Words can call Places into Being'[6]

The Anafiotika currently face the prospect of the end of their social reproduction as a spatially bounded and based community. In response to this, the residents reinforce their symbolic boundaries (Cohen 1985) by telling stories of themselves and their settlement, constructing a counter-discourse of space, time and history based on shared collective and individual memories that have been fundamental in creating a 'community of participation' and enabling them to develop and sustain a sense of distinct cultural identity.[7]

A Poetics of Place and Time

Narrating how the settlement came to be built, the residents tell of the master builder from Anafi who, having finished his work, told King Otto he was going back to his island to take care of his younger unmarried sister. In this *tête-à-tête*, as it is often called, the king pleaded with him to stay and bring his sister and

---

5. Over the last twenty years, most of the houses have been expropriated by the Ministry of Culture.

6. Yi-Fu Tuan, 1991.

7. The conditions of emergence of 'hidden transcripts' outlined by Scott (1990: 134–5): '"communities of fate" characterized by features such as the homogeneity and isolation of their community and work experience, close mutual dependence and relative lack of differentiation ...' are quite similar to the situation in the Anafiotika.

build her a house wherever she liked. The builder's sister duly arrived in Athens and was received at the palace; looking at the view of the city through a window, she pointed to the rocky slope of the Acropolis and, saying it reminded her of the heights above her home village in the Cycladic island of Anafi, expressed her desire to live there. The king gave his permission and the settlement was built.[8]

This narrative reads space in quite a different way from the hegemonic one; it foregrounds the migrants' carrying of homeland memories and the investing of new, as yet unchartered, living space with them, thus symbolically appropriating it and bridging the distance between the homeland and the new settlement. It can also be seen as a skillful manipulation of time, at odds with official history, since it was during the first decade of Otto's reign that the area was declared archaeological, yet it was during his reign that he himself overruled the prohibitions surrounding these grounds, thus legitimizing the residents' claims to place.

Divesting the foremost monument of classical antiquity of its sacredness and uniqueness, reinvesting it with aspects of the local and the vernacular, the Anafiot narrative offers an alternative, 'Greek' reading of a sacred site, constructing it as a familiar, lived-in and taken-care-of homeplace, in contrast to the unfamiliar, 'frozen' and prohibited aspect more and more monumental sites are taking on. For all the vicissitudes that archaeological concerns have brought them, the residents' narratives testify to a warm relation with the monument above them; they tell of helping the archaeologists in their work on the Acropolis as children, finding 'bits and pieces' of statues, of dressing up in sheets and 'playing at being ancients' in the Dionysos theatre.

The active appropriation and creation of place by the Anafiots is more than a narrative product; when the first settlers arrived, they restored two half-ruined chapels, placing in that of St Symeon a copy of the miracle-working icon of Anafi's patron, the Virgin Mary of the Reeds, as well as a stone tablet bearing the words: 'St Symeon of the Anafiots', thus investing a pre-existing landmark with symbols of their local identity. On 3 February (St Symeon) and in early September (on the nameday of the Virgin), the chapel celebrates: though the feasting and dancing of old days are over, both events are attended by many visitors and Anafiots from all over Athens. These two celebrations involve more than a religious duty: by attending the event, residents and visitors actively participate in the community's affirmation of its identity and collective sense of attachment to place; news of resident families are discussed, the whitewashing and decoration of the chapel are commented on, the story of the tablet and the icon are recounted. Such events are usual practice among internal immigrant groups; in the case of the Anafiot celebrations, however, the spatial referent is a double one since both the island of

---

8. The residents often point out that if the first settlers had built elsewhere they (their descendants) would now be millionaires.

origin and the settlement itself are celebrated. This dual sense of attachment also emerges in residents' discourses; during a conversation on 'homeland', a man explained that he saw both the island and the settlement as 'home', while another resident who is not from the island said 'I am an Anafiot too; I love the Anafiotika'.

The residents speak repeatedly and forcefully of their ties to the settlement, their care for it and their holding onto it. A strong sense of place is a prominent feature in individual life histories; it is striking that while, especially among the older residents' narratives, the time-location of events appears as unimportant (decades are confused; whether something happened before or after the war is unclear), the spatial setting is sharply defined, often in terms of a precise, pointed-to, part of a wall or rock or staircase. As Tilley (1994, 59) notes: 'Events are anchored and given significance in terms of particular locales . . . Particular locales are of essential importance in "fixing" events and acting as mnemonics, thus creating a sense of social identity and establishing linkages between past and present . . .' Conversely, place comes to life through being narrated; individual stories told by residents construct the Anafiotika and specific parts of it as lived-in, as existing through people's everyday bodily experience and intimate connection to them. Their stories take on sarcastic undertones, when they tell of knowing the grounds far better than the archaeologists, or when they contrast their local knowledge and attachment to place to that of the wealthy people who have recently built large houses beneath the settlement, 'now they've discovered the area and they like it'. When shown photographs of the Anafiotika taken in the 1920s even younger residents unhesitatingly identified the exact location of houses demolished decades ago and took me to the exact spots where these photographs had been taken from, urging me to take new pictures that would illustrate 'what had been done' to the community. Family names, genealogies and stories of the people who had been dispossessed and relocated, the cases of some elders who pined away and died in their new homes were readily proffered.

The various forms of exclusion and dispossession the residents have experienced appear to have generated intense feelings of belonging and of the rightness of their cause, as well as their conviction of possessing a distinct identity among the Athenians. By a skillful manipulation of the concept of 'tradition' residents present their community as the real bearer and embodiment of tradition; 'our tradition is our way of life that we still keep, it is from our parents', a communal, socially harmonious way of life handed down through successive generations, an antithesis to the commercialized and individualist way of life of their metropolitan surround-ings. Religion is another symbolic resource the residents draw on in their narratives: referring to the razing of the neighborhood Vlastarou in the 1930s by the ASCS for the excavation of the Agora, a deeply religious woman spoke of 'the sacrifice of Byzantium', referring to the numerous demolitions of Byzantine churches in the nineteenth century by archaeologists. By drawing this parallel between the treatment of Byzantium (Christianity) and the old neighbourhoods wholly or partly razed by the archaeologists, she was recasting the history of the Anafiotika as yet another victim of the enmity against the Christian period of national history, placing the vernacular and the local under the overarching theme of Orthodox Christianity.

Collective solidarity, cleanliness, hospitality, egalitarianism 'we were all poor' are presented as ubiquitous, unchanging features of the community's identity. The metaphor of rootedness invoked and the value accorded to status conferred by birth in the settlement and family genealogy – the oldest the better – convey an essentialized, unchanging version of past and present identity. Much as the hegemonic discourse does, the residents' narratives occlude what is construed as not good for their aims; they carefully, for instance, banish from their stories the social distinctions and antagonism that emerged among residents at the time of their eviction.

By defining themselves culturally in opposition to the surrounding metropolitan ways of life the Anafiots reassert the symbolic boundaries upholding their sense of difference and, negotiating the position of an essentialized 'other' constructed by the official discourse, invert its meaning, turning this 'otherness' and their marginalization into positive self-enhancing values.

In their attempts to reconfigure a monumental landscape, the agents involved in imposing an 'appropriate' reading and uses of Greece's most prestigious monument have engaged with an 'inappropriately' located community, striving to discipline and disempower its tenacious claims to, and sense of, place. They have encountered little organized resistance at the level of social and political action. The Anafiots' collective experiences and understanding of their predicament has led them, rather, to seek ways of articulation and defence of their history and identity in the space of story telling, the space that 'protects the weapons of the weak against the reality of the established order, hiding them from the social categories which "make history" because they dominate it' (de Certeau, 1988: 23).

Acknowledgements

The research was funded by the National Centre for Social Research. Special thanks to the director of the Centre's Institute of Urban and Rural Sociology, Professor Charalambos Kasimis for his support. I would like to thank Barbara Bender (UCL) for her suggestions on a first version of this chapter and the participants at the University of Hull's International Workshop on Landscape Modernity and Exclusion held in September 1999 in Dubrovnik for their constructive and helpful observations and comments on the material I presented there. My greatest debt is to the Anafiotika residents. Special thanks to Nikos Sachas, Eleni Vlachou, Georgia Michaloliakou, Christos Papoulias, Alexandra Katsourani, Nikos Gavalas, Theodosis and Soula Degaiti.

References

Alonso, A-M. 1994. The Politics of Space, Time and Substance: State Formation, Nationalism and Ethnicity. *Annual Review of Anthropology* 23: 379–405.

Anderson, B. 1991. *Imagined Communities*. London and New York: Verso.

Angelomatis-Tsougarakis, H. 1990. *The Eve of the Greek Revival: British Travelers' Perceptions of early Nineteenth-Century Greece*. London: Routledge.

Asad, T. 1993. *Genealogies of Religion: Discipline and Reasons of Power in Christianity and Islam*. Baltimore: Johns Hopkins University Press.

Augustinos, O. 1990. *French Odyssey: Greece in French Travel Literature from the Renaissance to the Romantic Era*. Baltimore: Johns Hopkins University Press.

Bauman, Z. 1997. *Life in Fragments: Essays in Postmodern Morality*. Blackwell.

Bender, B. 1992. Theorizing Landscapes and the Prehistoric Landscapes of Stonehenge. *Man* (n.s.): 735–55.

Boyer, C. 1996. *The City of Collective Memory: Its Historical Imagery and Architectural Entertainments*. Cambridge, Mass.: MIT Press.

Buck-Sutton, S. 1995. The perception and making of an ancient site. *Σημείον Αναφοράς* **3,** (1), pp. 14–21.

—— 1997. Disconnected landscapes: ancient sites, travel guides and local identity in modern greece. *Anthropology of East Europe Review* **15** 27–36.

Cohen, A. 1985. *The symbolic construction of community*. London: Tavistock.

de Certeau, M. 1988. *The Practice of Ordinary Life*. Berkeley, Los Angeles, London: University of California Press.

Douglas, M. 1966. *Purity and Danger: An Analysis of the Concepts of Pollution and Taboo*. London: Routledge.

Durham-Peters, J. 1997. Seeing bifocally: media, place, culture, in A. Gupta and J. Ferguson (eds) *Culture Power Place; Explorations in Critical Anthropology*. Durham and London: Duke University Press 75–92.

Edholm, F. 1993. The view from below: Paris in the 1880s, in B. Bender (ed.) *Landscape: Politics and Perspectives*. Oxford: Berg 139–68.

Fabian, J. 1983. *Time and the Other: How Anthropology Makes its Object*. New York: Columbia University Press.

Foucault, M. 1980. The Eye of Power, in C. Gordon (ed.) *Power/Knowledge*. New York: Pantheon Books 146–65.

—— 1996. Space, knowledge and power, in S. Lotringer (ed.) *Foucault Live: Collected Interviews, 1961–1984*. New York: Semiotext(e) 335–47.

Gupta, A. and Ferguson, J. (eds) 1997. *Culture Power Place: Explorations in Critical Anthropology*. Durham and London: Duke University Press.

Harley, J.B. 1988. Maps, knowledge and power, in D. Cosgrove and S. Daniels (eds) *The Iconography of Landscape: Essays on the Symbolic Representation,*

Design and Use of Past Environments. Cambridge: Cambridge University Press 277–312.

Herzfeld, M. 1982. *Ours Once More: Folklore, Ideology and the Making of Modern Greece.* Austin: University of Texas Press.

—— 1989. *Anthropology through the Looking-Glass: Critical Ethnography in the Margins of Europe.* Cambridge and New York: Cambridge University Press.

—— 1991. *A Place in History: Social and Monumental Time in a Cretan Town.* Princeton, N.J.: Princeton University Press.

Just, R. 1989. The triumph of the ethnos, in E. Tonkin, M. McDonald and M. Chapman (eds) *History and Ethnicity.* London and New York: Routledge 71–88.

Kambouroglou, D. 1920. *Rizokastron: A Historical Guide*, Athens: Hestia (in Greek).

Kyriakidou-Nestoros, A. 1978. *The Theory of Greek Folklore.* Athens: Association of Studies of Modern Greek Culture (in Greek).

Leontis, A. 1995. *Topographies of Hellenism: Mapping the Homeland.* Ithaca and London: Cornell University Press.

Loukakis, A. 1997. Whose Genius Loci? Contrasting interpretations of the Sacred Rock of the Acropolis. *Annals of the Association of American Geographers* **87**(2) 306–29.

Lovell, N. 1998. *Locality and Belonging.* London/New York: Routledge.

Malkki, L. 1997. National Geographic: The rooting of peoples and the territorialization of national identity among scholars and refugees, in A. Gupta and J. Ferguson (eds) *Culture Power Place: Explorations in Critical Anthropology.* Durham and London: Duke University Press 52–74.

Nzegwu, N. 1996. Bypassing New York in re-presenting Eko: production of space in a Nigerian city, in A. King (ed.) *Re-Presenting the City: Ethnicity, Capital and Culture in 21st Century Metropolis.* London: Macmillan 111–36.

Olwig, K. Fog and Hastrup, K. 1997. Introduction, in K. Fog Olwig and K. Hastrup (eds) *Siting Culture: The Shifting Anthropological Object.* London and New York: Routledge 1–14.

Papageorgiou, A. 1965. Plaka: A proposal concerning the old town. Reprint from vol. 10, Technical Chamber of Greece (in Greek).

Sciorra, J. 1996. Return to the future: Puerto Rican vernacular architecture in New York City, in A. King (ed.) Re-Presenting the City: Ethnicity, Capital and Culture in 21st Century Metropolis. London: MacMillan 60–92.

Scott, J. 1990. *Domination and the Arts of Resistance: Hidden Transcripts.* New Haven and London: Yale University Press.

Shields, R. 1996. A guide to urban representation and what to do about it: alternative traditions of urban theory, in A. King (ed.) *Re-Presenting the City: Ethnicity, Capital and Culture in 21st Century Metropolis.* London: Macmillan 227–52.

Tilley, C. 1994. *A Phenomenology of Landscape: Places, Paths and Monuments.* Oxford: Berg.

Tuan, Yi-Fu 1991. Language and the making of place: a narrative-descriptive approach. *Annals of the Association of American Geographers* **81**(4) 584–696.

Vikelas, D. 1897. Public spirit in modern Athens. *The Century Illustrated Monthly Magazine.* **LIII**(3) 378–92.

Zerubavel, E. 1993. *The Fine Line: Making Distinctions in Everyday Life.* Chicago and London: University of Chicago Press.

–2–

Matter and Memory in the Landscapes of Conflict: The Western Front 1914–1999
Nicholas J. Saunders

Engaging Landscapes

The Western Front is a symbolic landscape for our time. In many ways it stands as a metaphor for the defining human activity of the twentieth century – industrialized war – and at the end of the century remained one of the few artefacts visible from space (Webster 1998: 63). The human experiences of Western Front landscapes between 1914 and 1918 were deeply formative. They impressed vivid imagery onto individual and collective memories, and crystalized into phrases of enduring currency: we still talk of going 'over the top', suffering shell-shock, and the dangers of 'No Man's Land'.

Hitherto, the Western Front has been seen mainly in terms of military history – as a place of stasis and attrition, human misery, and eventual victory (e.g. Brown 1993; Keegan 1998). Such assessments have tended to see landscape as inert – an empty backdrop to military action. However, it is evident that the study of any landscape crosses the boundaries between geography, anthropology, archaeology, art history, and other disciplines (Gosden 1999: 153). By changing focus – altering our theoretical engagement – we see the Western Front as not just a series of battlefields, but as a palimpsest of overlapping, multi-vocal landscapes. Each is contested by different groups who engage with its materiality in different ways (Layton and Ucko 1999: 1), and whose experience of 'being in' *their* landscape produces a sense of place and belonging (Tilley 1994: 15). The Western Front is a prime example of the social construction of landscape, of landscape as ongoing process, which has implicated the lives of a succession of people since 1914 (see Hirsch 1995: 22–3).

Regarded in this multi-dimensional way, the Western Front is composed, variously, of industrialized slaughterhouses, vast tombs for 'the missing', places for returning refugees and contested reconstruction, popular tourist destinations, locations of memorials and pilgrimage, sites for archaeological research and cultural heritage development, and as still deadly places full of unexploded shells and bombs.

The ways in which the architecture of matter can embody memories, and the ways in which memories can stimulate the production and shape of matter are important elements in this discussion. The Great War brought cataclysmic disorder to large areas of northern France and Belgium, banishing the images of a prosperous mainly pastoral past, and replacing them with those of total war. The destruction of land and life created new landscapes infused with new meanings – a reordering of existence whose memories and associations came into conflict with other realities after 1918, and continue to do so today.

Whose images of which past should take precedence in the reconstitution of matter? What kinds of memories and images can a reconstituted materiality invoke, encourage, or constrain in the minds of subsequent generations? These questions are the tip of an iceberg, for as physical place and cultural image, the Western Front is neither a single concept nor a solely historical entity. Like Stonehenge, the Soviet gulags, or the Golan Heights, the Western Front is 'something political, dynamic, and contested, something constantly open to renegotiation.' (Bender 1993: 276).

Destruction/Creation

Despite the largely static nature of trench warfare, Western Front battlefields were metaphysically unstable places. Once tilled for crops, they had been 'drenched with hot metal' (Terraine 1996: 9), the ground shattered, pastoral settings transformed into lunar landscapes of endless craters, barbed wire, devastated buildings, and blasted trees (Figure 2.1). The fields of Picardy, Artois, and Flanders had been industrialized by force, transformed from rural idyll to unrecognizable wasteland. Where before the war, and since medieval times, the texture of the sensory environment in such areas had been determined by the rhythms of nature and the structured peal of innumerable church bells (Corbin 1999: 4–5), there was now an

> . . . otherworldly landscape, [where] the bizarre mixture of putrefaction and ammunition, the presence of the dead among the living, literally holding up trench walls from Ypres to Verdun, suggested that the demonic and satanic realms were indeed here on earth (Winter 1995: 68–9).

There was a sense in which, through the agency of destruction, soldiers experienced 'being in' the landscape and contributing to its transformation through their own (often unnecessary) woundings and deaths. British and French shells fired at the enemy more often than not simply churned the ground over which their own soldiers had to advance, making progress a slow and deadly affair, if not impossible. Here, in Gosden's (1999: 161) reformulation of Foucault, the soldiers were '. . . formed as subjects by the technology they use[d]'. Personal accounts of this new kind of landscape formation were vivid.

> Showers of lead flying about and big big shells its an unearthy (sic) sight to see them drop in amongst human beings. The cries are terrible . . . (Papers of Miss Dorothy Scoles, quoted in Bourke 1996: 76).

When a barrage lifted or an attack ended, the land had been transformed. Trenches, dugouts, battlefields, and rear areas alike were strewn with the detritus of industrialized war – spent shells, cooling shrapnel, smashed tanks, lingering gas, and unexploded ordnance. Interspersed with these were the equally fragmented remains of the soldiers themselves. Through memoirs, newspaper reports, and even official accounts, there is a complex layering of language to describe such events. The desolation of landscape is described by such words as 'skeleton', 'gaunt', and 'broken' in such a way that imagery phases in and out between landscape, village, and human corpse. The result was 'a close connection, an osmosis between the death of men, of objects, of places' (Audoin-Rouzeau 1992: 81).

For French infantrymen, their Catholic faith made bomb-shattered churches and calvaries places of spiritual unease.

> At the centre of the cemetery stands a large wooden figure of Christ. One arm has been broken by a shell and hangs sadly, held on to the cross by the nailed hand. And the face, dripping with rain, appears to reflect an infinity of suffering and sadness (*La Saucisse* June 1917, quoted in Audoin-Rouzeau 1992: 85)

The physical and psychological intensities of these experiences produced a different view of the world for many soldiers. In a universe of trenches, dugouts, deafening artillery bombardments, and blind advances across No Man's Land, the visual was often denied, and replaced by other elements of sensory experience, such as smell and touch (e.g. Howes 1991: 3–5; Eksteins 1990: 146, 150–1). These new landscapes of the senses are captured in memoirs and war poetry (e.g. Blunden [1928] 1982; Sassoon [1930] 1997). If, as Tilley (1994: 10–12) and others (e.g. Hillman and Mazzio 1997; and see Stewart 1993: 125) indicate, the human body is a way of relating to and perceiving the world, then the fragmentation of human bodies and landscape on the Western Front joined together to fragment reality.

If there was any doubt as to the scale of the devastation/creation which soldiers experienced then statistics quickly dispel them. In 1920, Albert Demangeon (quoted in Clout 1996: 3–4) called the Western Front 'a zone of death, 500 km long and 10–25 km broad . . .' In the worst areas official estimates reported that more than 1,000 shells had fallen per square metre. The area around Verdun, for example, was so thick with unexploded ordnance that in November 1918 the French government closed off around 16,000,000 acres (Webster 1998: 12–13). It was estimated that some 330,000,000 cubic metres of trenches scarred the French landscape as did some 375,000,000 square metres of barbed wire (Clout

1996: 46). An estimated total of 794,040 buildings were destroyed or damaged (ibid. 49).

Matters of Memory

Landscapes exist as cultural images (i.e. graphic representations) as well as physical places (Daniels and Cosgrove 1988: 1). Between 1914 and 1939 on the Western Front, images and constructions (more accurately re-presentations and re-constructions) were multi-vocal, contesting each other as different conceptions of the world (Layton and Ucko 1999: 1).

Re-presentations 1914–1918

Visually, the war was re-presented to the British public through official drawings, paintings, photographs, films, and maps (e.g. Gough 1997). Many painters struggled to represent what they saw in the traditional pre-war manner of romanticized heroics and pastoral landscapes. These stood in stark contrast to the works of Paul Nash and Wyndham Lewis who grasped the change in perceptions of reality produced by the de-rationalization of space (e.g. Gough 1997: 417–20; Cork 1994). For Nash, Lewis, and others, the war appeared a valueless, formless experience, which could not be rendered by the conventions of the day (Hynes 1990: 108; and see Nash 1998: 29–30). It was as if the Western tradition of landscape art had broken down, and been replaced by something more akin to indigenous non-Western art, where landscape was memory and process (see Küchler 1993: 85–6). 'In a land where Nature was dead, paintings were more like elegies for the death of landscape.' (Hynes 1990: 199).

The contest of canvas images was paralleled by competing representations on photographic paper. Carrying a camera and taking photographs was prohibited by the military authorities who sought to conceal the terrible scenes of carnage (Eksteins 1990: 233). Official photographers also were constrained, the *quid pro quo* for access being adherence to the policy that images of British dead were unacceptable (ibid.). These restrictions produced a sanitized if not bizarre view of the war – landscapes of dreadful destruction peppered with enemy dead but few if any allied casualties. For the bereaved, the vast numbers of 'the missing' (in battle) were pre-figured by the even larger numbers of 'the invisible' (in photographs). Civilian notions of Western Front landscapes consequently bore little resemblance to those of soldiers – a fact which contributed to the (sometimes bitter) alienation felt by many servicemen returning home on leave (see Hynes 1990: 116).

There was also a new dimension to photography – one which adopted a highly symbolic vertical perspective. The development of reliable aircraft and the innovation of aerial photography produced monochrome images of landscapes

Figure 2.1 Cratered devastation in the Ypres Salient, 7 June 1917. Aerial photograph shows British trenches and the Hill 60 Crater below the railway cutting, which runs left to right, with Caterpillar Crater above (photo courtesy of the Imperial War Museum, London, No. Q64641)

which often appeared identical to contemporary colourless photographs of the cratered surface of the moon (Figure 2.1). Both landscapes were 'other-worldly', and both seemed inimical to human life. Equally poignant at the other end of the scale were detailed trench maps which measured the terrible human cost of miniscule territorial gains.

Perhaps the most symbolic of these detached, bird's-eye re-presentations of landscape was the 1919 mapping of devastated areas. In France, damage was assessed, graded, and shown on maps coloured in blue, yellow, and red to signify areas of increasing devastation (Clout 1994: 24). The worst affected areas, the *zones rouges*, had between 80 and 100 per cent of the land destroyed and were considered too dangerous to rebuild or reoccupy (Holt and Holt 1996: 24, 44). This multi-coloured paper landscape resonates with Whalen's (1984: 38) report, that during the 1920s French films were filled with blood 'because northern France was soaked in blood' (and see Starling 1998).

Aerial photographs and maps can be seen as the triumph of contemporary technology in producing the 'Western Gaze', a god-like view of landscape which, by skimming the surface, exercised control over the perception and experience of the world (Bender 1999: 31).

Re-constructions 1919–1939

After the war, the contest between matter and memory centred on the shape and ownership of landscapes. Whose memories, and of what past, should be given precedence in reconstruction? The politicization of these issues was as pointed as any late twentieth-century dispute over indigenous land rights and the status of sacred places in Australia, North America, and elsewhere (e.g. Layton 1998; Morphy 1993).

From 1919 until 1939, and in some cases down to the present, there were tensions between local farmers who wanted to return as soon as possible to work the land, and other civilians, the military, and governments who, in part at least, wished to retain war-torn landscapes as a testament to German aggression and the sacrifice of so many men, and in part had to recognize officially that *zones rouges* would forever be unsafe. The French farming peasantry nevertheless repeatedly contested such official assessments and their petitions led to ever downward revisions of the *zones rouges* in the decade after the armistice (Clout 1996: 28–9). As Clout (1996: 28) has also noted, there were those who considered that *zones rouges* should be cleared of unexploded ordnance, and afforested as a national monument or alternatively provided with a *voie sacrée* lined with monuments and cemeteries.

There are many examples of such disputed views of the future – from whole towns, like Ypres in Belgium, to individual features of battle, such as the huge Lochnagar Crater at La Boiselle outside Albert on the Somme (FL n.d.). Here, the local farmer's desire to fill in the crater to increase his farmland was opposed by those wished to retain it as a memorial to all who fought in the Battle of the Somme in 1916. The situation was only resolved in 1978 when the site was bought by an Englishman (Middlebrook and Middlebrook 1994: 124) after other nearby craters had been filled in and the landscape of war looked like disappearing for ever.

Events surrounding the re-construction of the medieval Belgian town of Ypres (now Ieper) are especially (perhaps uniquely) illustrative of competing memories and the shape of the future (Anon. 1999). Some, such as the architect Eugène Dhuicque said, '. . . leave the ruins as they are. Why should the 13th or 14th centuries be of more value than the four years of the World War' (Vermeulen 1999: 10). This view was expressed also by the British military authorities and veterans' associations, who believed the ruins should be holy ground held in memoriam for soldiers who had died in the Ypres Salient (see Willson 1920).

Nevertheless, the post-war shape of Ypres was not determined by the voices and memories of soldiers who had lived in, passed through, and fought around the city from 1915 to 1918, nor of those citizens of Ypres who believed in looking forward rather than backward. 'Instead of modern town-planning there was much pre-war town-scaping . . . [which produced] an ersatsz replica of what was lost forever' (Derez 1997: 450). The debate continues today: 'Ieper is a lie, a missed opportunity. [It could have been] . . . the first modern city of this century, a symbol of regrowth, forgiveness and inventiveness.' Instead, 'people prefer the sheltering past to the present and future' (Vermeulen 1999: 9–10) (Figure 2.2). One ironic consequence is that 'modern' Ypres depends on battlefield tourism for its prosperity, yet appears a characterless anachronism largely devoid of any memories or meaningful associations.

Memories of Matter

Landscapes of Pilgrimage, 1918–1939

As matter was being re-ordered through reconstruction in line with the memories and aspirations of returning refugees, the Western Front was becoming also a landscape of remembrance for thousands of battlefield pilgrims and tourists (Lloyd 1994). Their associations were less with the physical landscape than a symbolic

Figure 2.2 The Cloth Hill at Ypres (Ieper), Belgium, August 1998. The original was built in the thirteenth century, destroyed in 1915, and reconstructed as an exact replica during the 1920s (photo: N.J. Saunders)

one full of memories of loved ones – located and glimpsed through letters, postcards, souvenirs sent home, and (sometimes) home-leave conversations. Money brought in by pilgrimage tourism contributed to local economies and strengthened the financial basis of reconstruction. As Lloyd (1994: 50) observes, 'Both Belgium and France looked to tourism to help rebuild their shattered economies.'

Armed with the ubiquitous Pickfords or Michelin Battlefield Guides (see Eksteins 1994), whose illustrations portrayed devastated villages and countryside, visitors tramped across the landscape looking for places associated with their loved ones. In 1918, there were half a million unmarked British graves spread across the war zones of France and Belgium (Bourke 1996: 235). As pilgrims sought to correlate photographic images with reality they increasingly encountered discrepancies as reconstruction changed the face of the land again (e.g. Elise Guyot quoted in Clout 1996: 44). Battlefields were cleared, villages rebuilt, and cemeteries and memorials began to focus the sense of loss away from land and towards architecture (Figure 2.3). For many pilgrims, there was disappointment, fulfilment, and irony in varying parts. The reconstruction which so changed the face of the land and disoriented pilgrims was partly funded with money raised by British towns. After sacrificing their menfolk many now donated money for rebuilding, formalizing the process by officially pairing themselves with French towns, such as Birmingham and Albert, and Ipswich and Fricourt.

Figure 2.3 The Menin Gate Memorial to the Missing at Ypres (Ieper), Belgium, August 1998. It was unveiled on 24 July 1927. Despite its size, there was only room for 54,900 names; the remaining 34,888 were inscribed on the nearby Tyne Cot cemetery (photo N.J. Saunders)

Landscapes of Tourism, 1946–1999

The Second World War together with a changing society contributed to the distancing (perhaps alienation) of the unique circumstances of the Great War in post-1945 memory. This dissociation was particularly marked during the 1950s and early 1960s, which saw the nadir of public interest in the Great War, and in visits to the battlefields, cemeteries and memorials of France and Belgium (Lloyd 1994: 288; Walter 1993: 63). During these years, the Western Front became a largely forgotten landscape.

In 1964, commemorations of the fiftieth anniversary of the start of the Great War and the broadcasting of several television histories – notably the BBC's monumental *The Great War* – brought the 1914–18 conflict into countless homes. Public awareness of events was potentially deeper and more widespread during the mid-1960s than at any time since the war itself. In one sense, the Great War was the first 'television war', pre-empting daily coverage of the Vietnam conflict. The impact was immediate. Re-branded as 'cultural memory', television images stimulated the desire to visit the battlefields and memorials of the Western Front.

The early 1970s saw some 50,000 visitors a year. By 1974, this had increased to 250,000 (Lloyd 1994: 289). Similarly, personal enquiries concerning the whereabouts of a grave made to the Commonwealth War Graves Commission (CWGC) rose from 1500 a year in the mid 1960s to 8,000 in 1980 and an astonishing 28,000 in 1990 (Walter 1993: 63). Numbers continued to grow during the 1980s and 1990s, as indicated by the mushrooming of commercial tour companies specializing in battlefield tours (Walter 1993: 63, 67–9). The increase in tourists began to change both the physical and cultural landscapes in terms of re-presenting Great War sites to a late twentieth-century audience.

The 'Western Front Experience' in the Somme département is now part of an integrated tourist circuit as conceived and promoted by the official tourist office at Amiens (e.g. CDTS n.d.; and see HGG 1997). Great War battlefields are now 'of a piece' with the nearby attractions of Euro-Disney, Parc Astérix, and the archaeological theme park at Samara (SG.n.d.; Dieudonné 1999). A similar integration of Great War sites with other local attractions is found at Ypres in Belgium (Holt and Holt 1997: 54–5).

Battlefield tour itineraries create landscapes within landscapes – selected tourist 'stops' that all visitors 'know' through personal experience. These are a mix of 'preserved battlefields' (see below), impressive or newly erected memorials, café-museums, unusual or scenic CWGC cemeteries, and the major museum of the area – i.e. *In Flanders Fields* at Ypres, and *L'Historial de la Grande Guerre* at Péronne on the Somme.

The social worlds and symbolic landscapes of the 1920s have been overlain by and integrated within a reconfigured economic reality. New kinds of tourists now visit the Western Front. They struggle to imagine the verdant woods and fields as monochrome images of Hell, just as returning refugees in 1919 struggled to imagine devastated landscapes as fertile pastures and farms. Each is/was in one landscape imagining being in another.

Today, in a manner akin to that of the sacred places of traditional societies (Carmichael *et al.* 1994), the Western Front has become a symbolic landscape of remembrance (Winter 1995) – a place where personal and cultural identities are explored and created (Tilley 1994: 15, 26). 'The missing' dominate this landscape both as a spiritual presence and physically – in huge memorials such as Thiepval on the Somme and Tyne Cot near Passchendaele. Over 100,000 scattered and lost remains (of all participating nations) still lie beneath the reconstituted fields of the Somme alone (Middlebrook and Middlebrook 1994: 356).

Ambiguous Landscapes: the Western Front Today

Until the twentieth century, landscapes of war were of a piece with others – physical places whose symbolic dimensions endured only as long as personal or group memory allowed. They did not arbitrarily or autonomously generate new associations, though new meanings and significances could be renegotiated and revitalized at any time by human groups who occupied them or knew of their existence. From Megiddo (Armageddon) to Agincourt and Waterloo, such landscapes were deadly only to the protagonists and only while fighting continued.

The Great War of 1914–1918 changed this for ever. Battlefield landscapes retained previous significances, but now became 'live' and pro-active by virtue of the vast quantities of unexploded ordnance left in the ground. These landscapes could now kill and maim indiscriminately, long after conflict had been resolved, and long after the original protagonists had passed away and direct memory of events faded.

Déminage

Today, unexploded ordnance is the defining feature of the Western Front. Over 28,000,000 artillery shells, bombs and grenades from both world wars have been collected in France alone. In 1991, a total of 36 French farmers were killed when their machinery hit unexploded shells (Webster 1994: 29), and between 1946 and 1994, 630 French *démineurs* died during attempts to retrieve and defuse ordnance (ibid.: 28).

In the late 1990s, an average year on the Somme yielded around 90 tonnes of dangerously volatile 'hardware' – known as the 'iron harvest' (Holt and Holt 1996: 12; and see Coombs 1994: 6), and throughout France some 900 tons of shells, of which 30 tons are toxic, are recovered annually (Webster 1998: 24). In Belgium, in the area around Ypres, up to 250,000 kgs of such materials can be recovered in a year – disposed of by the Belgian Army in two or three controlled explosions a day (Lt. Col. L. Deprez-Wouts, pers. comm. 1998; and see Derez 1997: 443). In the early 1990s, more than a million German grenades were found in a lake in Alsace (Webster 1998: 50). Not even the cultural paradise of the beach (Lenček and Bosker 1999) escapes the ambiguity. At Le Crotoy on northern France's Opal Coast, ordnance is buried in the sand at low tide and exploded at high tide at the rate of six tons of bombs a day, five days a week, for one week per month (Webster 1998: 56).

Occasionally, shells rise to the surface inside war cemeteries – pockets of French or Belgian land ceded in perpetuity to the British, Commonwealth, and American governments. In France, these shells are the responsibility of the nation to which the land has been given and the *Département du Déminage* is forbidden to intervene (Webster 1998: 32). In Belgium, more pragmatically, the local gendarmerie inform the Commonwealth War Graves Commission office in Ypres, and then the Belgian Army's bomb disposal unit enters the cemetery and removes the shells (Snr. Capt. A. Vander Mast, pers. comm. 1999).

Unexploded ordnance has given rise also to two other kinds of landscape where public access is restricted. The first contains the *villages détruits*, such as Louvemont near Verdun (Webster 1998: 63), and the five villages whose remains now lie within the French Army training area of Camp de Suippes in Champagne (Fair 1998). Related to these are places which exhibit a strange arrangement of death and leisure. In the midst of some prohibited regions are areas cleared of ordnance with signs announcing their suitability for picknicking (Webster 1998: 64). Mount Kemmel, near Ypres, was devastated by German bombardment in April 1918. Today it is a popular weekend leisure spot. Belgian and French families picnic and walk along narrow paths on its forested slopes separated by flimsy wire fences from untold thousands of volatile unexploded shells and bombs lying just inches away. Eighty years after that war, as the French *démineur* Remy Deleuze was able to say, 'Any dreams France [or Belgium] has of feeling completely safe from the First War . . . are exactly that: dreams.' (quoted in Webster 1994: 30).

Archaeologies

The old Western Front today is increasingly contested by those who retrieve the physical remains of the conflict of 1914–18, and to a lesser extent of that of 1939–45. First, there are those who scavenge the battlefields for mementoes – out of personal interest, or for commercial gain. Their activities range from casual field-walking to metal-detecting, from clandestine digging to stripping human remains of personal effects and military paraphernalia. Such behaviour, and the consequent scattering of human remains, almost always precludes the possibilities of identification and burial in a military cemetery. Astonishingly, there have been attempts to justify and dignify such morally dubious and illegal activities as a kind of archaeology: '. . . the [battlefield] visitor needs nothing more than a good guidebook to become an "archaeologist"' (Laffin 1987: 70) and 'There is nothing sacrilegious about digging relics from battlefields . . .' (ibid.:10). The relatives of the tens of thousands of 'the missing' might well disagree.

More recently, there have been moves towards establishing a scientifically credible sub-discipline of battlefield archaeology on the Western Front (see Saunders n.d. for overview), and an associated concern with the regions' geologies in relation to war (e.g. Doyle 1998; Rose and Rosenbaum 1993). To date, this has taken the form of thorough and sometimes innovative excavations of widely varying structures (e.g. Bostyn 1999) though currently on a necessarily ad hoc basis rather than as part of a systematic programme of investigation (Figure 2.4). There is great potential for such investigations, as the speed of post-war reconstruction left whole systems of trenches, dugouts, *matériel*, and human remains (often perfectly) preserved just centimetres beneath the modern household and crop-growing surface.

Figure 2.4 Excavations at Beecham Farm, near Passchendaele in the Ypres Salient, Belgium, August 1999. The site was an elaborate system of underground wooden dugouts, used by both sides at different times. Finds included a bandolier stamped '156th Brigade Royal Field Artillery', and a newspaper of 24 January 1918 (photo Johan Vandewalle, copyright Association for Battlefield Archaeology in Flanders, Zonnebeke)

Archaeology creates a tension between past and present. Complex issues of whether to excavate, how to treat human remains, and where to place them, are well known from repatriation and reburial cases concerning indigenous peoples in Australia and the Americas (e.g. Price 1991). The Western Front is no exception – indeed it manifests a unique mix of reburial issues. There are four national (Christian) burial/re-burial policies (i.e. British and Commonwealth, French, Belgian, and German), but also a multitude of non-European soldiers and service personnel (from Native America, India, Africa, and China), most of whom possessed different languages, religions, worldviews, and attitudes towards the soul and treatment of the dead. Such diversity is dealt with by the Commonwealth War Graves Commission by the interment of identified bodies with military honours in a CWGC cemetery (e.g. Brazier 1998), with due respect given to non-Christian mortuary practices and beliefs wherever possible.

Equally problematic is the disinterest/disrespect for the dead among modern inhabitants of battlefield areas. In France, battlefields are sacred ground, and unofficial disturbance an offence. Yet, whereas around Verdun enforcement appears strict, elsewhere application seems selective. When the remains of British and Imperial soldiers were discovered on the Somme during construction of the TGV railtrack from Paris to Calais, many were ignored and unceremoniously covered over so as not to disrupt deadlines for completion (and see, Desfossés 1999: 39–41).

Heritage

Apart from a credible archaeology, the most recent development to contest Western Front landscapes has been that which combines elements of preservation, re-construction, and re-presentation of parts of Great War battlefields as more or less emotionally charged aspects of cultural heritage (e.g. Coombs 1994: 91; Fair 1998). The major stimulus has been the recent surge in battlefield tourism (see above) which requires key locations for tour itineraries, where tourists can 'experience' an 'authentic' battleground (i.e. usually a trench system). The 'preserved trenches' at Sanctuary Wood Museum/Café outside Ypres, and the more dignified Newfound-land Memorial Park at Beaumont Hamel on the Somme, are two different approaches to re-presenting the war to a new generation of visitors.

If the Second World War's legacy of pill boxes, airfields, and gun emplacements can be seen as having transformed Britain's landscape (Layton and Ucko 1999: 15), how much more did the Great War transform – and, through *déminage*, memorialization, pilgrimage, tourism, and archaeological research, continue to transform – the landscapes of France and Belgium? The Western Front is a complex series of landscapes, made poignant by the vast quantities of dead it produced, and in large part still conceals. Only in the late 1990s were scholars responding to the challenge of understanding its many layers of meaning, the visceral elements which constitute our cultural memory of war.

Acknowledgements

For invaluable help and advice in researching the issues dealt with here I would like to thank the following: Senior Captain A. Vander Mast (Langemark-Poelkapelle), Johan Vandewalle and Franky Bostyn (Zonnebeke), Hugh Clout and Barbara Bender (UCL), Annette Becker (Paris X Nanterre), Jan Dewilde (Stedelijke Museum, Ieper), Peter Doyle (Greenwich). I gratefully acknowledge the financial support of University College London, and of the British Academy through its award of an Institutional Fellowship.

References

Anon. 1999. Verwoest Gewest, Ieper 1919– *Flanders Fields Magazine* **1**(2) 12–15.

Audoin-Rouzeau, S. 1992. *Men at War 1914–1918: National Sentiment and Trench Journalism in France during the First World War*. Oxford: Berg.

Bender, B. 1993. Stonehenge – contested landscapes (medieval to present-day), in B. Bender (ed.) *Landscape: Politics and Perspectives*. Oxford: Berg. 245–79.

—— 1999. Subverting the Western gaze: mapping alternative worlds, in P.J. Ucko and R. Layton (eds) *The Archaeology and Anthropology of Landscape: Shaping your Landscape*. London: Routledge. 31–45.

Blunden, E. [1928] 1982. *Undertones of War*. Harmondsworth: Penguin.

Bostyn, F. 1999. *Beecham Dugout, Passchendaele 1914–1918*. Zonnebeke: Association for Battlefield Archaeology in Flanders, Studies 1.

Bourke, J. 1996. *Dismembering the Male: Men's Bodies, Britain and the Great War*. London: Reaktion Books.

Brazier, J. 1998. Re-burial of 27 soldiers from 13th Bn Royal Fusiliers at Monchy-le-Preux. *The Western Front Association Bulletin* **50** 39.

Brown, M. 1993. *The Imperial War Museum Book of the Western Front*. London: Sidgwick & Jackson.

Carmichael, D.L., J. Hubert, B. Reeves, and O. Schanche (eds) 1994. *Sacred Sites, Sacred Places*. London: Routledge.

CDTS. n.d. *Not to be missed: 16 places of interest in the Somme*. Leaflet produced by the Comité Départemental du Tourisme de la Somme. Amiens.

Clout, H. 1996. *After The Ruins: Restoring the Countryside of Northern France after the Great War*. Exeter: University of Exeter Press.

Coombs, R.E.B. 1994. *Before Endeavours Fade* (7th edn). London: Battle of Britain Prints International Ltd.

Corbin, A. 1999. *Village Bells: Sound and Meaning in the Nineteenth-century French Countryside*. London: Papermac/Macmillan.

Cork, R. 1994. *A Bitter Truth: Avant-Garde Art and the Great War*. New Haven: Yale University Press.

Daniels, S. and Cosgrove, D. 1988. Introduction: iconography and landscape, in D. Cosgrove and S. Daniels (eds) *The Iconography of Landscape*. Cambridge: Cambridge University Press. 1–10.

Derez, M. 1997. A Belgian salient for reconstruction: people and *Patrie*, landscape and memory, in P.H. Liddle (ed.) *Passchendaele in Perspective: The Third Battle of Ypres*. London: Leo Cooper. 437–58.

Desfossés, Y. 1999. Préserver les traces. *L'Archéologie et la Grande Guerre Aujourd'hui. Noêsis: Revue Annuelle D'Histoire* **2** 37–51.

Dieudonné, G. 1999. Experimental archaeology and education: ancient technology at the service of modern education at SAMARA, France, in P.G. Stone and P.G. Planel (eds) *The Constructed Past: Experimental Archaeology, Education and the Public*. London: Routledge. 206–16.

Doyle, P. 1998. *Geology of the Western Front, 1914–1918*. London: The Geologists Association.

Eksteins, M. 1990. *The Rites of Spring: The Great War and the Birth of the Modern Age*. Boston: Houghton Mifflin.

—— 1994. Michelin, Pickfords et La Grande Guerre: le tourisme sur Le Front Occidental: 1919–1991, in J-J. Becker, J. Winter, G. Krumeich, A. Becker and S. Audoin-Rouzeau (eds) *Guerre et cultures, 1914–1918*. Paris: Armand Colin Éditeur. 417–28.

Fair, C. 1998. The Lost Villages of the Camp de Suippes, Champagne: La Journée des Villages Détruits. *The Western Front Association Bulletin* **51** 32.

FL. n.d. *An Invitation to Join the Friends of Lochnagar* (Leaflet). Pinner: The Friends of Lochnagar.

Gosden, C. 1999. *Anthropology and Archaeology: A changing relationship*. London: Routledge.

Gough, P. 1997. An epic of mud: artistic impressions of Third Ypres, in P.H. Liddle (ed.) *Passchendaele in Perspective: The Third Battle of Ypres*. London: Leo Cooper. 409–21.

HGG. 1997. *Visitez L'Historial de la Grande Guerre: Premier Musée International Trilingue sur la Première Guerre Mondiale en Europe*. Leaflet produced by the Historial de la Grande Guerre. Péronne.

Hillman, D. and Mazzio, C. 1997. Introduction, in D. Hillman and C. Mazzio (eds) *The Body in Parts: Fantasies of Corporeality in Early Modern Europe.* London: Routledge. xi–xxix.

Hirsch, E. 1995. Introduction: landscape: between place and space, in E. Hirsch and M. O'Hanlon (eds) *The Anthropology of Landscape: Perspectives on Place and Space.* Oxford: Oxford University Press. 1–20.

Holt, T. and Holt, V. 1996. *Major and Mrs Holts Battlefield Guide to the Somme.* London: Leo Cooper.

—— 1997. *Major and Mrs Holts Battlefield Guide to the Ypres Salient.* London: Leo Cooper.

Howes, D. 1991. Introduction: to summon all the senses, in D. Howes (ed.) *The Varieties of Sensory Experience.* Toronto: University of Toronto Press. 3–21.

Hynes, S. 1990. *A War Imagined: The First World War and English Culture.* London: The Bodley Head.

Keegan, J. 1998. *The First World War.* London: Hutchinson.

Küchler, S. 1993. Landscape as memory: the mapping process and its representation in a Melanesian society, in B. Bender (ed.) *Landscape: Politics and Perspectives.* Oxford: Berg. 85–106.

Laffin, J. 1987. *Battlefield Archaeology.* London: Ian Allan Ltd.

Layton, R. (ed.). 1998. *Conflict in the Archaeology of Living Traditions.* London: Unwin Hyman.

Lenček, L. and G. Bosker. 1999. *The Beach: The History of Paradise on Earth.* London: Pimlico.

Lloyd, D.W. 1994. *Tourism, Pilgrimage, and the Commemoration of the Great War in Great Britain, Australia and Canada, 1919–1939.* Ph.D Thesis, Cambridge University.

Middlebrook, M. and M. Middlebrook, 1994. *The Somme Battlefields: A Comprehensive Guide from Crécy to the Two World Wars.* Harmondsworth: Penguin.

Morphy, H. 1993. Colonialism, history and the construction of place: the politics of landscape in Northern Australia, in B. Bender (ed.) *Landscape: Politics and Perspectives.* Oxford: Berg. 205–43.

Nash, P. 1998. Letter by Paul Nash, Official War Artist, 18th November 1918, in *Flanders Fields Museum, Cloth Hall, Market Square, Ieper: Eye Witness Accounts of the Great War: Guide to Quotations.* Ieper: Province of West Flanders.

Price, H.M. 1991. *Disputing the Dead: US Law on Aboriginal Remains and Grave Goods.* Columbia: University of Missouri Press.

Rose, E.P.F. and Rosenbaum, M.S. 1993. British military geologists: The formative years to the end of the First World War. *Geologists Associations Proceedings* **104** 41–9.

Sassoon, S. [1930] 1997. *Memoirs of an Infantry Officer.* London: Faber & Faber.

Saunders, N.J. n.d. *Archaeology, War, and the Great War 1914–1918.* Mss in preparation.

SG. n.d. *Samara: The Guide.* Amiens: La Communication et La Culture du Conseil Général de la Somme.

Starling, R. 1998. Rethinking the power of maps: some reflections on paper landscapes. *Ecumene* **5**(1) 105–8.

Stewart, S. 1993. *On Longing: Narratives of the Miniature, the Gigantic, the Souvenir, the Collection.* Durham: Duke University Press.

Terraine, J. 1996. The substance of the War, in H. Cecil and P.H. Liddle (eds) *Facing Armageddon: The First World War Experienced.* London: Leo Cooper. 3–15.

Tilley, C. 1994. *A Phenomenology of Landscape: Places, Paths and Monuments.* Oxford: Berg.

Ucko, P.J. and Layton, R. 1999. Introduction: gazing on the landscape and encountering the environment, in P.J. Ucko and R. Layton (eds) *The Archaeology and Anthropology of Landscape: Shaping your Landscape.* London: Routledge. 1–20.

Vermeulen, B. 1999. Ieper is a lie, in *Flanders Fields Magazine* **1**(1) 9–11.

Walter, T. 1993. War Grave pilgrimage, in I. Reader and T. Walter (eds) *Pilgrimage in Popular Culture.* Houndmills: Macmillan Press. 63–91.

Webster, D. 1994. The soldiers moved on; the war moved on; the bombs stayed. *Smithsonian Magazine* February 26–37.

—— 1998. *Aftermath: The Remnants of War.* New York: Vintage Books.

Whalen, R.W. 1984. *Bitter Wounds: German Victims of the Great War, 1914–1939.* Ithaca: Cornell University Press.

Willson, Lt.-Col. H.B. 1920. *Ypres: The Holy Ground of British Arms.* Bruges: Bayaert.

Winter, J. 1995. *Sites of Memory, Sites of Mourning: The Great War in European Cultural History.* Cambridge: Cambridge University Press.

–3–

Contested Landscapes in Inner Mongolia:
Walls and Cairns
Caroline Humphrey

Introduction

Following Hirsch (1995: 1), I use 'landscape' to refer to the meanings imputed by local people to their cultural and physical surroundings. This chapter provides a brief introduction to one region of Inner Mongolia settled by both Mongols and Chinese, each people seeing a very different landscape in the same territory. These landscapes arise within ways of life and memories; they are sedimented outcomes of many centuries of difference. I have shown elsewhere (Humphrey 1995) that there is no such unified perspective as 'the Mongolian landscape', since people may switch between at least two dominant kinds of landscape conception depending on the social context in which it is invoked (I called these 'chiefly' and 'shamanic' landscapes). In this chapter, the concept of landscape is yet further complicated. It is suggested that even rather abstract spatial relations within landscapes, when they appear in the form of built constructions, may be 'motivated' by an opposi-tional politics of confrontation with the landscape of another culture. To demon-strate this I take the example of the Chinese wall (or walled enclosure) and two Mongolian constructions, the *sach* (a protective shrine) and the *oboo* (a sacred cairn).

A field study was conducted in summer 1998, based at the Mongolian Buddhist monastery of Mergen Süm, just to the north of the bend of the Yellow River (Xuang-he), which flows west to east and curves round the Ordos grasslands. Some 25 kilometres from the river and parallel to it rise the craggy Mona Uul mountains (*c.* 6,000 feet). From north to south the region consists of a series of ecologically contrasted bands: a high, hilly, sandy steppe to the north of Mona Uul, historically home to Mongol pastoralists; the precipitous mountains with their caves, bubbling springs, pockets of grass, and luxuriant juniper trees; a strip of stony pasture to the 'front' where mountain streams run off and disappear into the plain; and the fertile, now densely-farmed, valley floor of the Yellow River. Mongols are aware of the dynamic possibilities of this physical situation: the Yellow River changed its main course around 150 years ago; then a band of moving sand spread from

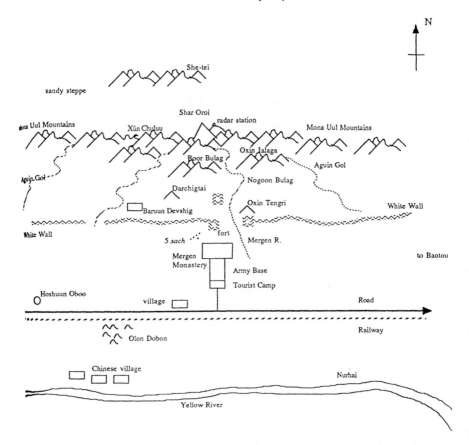

Figure 3.1 Sketch map (not to scale) of the environs of Mergen Monastery, Inner Mongolia

west to east across the northern steppe within living memory; and torrents and landslides are frequent occurrences that change land configurations and constantly threaten shepherds living in the mountains. Such physical events are incorporated conceptually into a cultural 'landscape' that itself generates ideas of danger, sacredness, avoidance, and worship. The dynamics of wind directions and rain patterns are also highly salient. Mongols are very sensitive to position, movement, direction and spatiality. Some ritual objects are constructed and sited for no other reason than to 'contain' or 'repel' supernatural influences following certain land contours and weather events.

This whole terrain is densely scattered with ritual places. Mountain, caves, rivers, trees, springs, crags and stones, and combinations of these objects, are thought to be the dwelling places of powers and spirits. Material constructions at such places are numerous, including cairns (M. *oboo*), stone altars, small temples, pagodas

Figure 3.2 A temple inside Mergen Monastery (photo: B. Zhimbier)

and shrines, and ephemera such as ribbons tied to sacred trees. The Chinese and Mongols have strikingly different ideas about sacred aspects of the natural world, and even when one might imagine they are similar (for example, both peoples in the region have cults of mountains), the ritual practices and entire conceptualization of the worship are different. Systems linking topographies to human decisions (astrology in the case of the Mongols and *feng-shui* in the case of the Chinese) also differ.

This region has been a shifting frontier of confrontation between different ways of life. The Mongols are pastoralists, and until the 1950s–60s mostly lived in a dispersed, mobile and scattered way. The Chinese on the other hand are settled, village-based agriculturalists, who nevertheless have advanced and retreated over these border lands for millennia. The idea of 'the Great Wall' as the boundary of civilization is important for them, and several, mostly ruined, walls in the region mark the lines of these advances and retreats. The Mongols tend to pass over the land, allowing pasture to regenerate and constructing few buildings. They have what one might call a negative cult (strict avoidance, fear) of graves and remains of ancient habitations. The only exception to this are the ritual cairns (*oboo*) associated with noted ancestors who are held to have become spirit-masters (M. *ejin*, pl. *ejid*) of the land, in which case the cairn is not considered to be a grave. The Chinese, on the other hand, revere their graves and clean and rebuild them each year at a ceremony in spring. At the present time, the Mongols are far more prone than the Chinese to sacralize natural objects. The Mongols are mostly quite devout Buddhists and they all take part in the sacrifices at *oboo* cairns. The Chinese of this area, on the other hand, mostly ignore the mixture of Daoism and folk-religious practices that was common a couple of generations ago and have only a spectator-type interest in Buddhism. In general, the Mongols and Chinese in rural areas today lead separate social lives and intermarriage is disfavoured. This reflects different, deep-rooted 'ecological identities',[1] which have persisted despite centuries of interaction.

Walls

The main line of the well-known 'Great Wall' was built to the south of the studied area between 1470 and 1480 during the Ming Dynasty (1368–1644). However, far earlier, the Chinese had extended their rule up to the Mona Uul mountains. We observed an ancient wall, immediately to the south of the mountains, known locally as the White Wall, which seems to have been built under the Zhao (Chao) around 300 BC (Waldron 1990: 15). This section of wall later formed part of the extensive imperial Qin (Ch'in) wall, and it was subsequently rebuilt during the Western Han Dynasty in the second century BC during the Chinese expansion against the pastoralist Xiongnu (Hsiung-nu). The wall subsequently fell into desuetude with repeated 'barbarian' conquests of northern China. It was essentially an earth rampart, and like other early walls bears little similarity to the magnificent stone fortifications of the Ming 'Great Wall'. Today, the White Wall consists of a double line of large boulders (many removed for building purposes) enclosing packed whitish earth, and it looks in places like a weather-beaten road base. At points where rivers flow down from the mountains the wall is interrupted, and there are raised square constructions on both banks which seem to have served as forts and beacons.

In general, the sporadic Chinese occupation of the area north of the Yellow River can be characterized as military and defensive, while, at least in recent centuries, the Mongolian front has been a religious one. A series of Buddhist monasteries, built in the seventeenth to eighteenth centuries, are situated along the south face of the Mona Uul and Da Qing Shan Mountains. The Mergen monastery was sacked by the Chinese army in 1913 when the Mongols declared allegiance to Outer Mongolia. Chinese military occupation again erupted on the scene in the 1960s with the Sino-Soviet split. The monastery was occupied by the

---

1. See Williams (1996), in which the idea of 'ecological identity' accounts for the way in which the cultural representations of ecology of the Mongols and Chinese ground intersubjective experiences of identity and meaning for local residents.

People's Liberation Army, which made it a forward base for anti-Soviet operations. (At this time, Soviet Red Army troops were based over the border in Mongolia.) The PLA attempted to build a radar installation on the highest peak of Mona Uula range, a mountain sacred to the Mongols and known as Shar Oroi. However, initial dynamiting to level the peak was followed by the death of several soldiers and it was decided to build the base on a nearby mountain. Mongolians attribute these deaths to the revenge taken by the 'master spirit' of Shar Oroi, a deity called Mona Khan.

During the Cultural Revolution, 1968–72, the temple buildings were again sacked; this time, however, by local Mongol enthusiasts. All sacred books and ritual items were removed and destroyed. *Oboo*s, pagodas and small temples in the hills were attacked. The few remaining lamas were punished or jailed. The army also demolished many structures, and then built barracks and a solid 4m high stone wall round the entire army–monastery complex.

In 1983 a miraculous event occurred, or so it is seen by local Mongols. A fantastic spring wind blew down the front wall built by the army. The few remaining lamas, old men living scattered in nearby settlements, had earlier noted portents of the revival of Buddhism. They were ready for this event, and seizing the sacred ashes (*sharil*) of the last 8th Reincarnation of the Mergen Gegeen, they stormed over the ruined wall into the monastery, ignoring the protests of the soldiers. The ashes were placed in the Temple of Ashes, and the lamas refused to go away. In 1994 the army left the monastery and abandoned the radar station, although the military still retains ownership of the complex today.

Evidently, walls having quite different meanings for the Mongols and the Chinese. For the Chinese, the local and barely visible White Wall fed into[2] the concept of 'The Wall', which they commonly referred to not as Chang Cheng (Great Wall) but by the terms 'inside the gate' (*kou-li*) and 'outside the gate' (*kou-wai*). So people would say, 'He went to *kou-li*', or 'My grandfather came from *kou-wai*.' The 'gate' does not refer to a definite gate in a section of wall, but to an understanding that certain regions were 'inside' – inside, people implied, real China.

At the same time, for the Chinese, walls and gates signify order, safety and control wherever they are located. This is why the episode of the miraculous blowing down of the army-built monastery wall and its storming by the lamas has such resonance for the Mongols.

The area of Mona Uul was definitely located outside the conceptual China of *kou-li*. For local Chinese, notwithstanding the presence of the White Wall and walled cities dating back to the third millennium BC, this whole region was still seen as a frontier area waiting for economic development. Thus, they often referred

---

2. It was said by local people to join up with a high, well-built Ming wall at a place called Badaling.

to the village of San-ding Zhanfang ('three yurts') by another name, Heliangdi ('good wetland'). This contrasted directly with the Mongol understanding that this was their pasture land. 'All the land up to the Yellow River is ours,' the Mongols often said to us.

The literature on the Great Wall undermines a constant monocausal explanation (walls were built by Chinese for defence against nomad raids) by proposing that they had different purposes at different periods. At times they may have been constructed less for defence than as boundary markers of the Sinic culture, which was universalistic in principle but floundered when faced with aggressive nomads with different values (Waldron 1990: 32–3). Another theory is that the early walls were built in order to define populations at the period of the first Qin consolidation of the Chinese state, in effect to keep the Han Chinese in and prevent them escaping to become nomads (Lattimore 1940). While the idea of 'inside and outside the gate' lends some support to such theories, they do not apply to present-day local Chinese understandings of the White Wall, which according to residents was built in ancient times as part of a straightforwardly defensive strategy against barbarians.

Nevertheless, Mongol interpretations of the local White Wall differ from those of the Chinese. First, Urad intellectuals living in Huhhot queried its position: if you are defending against warlike enemies from the north, why build a wall at the very foot of steep mountains, from which it is only too easy to shoot above and over any wall? Might this wall not have been been built by the Mongols, e.g. to keep their flocks in? Local Urad Mongols, however, did not have this idea, but rather saw the wall lineally, that is from the point of view of those building it. They called *Pao-ma-bie-chang* ('running horse compression wall'). It was constructed, they said, by the Chinese Aimtugai Khan (Frightened King), who insisted that the workers build as much wall in a day as a horse could run. The workers built madly and died day by day, filling the wall with their corpses and bones. The wall thus had in principle a sacred aspect. Furthermore, people said that the whitish mud inside the wall is not local earth but something different with special qualities. One place we were shown was called *tai shoroo* (pagoda earth), and this, the crumbled remains of a tall pagoda-like point in the wall, was said to provide a powerful medicine curing serious illnesses such as hemiplegia.[3]

This idea of the wall as *a way*, is found elsewhere in Mongol cultures,[4] and accords with the importance given to movement and direction among the

---

3. When a person falls ill, someone is sent to fetch earth from the *tai shoroo* in the White Wall; this is then put in a bottle of alcohol, and when the alcohol's colour changes to red it is drunk for a cure.

4. See, for example, the Daur story of the competition between the Khan and his daughter-in-law to see which of them can build a wall to Beijing most quickly. This is an explanation for an ancient wall in the Morin Dawaa region (Humphrey 1996).

pastoralists. The wall itself appears in the story above as a process of movement in space-time.

The different conceptions of the White Wall, as a barrier (Chinese) and as a way (Mongol), are reiterated in other built structures of the two peoples in recent centuries and the present. The Chinese surround their buildings with walls, not just as for their houses, cities and villages in the past, but also in the present for the military compound and the tourist camp located near the monastery. The Mongols are less likely to do this,[5] and their ritual sites in particular are in built in the open. The Mergen Monastery had no surrounding wall but rather a circumambulation path called *gorio*.[6] Similarly, the Mongolian *oboo* is a cairn that stands in the open, encircled by the invisible path of the worshippers.

Oboo Cairns

An *oboo*[7] is a rounded cairn of stones, often shaped like an inverted Mongol yurt, piled over a cone of pressed earth. There are several kinds of *oboo*. Sacrificial (*taxidag*) *oboo*s are sites for large, regular, collective sacrifices for the purpose of obtaining blessings for the community. In most parts of Mongolia, *oboo*s are sited on sacred mountains. The spirit recipients of the sacrifices are numerous and varied, including ancestors (often mythic ancestors) whose souls have become spirits of the land, as well as land-masters of heavenly origin, and *luus* (gods of water, dragons). As well as the spirit of the given *oboo*, prayers call on the masters of numerous other places thus invoking the wide spirit-topology of the worshippers. The other kinds of *oboo* found in the Mergen area are those erected by the lamas,[8] wayside (*zamyn*) and defile (*xöteliin*) cairns, where passers-by make small offerings to land spirits.

Our research team had anticipated that *oboo*s might be very old structures, since worship of mountains is documented among the Mongols from the thirteenth century and their nomadic forebears the Qidan and Xianbei. We thought that archaeological sequencing of *oboo* structures might enable us to discover continuities in mountain cults through the series of different peoples inhabiting the region. However, the spatial disjunction between the sacred mountain of Shar Oroi and

---

5. Mongol settlements and towns often had wooden fences (*xüree*), but pastoralists' camps are set up in the open. The banditry affecting the Mergen area in the 1930s–40s drove Mongols either to protect their settlements with walls or to flee into the mountains.

6. The *gorio* was at the same time a kind of ritual boundary. Impure beings, such as women and donkeys, were not allowed within it, and lamas were instructed to defecate outside it.

7. Written Mongolian *oboga*, meaning a heap or pile.

8. North of the monastery is Lamxain Oboo (Lamas' Oboo) and to the west, just outside the army wall, is a large *oboo* called Olon Huvragiin Oboo (Oboo of the Many Student Lamas).

the *oboo* presented some problems for this idea. Furthermore, we had not paid sufficient attention to what the Mongols themselves say, which is *both* that *oboos* are timelessly ancient *and* that a given *oboo* is linked with a specific ancestor who is often datable historically. It is probable that while the idea of an *oboo* (or some ontologically equivalent structure) is rather old, the *oboos* as physical objects in the Mergen area are not ancient but were constructed in the seventeenth century, as local people say, with the arrival of the Urad ancestors.

The main *oboo* of the Mergen area is called Banner (Hushuun) Oboo. It consists of one main cairn, some 20ft high, with twelve small cairns in a line directed to the north-east. Threaded among the stones of the main cairn is a long rope of strips of ox-skin, which symbolizes the belt holding together the scattered people of Urad. Anyone approaching the *oboo* is supposed to add stones ('so it grows large over the years') and to make a clockwise circumambulation three times. In the past, only males attended the annual rites[9] and the mass circling of the cairn was done on horseback.

The Hoshuun Oboo as a holy site is the focus of several bitter histories of recent times illustrating the idea of punishment-misfortune. One Mongol who had led the Red Guards in their orgy of destruction was called Tulga. When the *oboo* was rebuilt he felt regret for his actions and he offered to give a horse as a consecrated animal (*seter*) dedicated to the *oboo* spirit. The people agreed, but when the horse was ritually dedicated and set free it ran away to the mountains and was lost. Later, Tulga went to the mountains, found the horse and sold it without telling anyone. Soon, he was beaten up by unknown people and died. His corpse strangely decomposed within a day, so he had rapidly to be buried (against Mongol custom). People saw thirteen snakes crawling from his grave, one snake for each of the thirteen cairns of the Banner *oboo*. This death, people say, was clearly a supernatural punishment.

Along the front of the Mona Uul range, the same 'landscape' is repeated at each major valley. There are sacred peaks in the mountains, a Buddhist monastery in the foothills, a section of White Wall with medicinal earth nearby, a sacrificial *oboo* in the plain in front, and several worshipped springs and trees in the vicinity. All of these objects stand in the open, not protected by walls. Instead, Mongol landscape ideas link them to ways and directions.

---

9. Adult women were wives, who by definition in this exogamous clan society came from outside groups. Their foreign presence was held to be polluting in the context of clan festivities. Young girls, who were daughters/sisters in the clan, could attend in the capacity of children, but it was expected that they would be married out by the time they reached adulthood.

Losing the Way, Disorder and the Suppression of Devils

Perhaps partly because the mountains are so dangerous[10] and so bemusing with their twisting defiles leading to blank cliffs, 'losing the way' is an everyday preoccupation of Mongols. However, causing people to lose the way was also attributed by our respondents to graves and ghosts. There was a Mongol burial place 3km to the east of Mergen, Xavagiin Enger, where passers-by regularly became disoriented. Some time in the past, a lama went there with several disciples to quell the ghost by reading the Lui-Jin prayer. 'Look in my arm-pit if you want to see what kind of ghost this is,' said the lama. The disciples peered and saw a woman with her hair standing on end. Such accounts seem fanciful, but still today people are affected by them. We met a woman who said she had experienced getting lost at Xavagiin Enger. She was charged with delivering urgent mail and therefore had to travel at night. Starting at 10 o'clock in the dark, with two companions and taking a torch, she first lost her way at Xavagiin Enger, then reached Aguin Gol where she was again bewildered, then struggled down to the fields and then again couldn't find her trail. The feeling was so strange, she said, because she knows this land like the back of her hand. She was lost 'till the crowing of chickens' (i.e. till dawn, when ghosts lose their power).

The lama was able to suppress the Xavagiin Enger devil, but people told us that the Revolution was incomparably more powerful than Buddhism in this respect. 'After Liberation, the ghosts became afraid,' they said, 'And then Mao with his great power suppressed both Buddhism and the devils.' One woman added, 'But after the death of Mao and with the Open Door policy those ghosts and Buddhas have got more freedom again. New devils have arisen to plague us.' So who are the 'new devils'? We gradually learned that the Cultural Revolution itself is held to have produced many tortured and unhappy souls – that is, the people who were wrongly executed or killed themselves in the campaign against the Nei Ren Dang[11] and the people who died feeling guilty at the role they themselves had played in the destruction. These statements shows how state power for these people does not inhabit a separate mental universe from that of the stories about devils and their disorienting effects. State power repressed certain old demons, but only to produce in its excesses some new ones. This is not just an abstract idea: people were telling us about how they themselves experienced both Maoist order/terror and the frightening feeling of being lost in one's own well-known countryside.

---

10. Every year people die in accidents (falls, loose boulders, floods) in these mountains.

11. The Nei Ren Dang is the Inner Mongolian Revolutionary Party said to have taken a counter-revolutionary nationalist line during the Cultural Revolution.

Devils and ghosts (Mongolian [M.] *chötgör, shulmus, bon*) are said to have their own invisible ways called *güidel* (running-tracks). These *güidel* cross-cut human tracks. When traversing the countryside, people also avoid places where sheep-devils and goat-devils are said to lurk. All this coexists with a very strong sense of orientation and the 'right' (i.e. auspicious) direction for journeys of various kinds.

There are several 'mental maps' by which Mongols orient themselves. Apart from the avoidance of known *güidel* and devil haunts in the area, there are also two abstract systems whereby people relate the direction they take to time. One of these is the system of the Black Dog's Mouth (M. *xar noxoin am*). The Black Dog is a notional cosmological creature lying on its side, which moves round the directions (north, east, south, west) as it were like a timepiece, so that its mouth gradually moves from one direction to another during the seasons of the year. The direction of the Dog's Mouth is always a bad direction to take. The dog's chest faces a good direction, we were told, but the tail is unpredictable: 'One wag of the tail may sweep away your house.' People in rural Urad, in fact throughout rural Inner Mongolia, always know the direction of the Black Dog's Mouth in any given period of the year.[12] The Black Dog system applies to everyone, but the other system, that of the Eight Seats (M. *naiman suudal*) applies to people differently according to their date and time of birth, their age and their sex. The Eight Seats are astrological sites linked to the eight cardinal directions; they determine which will be auspicious and inauspicious directions for individual people to take at a given time.[13]

The two systems of orientation just mentioned are notably symmetrical, yet the physical land people live in cannot be so. We gained the impression that for the local Chinese a jumbled mountain landscape was unproblematic in the sense that this is what was expected of wild, alien country as opposed to the order of the fields and village. For the Mongols, however, the mountains are their world and attempts are made to see order in the peaks and valleys.

The system of mountain cults of the Urad Mongols is one of relatively long-maintained social ordering. Three peaks are worshipped today and have been so since the seventeenth century: *Mergen Shar Oroi* (Yellow Peak) is the sacrificial

---

12. The direction of the Black Dog's Mouth is not much taken into account for everyday movement, but it is a serious matter for important journeys such as fetching a wife, building or moving house, or taking out a corpse for burial. In these cases, one solution is to wait until the Dog's Mouth has moved on.

13. We have full information on the Eight Seats system which will be provided in the final report on this project. The system might in principle regulate every journey people take. Because this is impractical, people normally 'open my right direction' (*zügden gargax*) once at the beginning of the year, i.e. they take a short journey in the direction that is auspicious for them and return along it. 'If I open my lucky direction now,' people say, 'I don't have to worry so much when I go out every day.'

site of the West Banner, *Suburgan Chuluu* (Pagoda Stone) is the site of the Middle Banner, and *Avtar Chuluu* (Box-chest Stone) is the site of the East Banner. These mountains are said to be 'brothers', like the three founding ancestors of the Urad clans forming the Banners. The offerings are 'red' (i.e. blood sacrifices) and made by male elders and cadres, with lamas invited to read the prayers. This clannic-administrative ordering of the mountains is paralleled by a religious one called the Three Objects of Veneration (*gurban shüteen*): Shar Oroi is the symbol of 'body' (*bie*), Avtar Chuluu is the symbol of 'tongue' (*xel*), and Suburgan Chuluu is the symbol of 'mind-heart' (*setgel, zurx*), where each of these 'symbols' stands not for the body as such but for a type or means of religious veneration.

Mongolian ideas of direction are symmetrical and related to the four cardinal points. The interesting question, then, is how direction relates to the social order seen in the landscape. The monastery is built, like all Mongolian dwellings, with its 'front' (doors, windows) facing directly south and its 'back' (blank walls) facing north. The monastery was built more or less directly south of Shar Oroi, which is in fact a notably symmetrical, pyramidal shape and as it were provides benign protection from the north. However, we were told one day of a bent crag to the north-west along the crest of the Mona Uul range called Xün Chuluu (Human Stone). This crag is said somehow to peer intrusively and exercise a malign surveillance over the land below, including the monastery.[14] (At first we thought this might be imaginary, but we were lent binoculars to verify the presence and oddly leaning shape of the stone). To protect the monastery from its evil influence, Mergen Gegeen in the eighteenth century erected a luck-giving flag (*darchig*) on a hill to the NW and reinforced this with five small shrines (*tavan sach*, five mini-pagodas) built in a horizontal line across the NW–SE axis. Subsequently, the lamas also set up another four small *sach* shrines at the four corners of the monastery. In other words, the monastery was without an encircling wall, but it was protected on its diagonal axial by religious counter-constructions, and triply so to the north-west. It is notable that this disposition of sites is not narrativized and has no story to account for it. Today people are still highly conscious of the diagonal line even though the flag has been removed and the five mini-pagodas are now just piles of stones.

If you have a four-square notion of direction, then diagonals or corners may be seen as points of vulnerability/threat. We were told that someone should not sit at the corner of a rectangular table at mealtimes, especially someone in the 'sister's son' (*zee*) category of kin. Interestingly, the *zee* could be seen as having a 'diagonal' relation to the clan, not being related in the direct patriline and being one generation

---

14. Mongols, we were told, hate being overlooked. If a goat jumps on the roof or onto some high storehouse so that it may look into one's house, this is considered a very bad omen.

below that of Ego. The *zee* is also forbidden to stand in the main doorway blocking the light from the south.[15] Perhaps in the first case (corners) the *zee* reinforces threat from diagonals, while in the latter (the front door) he intrudes on what should be a 'straight' category of space. The question of diagonals and blocking of such lines also arises with the disposition of luck-giving 'wind-horse' (*xii mori*) flags. Most Mongol houses have a pole with such a flag (in the past, all did). Interestingly, the Urad Mongols place their flags at the corner of the yard, to the NW or NE.

Evidently, the mountains are thought in some complex processual way to cause both protection and threat towards living beings, and these processes are related to (derived from?) physical contours and hollows. Mountain influences, sometimes personified as 'spirits', are held to be different from yet subject to a certain containment by human practices. Buddhism in this respect does not provide a cosmology that encompasses and takes over 'natural causality': lamas, however respected, are no different from other living beings in their relations to the land. The constructions of pagodas, *sach* shrines, and *oboo*s are but feeble attempts to hold at bay the inexorable results of the clash between mountain configurations/ influences and human needs. The siting of Mongolian settlements as well as numerous minor *oboo*s can be seen in this light.

We were told, for example, that dwellings should not be sited at *xeltegei gazar* (broken, 'incomplete' land) nor at the 'mouth' (*am*) of rivers and valleys. 'Reasons' for this could be practical: *xeltegei gazar* may indicate subsidence/erosion, and the mouth of a valley may be subject to unpredictable floods. Yet at the same time 'reasons' can be conceptual, i.e. broken, incomplete land violates the idea of symmetry and wholeness, and to place oneself in the 'mouth' is to get in the way of mountain channels of influence. In one particular geographical situation people should build an *oboo*. This is when they settle in a *xötel*, a narrow mountain pass. The *oboo* should be built in the centre of the pass, such that people coming up add stones from the right side and people going down add stones on the other side, so the cairn constantly increases in size. The point of the cairn is not to fill the valley, but to make a *darlag*, literally something that oppresses or suppresses something else. A *xöteliin oboo* is meant to suppress 'bad influences' coming up and down the defile. The *xöteliin oboo* is thus similar to the 'five *sach*' shrines built by the Mergeen Gegeen to counteract the Human Stone.

Conclusion

This preliminary sketch has described some geographical ideas of the Mongols and Chinese, especially as they relate to sacred sites. I have shown how Chinese

---

15. No reason was given for this prohibition. *Zee* people are simply ordered to move away if they linger in the doorway.

military-strategic and productive-extractive relations to the land confront a Mongolian 'landscape' dominated by magical-religious relations. The Chinese cultural preoccupation with walls is even now countered by Mongol breaching of walls (cf. the lamas' storming of the army wall). I hope to have explained to some extent why, in this landscape, certain sacred constructions are sited where they are.

The Mongols have a strong sense of 'place', that is, particular, meaningful, named sites to which things belong (cf. cases in which objects were returned to that rightful places by people guilty of theft during the Cultural Revolution). They also have ideas of geographical configurations that are ontologically related to human activities, from the hollow (*xotxor*) that measures the number of sheep in flocks to the defile (*xötel*) that is a guide-line for travel. However, most important of all for the Mongols is their sense of direction and symmetry, according to which bent and crooked physical landmarks generate evil influences and diagonals are lines of threat. Narrativized magical travels across this landscape are seen in the light of prevailing political relations, in particular the military-strategic landscape constructed by the Chinese. The reinterpretation of ancient walls as ways and the miraculous breaching of modern walls are examples of this confrontation. At the same time, we have evidence of the Mongols' non-narrativized actions (such as building *sach*) to contend with physical surroundings seen as dynamical configurations. This suggests that 'hindrance' versus 'powerful directed movement' is a binary pair which is deeply rooted in Mongol conceptual geography and that the confrontation with the configurations of the settled agriculturalists, which has the same structural form, is not incidental but central to Mongol culture.

Acknowledgements

I would like to thank the MacDonald Institute for Archaeological Research (Cambridge) for supporting the research on which this article is based.

References

Hirsch, E. 1995. Landscape: between place and space, in E. Hirsch and M. O'Hanlon (eds) *The Anthropology of Landscape: Perspectives on Place and Space.* Oxford: Oxford University Press.

Humphrey, C. 1995. Chiefly and shamanist landscapes in Mongolia, in E. Hirsch and M. O'Hanlon (eds) *The Anthropology of Landscape: Perspectives on Place and Space.* Oxford: Oxford University Press.

—— 1996. *Shamans and Elders: Experience, Knowledge and Power among the Daur Mongols.* Oxford: Oxford University Press.

Lattimore, O. 1940. *Inner Asian Frontiers of China.* New York: American Geographical Society.

Waldron, A. 1990. *The Great Wall of China: from History to Myth.* Cambridge: Canto, Cambridge University Press.

Williams, D.M. 1996. The barbed walls of China: a contemporary grassland drama. *Journal of Asian Studies* **55**(3) 665–91.

–4–

Negotiating the River: Cultural Tributaries in Far North Queensland
Veronica Strang

One of the central issues in modern anthropology is the need for theoretical approaches which deal with the complex dynamics of industrialized societies, in which there are multiple subcultures and 'contexts' of social being. Often such 'cultures within cultures' are defined by a particular economic or recreational activity which 'absorbs focus and percolates all activities' (Simmel 1955: 185). Within subcultural or occupationally defined groups, the activities central to the identity of each are linked with definable patterns of beliefs and values. This chapter proposes that, concretized in material culture, embedded in cultural landscapes, and promulgated by internal cultural forms, these values create a particular mode of environmental interaction, and maintain a trajectory of cultural adaptation which is specific to each group.

In arguing that subcultures and occupationally defined groups have their own adaptive trajectories, a potential problem is that membership in such circles is not always continuous. Individuals in post-industrial societies have a multiplicity of social identities or alternative professional occupations, and they shift regularly between these. However, these persona are generally complementary to each other. Individuals' engagement with different arenas may bring commensurate shifts in the values which are foregrounded at the time, but because values are learned within social milieux, embodied and integrated into personal identity, people do not undergo value transformations in shifting between related contexts.[1] On the contrary, most individuals construct a personal constellation of 'action frameworks' which, being situated within their particular sphere of social relationships, tend to have values which are mutually reinforcing. It is therefore feasible to consider subcultures or primary industries more dynamically, as dominant elements within clusters of interrelated contexts. Each such 'cluster' – though it may contain diversity within certain parameters – is defined by an identity which is, in the end, based upon shared beliefs and values.

1. It is reasonable to suppose that individuals can and do change their values over time, but it is also fair to say that this is most often achieved when they make major shifts from one social group to another.

Inevitably, in a complex society, some groups or 'clusters' have internal cultural forms which encourage considerable continuity in their beliefs and values, and thus in their particular trajectories, while others are more open to change. However, the ethnographic example that follows suggests that there are factors which maintain shared values and definable identities even in the most mobile and dynamic groups. There appear to be two vital influences: the potential for multiple 'sideways shifts' of identities within groups (i.e. their relative fluidity and degree of prescription) and, perhaps most crucially, each group's relative 'rootedness' in the land – the longevity and intimacy in its interaction with the land.

No group develops its cultural trajectory in isolation. The diverse subcultural groups of which complex societies are composed meet in various fora, where they enact, represent and negotiate their values. Their discourses, and the actions that emerge from them, define the strategies of the wider community. Thus the environmental interaction of a particular society may be seen as the outcome of their negotiations. Clearly much depends on the relative power held by each group, politically, economically and socially, but this is always emergent from the process of debate. As illustrated in the following example, small groups with little power and status can gain influence and renegotiate their position by focusing their self-representation on particular aspects of their culture and stressing their alignment with the values and aspirations desired by a majority, or by other, more powerful groups.

Negotiating the River

The case study is drawn from ethnographic research in the Mitchell River catchment in Far North Queensland. The watershed contains diverse groups, whose levels of mobility and 'rootedness' differ considerably. It includes:

the Aboriginal community in Kowanyama
European Australian pastoralists
Miners
A commercial fishing industry
Environmentalists and National Parks rangers
Tourists

Each of these groups may be regarded as having an 'internal culture' or as Douglas (1987) would put it, a 'fictive institutional personality'.[2] Each is represented in the Mitchell River Watershed Catchment Management Group (MRWCMG), which

2. Although only one of the groups has a distinctive 'ethnic' identity, each conforms at least partially to Parkin *et al.*'s (1996) criteria for distinctiveness, though they are not entirely self-sufficient economically: they all have some economic independence, are residentially segregated, are somewhat insulated from the dominant values of the wider population, and are specialized in their occupations.

provides a useful forum for – and a demonstration of – their interactions and their constructions of identity. Both Turner (1982) and Gell (1998) have underlined the recursive relationship between performance and identity, and Hastrup (1995) and others (e.g. Foucault 1978; Moore 1994) have argued that it is through performance that identity is embodied. It is perhaps better, therefore, not to draw a line between formal performance and activities which, according to Strathern, are essentially performative: 'Work cannot be measured separately from performance . . . Action is understood as effect, as a performance or presentation, a mutual estimation of value' (Strathern 1988: 160, 174).

As Bailey notes, it is in people's everyday actions that 'off-stage' values and beliefs can be discerned (1996: 16–17). Thus the everyday activities of each group, as well as their more formal representations of these within the MRWCMG, enable the inculcation and the performance of particular values, and in the process, group identity is expressed and perpetuated. Many writers (e.g. Simmel 1955) have pointed out that the relationship between different contexts is often a defining influence. Eriksen observed that group identity 'is an aspect of relationship, not a cultural property of a group' (1993: 34), and as Cohen (1974) has shown, performance of a particular identity is critical in social and political negotiations within and between groups. Representation is not merely of, it is also to. Thus the groups in the Mitchell River area define themselves partially in relation to each 'other', their representations defining the qualities and actions that they own or disown.

The MRWCMG was formed in the early 1990s in an astute initiative by the Aboriginal community in Kowanyama. The objective was to bring together land users in the watershed, ostensibly to discuss common environmental problems, but implicitly to facilitate dialogue and negotiation. The MRWCMG now contains representatives from every group in the catchment area.[3]

Within the MRWCMG, some of the emergent relationships are unexpected: value trajectories that until recently appeared to be heading in opposite directions – for example those of the Aboriginal groups and the miners – have begun to converge. Others which ran parallel in a more co-operative era – such as the pastoralists' and the Aboriginal community's – are now diverging widely. It is apparent that the groups differ in their ability to change direction. They also have radically different rates of change in their internal adaptations, and it is clear that a key influence on each group's relative stability is its particular interaction with the land and its resources.

---

3. The MRWCMG is not an isolated case: there are similar organizations elsewhere in Australia, and in 1992 the Queensland Government underlined its support for such endeavours by allocating $3.5 million for an integrated Catchment Management Programme. However, the Mitchell River group is the only such organization to have been initiated by Aboriginal people, giving them a strong position at the negotiating table.

Figure 4.1 Fishing for yabbies near the Mitchell River (photo: V. Strang)

The Mitchell River Watershed

The Mitchell River runs from the Dividing Range in eastern Cape York to the savannah country on the west of the Peninsula. Until recently the watershed was a 'remote area' inhabited only by the Aboriginal community, a scattering of fishing camps along the Gulf coast, vast cattle stations, and a few mines. However, the tourist industry has now boomed along the eastern seaboard, encouraging the use of previously neglected National Parks along the Mitchell and focusing the attention of conservation groups on the regional ecosystem.

Infrastructural development has brought increasing interaction between the different land users. Various environmental issues affect all of them and are, undoubtedly, caused or exacerbated by some of their activities.[4] There are also major economic and social issues surrounding the massive programme of development of the Peninsula, initiated by the State Government in 1991.[5]

4. Environmental problems in the watershed include weed infestations, inadequate fire manage-ment, water shortages or salination, land degradation, feral animals and loss of biodiversity.
5. The Cape York Peninsula Land Use Strategy, though presented as protective management of the area, has been cynically nicknamed the Cape York Development Strategy, reflecting the reality in which it has done much to encourage the development of the region.

Figure 4.2 Negotiating the Mitchell River (photo: V. Strang)

The MRWCMG provides a public forum for tackling these problems and resolving differences. Its participants share a desire to keep up with local events, to keep an eye on each other's activities, and – at times – to have a united and thus stronger voice in opposing external pressures and incursions into the watershed. However, their aspirations differ considerably, and outside the MRWCMG's nominally neutral space they are often locked in conflicts over land ownership, access, use and management. The MRWCMG is important in that it enables change and development in the relationships between the people involved. A key part of this process is their representations of themselves reflexively and to each other, which may entail particular 'cultural compressions'[6] of their internal characteristics. The regular meetings of the group are quite formal, providing a stage on which the participants can perform, legitimize and negotiate their cultural values (see Turner, 1982).

Performing Principles

Within the MRWCMG, the community in Kowanyama performs values which reflect wider Aboriginal concerns. The community is anxious to protect its land

6. Though the term 'cultural compression' has normally been applied to cultural identity and representation at an ethnic or subcultural level, this analysis suggests that it may be as usefully employed to consider smaller groups such as particular industries.

Figure 4.3 Bull catching at Rutland Plains Station (photo: V. Strang)

and resources, to regain control over traditional land (much of which is held by neighbouring cattle stations), and to achieve economic self-sufficiency and greater social stability. The MRWCMG offers a way of attaining status as land managers and re-establishing a position in accordance with Ancestral Law, which prescribes a stable and permanent environmental interaction, in which people and land cannot be alienated from each other. Even today, the internal cultural forms of Aboriginal communities such as Kowanyama continue to be mediated by and based upon continual interaction with the land. This massively stabilizing influence on Aboriginal values has enabled the community to resist external influences, and members of the community prioritize and perform values which remain intensely concerned for the well-being of their local environment.

Ironically, this deeply affective relationship with land has been supported by the community's interactions with the other land users in the watershed. The settlers who dispossessed Aboriginal people and colonized Cape York initiated a secular and combative interaction with the environment. In defining themselves oppositionally to this and in dealing with a repressive political reality, Aboriginal people have tended to emphasize and thus affirm their spiritual and affective relations with land.

These values are foregrounded in the meetings of the MRWCMG with representations evoking Ancestral Law and stressing the longevity and closeness of

Aboriginal relations with land. Thus when the community hosts workshops and conferences for the MRWCMG, 'educational' trips are made to 'story places' such as an increase site situated right beside the homestead of the nearest cattle station:[7] 'This sugarbag [honey] country, this here . . . They [Aboriginal people] want to come here get sugarbag, they come hit this tree here . . .' (Banjo Patterson, Jerry Mission, 1992).

Though political realities have forced Aboriginal people to focus on spiritual rather than economic interactions with land, this representational focus has created very different kind of relationship with more recent land users in the catchment area (see Strang 2000a, b). Tourists and conservationists, rather than approaching the land merely as an economic resource, are in search of a more experiential aesthetic, or what Turner (1982) calls 'communitas'. For them, Aboriginal knowledge and spirituality, backed by the weight of millennia, offers a way to meet their own aspirations for balance and reunification with Nature. By fore-grounding these values in fora such as the MRWCMG, the Aboriginal community has been able to garner considerable support for claims to the land, and some of the social status critical to political influence.

The Politics of Pastoralism

The pastoralists see the MRWCMG partly as a political platform, but also hope that it will help them gain financial assistance, ostensibly for dealing with ecological problems, but in reality to provide more general subsidies. Like other landholders in the watershed, they hope to control access to their land or at least to profit from tourists' use of it. They want to be part of the wider decision-making process, ensuring that environmental groups do not persuade the Government to support 'expensive and unnecessary' conservation measures, or even – as has been suggested – halt cattle grazing in the watershed.

Like the Aboriginal community, the pastoralists attempt to validate their position by pointing to their historical interaction with the land. It is a very different kind of history though: in contrast to the sustainable hunting-and-gathering 'Eden' astutely represented by the indigenous population, the pastoralists' imagery focuses on a pioneering battle with a 'hostile' environment. This colonial endeavour and the economic investment of labour in the land form the basis of their performances to the MRWCMG. There is an obvious consonance between their economic activities and these representations. Stock work offers a highly combative

---

7. It is by no means coincidental that such important sacred sites are often positioned close to pastoral homesteads. As Morphy (1993) has pointed out, both cattle station homesteads and sacred sites cluster around primary resource places. In this instance though, the choice of site for 'performance' also provides a clear political message to the MRWCMG.

interaction with the environment which, physically and metaphorically, supports the pastoralists' identity as 'battlers' and reaffirms this resistant stance. The pastoralists therefore share common ground with the Aboriginal population, in that their cultural trajectory is similarly stabilized by the continuity of their interactions with the land and a strong identification with the past.

Until recently, representations foregrounding the pastoralists' historic role have been highly successful, providing key symbolic imagery for the wider population and its national identity. Broadly, it may be said to represent a European battle for control over the continent, the indigenous population and the larger forces of Nature. This control is not only composed of exclusive 'ownership' of the land, but also relies on the authority of the pastoralists as land managers. Thus, within the MRWCMG, the pastoralists stress their practical, everyday experience in managing the land – as opposed to the 'theoretical' knowledge of other groups (such as bureaucrats or conservationists) or 'non-productive' Aboriginal bush knowledge.

When their economic activities (aided by cheap Aboriginal labour) were profitable, their pioneering past was celebrated, their land management was respected, and their social status was high. Today few properties are truly viable financially, and the wider population is anxious to distance itself from the emergent realities of colonialism. Conservationists are drawing attention to the environmental problems caused by cattle farming, and with a more highly educated urbanized population, semi-literate farmers are no longer esteemed. As one station manager said: 'they think we are all myalls [rednecks]' (David Hughes 1993).

This widening gap illustrates the relative flexibility of the trajectories of rural and urban groups, and the anchoring influence of land-based occupations. However, while the Aboriginal population has drawn upon its highly stable environmental relationship to resist change relatively successfully, the pastoral industry has been disempowered and marginalized. While they have maintained a conservative subculture out in the remote areas, the wider Australian population has moved on, liberalizing, becoming concerned about environmental issues, and rejecting adversarial modes of land management. Indeed, many Australians find more common ground with Aboriginal representations of a spiritually and socially based landscape which provides a basis for affective attachment. Accordingly, they have become increasingly sympathetic to Aboriginal land claims.

Inevitably the pastoralists feel betrayed. They are fighting hard to protect their tenure and their position as land managers, but their position is defensive. In the Mitchell River, as elsewhere in Australia, they feel besieged by a host of external pressures. This may be a familiar stance, but the 'battle' is no longer against the hostile forces of nature, but against forces of economic and social change. As such, it pits them against the wider population, and this divergence is demonstrated by the pastoralists' alliances with increasingly extreme political parties.

Right-wing political groups have persisted with representations of pastoralism which draw heavily on romantic visions of its pioneering past, and on the 'bush knowledge' gained by 'real' experience. They continue to try to instil in the mainstream population a 'proper' appreciation of the 'outback battlers'. This is not entirely unsuccessful, given that – whatever the wider angst about colonial history – the pastoral industry continues to 'hold' the land on behalf of the European Australian majority. More recently, attempts have been made to modernize these representations by stressing the pastoralists long-term emotional ties to the land, and their place in the 'national heritage'. There is some evidence to suggest that the growing discourse about 'heritage' merely offers new euphemisms for validating European claims to the land, designed to assuage post-colonial guilt and create effective competition for Aboriginal claims of attachment (see Strang 1997, 2000).

This modernization has yet to persuade the pastoralists in the Mitchell River area to soften their representations greatly. Politicians may blithely discuss affective issues, but such behaviour would entail a major shift in self-image for stockmen and station managers, who would find it alien to express their attachment to the land in highly emotive terms at meetings of the MRWCMG.[8] It is unfortunate that their subculture is so repressive, because by foregrounding values of aggression and control and emphasizing their economic role they are, in effect, hoist with their own petard.

Mining Matters

Though the mining industry has been much more astute than the pastoralists in its self-representations, there is some similarity in their values and in their performed identities. Physically and symbolically, mining also provides a combative environmental interaction which is largely economic – concerned not with living in or connecting with the landscape, but with searching out specific sites, exploiting their resources and departing, often leaving a legacy of environmental degradation. In many parts of Australia, mining is still celebrated as a quintessentially masculine 'frontier' activity, a hegemonic treasure hunt. Representations of the industry remain laden with concepts of 'virgin territory', forcible entry and colonial control (see Bird-Rose 1992). In this sense mining appears to be diametrically opposed to the environmental interaction of hunters and gatherers, and with such disparity in values it is unsurprising that the mining industry has consistently offered the most powerful – and vitriolic – opposition to Aboriginal claims to the land.

---

8. Though public displays of tender emotional issues may be considered beyond the pale for pastoralists (see Strang 1997 & in press b), it is interesting to note that the most astute station managers have begun to make use of this discourse more privately, for example, by making explicit comparisons between Aboriginal attachment to land and their own desire to be buried near the homestead.

By defining their identity in opposition to that of the Aboriginal population, miners have attempted to frame their activities as 'progressive' and 'civilizing'.[9] Like the more astute pastoralists, they have also begun to validate their claims to the land by underlining their affective links with 'the national heritage': 'We're all very proud of our mine . . . and we want to be proud of what we leave behind, because today's workings are tomorrow's cultural heritage' (Bruce McCarthy, 1992).

For the Aboriginal community, mining represents the most extreme form of interference with the land. Physical disturbance of ancestral forces violates spiritual laws, and runs contrary to the values inherent in a non-invasive environmental interaction.[10] Mining also generates anxiety about the symbolic and physical pollution of the landscape. (Strang, in press a.) The elders in Kowanyama are well aware that the gold mines upstream use poisons (e.g. cyanide), and are afraid that these will seep into the river: '. . . then it will all be gone, finish. All the fish, all the animals – everything finish' (Kowanyama Counsel of Elders, 1992).

It would be reasonable to expect that this conflict would emerge forcefully within the MRWCMG; however, this is not the case: local mining companies, along with many in Australia, have altered their trajectory of environmental interaction considerably, and this is reflected in their activities and performances, and in their relationships with other groups. They now represent their activities as being highly localized,[11] by talking about compartmentalization, containment and

---

9. These values are clearly expressed by the Australian Mining Council (AMIC): 'From the dawn of history, human progress has been associated with the ability to extract and utilise minerals . . . Without a minerals industry, Australia would be a poor nation . . . the mining industry has played a major role in developing Australia's outback areas . . . Such development supports general government decentralisation policies and is of defence significance. Without mining development, much of Australia's interior and north would remain isolated and unproductive' (AMIC 1989: 12–19).

10. It is mining that has sparked the most anguished protests, such as this letter to the Government from the people of Noonkanbah: 'We Aboriginal people of Noonkanbah Station truthfully beg you important people that you stop these people, namely CRA and AMAX, who are going into our land. These people have already made the place no good with their bulldozers. Our sacred places they have made no good. They mess up our land. They expose our sacred objects. This breaks our spirit; we lose ourselves as people. What will we as people do if these people continue to make our land no good? Today we beg you that you will truly stop them' (*The Australian*, 17 May, 1979: 13).

11. One of the most frequent comments is that mining requires the sacrifice of only small areas – less than 0.02 per cent of the country's land area, and this is held to be morally justifiable in light of the economic gains. As Bruce McCarthy, the environmental director at Red Dome gold mine puts it: 'We've produced 273 million dollars worth of revenue for Queensland since we started, for around 270 hectares disturbed' (1992). This is also his argument for pushing the Government to permit mining in the National Parks: 'The actual impact of mining, although it is very obvious in a small area, is only on a small area. If we can keep everything on site and minimise our impacts . . . why not allow [us] to go and mine these areas?' (Ibid.)

Figure 4.4 Red Dome Gold Mine (photo: V. Strang)

careful decommissioning. 'Environmental responsibility' has become their new mantra, chanted with varying degrees of enthusiasm and sincerity, and there are serious efforts to work alongside rather than against other groups.

Various factors have contributed to these changes. One is simple pragmatism: mining companies now meet effective opposition to their activities, not just from a more outspoken Aboriginal community, but also from a large and vociferous environmental movement. Widespread sympathy for these concerns has made it unwise to ignore their protests, and led to more stringent environmental legislation, forcing miners into activities which 'repair' the landscape and thus foreground quite different values.[12]

At the same time, increasing technological complexity has changed the social composition of the industry, bringing in many well-educated and relatively middle-class liberals and a new institutional culture. Most have trained as chemists, biochemists, geologists or engineers, and their work focuses on specialized technical or scientific aspects of the mining process. This encourages a less combative and more scientific vision of a landscape which can be (literally) deconstructed, processed and rehabilitated. Thus changes in key cultural forms within the mining industry have altered the trajectory of its values and the ways in which these are represented.

The mining industry has a significant advantage in that, while the pastoral industry is economically weak, mining remains critical to the State and also the national economy.[13] Its commensurate political status gives the industry a powerful position in the MRWCMG, which it sees as an opportunity for renegotiating its relationships with other land users, and improving its access to land. It is clear that the miners hope to persuade the other groups that increased exploration and mineral extraction will be painless and profitable all round, and they are also eager to shed the industry's image as despoilers.

The performance of this (some would say) new persona has significantly altered the miners' interactions with other land users in the Mitchell River catchment area, improving their relations with the Aboriginal groups, the tourist industry, and even making it feasible to find some common ground with the conservationists. This is partly because the trajectories of these groups are also diverging slightly to meet them. For example, the Aboriginal community, while successfully asserting its own values, has also begun to adopt European land-management techniques and to acquire the accompanying language.

Conserving the River

The influential environmentalist contingent in the watershed is by no means homogenous, being composed of National Parks or Government employees,

12. Red Dome Gold Mine, near the headwaters of the Mitchell River, expects to spend 1.7 million dollars on decommissioning and rehabilitating its mine site when operations are completed. The dam will become a 'sustainable aquatic ecosystem' with the introduction of flora and fauna from the nearby river, so that tourists and fishermen will inherit a 'recreational lake'. The National Parks Department will be given the plant nursery, and neighbouring pastoralists will benefit from the improved grazing and water bores that Red Dome has created.

13. In the Mitchell River catchment there are over 350 mining tenders for gold, silver, copper, zinc, lead, tin, bauxite, coal and mineral sands.

scientific groups, and a variety of conservation organizations.[14] Those linked with Government departments are generally keen to encourage local tourism, provided that it is 'controlled', while others are determined to resist development and keep human interference with the 'natural' environment to a minimum. Their relations with Aboriginal people also differ: Governmental Departments are still trailing the baggage of a paternalistic relationship, making it difficult for them to consider joint land-management schemes with equanimity. The more radical activists, on the other hand, having grown out of their idea of recreating a dehumanized 'wilderness', tend towards a romantic vision of Aboriginal people as a representation of ancient and sustainable relations with the land.

The activist groups oppose mining in the watershed, maintaining – with considerable evidence – that many mines have dumped toxic chemicals into the aquatic systems. They see cattle over-grazing as responsible for a steady degradation of the land, and are concerned that tourism is leading to untrammelled development and excessive pressure on the catchment area.

In recent years the conservationists' environmental trajectory has shifted direction. Like the miners they have adopted a more 'scientific' approach, and gone from hugging trees to counting them. This may be due to a partial 'establishment take-over' of what was a liberal and sometimes extreme political movement. More generously, it could be said that environmental issues are now 'mainstream'. Whatever the cause, the conservationist's vision of the watershed has become increasingly abstract and generic, classifying the landscape in terms of its geomorphology, topography, soil types, flora and fauna. In the forum of the MRWCMG they focus on the physical environmental problems such as weeds, pollution, feral animals and soil degradation, and their major concern is to control, manage and protect the biodiversity of the region. This new discourse, however, is still underpinned by complex issues of morality and stewardship. These values, central to the environmentalists' identity and self-representation, give them moral high ground and political influence.

There has been much talk of a 'Black–Green' alliance in Australia (see Horstman 1992), and in the MRWCMG there is certainly a subtle alignment of the interests opposed to pastoralism and mining. For many Aboriginal groups though, conservationists who want to play a central role in managing the environment seem little different from other invaders. People in Kowanyama have therefore approached any supposed alliance with caution, and this has paid off: the conservationists

---

14. The National Parks Department has now been subsumed within the Department of Environment and Heritage, which has a very broad remit. Most of the scientific groups (for example, the Tropical Weeds Research Centre) have Government funding. The conservation groups, such as the Cairns and Far North Environment Centre, operate more independently.

now more commonly represent their role in the MRWCMG as being merely supportive and advisory to local Aboriginal interests.

Outback Tours

With the primary industries in the region faltering, tourism has become one of Queensland's most profitable industries. Cairns and Port Douglas are used as jumping-off points for 'outback tours' and people are visiting the Mitchell River area increasingly for recreational purposes. For the industry, Aboriginal people and cattle ranchers are both an obstacle and a marketing opportunity: one of the major reasons for its involvement in the MRWCMG is to persuade them to welcome tourism.[15]

For the other groups along the Mitchell the jury is still out on this. Some members of the Aboriginal community hope to create small-scale tourist ventures, but see this as an independent activity. Similarly, pastoralists reduced to dude-ranching are dubious about linking such activities with agents in Cairns. Both groups recognize, however, that they can 'piggyback' on more intensive tourist ventures on the east coast.

For the tourists, Cape York represents 'the great escape' from the restraint of their daily lives (see Strang 1996). Their interactions with the watershed centre upon play, encouraging experimentation with a range of assumed identities. Released from their domestic lives, men favour 'bush-bashing', rally-driving, pig shooting, and other 'man-the-hunter' posturings. Family groups tend towards more benign activities such as birdwatching. There is growing demand for ecotourism and ethereal 'oneness with Nature'.

Despite this diversity, tourist activities share some important features: they permit creative expression, they represent freedom, and they involve 'experiencing' the landscape sensually and aesthetically rather than in economic or managerial terms. They therefore tend to engender affective responses to the landscape, providing crucial common ground with the Aboriginal groups. It is this representation of Aboriginal relations with 'nature' which tourists are most anxious to appropriate, or at least to share. In their interactions with the landscape, tourists thus perform values which resonate with Aboriginal aspirations, encouraging greater respect and sympathy for these. In this sense the trajectory of their environmental relations

---

15. The Aboriginal community and the pastoralist share highly mixed feelings about the tourist industry. Often they get only the pain and none of the gain from the visitors who get bogged in the creeks in their hired vehicles (and have to be rescued); drive through the wire fences which order the distribution of cattle; take freezer-loads of fish from the waterholes and rivers; leave litter at campsites and as one person commented in Kowanyama: 'stare too much and photograph everything in town – make me feel no good'.

has moved closer to that expressed by Aboriginal groups. Their activities may be temporary, but values are of course permeative, and it is uncontroversial to propose a relationship between increased recreational use of land and wider concern for its well-being.

Conclusion

The multi-vocal exchanges within the MRWCMG support the proposal that even small subcultural groups and industries have definable internal cultures and values which create particular trajectories of environmental interaction. They also have quite varied abilities to change the direction of these trajectories, and quite different internal rates of change.

Several factors appear to enable continuity: the most crucial is the relative intimacy of the groups' interactions with the land. The Aboriginal trajectory, for example, is massively stabilized by the fact that all of its internal cultural forms are mediated by the land. Daily activities involve intimate physical, emotional and spiritual involvement with the landscape, and the spatial location of social and spiritual identity accords with Durkheim's original argument (1995 [1912]) that the projection of social forms onto Nature is inherently conservative. The complexity and density of these ties means that despite the traumatic disruptions in the last century, Aboriginal values today remain consistent with those described by Lauriston Sharp's ethnography of the Yir Yoront community over 60 years ago (1937). In the forum of the MRWCMG the community has kept faith with these principles, but astutely foregrounded the values which have resonance for many sectors of the Australian population. In this sense, their trajectory exerts a magnetic pull on other, more malleable groups.

The other most firmly conservative group in the MRWCMG is the pastoralists, who although less tied to particular places, are closely involved with the land. They are, to some degree, locked in combat with a long-term investment in values inherently resistant to change. Their identification with a 'glorious' pioneering past is a weighty legacy which locates their social identity within the landscape. There are echoes here of Gellner's (1991) 'potato principle' – the idea that territorial identity and 'rootedness' stabilize rural societies.

Both the Aboriginal community and the pastoralists are part of well-established social networks, and this too contributes to the consistency of their self-representation, identity and values. As Douglas points out, the dense interpersonal ties which characterize small-scale societies are a stabilizing force. Conversely, 'large scale industrial processes are their own institutions. They cannot be embedded in the patterns of local, community control'. (Douglas 1987: 108)

Such stabilizing factors are missing from the activities of the mining industry, whose interaction with the land is site-specific and highly temporary, and whose social organization and other cultural forms are highly fluid. Its trajectory is commensurately flexible, as has been demonstrated by the rapid adaptations it has made to changing circumstances, its new representations and its purported changes in values.

The most radically altering trajectories are those of the groups whose involvement with the land is neither continuous nor based on key cultural forms such as economic activities. Environmentalists and tourists alike, with their vast range of potential persona, bring to the MRWCMG representations which illustrate considerable diversity and adaptivity.

Social multiplicity has long been a recurring theme in the literature on modernity. Gellner comments that modern man 'makes his own position' (1994) and Simmel suggested that freely chosen affiliation has a greater potential for change:

> Any association which is based on local relationships or is otherwise brought about without the individual's participation, differs from affiliations which are freely chosen, because as a rule the latter will make it possible for the individual to make his beliefs and desires felt (1955: 130).

On this basis it will be the groups whose identity is most potentially flexible and diverse, and whose activities are least embedded in the land, who will have the capacity to change direction most radically and rapidly. The cultural representations within the MRWCMG suggests that this is indeed the case. The MRWCMG therefore houses a creative tension between the values which stabilize relations to land and those which encourage dynamic change.[16] It also provides a relatively neutral and egalitarian forum in which groups previously divided by deep hostility and massively unequal power relations can perform their particular identities, develop social and political relationships, redefine their cultural landscapes and exchange values and 'symbolic capital' (Cohen 1974). Organizations such as the MRWCMG are thus an essential part of the process through which the trajectories of all its constitutient groups are negotiated. As the MRWCMG develops its own identity as an organization, and performs this through concerted actions, it becomes increasingly possible for its members to consider joint policies and other forms of co-operation within the watershed. In debating the environmental management of the catchment area, the MRWCMG is to some extent defining its own trajectory

---

16. Obviously one of the most central issues in constructing continuity in relations to land is the matter of land rights, and the debates over Native Title and security of tenure. Though this is rarely raised explicitly at meetings of the MRWCMG, the wider battles over land ownership are implicit in all of the group's discussions. In many respects, organizations such as the Management Group are part of this process and provide a level of interaction at which many of the issues which problematize Land Rights negotiations, such as access and control, can be negotiated.

which, over time, will enter – and influence – the discourse through which each group negotiates its way forward.

Acknowledgements

I would like to thank Howard Morphy (ANU), Barbara Bender (UCL) and Marcus Banks (Oxford) and other colleagues in Oxford and Lampeter for their advice on emergent versions of this chapter, and the WAC participants and referees, whose comments helped enormously. I would also like to express my gratitude to the many people along the Mitchell River who have been unfailingly generous with both information and hospitality. The work was made possible with funding from the ESRC and Linacre College Oxford.

References

Australian Mining Council (AMIC) 1989. *What Mining Means to Australians.* Canberra: AMIC.

Bailey, F.G. 1996. Cultural performance, authenticity and second nature, in D. Parkin, L. Caplan and H. Fisher (eds) *The Politics of Cultural Performance.* Providence and Oxford: Berghahn Books. 1–17.

Bird-Rose, D. 1992. Nature and gender in outback Australia, in *History and Anthropology.* **5**(3–4) 403–25.

Cohen, A. 1974. Two-Dimensional Man: An Essay on the Anthropology of Power and Symbolism in Complex Society. London: Routledge and Kegan Paul.

Douglas, M. 1987. *How Institutions Think.* London: Routledge and Kegan Paul.

Durkheim, E. 1995 [1912]. *The Elementary Forms of the Religious Life.* Transl. K. Fields. New York: Free Press.

Eriksen, T.H. 1993. *Ethnicity and Nationalism: Anthropological Perspectives.* London and Boulder, Colo.: Pluto Press.

Foucault, M. 1978. *The History of Sexuality,* Vol 1. Harmondsworth: Penguin.

Gell, A. 1998. *Art and Agency.* Oxford: Clarendon Press.

Gellner, E. 1991. Le nationalisme en Apesanteur, in *Terrain* **17** 7–16.

—— 1994. *Encounters with Nationalism.* Oxford: Blackwell.

Hastrup, K. 1995. *A Passage to Anthropology: Between Experience and Theory.* New York: Routledge.

Horstmann, M. 1992. Cape York Peninsula: forging a Black-Green alliance, in *Habitat Australia.* **20**. April 1992. 18–25.

Moore, H. 1994. *A Passion for Difference: Essays in Anthropology and Gender.* Cambridge: Polity Press.

Morphy, H. 1993. Colonialism, history and the construction of place: the politics of landscape in Northern Australia, in B. Bender, *Landscape: Politics and Perspectives.* Oxford: Berg. 205–43.

Parkin, D., Caplan, L. and Fisher, H. (eds) 1996. *The Politics of Cultural Performance.* Providence, Oxford: Berghahn Books.

Sharp, L. 1937. The Social Anthropology of a Totemic System of North Queensland. PhD thesis, Harvard University.

Simmel, G. 1955. *Conflict and The Web of Group Affiliations.* Transl. Reinhard Bendix. London: Free Press of Glencoe.

Strang, V. 1996. Sustaining tourism in Far North Queensland, in M.F. Price (ed.) *People and Tourism in Fragile Environments.* London: John Wiley.

—— 1997. *Uncommon Ground: Cultural Landscapes and Environmental Values.* Oxford: Berg.

—— 2000a. Not so black and white: the effects of Aboriginal Law on Australian legislation, in A. Abramson and D. Theodossopoulos (eds) *Mythical Land, Legal Boundaries: Rites and Rights in Historical and Cultural Context.* London: Pluto Press.

—— 2000b. Showing and telling: Australian land rights and material moralities, in *Journal of Material Culture* 5(3) 275–299.

—— (in press a.) Poisoning the Rainbow: cosmology and pollution in Cape York, in A. Rumsey and J. Weiner (eds) *Mining and Indigenous Lifeworlds.* Adelaide: Crawford House Publishers.

—— (in press b.) Of Human Bondage: the breaking in of stockmen in Northern Australia (*Oceania*).

Strathern, M. 1988. *The Gender of the Gift: Problems with Women and Problems with Society in Melanesia.* Berkeley: University of California Press.

Turner, V. 1982. From ritual to theatre: the human seriousness of play, in *Performing Arts Journal.* New York.

–5–

Crannogs: Places of Resistance in the Contested Landscapes of Early Modern Ireland

Aidan O'Sullivan

Introduction

Landscape has long served as both a metaphor and a source of imagery for the forging of Irish identities by artists, poets, playwrights, politicians, historians and geographers (e.g. Evans 1981). Since the 'Celtic revival' of the late nineteenth century, Irish nationalists in particular have argued that the Irish identity was essentially rooted in the landscape, preferably that of the wild and purer west of the island (Duffy 1997; Leersen 1994). Moreover, the Irish 'sense of place' was seen as being peculiarly strong and timeless, drawn from an immense, unchanging tradition of landscape appreciation and lore. Ironically enough, it could be argued that the traditional Irish rural 'hunger for the land' (ominously depicted for example in John B. Keane's (1966) play *The Field*, or in the rural-based novels of Patrick Kavanagh and Liam O'Flaherty) springs largely not from an ancient Irish tradition but from the relatively recent historical experience of the Great Famine in the 1840s. During these years, hundreds of thousands of landless labourers were swept away by starvation, disease and emigration. Because of this until recent times in rural Ireland, ethnic travellers (traditionally known as 'tinkers'), transient and seasonal labourers or other people without land or a visible means of economic security, were typically seen as the feckless poor while the strong farmer was at the heart of Irish society. In modern Irish society therefore, settlement stability was prized over settlement mobility. It is only in recent years, as people move to the cities, that this common link with 'the land' has begun to be eroded and replaced. In other words, landscape and place in Ireland, as elsewhere, can be seen to be culturally constructed, historically contingent and constantly contested and in flux.

Indeed, as modern Irish society changes, geographers and historians have started to explore more diverse senses of place and more fluid senses of Irish identity, focusing in particular on other communities (in terms of ethnicity, gender, age and social class) not previously considered. Modern Irish geography is increasingly studying the contested identities of a new, often urban, Ireland (Graham 1997; Graham and Proudfoot 1993). Irish archaeology too has recently come to grips with landscape both as a multi-disciplinary approach and as a theoretical stance (e.g. Cooney 1999, 2000). However, it is likely that whether in geography, history or archaeology, space and place will continue to remain key contexts for exploring negotiations of power and dispute in Ireland. Indeed, it can be seen that the Irish landscape itself is, and has always been, vigorously contested between different ethnic, political and social groups.

For example, post-colonial studies of the early modern period (AD 1534–1700) in Ireland (wherein lie the historical roots of Northern Ireland's profound ethnic, political and social divisions between Catholic and Protestant, or nationalist and loyalist communities) now increasingly emphasize the study of topography and cartography. In this chapter, early modern Irish archaeology, history and cartography will be used to explore how a particular type of settlement site, the crannog or lake-dwelling, can be used as a metaphor to explore the clash between Gaelic Ireland and the English Tudor government in the late sixteenth century. In particular, the opposing perceptions of these island dwellings can be shown to reflect two profoundly different views of landscape, place, culture and identity.

The Tudor Re-conquest and Plantation of Ireland, AD 1534–1602

The early modern period (AD 1534–1700) was one of great social, economic and political change in Ireland, witnessing religious and cultural conflict between the dispossessed Gaelic Irish, the Old English and the new Scottish and English colonialists. The historical and political background to the transformation of the Irish landscape in this period can first be briefly sketched out (MacCurtain 1972; Moody *et al.* 1976; Cullen 1981; Brady and Gillespie 1986; Canny 1987; Loeber 1991; Gillespie 1993; O'Brien 1998; Ellis 1998).

In the mid-sixteenth century, the English Tudor government, realizing that Ireland was a potential source of revenue and a means of defending itself against its European enemies, embarked on a programme of colonial intervention and experimentation on the island. Indeed, sixteenth- and seventeenth-century Ireland became a testing ground for England's colonial adventures in the Americas. Throughout the sixteenth century, attempts to persuade the Gaelic and Old English (who were descended from the original Anglo-Norman colonizers of the twelfth century) natives to accept new English political, legal and land-owning systems, were interspersed with bouts of military conquest and large-scale land confiscations and plantation.

Gaelic and Old English resistance led to several periods of rebellion, culminating in the Nine Year War between 1593–1603, this being known as the Earl of Tyrone's 'Great Rebellion'. The defeat of the last of the Gaelic chieftains by the end of that war, followed by the flight of some out of the country in 1607, enabled the crown to begin the plantation of Ulster in earnest. During these various sixteenth- and seventeenth-century plantations, land was mostly granted to new English and Scottish protestant landowners. These new settlers were encouraged to build strong defended houses and masonry castles and to introduce English-style agricultural and industrial management practices. Market towns and villages were planned and laid out in orderly fashion. The main aim of the plantations was to transform the wild Irish landscape into a model of English settlement and to exploit in a much more organized and entrepreneurial way its rich resources of woodland, river and land.

Tudor Perceptions of the Gaelic Settlement Landscape

One of the difficulties in reconstructing the sixteenth-century Gaelic settlement landscape lies in the fact that much of our historical descriptions of it come from English observers, who of course had an agenda of their own and so deliberately stressed its political instability and economic wastefulness. Both Gaelic and English historical sources make it clear that during the sixteenth century, Gaelic society was largely structured around dozens of regional and local lordships, where chieftains of ruling clans controlled large territories and a landowning class owned and managed their own estates that were cultivated by landless tenants. However, these lordships were more 'of men than land', and a chieftain's real wealth lay in the number of farmers who lived under his protection and of the cows they tended (Ellis 1998). The Gaelic settlement landscape was dominated by the dwellings of lords and chieftains, who generally laid little stress on large houses, but inhabited small fortified masonry castles (towerhouses) that could resist small-scale attacks, as well as crannogs and earthen ringforts (both types of settlement originating in the early Middle Ages).

It seems likely that there was at least some settlement mobility in the Gaelic Irish landscape (although its role in Irish society is contested among Irish historians), with lords moving around their territories through the year, from residence to residence. The dwellings of the native tenants of these Gaelic lords have yet to be traced archaeologically, but some Irish geographers and historians argue that the ordinary people must have lived in *clachans* adjacent to towerhouses, nucleated settlements of numerous wooden houses capable of being disassembled rapidly. Arable agriculture was known among the Gaelic Irish and landowners cultivated their own lands with the aid of labourers, who were probably paid with a share of the crops (Nicholls 1972: 115; 1993). Wheat and rye were grown on good land, barley harvested for brewing and distilling and oats grown on the poorer lands of the west (Mitchell and Ryan 1997: 316). However, although arable farming was certainly important on Gaelic estates, native land-tenure practices (with the periodic re-distribution of lands among co-heirs according to Gaelic law and custom) and the vulnerability of crops to the endemic warfare of the period meant that there was little incentive for the Gaelic lords to practise the intensive farming methods proposed for the new English settlers. However, there were certainly exceptions to this, and settlement studies in south Ulster indicate the scale and complexity of Gaelic land-holdings.

The Tudor observers derived even more sustenance for their beliefs about the mobility of the Gaelic settlement landscape in cattle transhumance practices and in the mobile tactics of Gaelic warfare. Gaelic lords typically had enormous herds of cattle, which were important in both social and economic terms (Aalen 1978; Nicholls 1972: 114). The herds and those who drove them were known as *caoruigheachta* or 'creaghts' and these were typically moved through the landscape as part of a 'booleying' or transhumance system. These nomadic Gaelic pastoralists, driving their huge herds of cattle through the landscape, often moving from the protection of one lord to another, were a source of particular fascination to English commentators. In fact, modern Irish historians believe that English observers were actually witnessing something which was a product of unsettled times, as endemic warfare and the constant loss of arable crops exaggerated the normal traditions of seasonal cattle transhumance. Indeed, some Gaelic lords themselves were attempting to convert these mobile cattle herders into rent-paying farmers, not always successfully (Mitchell and Ryan 1997: 315). In any case, Tudor commentators made great play of this perceived inefficiency of Gaelic land-use and economy in their calls for the transformation of the Irish landscape.

Gaelic warfare tactics were also highly mobile in the period, as can be seen in various sixteenth-century descriptions of cattle raids; whereby Gaelic forces usually made a sudden attack followed by a quick retreat into the woods, lakes and marshes, the landscape being their own natural fortress. English commentators argued that if only this Gaelic settlement system could be changed and the 'wandering Irish' anchored to the land on tillage farms, or preferably replaced by settled Englishmen living in manor houses at the centre of farmed estates or in orderly market towns and villages, then the Irish landscape could finally be pacified and stabilized.

The Role of Cartography in Imposing English Order on the Gaelic Landscape

This English view of the Gaelic landscape was typical of the colonialist European nations in the sixteenth century, where there were ongoing debates about 'culture', 'nature' and 'civility'. At this time 'European man' was presented, through the discovery of the New World, with a perplexing new variety of cultural forms as well as a challenge of imposing order on distant primitive landscapes and societies. The outcome was that places such as Ireland would now be treated in the same way as the new lands beyond the Atlantic (both the Irish and the Iroquois would be civilized). Tudor soldiers, government officials and entrepreneurs all saw the Irish landscape as barbarous and unstable, as did such scholars as Edmund Spenser (author of the *The Faerie Queene*), William Camden (who wrote about Irish geography and landscape), and Fynes Moryson (an early English travel-writer) (MacCurtain 1981).

It was also the case that the landscape of Gaelic Ireland remained largely unknown to the English government. At the end of the sixteenth century, most of the north and west of the island remained *terra incognita*, from which stories came of great lakes (the north-west is actually largely lake-bound), mysterious off-shore islands (mostly non-existent!) and a mountainous interior (the Irish midlands are entirely low-lying). This lack of knowledge of the landscape during the early part of the colonial enterprise created a great need for maps and accurate geographical descriptions of the conquered territories. Thus several cartographic surveys were carried out, so that by the end of the seventeenth century, Ireland was one of the best-mapped countries in the world. Most of these maps and surveys aimed to delineate territorial boundaries and economic resources, to facilitate the elaborate task of land apportionment among the new settlers. They aimed to transform the native Gaelic oral knowledge of the landscape into a cartographic knowledge, which could then be used for political ends.

These Tudor maps vary in detail and usefulness for reconstructing Gaelic settlement patterns, but a particularly striking set are the pictorial maps produced by Richard Bartlett at the beginning of the seventeenth century. Bartlett was an English cartographer engaged to supply military charts of Irish territories during Lord Mountjoy's campaign against Hugh O'Neill, Earl of Tyrone in 1601–1603. His maps are of enduring geographical interest, with their detailed drawings of the land, its settlements, woodlands, farmland, forts and crannogs (Hayes-McCoy 1964; Aalen 1978: 150). However Bartlett's maps can also be seen to be full of political meaning, intended as they were to symbolize the Irish defeat and provide cartographic proof of the overthrow of the old Gaelic order.

Bartlett's maps were created by, but they also sustained, the colonial enterprise (see Bender 1999 and Harley 1988 for discussions of maps and colonialism). They served first of all to illustrate the success of the English soldiers and entrepreneurs, who of course had financial and political supporters to impress back in London (i.e. the English soldiers in Ireland had not only to defeat the Irish, but also their rivals at home in the Elizabethan court). The maps also serve as an analogue for how the Irish landscape would be framed, acquired and managed. In Bartlett's maps, the subjective viewer is provided with a birds-eye view of an objective landscape, which is framed within the cartographer's chosen boundaries. The maps are about control, where the observer is controlled and the Irish are also seen to be under control, as the viewer is presented with the 'truth' of a particular historical

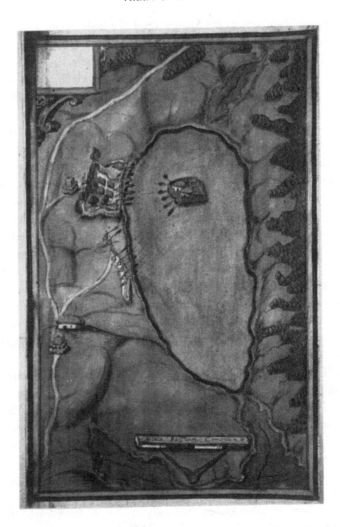

Figure 5.1 Interpreting Richard Bartlett's pictorial map, 'attack on a crannog'. It is 1 July 1602, and a crannog belonging to the leader of the Ulster rebellion, Hugh O'Neill, the Earl of Tyrone, is under fierce attack by Lord Mountjoy's English forces. Richard Bartlett has drawn the English forces as orderly, disciplined and well-armed with their small cannon pounding the wooden palisade of the Gaelic crannog. English re-enforcements can be seen to be on the way, spelling the end for the island's defenders. In contrast, the Gaelic forces are hidden, unseen and unruly, their muskets blasting across at the English soldiers. Their small huts are clearly depicted, as well as a mysterious rectangular structure (the function of which is unknown to us today, but may have been a gallows). To further emphasize the dark, wild character of the Gaelic rebels, Bartlett has depicted deep, dark woodlands on the opposite lake-shore, those ungovernable places into which the Irish were often known to retreat. In Edmund Spenser's *The Faerie Queene*, in Canto IV, the woods of southern Ireland assume a sinister and dark aspect. Here in Ulster, in Bartlett's map, these Irish woods reach out towards the English with menacing, splaying leafy fingers, much in the same way as the hidden Irish defenders blast out their muskets of rebellion. (Reproduced courtesy National Library of Ireland)

Figure 5.2 Interpreting Richard Bartlett's map, 'Monaghan'. Crannogs were not only defended strongholds for times of war, they were also lordly residences and summer lodges in times of peace. At the beginning of the seventeenth century, when the confiscated lands of Ulster were being surveyed, maps produced for the Monaghan district indicate that each crannog could be identified with a local chieftain. Richard Bartlett also illustrated crannogs in this map of Monaghan town, using an interesting technique that symbolized the transition from the earlier Gaelic rural landscape to the new English planter town. On the 'lower fold' of the map, the earlier Gaelic landscape with its crannogs can be seen, while on the 'overlying fold' the English town of Monaghan is shown with its earthen banked enclosure and its tidily laid-out houses and streets. Bartlett is again using crannogs to symbolize the reality of the newly transformed landscape. (Reproduced courtesy National Library of Ireland)

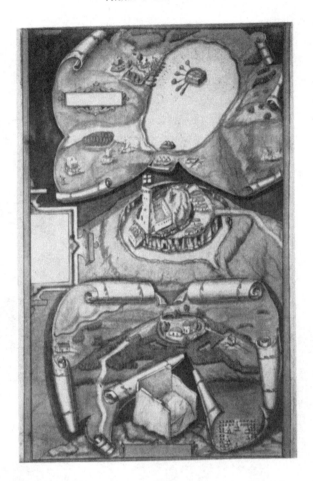

Figure 5.3 Interpreting Richard Bartlett's map, 'Attack on a crannog, Dungannon and Tullahoge'. Richard Bartlett depicted these various types of Gaelic Irish settlement in another one of his maps of captured Irish places. An Irish crannog at Lough Roughan is shown under attack at the top, Hugh O'Neill's towerhouse at Dungannon is shown in the middle, after its capture, and around it are the simple huts of his followers. A ringfort and the O'Neill clan's royal inauguration chair is shown at the bottom. The crannog is situated in a lake set among low hills with small patches of woodland. There is a second, abandoned crannog or lakeshore settlement with an unroofed house at the opposite end of the lake. The crannog is again being attacked (it may in fact be the same event depicted) by English cannon, musketry and a small force of infantry, while its inhabitants are also defending themselves with musket fire. In any case, it seems likely the capture of the crannog marked a significant moment in the English campaign (as important as the capture of the O'Neill headquarters of Dungannon and the destruction, carried out by English forces, of the O'Neill's royal inauguration chair at their ancestral fort of Tullahoge). Historical accounts describe attacks on two crannogs at this time, at Roughan Lough, Co. Tyrone, and at Magherlocowe, Co. Armagh. Mountjoy himself described the attack on Roughan Lough crannog, stating that it was O'Neill's 'strongest island fort'. The three scrolls again symbolize the destruction of the Gaelic past and the blank sheet thus left for the new English and Scottish planter future. (Reproduced courtesy National Library of Ireland)

event. An interesting aspect of Bartlett's maps too is the fact that the Gaelic population are rarely shown (although the English themselves are hardly more common, mostly indicated by military tents or English flags). The Gaelic Irish are shown as hidden behind their defences (see Figure 5.1); only their barking guns can be seen. Otherwise they are merely represented by abandoned forts or ruined buildings. In other words, they are gone, the land is now empty and thus open for exploitation.

Bartlett's pictorial maps depict a whole range of settlement and economic features, and in emphasizing crannogs in this chapter I do not wish to suggest that these predominate in his work. Gaelic towerhouses, forts and fields are also common. However, Gaelic crannogs do feature in several and are shown in key maps, emphasizing both their importance to the native Irish and their peculiarity to English eyes. Indeed, it seems that Richard Bartlett was using crannogs as a metaphor for the displacement of the old Gaelic social order and its replacement, through English and Scottish conquest and plantation, with an entirely new way of life. The Gaelic chieftains were well aware of the role of map-makers in this process of destruction of their way of life. Although Gaelic Ireland was literate, and had been so for many centuries, knowledge of the landscape would have been communicated orally, by means of praise poems, songs and stories, through which family genealogies, events and other traditions could be transmitted. Cartography in the modern accepted sense of the word was unknown, so the activities of map-makers in their territories would have been recognized as a source of danger, as can be seen in the poignant fate of Richard Bartlett himself. An early seventeenth-century account indicates how he met his end.

> Our geographers do not forget what entertainment the Irish of Tyrconnell [i.e. west Ulster] gave to a mapmaker about the end of the late great rebellion [i.e. the Nine Years War]. When he came into Tyrconnell the inhabitants took off his head, because they would not have their country discovered (Andrews 1997: 89).

The Destruction of Gaelic Crannogs by English Forces in the Sixteenth and Seventeenth Centuries

Why did Bartlett depict crannogs? Essentially, this occurs against the backdrop of the military campaigns waged by the Tudor government in Ulster. Apart from the need to defeat Gaelic rebels, Tudor commentators also realized that as a policy, before the land could be properly pacified and civilized, certain hot spots of rebellion would have to be broken down. Crannogs were seen as hot spots and a particularly obnoxious form of native settlement practice at that. Crannogs, a classic feature of the settlement landscape of early Ireland, are generally defined by archaeologists as artificially built islands in lakes, typically of circular plan, constructed of layers of stone, peat, brushwood, timber and earth and usually retained within a circular wooden stockade of post-and-wattle or cleft timber planks.

Crannogs were first constructed and occupied in Ireland in the early medieval period (AD 600–1200), when some served as royal residences, places for specialized crafts, especially bronze-working, iron-working and glass-working and for the redistribution into the wider landscape of high-status goods. There is also good archaeological and historical evidence that crannogs were occupied, reconstructed and strengthened in the late medieval period (AD 1200–1534) and early modern periods (AD 1534–1700) when they were used as lordly residences, defended strongholds, farmsteads, hospitals, prisons and gold/silver and ammunitions stores (e.g. Wood-Martin 1886: 146–54, 236–8; Hayes-McCoy 1964: 9–10, 16, 20; O'Sullivan 1998; Barry 1987). The fact that many of these Early Medieval sites were still being occupied in the sixteenth century says a lot about Gaelic sense of tradition, continuity and belonging at particular places in the landscape.

The Gaelic Irish were little interested in resisting long sieges or fighting set-piece battles, and crannogs, due to their inaccessibility out on the lakes, could be easily defended and quickly abandoned. English soldiers were initially fooled by the light wooden defences of these islands, but their apologetic letters to Queen Elizabeth's council indicate that they often came off quite badly in frontal attacks on them. On some occasions, crannogs could be successfully attacked only by sending piles of burning brushwood drifting down onto the islands. The importance of these crannogs as Irish munitions stores and military bases can be seen in Fynes Moryson's (Lord Mountjoy's secretary) early seventeenth-century account of the defeat of Hugh O'Neill during the Ulster rebellion. He describes how Lord Mountjoy

> took some of Tyrone's (Hugh O'Neill) strongest Illands, namely one wherein he had a strong fort, where we recovered three peeces of his majesties artillery, and another Illand called Magerlowni, which next to Dungannon was the chiefe place of his aboade and magazins for his warre (Moryson 1908).

These attacks were not always successful. Sir Henry Sydney wrote the following passages to Queen Elizabeth I on 12 November, 1566 describing such a failed attack. The English attackers had had to retreat from the island with a few casualties. The letter describes a fortified lake island, about 100m from the shore, with a palisade of timber and stakes.

> So on the 21st of the same month, we removed and marched towards Ardmach, and in the way, having occasion to encamp hard by a logh, in which was an island, and in the same, by universal opinion and reports of divers of that country, a great quantity of the rebel's goods and victuals kept, only without guns, as it was thought, not greatly strong as it seemed but hedged about, and the distance from the main not being passed five-

score yards, the army coming timely to the camp, divers soldiers were very desirous to attempt the winning of it, which was granted to them . . . They found the place better manned than it was thought, and they of better courage than before that time the like men had ever shewed themselves in the like place. They found the hedge so bearded around with stakes and other sharp wood, as it was not without extreme difficulty scaleable, and so ramparted as if the hedge had been burned – for doing whereof the fireworks failed – without a long time it was not to be digged down (Wood-Martin 1866: 148).

Both Irish and English historical references indicate that crannogs were also being used by the Gaelic lords as hospitals and prisons or as safe places to keep gold and silver plate. English commentators were aware, or perhaps even very interested, in this practice. For example, in May 1567 the English soldier Thomas Phettiplace, when asked by the Queen Elizabeth's council what castles or forts Shane O'Neill possessed, replied

> . . . that fortification that he only dependeth upon is in ssartin ffreshwater loghes in his country . . . it is thought that there in ye said fortified islands lyeth all his plate, whc is much, and money, prisoners and gages (Wood-Martin 1886: 147).

In Marshal Bagenal's description of Ulster, AD 1586, a description of O'Neill's condition refers to a wetland settlement, 'You shall do verie well to see his lodgings in the fen, where he built his lodging, and kept his cattell, and all his men' (Wilde 1857: 232). Crannogs were also used as places of refuge, hospitals or as safe places for wounded and injured. Thus, in 1603, Hugh Boy O'Donnell having been wounded, 'was sent to *Crannog-na-n-Duini*, in Ross-Guill, in the tuathas (Donegal), to be healed' (Wood-Martin 1886a: 150; *Annals of the Four Masters*).

Even after the final defeat of the Gaelic rebellion in 1602, crannogs still signified rebellion and instability to the English commentators. Before the landscape could be properly populated and managed, these crannogs and lake-dwellings would have to be destroyed totally. Indeed, one observer recommended that Ireland could more easily be governed if (among other things) 'none of the Irish do build any houses on loughs, but be enjoined to build castles or houses upon the firm land, and those houses that now are built upon loughs to be defaced' (Hayes-McCoy 1964: 20).

Bartlett depicts crannogs, then, because their destruction was a key feature of the successful military campaign in Ulster. However, they also are depicted because they symbolized the wildness and peculiarity of the Irish, who instead of residing in proper English-style residences (for the most part) utilized these strange lake-dwellings. Perhaps we could trace comparisons and find similar interests in the documents with the strange dwelling places of the Iroquois, in North America.

Gaelic Crannogs and new English Settlements – Continuity and Accommodation in the Seventeenth Century

Despite all the efforts of the English government, the sixteenth-century plantations of loyal protestant settlers in Ireland were not entirely successful. In many ways, the plantations initially proved too ambitious. British settlers were difficult to attract in numbers. However, the defeat of the Gaelic Irish rebellion of the 1641 after twelve years of war enabled an even larger and more efficient English plantation scheme, with massive land confiscations which were often accompanied by major mapping surveys, such as the Down Survey implemented by William Petty in the 1650s (Andrews 1997). After the end of the short Williamite Wars of English succession (1689–1691), the Irish landscape was finally under total English control and witnessed a prolonged period of social and economic stability.

The Irish landscape was almost cleared of woodlands, organized into estates and fenced field-systems; cattle meat was exported and sheep grew in importance. The growth of demesne and estate villages went hand-in-hand with ideas of agricultural improvement, largely creating the modern Irish rural landscape of dispersed farmhouses with their large, enclosed field-systems: the landscape, ironically enough, with which most of the nineteenth-century nationalist artists, poets and writers would have been familiar, an Irish landscape of modern Anglo-Irish, landlord origins.

By 1691 the vast majority of the Irish landscape was firmly in the new English and Scottish settlers' hands and crannogs had been abandoned (although some few remained in use as hiding places for 'Tories', Roman Catholic outlaws and the dispossessed). Nevertheless, continuity in settlement and society was as important as change (Gillespie 1993). Most of the native Irish population remained as tenants to the new lords. For the Scottish and English settlers, there were also the pervading influences of the traditional Irish economy and way of life and the realities of the Irish landscape. The early seventeenth-century settlers often built fortified residences in the manner of the late medieval Irish tower-house, sensibly reflecting the unsettled nature of the times. After difficulties in early attempts at tillage and arable farming in the heavy, waterlogged soils of Ulster, cattle raising was found by the new settlers to be indeed more suitable for the landscape of west Ulster (Mallory and McNeill 1991).

Although the social and settlement landscape had certainly been transformed, it is possible to trace specific settlement continuities, often indeed relating to crannogs. For example, many of the new English and Scottish defended houses and masonry castles were built on the sites of earlier Gaelic Irish towerhouses or were placed adjacent to former Gaelic Irish lordly crannogs. At Monea castle, in Fermanagh in west Ulster, an early seventeenth-century Scottish plantation castle was built beside a crannog, thus illustrating the shift in power from the local Gaelic

Irish lord to the new Scottish landowner. The castle was captured by the Gaelic Irish in the 1641 rebellion and abandoned after 1750. This planter castle was itself, in turn, succeeded by a nineteenth-century landlord demesne house, itself symbolizing the further transition to the new Irish social and economic landscape.

Conclusion

In conclusion, the late sixteenth and early seventeenth centuries witnessed the end of the use of crannogs in Ireland, at a time when the Gaelic and old English lords were being largely displaced by the new English and Scottish entrepreneurs and landowners. The hostility of the English commentators, soldiers, map-makers and politicians towards these crannogs was because they were symbolic of Gaelic ethnicity, tradition, power and resistance in this bewildering landscape of woods and water. So much so, that the destruction of these crannogs was celebrated in Bartlett's maps and other commentators went so far as to recommend that the native peoples not be allowed build or live on them again. In general terms, two profoundly different views of landscape, place, culture and identity conflicted in the sixteenth and seventeenth, as one replaced the other. In particular, the destruction of Gaelic crannogs and their replacement by new settlements can be seen as metaphor for the passing of a traditional way of life and the emergence of a new one in the contested landscapes of early modern Ireland.

Acknowledgements

I would like to thank Barbara Bender (UCL), Eoin Grogan and Kieran O'Conor (Discovery Programme) for their helpful comments on this chapter. Thomas Herron (University of Wisconsin, Madison) made some inspiring comments on the textuality of the Bartlett maps. The maps are reproduced courtesy of the National Library of Ireland.

References

Aalen, F.H.A. 1978. *Man and the Landscape in Ireland*. London: Academic Press.
Andrews, J.H. 1997. *Shapes of Ireland: Maps and their Makers 1564–1839*. Dublin: Geography Publications.
Barry, T.B. 1987. *The Archaeology of Medieval Ireland*. London and New York: Routledge.

Bender, B. 1999. Subverting the western gaze: mapping alternative worlds, in P.J. Ucko and R. Layton *The Archaeology and Anthropology of Landscape*. One World Archaeology. London: Routledge. 31–45.

Brady, C. and Gillespie, R. (eds) 1986. *Natives and Newcomers: Essays on the Making of Irish Colonial Society 1534–1641*. Dublin: Irish Academic Press.

Canny, N. 1987. *From Reformation to Restoration: Ireland 1534–1660*. Dublin: Helicon History of Ireland.

Cooney, G. 1999. Social landscapes in Irish prehistory, in P.J. Ucko and R. Layton *The Archaeology and Anthropology of Landscape*. One World Archaeology. London: Routledge. 46–64.

—— 2000. *Landscapes of Neolithic Ireland*. London: Routledge.

Cullen, L.M. 1981. *The Emergence of Modern Ireland, 1600–1900*. London: Batsford.

Duffy, P.J. 1997. Writing Ireland: Literature and art in the representation of Irish place, in B.J. Graham (ed.) *In Search of Ireland: a Cultural Geography*. London: Routledge. 64–83.

Ellis, S. 1998. *Ireland in the Age of the Tudors*. London: Longman.

Evans, E.E. 1981. *The Personality of Ireland: Habitat, Heritage and History*, rev. edn. Belfast: Blackstaff.

Gillespie, R. 1993. Explorers, exploiters and entrepreneurs: Early Modern Ireland and its context, 1500–1700, in B.J. Graham and L.J. Proudfoot (eds) *An Historical Geography of Ireland*. London: Academic Press. 123–57.

Graham, B.J. (ed.) 1997. *In Search of Ireland: a Cultural Geography*. New York and London: Routledge.

—— and Proudfoot, L.J. (eds) 1993. *An Historical Geography of Ireland*. London: Academic Press.

Harley, J.B. 1988. Maps, knowledge and power, in D. Cosgrove and S. Daniels (eds) *The Iconography of Landscape: Essays on the Symbolic Representation, Design and Use of Past Environments*. Cambridge: Cambridge University Press. 277–314.

Hayes-McCoy, G.A. 1964. *Ulster and other Irish Maps, c. 1600*. Dublin: Government Publications Office.

Leersen, J. 1994. The western mirage: on the Celtic chronotype in the European imagination, in T. Collins (ed.) *Decoding the Landscape*. Galway: Centre for Landscape Studies.

Loeber, R. 1991. *The Geography and Practice of English Colonisation in Ireland from 1534 to 1609*. Athlone: The Group for the Study of Irish Historic Settlement.

MacCurtain, M. 1981. *Tudor and Stuart Ireland*. Dublin: Gill and MacMillan.

Mallory, J. and McNeill, T. 1991. *The archaeology of Ulster: from colonisation to plantation* Belfast: Institute of Irish Studies.

Mitchell, G.F. and Ryan, M. 1997. *Reading the Irish Landscape*. 3rd edn. Dublin: Town House.

Moody, T.W., Martin, F.X. and Byrne, F.J. (eds) 1976. *A New History of Ireland III: Early Modern Ireland*. Oxford: Oxford University Press.

Moryson, F. 1908. *An Itinery* . . . . vol III. Glasgow (First published in 1617).

Nicholls, K. 1972. *Gaelic and Gaelicised Ireland in the Middle Ages*. Gill and MacMillan: Dublin.

—— 1993. Gaelic society and economy, in A. Cosgrove (ed.) *A New History of Ireland II: Medieval Ireland 1169–1534*. Clarendon Press: Oxford. 397–438.

O'Brien, A.F. 1998. Ireland – conquest, settlement and colonisation, in D. O'Ceallaigh (ed.) *New Perspectives on Ireland: colonisation and identity*. Dublin: Leirmheas and Desmond Greaves Summer School. 9–21.

O'Sullivan, A. 1998. *The Archaeology of Lake Settlement in Ireland*. Dublin: Royal Irish Academy.

Wilde, W.R. 1857. A descriptive catalogue of the antiquities of stone, earthen and vegetable materials in the museum of the Royal Irish Academy. Dublin.

Wood-Martin, W.G. 1886. The Lake-dwellings of Ireland or ancient lacustrine habitations of Erin commonly called crannogs. Dublin: Hodges and Figgis.

−6−

Landscapes of Punishment and Resistance: A Female Convict Settlement in Tasmania, Australia

Eleanor Conlin Casella

Introduction

In January 1851, a letter was intercepted en route to Jane Walker, an inmate of the women's prison establishment at Ross, Van Diemen's Land. Written by Catherine Cass, possibly a sister-in-law, the note assured Jane that she 'will be well don [sic] for':

> Jane your uncal sends you a pound note and you may expect to see littel John . . . and he will tell you all about your uncal . . . Dear Jane your box will be up as soon as the letter so I hope you keep up your spirits and do not fret for the time will soon come Dear Jane I must conclud with my Kind love to you and hope to see you soon . . . . (Mitchell Library, Tasmanian Papers, Number 104).

After seizing this letter, the prison Superintendent forwarded the forbidden communication to the Comptroller-General of the Convict Department, who annotated the margins with orders to improve perimeter security at the Ross Establishment so as to prevent future communications, and to intercept any box illicitly traded into the prison.

When considered together, the presence of this letter and the reaction of the institutional authorities demonstrate overlapping landscapes of penal domination and inmate resistance that operated to create this site. Why was Jane denied access to her relatives outside the perimeter wall of the prison? Who enjoyed the privilege of access? And how did convicts intentionally circumvent and penetrate these disciplinary boundaries? This chapter is concerned with the spatial dynamics of such questions.

The Administration of Female Convicts in Van Diemen's Land

From 1803 to 1854, over 74,000 British convicts were transported to the Van Diemen's Land, an island penal colony isolated from the southern coast of mainland Australia by the treacherous Bass Straits (Eldershaw 1968: 130). Approximately 12,000 of these felons were women, primarily convicted of petty theft of goods stolen from their domestic employers (Oxley 1996). Upon their colonial arrival, most spent time incarcerated within the Female Factory System, a network of women's prisons scattered across the island (Brand 1990).

Named 'factory' as a contraction of the word 'manufactory', these penal institutions were designed along the model of the British Workhouse System, a nineteenth-century form of public social welfare which required standardized rates of labour from all inmates to hasten their social and moral salvation from delinquency, idleness and poverty (Driver 1993). Upon entry into a colonial Factory, female convicts were assigned to the 'Crime Class', and incarcerated for a minimum of six months. While serving this probationary sentence, the women were intended to 'reform' through Christian prayer and forced training in acceptably feminine industries, including sewing, textile production, and laundry work. Recalcitrance was punished through lengthy periods of confinement in Solitary Treatment cells, accompanied by severe reduction of food rations. Once they successfully served their probationary period, the 'reconstituted' women were reclassified into the 'Hiring Class', and awaited assignment to local properties, completing their convict sentences as domestic servants for free colonists (Ryan 1995; Oxley 1996; Damousi 1997; Daniels 1998).

The Ross Female Factory

Located on the southern edge of the Ross Township in the rural midlands of the island (renamed Tasmania in 1855), the Ross Female Factory operated from 1848 through 1854, when Britain ceased convict transportation to the Van Diemen's Land colony. The Ross site was then transferred to civilian management, and experienced a series of municipal and domestic occupations. It was gazetted as an historic reserve in 1980, and is now administered through the Cultural Heritage Branch of the Tasmanian Parks and Wildlife Service, Australia. Since 1995, the site has become the focus of historical, geophysical and archaeological research (Casella 1999). This chapter presents results from the Ross Factory Archaeology Project by integrating multidisciplinary evidence for coexisting landscapes of penal domination and female inmate resistance that created and shaped the Factory site.

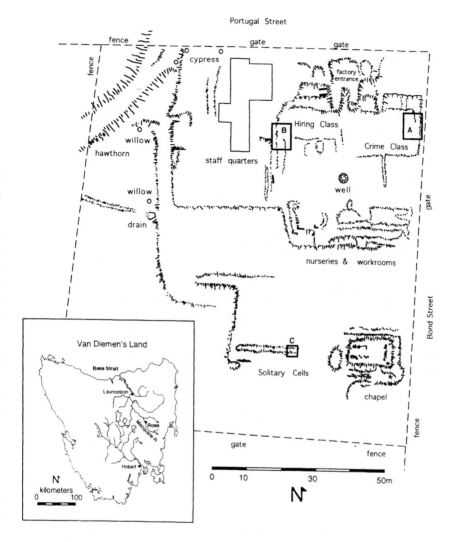

Figure 6.1 Site surface plan of the Ross Female Factory, Van Diemen's Land

A Cultural Landscape of Containment

In his analysis of gendered landscapes among the Berbers of Kabylia, Algeria, Pierre Bourdieu noted the role of segregated space in forming gender relations:

The reason why submission to the collective rhythms is so rigorously demanded is that the temporal forms or the spatial structures structure not only the group's representation of the world but the group itself, which orders itself in accordance with the representation: this may be clearly seen, for example, in the fact that the organization of the existence of the men and women in accordance with different times and different places constitutes two interchangeable ways of securing separation and hierarchization of the male and female worlds, the women going to the fountain at an hour when the men are not in the streets, or by a special path, or both at once. (Bourdieu 1977: 163).

The segmentation of space and time not only creates the disciplined bodies of institutional inmates, it also creates and reinforces a hierarchy of male and female spaces, through a temporal and physical ordering of their locales. Emphasizing a reflexive relationship between gender and the built environment, architect Daphne Spain similarly argued that the 'initial status differences between women and men create certain types of gendered spaces and that institutionalized spatial segregation then reinforces prevailing male advantages'. (Spain 1992: 6).

Through the demarcation of spaces within the Ross Factory landscape, inmates were limited to occupying appropriate interior locales at appropriate times. With functionally specific locales architecturally identified throughout the institution, the nature of boundaries and forbidden territories depended upon the exact classification of the inhabitant. Both Factory staff and inmate movements through the prison were strictly ordered through spatial and temporal regulations and procedures. As these inhabitants moved through the various segregated spaces of the Factory, they reiteratively mapped relationships of unequal social status onto the penal landscape. Thus, through the segregation of interior spaces, convict administrators fabricated an institutional landscape of order and reformation. Through this segmentation of movement in space and time, the threat of delinquency was – seemingly – eradicated and replaced by meticulously choreographed activity within the bounded institution (Foucault 1977: 150–1).

Mapping Domination: the Geography of Factory Staff

Not only did differentiated places within the Ross Factory order the inhabitants, the segregation of space also exerted social control by materially expressing relationships of dominant and subordinate status. Both subtle and overt statements of social inequality infused the monumental architecture of nineteenth-century Britain. Designs for institutions ranging from prisons and workhouses (Driver 1993; Evans 1982) to schools and museums (Seaborne 1971; Peponis and Hedin 1982) reflected and reified the unequal status of genders, races and social classes (Markus 1993). Thus, Factory fence lines, pathways, and entrance porches cemented the social hierarchy of this penal site.

A geography of occupant movement within the Ross Factory revealed subtle layers of differential status infused throughout the institutional landscape. This 'cultural map of political power' (Rodgers 1993: 48) began within the ranks of the Ross Factory staff. At the top of the hierarchy, the Factory Superintendent and

Matron, hired as a married couple, lived outside the Factory compound. Historical research suggested they occupied a house within the Ross township (Scripps and Clark 1991: 14). Besides encouraging their access to the outside colonial world, that location would have offered them a privileged degree of privacy from the Factory.

As the principal representative of the establishment, the Superintendent mediated the junction point between the inner world of the Ross Factory and the exterior colonial world of Van Diemen's Land. He provided all communication with the outside world, submitting frequent reports to the Comptroller-General of Convicts, hosting regular inspections by the Visiting Magistrate, and responding to all correspondence directed to the Factory. Arriving at the prison at 5:30 a.m., his hours of duty ended after the last, or 'silence', bell had rung at 8:30 p.m. At night, he was explicitly instructed to 'receive the [Factory] Keys and take them over to [his] house with [him]' (AOT MM 62/24/10774). Twice a week, he conducted surprise night-time inspections of the institution. As chief medical officer, the Superintendent directed activities in the Hospital Ward, classified and treated the health of inmates, regulated all medical supplies, and oversaw all births.

His personal interaction with female inmates was regulated by the Factory Matron, his wife. She maintained direct responsibility for all women within the institution, controlling interactions with both inmates and female officers. The Matron was required to accompany all dormitory inspections conducted by male officers, and 'attend to any just complaint of the women and if necessary bring the case before the Superintendent or Visiting Magistrate' (AOT MM 62/24/10774). Thus, issues of gender infused the political map of the Ross Factory. While the Superintendent controlled access between the institutional and free worlds, he was expected to inhabit only the administrative and hospital wards of the Factory. His wife controlled access to all locales directly related to the female inmates.

On the next tier of this hierarchical landscape were the Assistant Superintendent and Assistant Matron, also hired as a married pair. They lived within the boundaries of the Factory institution. Historic plans identified two rooms inside the Main Compound as the Assistant Superintendent's Quarters (Scripps and Clark 1991). This region was identified as Area B, and excavated during the 1997 season of the Ross Factory Archaeology Project (Casella 1997). Architectural and stratigraphic evidence suggested that the building had earthen floors, as no physical remains of stone or suspended wooden floors were recovered during excavation, and the two rooms contained compacted layers of sandy-silt containing high densities of nineteenth-century artefacts (Casella 1999). Since these brick quarters were relatively small, earthen-floored, and located inside the main compound of the prison, historians have suggested they functioned as an administrative office for the Assistant Superintendent, rather than as a primary residence for himself and the Assistant Matron (Terry 1998: 39).

Regardless of the exact function of this brick structure, the hierarchical status of the Assistant Superintendent's Quarters was materially emphasized by the introduction of a sandstone-flagged pathway delineating the entrance to the structure. Archival documents suggest this structure was installed sometime between 1848, when the Ross Female Factory was opened, and 1851, when the pathway first appeared in plans at the northern face of the Assistant Superintendent's Quarters. As with most convict-built architectural features, this sandstone pathway could be functionally interpreted as a labour-intensive construction scheme designed to occupy the male convict workers. The feature could also have been laid for safety or sanitary purposes within this densely occupied Establishment. However, this sandstone pathway also physically segmented space, and probably operated as a status marker within the cultural landscape of the Factory (Markus 1993: 95). Given a consistently inadequate supply of shoes for female inmates (AOT MM 62/28/12161; Scripps and Clark 1991: 51), winter musters within the pebble-packed earthen courtyards of the convict wards would have been cold, wet and muddy experiences of institutionalized subordination for the women convicts. The presence of a sandstone pathway for access to and from the Assistant Superintendent's Quarters could easily have provided physical communication between hierarchically ordered places within this penal environment (Markus 1993; Praetzellis and Praetzellis 1992).

The institutional duties of the Assistant Superintendent and Assistant Matron located them within the boundaries of the Factory. Whereas the Superintendent commanded the articulation of the prison with the external free colony, his Assistant regulated the internal boundaries and segmentations of this institution. Charged with the maintenance of Factory stores, he strictly governed the allocation of all non-medicinal resources, including daily food rations, firewood for cooking and heating, building materials used for additions and repairs, and water carried up from the nearby Macquarie River. He took charge of the keys at mealtimes, and evaluated the portions of food issued to inmates according to a March 1848 official scale of food rations (Scripps and Clark 1991). Each morning he would issue out quantities of wool, and every evening would meticulously collect, inventory, and secure unused portions of raw wool and all finished quantities of combed, carded, spun and woven textile produced by the Crime Class inmates that day. Regulating the segmentation of time within the Factory, the Assistant Superintendent supervised the bells for morning rise, morning muster call, dinner, evening muster, and night silence. He identified and categorized all prison inmates, ensuring the completion of:

> ... proper lists of the names of women in Crime Class with their sentence and ships, and of women in Nurseries and the Passholders ward and that this list is pasted on boards and hung up in each ward and corrected when required and that lists of the scale

of rations for each ward is hung up in it, also that the name, sentence crime & c. of each woman in Solitary is hung up on door of her Cell (AOT MM 62/24/10774).

Like the Matron, the Assistant Matron regulated interactions with the female inmates. However, her locale was limited to the Nurseries and Hiring Class, where she was directly responsible for 'preserving order, seeing [the wards] kept clean, the children, more especially the orphan children, properly provided for as regards nourishment and to see that those women who in the Nurseries may have Probation of work to do accomplish it . . . .' (AOT MM 62/24/10774). Again, gender and status intersected within the spatial hierarchy of the penal landscape.

The Male and Female Overseers and Constables formed a third tier in the Staff hierarchy. As the lowest-ranking employees of the Convict Department, their movements around the institutions were restricted to specific wards. Since the conjoined Georgian cottages immediately west of the Main Compound were identified as 'Staff Quarters' in archival plans, the Overseers probably resided within the boundary of the Factory, near the Assistant Superintendent and Assistant Matron. The Female Overseer escorted Crime Class inmates from their Dormitory to the Work Rooms, and chaperoned their labour. She accompanied them to dinner, to 'see they take their meals properly and that they use nothing which is not allowed' (AOT MM 62/24/10774). Using the lists created by the Assistant Superintendent, the Female Overseer called morning and evening musters to physically account for all inmates. Duties of the Male Overseer focused on the accommodation and supervision of the male convict labourers assigned to the Factory. He also appeared to play a coercive role within the Factory Main Compound, assisting the Constables to restrain female prisoners during violent altercations (AOT MM 62/26/11931; AOT MM 62/26/11946). Constables resided in the Guard House immediately north of the Main Gate. They exerted immediate disciplinary control over the female convicts through visual surveillance and physical coercion. Because of their immediate interaction with the inmates, and their role as purveyors of direct physical force, the Constables and Male Overseer occupied lower rungs of the Staff hierarchy (Foucault 1977b: 153–6).

Convict labourers constituted the lowest rank of Factory staff. 'Turnkeys' were Factory inmates selected from the promoted Hiring Class. They provided unwaged supervisory labour, and held privileged positions within the Factory. As convicts, their unfree labour was assigned to a specific task within a specific locale, such as night watch inside the Crime Class Dormitory, or childcare in the Nurseries. They were expected to occupy the Hiring Class ward when not on duty. Approximately twelve male convicts were assigned to the Ross Factory (Rayner 1980: 20). These men were accommodated in a fortified stone cottage at some undocumented location within the nine acres of gardens attached to the Factory. No remains of this structure were discovered during the Ross Factory Archaeology Project. The anonymous male convicts served as manual labourers and field hands for the Ross Establishment. By situating the men away from the main compound, the Ross Superintendent ensured strict sexual segregation of inmates, thereby enforcing a central tenet of post-medieval penal reform schemes.

Mapping Subordination: the Documentary Image of Inmate Geography

Incarcerated inmates also moved through segregated spaces, mapping their moral descent and redemption through the cultural landscape. Upon arrival, convict women entered the Factory by descending the steep slope of the alluvial terrace. Assigned to the Crime Class, they resided in one of two dormitories in the northwest ward of the Main Compound. By 9 a.m., after morning muster and breakfast, they were escorted across the Main Compound, past the enclosed Nursery Wards, out the southern side of the prison quadrangle. Marched to the Gothic-style sandstone Chapel, located on an elevated rise south of the Main Compound, they ascended the stairs for morning prayers. At 9:30 a.m. they descended from the House of God, and were escorted back across to the Main Compound.

Their days were spent either in the Work Room where they laboured at textile production, meeting predetermined Scales of Taskwork (AOT CO 280/699/268 p.162), or in the Wash House where they processed laundry for the institution and local private contracts. Six large rectangular windows were set into the southern wall of the Work Room. This architectural element was typical for nineteenth-century institutional designs, as the presence of large windows provided free light for work spaces. However, since the Work Room was located on the southern edge of the Main Compound, the commanding view from those windows was of the structures immediately south of the Main Compound (see Figure 6.1). While labouring at textile production, convict women gazed over a landscape of damnation and redemption – the topographically elevated Chapel towering over the bank of solitary punishment cells. At 5:30 p.m. their daily labour was assessed, and all unprocessed materials counted, weighed and secured in a locked storeroom by the Assistant Superintendent. They were escorted back to the Chapel for an hour of evening prayers. Descending once again from the monumental structure, they re-entered the Main Compound, marched past the secluded Nursery wards, and reassembled in the Crime Class Yard for evening muster at 6:30 p.m. After dinner, the inmates were encouraged to attend literacy classes in their Dormitories. Although this indulgence was not a mandatory requirement, attendance was noted, and regular attendance did appear to factor into evaluations of a particular inmate's morality. At 8 p.m., the silence bell was rung. All inmates were incarcerated within their assigned Dormitory, and expected to occupy their assigned bunk.

If a female convict deviated from this template, she was punished by a period of Solitary Confinement. Exiled from the Main Compound, she descended to the block of cells located on the southern side of the Factory, at the base of the alluvial terrace, approximately 3 metres below the Work Rooms. After serving her transformational sentence, she ascended the slope to rejoin the collective group of Crime Class inmates within the Main Compound. Once she had exhibited frequent enough performances of obedient behaviour to convince authorities of her compliance (Scott 1990: 29), she earned reclassification into the Hiring Class. This promoted ward was located immediately next to the Assistant Superintendent's Quarters, west of the Crime Class, in the northern half of the rectilinear quadrangle. While waiting for assignment to unwaged domestic labour for one of the local pastoral properties, she held the position of Turnkey within the prison. Intended to encourage reform of other prisoners through her good example, she performed limited supervisory duties within the Factory. When domestic assignment had been secured, the Ross Factory inmate completed her circle of transformation by ascending the slope of the alluvial terrace, through the northern Main Gate of the prison, rejoining the free colonial community on a probationary basis.

Both the movement of prison inhabitants through segregated spaces and the material demarcations of those locales communicated hierarchical status within the Ross Factory. Different classifications of inhabitants, the various ranks of both staff and inmates, were entitled to access specified locales within the prison. Their relative status determined the proximity of their residence to the institution, and provided varying degrees of spatial privilege and restriction throughout the segregated wards, workrooms, yards and pathways of the prison. Furthermore, as female inmates processed through the rectilinear quadrangle, they constituted a spatial map of transformation (Parham and Noble 1994: 72). Their moral descent and redemption became physically performed in their movements up and down the topographic elevations of the Factory site.

This geography of domination and subordination was mapped from surviving documentary evidence – the letters, proclamations, architectural plans, and regulations generated by the Factory Superintendent, staff of the colonial Convict Department, and members of the British Home Office. As such, it provides an official transcript for an ideal cultural landscape of institutional boundaries and regulated social control through the segmentation and classification of prison spaces. To consider the hidden transcript of inmate resistance, we must turn to alternative sources of evidence. Through the distribution of illicit objects within the Ross Factory site, we can map an alternate covert landscape. We can interpret the maintenance of a distinct and coexisting geography forged by the female convict inhabitants as they transgressed segmented spaces and moved through disciplinary boundaries of the ideal penal landscape.

Doing Trade: a Landscape of Resistance

This chapter will now explore the relationships among clothing buttons, alcohol bottles, and tobacco pipes, as evidence for a thriving black-market trade economy within the Ross Female Factory – an illicit form of networking that created an alternate and coexisting landscape of alliances and enemies within the Ross Factory site (Daniels 1998) and powerfully linked this site to the shadowy convict world of Van Diemen's Land penal colony.

On the Distribution of Buttons

During the Ross Factory Archaeology Project, 104 square metres were excavated, divided between three different areas of the site: the Crime Class, the Hiring Class, and the Solitary Cells (Casella 1997). After analysing the stratigraphic data, a number of female convict period deposits were identified, and their artefactual contents were subjected to further study. I will now turn to my analysis of the 67 buttons recovered from these female-convict-related deposits. Since my research considered the possibility of non-clothing-related functions for the button assemblage, I developed an abstract typological system for its classification (see Table 6.1). This three-tiered system enabled the categorization of buttons by their fabric type, their fastener type, and their diameter dimensions in millimetres. I then examined the spatial distribution of the button types through the three wards of the Factory site.

Constituting 47.7 per cent of the Ross collection, the two most prevalent button types were both large four-hole sew-through buttons, typically manufactured as fastenings for men's trousers and shirts, and for woollen jackets worn by either

---

Button Typology – three-tiered coding system:

1. Fabric type	2. Fastener type	3. Diameter dimensions
1. Ferrous	a. 4 hole	i. 8–12mm
2. Copper-alloy	b. 3 hole	ii. 13–16mm
3. Bone	c. 2 hole	iii. 17–20mm
4. Shell	d. 1 hole (button core)	iv. 21–24mm
5. Glass	e. 5 hole	v. 25–28mm
6. Other	f. shank loop	vi. 29–32mm
	g. shank sew-through (pedestal)	vii. diameter
	h. unknown	undetermined
		(broken or too
		decayed to measure)

Figure 6.2 Ross Factory Archaeology Project

men or women (Lydon 1993; 1995) (see Table 6.2). The third most common type consisted of small shell mother-of-pearl four-hole buttons, objects identified within industry catalogues as providing fastening for both men's shirts and women's dresses (Claassen 1994; Iacono 1996). Whether used in the standard regulation convict uniform, or related to non-uniform clothing, these buttons could easily have entered the site on laundry contracted from the local free community. Their presence might have represented accidental deposition during taskwork. The simple presence of these buttons at the Ross Factory site is in itself rather unremarkable. However, the artefact distribution pattern is potentially more revealing.

The largest number and greatest diversity of buttons were recovered from Area B. It contained both the Hiring Class and the Assistant Superintendent's Quarters. The earthen floors of this latter structure contained evidence of mixing between pre- and post-Factory periods of site use (Casella 1999). Erected in 1833 to accommodate male convict labourers during construction of the Ross Bridge, the brick structure was subsequently reoccupied by the Factory Assistant Superintendent after minimal modification of the original earthen floors. In addition to artefacts related to both pre-Factory and Factory periods of use, an 1866 Victorian penny was also recovered during excavation of these floors. Thus, artefacts from Area B could be least strongly related to the Factory period of site occupation.

In contrast, the stratigraphic, architectural and documentary evidence from Areas A and C suggested that the Crime Class Dormitory and Solitary Cells both contained a number of floor and underfloor deposits more directly associated with the Female Factory period of site occupation (Casella 1997: 83–4; Casella 1999). Extensive modifications of the Crime Class Dormitory floors during establishment of the Female Factory directly linked underfloor deposits of this structure to the Female Factory occupation period. Archival documents indicate that construction of the Solitary Cells occurred in Area C during the Factory period; no historic or archaeological evidence was recovered to suggest substantial re-use of the cellblock after closure of the Factory in 1855. Thus, artefactual assemblages recovered from Areas A and C could be stratigraphically related to the female convict inmates with a reasonable degree of certainty.

Returning to Table 6.2, if results from Area B are disregarded because of problems with stratigraphic association, the remaining data suggests that both a greater quantity and a greater diversity of buttons were recovered from the Solitary Cells compared to those found at the Crime Class Dormitory of the main penal compound. As only 16 square metres were excavated in Area C, compared with 48 square metres in Area A, these results could also suggest that a greater density of buttons was present within the Solitary Cells.

As detailed earlier within this chapter, a landscape of disciplinary segregation divided interior locales of the Ross Factory into strictly defined functional regions. The workrooms were isolated from living and punishment quarters by a series of

Description	Area A	Area B	Area C	Total	Per cent
Ferrous large 4hole trouser buttons (1.a.iii)	3	1	10	14	20.9
Ferrous other		1		1	1.5
Copper 4hole 'sinkies' (2.a.ii & 2.a.iii)	1	2	1	4	6.0
Copper shank loop (2.f.iii)	1	1		2	3.0
Copper 2hole base for textile buttons (2.c.ii)		2		2	3.0
Copper other		2		2	3.0
Bone large 4hole trouser buttons (3.a.iii)		17*	1	18	26.8
Bone small 4hole shirt buttons (3.a.i)	1	2	2	5	7.4
Bone small 3hole (3.b.i)			3	3	4.5
Bone 1hole core (3.d.i)			1	1	1.5
Bone 5hole (3.e.ii)		1		1	1.5
Bone other		1	1	2	3.0
Shell small 4hole shirt buttons (4.a.i)	3	2	1	6	8.9
Shell small 2hole shirt buttons (4.c.i)		3		3	4.5
Shell shank loop (4.f.ii)			1	1	1.5
Shell other		1		1	1.5
Glass small 4hole shirt buttons (5.a.i)		1		1	1.5
Totals	9	37	21	67	100

*note: 15 of these artifacts constituted special find 575

Figure 6.3 Distribution and Frequency of Button Assemblage

locked gates, courtyards, and nine-foot-high timber post and rail fences. Given this landscape of social, temporal and spatial control, the presence of non-uniform related buttons in substantial quantities in the Crime Class Dormitory and Solitary Cells may reflect intentional transport and possession, rather than accidental deposition during taskwork.

Particularly the Solitary Cellblock, by virtue of its intrinsic purpose, was strictly segregated from the work-related wards of the prison. While undergoing 'separate treatment' the female convict was supposed to be silently engaged in moral reflection and disciplinary social isolation. She was not engaged in laundry- or sewing-related taskwork. Thus, the significant presence of buttons, particularly non-uniform decorative buttons, in the Solitary Cells may represent evidence of non-clothing-related functions for this artefact assemblage.

It is significant to note the presence of two particularly unusual button types within the Solitary Cells. The one isolated occurrence of a bone button core within Factory-related deposits was recovered from Area C. These single-holed disks were used as the rigid core of a silk-thread decorative button, the colorful threads wrapped around the core, and a few loops left dangling for attachment to the article of clothing. Furthermore, all three specimens of a three-hole small bone button (Type 3.b.i) were recovered from occupation layers inside the Solitary Cells.

Preliminary comparative examinations of contemporary Australian archaeological sites have only located occurrences of this unusual button type within settlements occupied by male convicts, ex-convict labourers, and/or Aboriginal communities (Birmingham 1992; Greg Jackman, Nadia Iacono, Susan Lawrence, personal communications).

In her 1992 report on archaeological excavations at Wybalenna, the 1840s Tasmanian Aboriginal settlement on Flinders Island in the Bass Straits, Judy Birmingham argued that the high frequency of bone and ferrous four-hole sew-through buttons in occupation contexts related to the buttons' function as gaming tokens (Birmingham 1992: 110). By interpreting this particular function, Birmingham offered an alternative social and economic function for this class of artefacts. Extending this idea of the buttons as socio-economic objects, could they have held an exchange value in themselves? Could they have served as economic tokens? And if the buttons are trade tokens, what valued commodities would have fuelled the black-market economy of this convict landscape?

Illicit Objects: the Distribution of Bottles and 'baccy

My distribution analysis of artefacts related to tobacco and alcohol consumption also demonstrated some significant patterns (see Table 6.3). While the presence of the recreational indulgences on most archaeological sites would be unremark-able, at the female factories of Van Diemen's Land possession of alcohol and tobacco was strictly forbidden for prisoners. Thus, these two artefact assemblages were identified as 'illicit objects' within the specific context of the Ross factory.

Table 6.3 presents data on the frequency distributions of these objects recovered from the underfloor deposits of the Crime Class Dormitory, and the earthen floors of the Solitary Cells. As a common container for wine, beer and gin during the nineteenth century, olive glass bottles were specifically selected as a material representation of alcohol consumption because an insufficient number of diagnostic shards of clear glass were recovered to differentiate between vessels for alcoholic spirits (most commonly whisky) and food containers. In Table 6.3, the presence of kaolin clay tobacco pipe fragments and olive glass bottle fragments is demon-strated in terms of total weight (in grams) and percentage by weight of the total artefact fabric category. The minimum number of vessels (MNV) present in each context was also calculated, and is presented within this table.

Results of this analysis suggest that in terms of both relative frequency and MNV counts, more illicit materials existed within the Solitary Cells than in the Crime Class dormitory. A greater estimated number of kaolin clay tobacco pipes was found within the excavated solitary cells; these forbidden objects also comprised a higher percentage of the overall ceramic assemblage recovered from cell interiors. While a greater minimum number of olive glass bottles was recovered

Description	Crime Class	Solitary Cells
Total glass assemblage	2751g	406g
Olive glass alcohol bottle fragments	1529g (55%)	312g (77%)
Minimum Number of Vessels	15	10
Total ceramic assemblage	4,416g	1,547g
Kaolin clay tobacco pipe fragments	23g (0.5%)	74g (5%)
Minimum Number of Vessels	5	10
Total Area Excavated	48 square metres	16 square metres

Figure 6.4 Distribution of Illicit Objects

from the Crime Class dormitory, three times more area had been excavated in this region than in Area C. Therefore, while a larger number of illicit grog bottles was recovered from the Crime Class underfloor deposits, they occurred much less frequently than within the Solitary Cells. Comprising 77 per cent of the glass assemblage from Area C, olive bottle glass constituted only 55 per cent of the glass recovered from Area A.

These results could have been affected by such factors as occupation density, differential preservation of the record, and depositional processes. The greater presence of these artefacts within the earthen floors of the Solitary Cells might also have reflected the limited options for disposal of incriminating evidence. In her study of the glass assemblage from the Boott Mills of Lowell, Massachusetts, Kathleen Bond noted the significantly high quantity (by weight) of undiagnostic smashed glass artefacts in the courtyards that surrounded the workers' boarding-houses (Bond 1989). She suggested that this occurrence might indicate a 'smash and scatter' strategy employed by the mill girls to safely disperse all incriminating evidence of their illegal alcohol consumption. The lower frequency of tobacco pipes and alcohol bottles within the Crime Class Dormitory underfloors might indicate that a greater variety of options was open to those inmates for disposal of their 'indulgences'. But this archaeological evidence could also suggest an increase in prohibited activities within the Cells.

Subversion: the Convict Landscape

As places of ultimate punishment, the Solitary Cells were architecturally fabricated to discipline repeat offenders. Research by historians such as Kay Daniels (1998) and Joy Damousi (1997) has located these women at the apex of the underground economy of the Female Factories. The higher frequencies of tobacco- and alcohol-related materials within the Ross Factory Solitary Cells might reflect the flourishing of illicit trade within this edifice of confinement and punishment. While under solitary sentence, the factory 'incorrigibles' continued to maintain their access to forbidden indulgences, relieving the monotonous boredom, cold, and hunger of disciplinary confinement with a pipe and a bottle. Thus, when examined together, the significantly higher frequency and density of both illicit artefacts and buttons within the Solitary Cells may be related. These results archaeologically suggest a focal point within the black-market network. While inmates of the Crime Class actively engaged in economic 'trade', the most potent covert paths of this penal world seem to lead directly to the Solitary Cells, the very region of the prison designed for strictly bounded isolation. As inmate Mary Haigh noted in her 1842 deposition to the Parliamentary Committee of Inquiry, 'I have been in the dark Cells. That is bad punishment but even there Tea Sugar and etc [sic] can be obtained . . .' (AOT CSO 22/50). Thus, through black-market trade, the female convicts created an alternate and coexistent landscape of socio-economic networks. They negotiated the disciplinary segregation and classification of penal spaces through their movement of illicit materials around the bounded institutional landscape.

Conclusion

Inhabitants of the Ross Female Factory occupied a landscape of strictly defined and hierarchically organized locales. These places were spatially and temporally organized to maintain relationships of domination and subordination within the ranks of both staff and inmate inhabitants. However, the ideal organization of this institutional landscape was only partially realized. Archaeological evidence suggests that an alternate landscape simultaneously coexisted at the Ross Factory site. Networks of underground exchange subverted the documented institutional template (Daniels 1998; Damousi 1997). Through the covert landscape of barter and exchange, inmates and illicit materials circulated through the various bounded locales of the Factory site. Remarkably, archaeological evidence appears to suggest a dramatic inversion of the ideal template, with the dominant node of the black-market network located within the Solitary Cells – that region of the prison officially intended for strict isolation and disciplinary separation of female inmates. The Ross Female Factory never existed as one static cultural landscape. Through surviving documents and material culture, we can map the simultaneous and overlapped landscapes of both institutional domination and inmate resistance, as they negotiated, conflicted and intertwined to create this penal site.

Acknowledgements

Funding for the Ross Factory Archaeology Project was provided by the Wenner-Gren Foundation, and the Stahl Fund of the Archaeological Research Facility, UC

Berkeley. The Woodrow Wilson Foundation and the American Association of University Women supported the final stages of this research. The Parks and Wildlife Service of Tasmania, the Queen Victoria Museum and Art Gallery (Launceston, Tasmania), the Tasmanian Wool Centre of Ross, and the Riggall Family provided essential support and assistance. Finally, I would like to thank Barbara Bender (UCL) for her generous editorial advice.

References

Primary Sources:

Mitchell Library, Tasmanian Papers, Number 104.
AOT CO 280/699/268, p. 162. Colonial Office records. Revised Scale of Task Work . . . 29 December 1849.
AOT CSO 22/50. Colonial Secretary's Office. 1841–1843 Committee of Inquiry into Female Convict Prison Discipline.
AOT MM 62/24/10774. Miscellaneous Microfilm. October 1848. Duties of the Staff at the Ross Female Factory.
AOT MM 62/26/11931. Miscellaneous Microfilm. May 1849. Letter from Visiting Magistrate Stuart to Comptroller-General of Convicts.
AOT MM 62/26/11946. Miscellaneous Microfilm. May 1849. Investigations of Allegations made by Constable Taylor.
AOT MM 62/28/12161. Miscellaneous Microfilm. July 1849. Report by Visiting Magistrate to the Comptroller-General of Convicts.

Secondary Sources:

Birmingham, J. 1992. *Wybalenna: The Archaeology of Cultural Accommodation in Nineteenth Century Tasmania*. Sydney: The Australian Society for Historical Archaeology Incorporated.
Bond, K. 1989. The medicine, alcohol, and soda vessels from the Boott Mills boardinghouses, in M. Beaudry and S. Mrozowski (eds) *Interdisciplinary Investigations of the Boott Mills, Lowell, Massachusetts, Volume 3*. Cultural Resources Management Study, No. 21. Boston: National Park Service, North Atlantic Regional Office.
Bourdieu, P. 1977. *Outline of a Theory of Practice*. Cambridge: Cambridge University Press.

Brand, I. 1990. *The Convict Probation System: Van Diemen's Land, 1839–1854*. Hobart: Blubber Head Press.

Casella, E. 1997. 'A large and efficient Establishment': preliminary report on fieldwork at the Ross Female Factory. *Australasian Historical Archaeology* 15: 79–89.

—— 1999. Dangerous Girls and Gentle Ladies: Archaeology and Nineteenth Century Australian Female Convicts. Unpublished PhD dissertation, Department of Anthropology, University of California, Berkeley.

Claassen, C. 1994. Washboards, pigtoes, and muckets: historic musseling in the Mississippi watershed *Historical Archaeology* **28**(2).

Damousi, J. 1997. *Depraved and Disorderly*. Cambridge: Cambridge University Press.

Daniels, K. 1998. *Convict Women*. Sydney: Allen & Unwin.

Driver, F. 1993. *Power and Pauperism: The Workhouse System, 1834–1884*. Cambridge: Cambridge University Press.

Eldershaw, P.R. 1968. The Convict Department. *THRA* **15**(3): 130–49.

Evans, R. 1982. *The Fabrication of Virtue*. Cambridge: Cambridge University Press.

Foucault, M. 1977. *Discipline and Punish*. London: Penguin.

—— 1980. *Power/Knowledge: Selected Interviews and Other Writings 1972–1977*. Colin Gordon (ed.) New York: Pantheon Books.

Iacono, N. 1996. Cumberland/Gloucester Streets Site Archaeological Investigations 1994: Artefact Report, Miscellaneous. Unpublished report for the Sydney Cove Authority, Godden Mackay Heritage Consultants.

Lydon, J. 1993. Task differentiation in historical archaeology: Sewing as material culture, in H. du Cros and L. Smith (eds) *Women in Archaeology: A Feminist Critique*. Canberra: Department of Prehistory, Research School of Pacific Studies, the Australian National University. *Occasional Papers in Prehistory*, No. 23. 129–33.

—— 1995. Boarding-houses in the Rocks: Mrs Ann Lewis' privy. *Public History Review* **4** 73–88.

Markus, T. 1993. *Buildings and Power*. London: Routledge.

Oxley, D. 1996. *Convict Maids*. Cambridge: Cambridge University Press.

Parham, D. and Noble, B. 1994. Convict Probation Stations Archaeological Survey. Unpublished report to the Tasmanian Archaeological Society and the Philip Smith Education Centre.

Peponis, J. and Hedin, J. 1982. The layout of theories in the Natural History Museum, *9H* **3**: 21–5.

Praetzellis, M. and A. Praetzellis 1992. Faces and facades: Victorian ideology in Early Sacramento. A. Yentsch and M. Beaudry (eds) *The Art and Mystery of Historical Archaeology*. Boca Raton (FL): CRC Press. 75–100.

Rayner, T. 1980. *Historical Survey of the Ross Female Factory Site, Tasmania.* Unpublished report prepared for Cultural Heritage Branch, Parks and Wildlife Service, Department of Environment and Land Management, Tasmania, Australia.

Rodgers, S. 1993. Women's space in a men's house: the British House of Commons, in S. Ardener (ed.) *Women and Space.* Oxford: Berg. 48–50.

Ryan, L. 1995. From stridency to silence: the policing of convict women 1803–1853, in D. Kirkby (ed.) *Sex, Power and Justice.* Melbourne: Oxford University Press.

Scott, J. 1990. *Domination and the Arts of Resistance: Hidden Transcripts.* New Haven and London: Yale University Press.

Scripps, L. and Clark, J. 1991. *The Ross Female Factory.* Department of Parks, Wildlife and Heritage, Tasmania, Australia.

Seaborne, M. 1971. *The English School: Its Architecture and Organisation, 1370–1870.* London: Routledge & Kegan Paul.

Spain, D. 1992. *Gendered Spaces.* Chapel Hill (NC): University of North Carolina Press.

Terry, I. 1998. Ross Female Convict Station Historic Site: Conservation Plan. Unpublished report for the Tasmanian Parks and Wildlife Service, Department of Primary Industries, Water and Environment. Hobart, Australia.

–7–

Cultural Keepers, Cultural Brokers:
The Landscape of Women and Children –
a Case Study of the Town Dahab in South Sinai

Heba Aziz

Introduction

This chapter is about negotiating boundaries and reconstructing landscapes. It is about landscapes as dynamic socio-geographic entities that are constantly being reshaped by political, economic and social forces as well as shifts in moral and value systems. These changes are both creative of, and created by, people as they negotiate their place in the world.

People attach themselves to particular places, locales and landscapes but, of course, these places and people's sense of attachment are always in flux, and, particularly in the modern world, state and government intervention and the global penetration of capital have major effects on people's sense of self and of place.

This chapter will discuss the power of changing economic relations in shaping the socio-geographic landscape of Bedouin women and children. It is part of a wider research undertaken in the town of Dahab, South Sinai, Egypt. Dahab is located on the Gulf of Aqaba, an area of 3,460 square kilometres. The official population estimate of Dahab is about 2,048, of which 82 per cent are Bedouin and 12 per cent are migrants from the urban centres.

The main population of Dahab used to be the Mzeina Bedouin community; however, the authorities have constantly underestimated their numbers. Meanwhile, over 47,000 tourists visit the area each year (South Sinai Information Centre, 1996).

The tourist industry in Dahab has had dramatic repercussions and has witnessed the emergence of three landscapes (see Figure 7.1). The Beach: a landscape of tourists. The Interior: inhabited by the Bedouin of Mzeina whose economic base of pastoralism and fishing has been radically changed due to the emergence of the Beach. And finally The Road: the landscape of officialdom that intervenes between the Beach and the Interior. Beach, Interior and Road may be described as socio-geographic landscapes that are reconstructed physically, socially and perceptually via a dynamic and interactive set of relationships that take place between and across them.

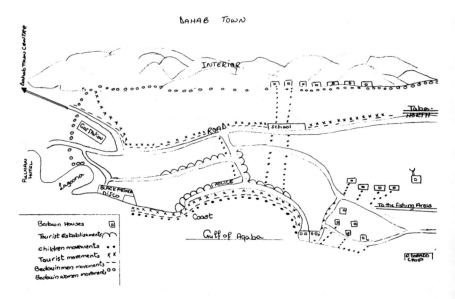

Figure 7.1 Sketch map showing the movement of Bedouin men, women, children and tourists across the landscape

A connection between the well-being of women and children and the introduction of economies based on capitalism and market forces has been accepted unquestioningly by governments in the developing world. The assumption is that the changing economy will pave the way for parallel development across the different socio-economic and gender groupings. Within the context of new market economies women are expected to move from the private to the public domain and to cross the boundary from passive to active involvement. These expectations need to be challenged, and in this chapter I begin to explore the socio-geographic landscapes of women and children on the move within a changing economy.

The Role of Women as Cultural Keepers

Bedouin landscapes have been in process of rapid change over the last few decades. Tourism has expanded rapidly in the last ten years. Before this expansion Bedouin men frequented the nearby towns and cities to work as wage labourers for six months of the year.[1] The cash income generated during this period was used to

---

1. The tradition of Bedouin men going to nearby towns was exercized until 1967. Then the Israelis occupied Sinai. As the road-construction programme got under way, the Bedouin were offered work in Eilat and other borderline Israeli cities. They worked in South Sinai until the Egyptian authorities regained Sinai in 1982. The Bedouin then returned to work in towns closer to home.

supplement the pastoral economy that the Bedouin considered to be their main and stable source of income – and pride. For the Bedouin, land and flocks were the symbol of their identity and culture – members of the community would look down upon a man without a flock. Marx (1984) notes that Bedouin men, regardless of how wealthy they became in the urban centres, were not happy with their dependent status and disliked having to work for an Egyptian individual or organization. The land and the flocks remained their security and the base to which they eventually returned.

While the men were away for six months of the year, the women remained in the Interior pasturing and moving the flocks with other women from one spot to the other and bringing up the children. The women's role as cultural keeper was realized in two forms. The first, and the one which gave them power, lay in their being in control of the most valuable assets of the Bedouin – livestock, land and the kin-group. Secondly, women shouldered the responsibility of realizing, or demolishing, concepts of shame and honour.

Bedouin women have always been associated with honour and shame, even to the extent that women are referred to as 'shame' (*Aar*) among certain Bedouin communities. They are not shameful in themselves but they may bring shame to their families and communities. Strict social, religious and local legal codes exist to curb any shame occasioned by women's behaviour from being associated with the Bedouin community. Abou Zeid (1966) argued that the women, who occupy a secondary position in relation to men, are regarded as something sacred and to be protected from desecration. In fact much of the honour of the nuclear family and the wider community to which the woman belongs depends on observing this sanctity, and in this sense the woman plays a vital and unique role in preserving the honour of her family and her social group. The reputation of a woman and her social group thus depends mainly on her willingness to observe the rigid and severe rules governing sexual relationships and on her ability to preserve her chastity. During the period when the women took over the maintenance of the flocks, the need to find pasture, and also water and firewood, meant that they were often far from home, family and neighbours. In such situations and within such a vast space, the protection of women's honour was not easy. It was based on mutual avoidance between the genders and knowledge of the repercussions, whether social or legal, if a man decided to harass a woman while she was out with the flocks.

The Reconstructed Landscape of Women

During the last ten years, the introduction of tourism as a new and the main economic activity in Dahab has affected the socio-geographic landscapes within which women operate. There has been increasing State intervention in an attempt to regulate the relationship between the local community and the newcomers.

With increased demand for land, and thus escalating land values, the State has had to intervene in an attempt to secure a smooth transfer from the Bedouin 'traditional' land-intensive pastoral economy to a tourist economy which is equally land-hungry.

Since Bedouin nomadism makes the process of control and integration in the wider civil system problematic, the State's encouragement of the Bedouin to settle serves both political and economic ends. On the one hand, it makes control easier, on the other, more space is made available for the facilities required to implement the new economic system.

The method of enforcement of Bedouin sedentarization revolves around land ownership. The state law did not recognize the traditional proofs of ownership such as palm trees or wells. The Bedouin found their livelihood at stake with the incursion of newcomers represented by Egyptian migrant labour, investors and tourists. The way round this problem was to prove their ownership of land with evidence acceptable to the state: a concrete house.

The symbolic move from the portable house as the main domestic space to the concrete house was accompanied by significant change in the overall social life. The problems over land made the move away from the house for long periods for pasturing rather risky: any uninhabited house in a prime location was under threat of being taken over by the authority or an investor.

Meanwhile, the government introduced various services that were desirable for the Bedouin, such as medical facilities, schools, education and electricity. The need to be next to such facilities made the Bedouin settle closer to the Road. Most of the Bedouin families now cluster together in the two villages, Assala and Masbat, and as opposed to having vast spaces around their tents, the space available has become very limited and the idea of keeping a flock inside or outside the house is no longer very feasible.

The facets of modernity introduced by the Road, and the presence of Egyptians and tourists, made the option of possessing valuable household equipment a necessity rather than a luxury. Most Bedouin houses possess a radio, television, washing machine, fridge, gas cooker and a sewing machine. These too, serve to anchor – they are impossible to move and risky to leave behind.

These circumstances makes pastoralism a non-viable option. The processes of urbanization and sedentarization have nearly put an end to pasturing and grazing as an economic base, and entering the cash economy therefore becomes vital. Men now work on the Beach within the tourist economy. Although they have become physically closer to their families, their lives are more distant. They are associated with the Beach; the lives of their women have become more confined to the Interior. With the growing dependency on the cash economy and the fading importance of pasturalism, women have ceased to be productive and have lost their power over the economy and the freedom they had had before the spread of tourism.

Urbanization and sedentarization have worked together to restrict women's movements. Their space becomes restricted to the private and domestic. Lewando-Hundt (1984) has described the way these two processes have resulted in a greater segregation of gender roles and constructed a confined and curbed women's space in the Interior. The spatial re-ordering has altered women's role from a mainly productive to a consumerist one.

The arrival of large numbers of newcomers to Dahab has further altered and restricted women's movement. The presence of Egyptian workers from the Nile Valley and tourists who are unfamiliar with the Bedouin culture and social rules made the process of protecting women's freedom, safety and space increasingly problematic. Where before the protection of women was based on mutual avoidance between the genders, and the sanctions for transgression were understood, the newcomers neither understand nor abide by such customary practice and law. Given the new socio-spatial order, women avoid moving across the Beach or the Road. It is now considered shameful to see a Bedouin woman walking along the Beach or the Road.

Of course there are exceptions – which then have to be accounted for. Sheikh Gomaa's (one of the elderly members of the community) sister is the only older woman to be seen on the Beach. She sells bracelets and beads and collects the tourists' leftover bread to feed the goats. Members of the community have normalized Hajja Selima's presence on the Beach, justifying it by the fact that everyone has to find his *rezq* (income). She does not have any young daughters whom she could send to the Beach and her husband, an old man of 85, has been paralysed for years. The woman herself says that even her two sons cannot support her as they have to look after their own families. Selling beadwork and bracelets is the only way that Hajja Selima can get six or five pounds a day, hardly enough to provide for her and her husband. The majority of people I met from the community did not consider the presence of Hajja Selima on the beach shameful but rather a necessity due to her personal circumstances.

The changes that have occurred in the economic and spatial order among the Bedouin of Dahab have altered other related systems such as diet, for example. The few goats and sheep available in each household are left to graze in the surroundings of the house. Plastic water bottles, paper, rubbish and tourist leftovers are the only pastures available for them. It is very rare that Bedouin women feed their families from their own flocks, for once the flocks stop grazing on pasture the quality of the meat deteriorates. Women shop at nearby supermarkets for tins of corned beef and vegetables. However, they still use dried fish in their daily consumption of food.

The constant presence of men on the Beach has caused women immense insecurity. Women used to be able to use sex as part of their negotiation of their relationship with men, but the construction of the Beach and the day-to-day interaction between female tourists and Bedouin men has weakened this power. Selouh, a woman informant who is fairly powerful among her female friends and neighbours, was surprised to see construction work for a new house in her own backyard. Her female friends teased her by saying that her husband was probably building this for his new wife whom he has chosen from the Beach. The availability of sex and other forms of relationship on the Beach have given Bedouin men the opportunity of experiencing new forms of gender relationships. Such relationships reflect rather negatively on family life and the status of wives within the family life.

The Mzeina Bedouin women spend hours in front of the television that bombards them with commercials about various consumer items – bathroom suites, dresses, corned beef, tuna tins and make-up. Possession of items other than the flocks has become a novelty and a sign of status, and Bedouin women aspire to possess such items. Meanwhile, with the construction of the Road (in a physical sense) traders from different parts of Egypt have exploited the markets in the newly constructed urban centres. Trucks loaded with beads, materials, creams, perfumes and other 'modern' products drive into the Bedouin population centres. They use speakers to advertise their products, and women whose needs have been shaped by television or by what other women in the vicinity buy purchase goods from these trucks. But these items have to be bought with cash rather than bartered with dates or dried fish. The women, no longer in charge of the economy, and dependent upon their husbands for food and household items, cannot usually find the amounts required and therefore pay by instalments, thus running up debts. Under these changing socio-economic conditions, the women turn to their children. It is they who become the new cultural brokers.

Children as Cultural Brokers

Available sources that discuss children's socio-geographic space are rather limited. Research conducted in the Sinai has an insignificant number of references to children's lives and roles (Lavie 1990; Wickering 1991). It is only with tourism that children start to play a major role in the life of the community and operate at the cutting edge of change in Bedouin life.

Lewando-Hundt (1984) suggests that children are one of the principal resources for Bedouin mothers. When men were wage labourers the women had complete responsibility for the running of the home and the care of the children. They use their children as information-gatherers and messengers. Both boys and girls prior to puberty have a degree of physical and social freedom which is not usually available for their mothers. Children are sent to pick up material from their aunts, to tell their married sisters that their mother is ill or that certain guests are expected. Mothers also keep themselves informed about the identity of guests and topics of conversation in the guest section by sending their young children to fetch and carry and at the same time observe and report on who has arrived and what is going on. Thus mothers, sequestered in their houses, utilize their children to keep in contact with each other and informed about events occurring beyond the occasional confines of their domestic spheres.

But in the newly constructed socio-geographic landscape of Dahab, children have become resourceful in other ways and have acquired new responsibilities. They are able to cross the boundaries between the landscapes as non-gendered cultural-brokers. They live in the Interior, they go to school on the Road and they work on the Beach.

The presence of children on the Beach has accompanied the introduction of tourism and increased with its development. Children visit the Coast regularly either as part of their movements across the landscape or because they are encouraged by their mothers to find bases of raising cash among the tourists. The cash required by women to make their purchases and pay off their debts is generated by their children. Under pressure to help, the children become adroit in finding ways to make money. They have mastered weaving the friendship bracelets and plaiting tourists' hair, neither of which are Bedouin practices but which the young backpackers want to take back from their visit and stay in Dahab as some kind of a reversed souvenir, a souvenir of their own culture.

The presence of children on the coast (see Figure 7.2) is tied to the tourist calendar. Children know well when it is Passover, Christmas, Easter and other important holiday times as these are peak periods for earning more cash. They work either individually or, more usually, in mixed groups; both boys and girls work together with no gender boundaries. Thus young Bedouin boys, realizing that girls were generating an income by weaving and selling bracelets, got the girls to show them how to do these things.

Particular groups of children are associated with particular coffee shops, and concepts of autonomy and competitiveness are expressed. Thus, for example, certain groups – usually the ones seen to be the most aggressive and hence powerful – have a monopoly over popular coffee shops on the Beach. The children are quick to gauge the possibilities of individual coffee shops, both in terms of the number of tourists who frequent them, and the attitude of the Egyptian owner towards Bedouin children. Owners or waiters may try to keep them from 'bothering the tourists', and the coffee shop owners may put bracelets and seashells on sale for the tourists to buy and thus minimize the opportunities the children might have to sell their own products. They may kick the children out and refuse to give them water to drink. The children play a game of hide and seek with the owners in order to avoid being beaten or sworn at. The children are also experienced enough to identify and segment their market. For example, they prefer Italian tourists to Israelis, as they are more generous.

Figure 7.2 Bedouin children weaving friendship bracelets on the Beach

The workload is distributed among the groups as follows: girls who are not attractive or witty are the bracelet weavers and those with more social gifts are the salespeople. The profits are divided among the children within one group. Children can make between 10 and 70 Egyptian pounds a day depending on the number of tourists, the nationality of the tourists, and the season. They use some of the money to buy ice cream or sunglasses or to rent a water-paddle. The rest of the money goes to the mother who, as we have seen, uses it to pay off her debts or to save towards new clothes for the feasts. This relationship between the children and their mothers is part of a secret economy from which the fathers are excluded. Not only are they excluded, but they often refuse to acknowledge the fact their daughters spend their days on the Beach. Because of their absence from the family set-up they are generally unable to exercise authority over their daughters' movements.

Shifting and negotiation of Bedouin moral boundaries takes place on the Beach. What is shameful for a girl or a young woman to do in the Interior is not equally shameful if it takes place on the Beach. A moral quality like shyness that is integral to a woman's honourable behaviour in the Interior is not observed on the Beach. Tourists (both male and female) describe the girls' behaviour on the Coast as pushy and aggressive. Girls argue and negotiate with the tourists over prices and are in physical contact with them. Children's behaviour on the Coast, especially that of girls, would be considered shameful if it took place in the Interior.

Children exercise their sales skills and initiate a friendly relationship with the tourists on the Beach while holding well-founded prejudices about them. Such a dichotomy confines the children/tourists relationship, and to a certain extent the Bedouin/tourists relationship, to a commercial one.

Shadia and Ria are two of the girls who work on the Beach. Their fathers have recently asked them not to go any more. The reason for that was nothing to do with the Bedouin moral and ethical code that is difficult to observe on the Beach, but rather fear of the Egyptian police. According to Shadia: 'When anything gets stolen from the tourists on the Beach, the police come round and imprison all the children who were around; that is why my father does not want me to go there.' Ria and a number of other girls who were in the same position told me the same story. The juxtaposition of the Beach, the Road and the Interior, each of which has its own system, has put the Bedouin in a weak position to seek, or know, their rights. Their limited knowledge of the Road's legal system leads them to avoid situations that might result in conflicts with the authorities.

But avoidance of conflict is not always possible, especially at this transitional stage of the Bedouin community in Dahab, where there are at least three different landscapes, each with its own rules and codes, coexisting in the same place. The legal system that provided women with safety and security is not suitable for protecting young girls as they go to the Beach to pursue a completely different economic activity from herding the flocks. Their work on the Beach put them in contact with Egyptians and tourists in different contexts; their working hours may extend beyond daylight. Working under such circumstances, elderly members of the community and the judges of honour are in doubt about these young girls' safety and honour.

I witnessed a discussion that was of great significance in demonstrating how it is that women fall out of a system that was designed to protect them. Although selling bracelets to the tourists or herding the goats both require young women being away on their own for lengthy periods of time, the law that protects women's space in the Interior is not applicable on the Beach. A Bedouin judge stated that the local legal system was one of the main feature that unites the Bedouin. The issue of tourism was brought into the conversation and the group attending the discussion disagreed on whether the local legal system protects a girl who gets attacked on the Coast. The Bedouin judge said that the girls who leave the Interior and mix with men and naked women on the Beach are not supposed to be protected by the same legal framework that was set up to protect women observing a 'respectable traditional' way of living. He added that if a man chooses to send his girl to the Beach then he should not expect a customary-law judge to protect her. He also added that customary law only works when all members involved in any interaction understand it: those who come from outside the community cannot be made accountable in terms of customary law.

Those taking part in this conversation became rather angry and disappointed. They argued that the majority of girls in Dahab now go to the Beach to work and that the money they make is important for the subsistence of their families. They are disappointed that their own legal system declines to protect the women in their new setting. Other senior members of the community, like Sheikh Salem, the head of the Mzeina, perceive the situation in a different light, and understand that people are obliged to send their daughters to the Beach for economic reasons. Confused and contradicting views were widely expressed. Bedouin's pride and belief in their traditions and clear definitions of what is acceptable and what is not works alongside their full appreciation of the scale of change that is currently happening.

As part of these changes, the children's role as cultural brokers and money earners has led to them acquiring social and economic power within the family setting. Children, principally the girls, are becoming more powerful and forthright. Traditionally children are followers and subordinate to their parents, but their time on the Beach and on the Road has given them power and knowledge not available to their parents. The children become their mothers' window to the outside world, and selectively provide them with information in a way that seems appropriate to them.

Conclusion

I argue here that the role of both women and children has been significantly altered by the economic and social changes that have occurred since the construction of both the Road and the Beach and the reconfiguration of the Interior. This chapter is as much about boundaries as it is about landscapes. The changes that I have discussed are linked to the constant negotiation and shifting of boundaries – not just physical boundaries, but those associated with gender and age as well as moral and ethical boundaries.

I have been primarily concerned with the landscape of women, by which I mean women's spatial, social and cultural space, and by how this is affected by the rapidly changing economic and social systems. I challenge the concepts of private and public.

The confinement of women to one particular space – that is, the Interior – only occurred after the introduction of the market economy, urbanization and tourism. Bedouin men often still perceive the women as keepers of symbolic facets of a lifestyle that has ceased to exist. Women's presence in the Interior, away from both the Road and the Beach, and the way they appear less obviously affected by change, for example in their dress, makes them capable of representing the Bedouin culture. A Bedouin man, working on the Coast, said that he only feels that he is still a Bedouin when he goes back on occasional visits to his family in the Interior.

As we have seen, the marginalization of women has led to them using their children as resources in a financial and cultural sense. Children are now the main contributors to family budgets. They bear the responsibility of returning home every day with a substantial amount of money. Their non-gendered situation makes them capable of running across the landscape, but the responsibilities they shoulder makes their ability to move freely across the landscapes a strenuous one – the Beach (that is, the landscape of leisure and freedom) is, for the children, the workplace that they long to quit. The issue of landscape and identity comes to the forefront in this discussion: children are involved in a complicated set of shifting identities and relationships. On the Beach they play the role of adults and become the breadwinner; on the Road they attend schools and are integrated in an education system provided by the government, and hence they are supposed to follow a system that their wider family rejects in many ways; and in the Interior they are the children.

Women and children reconstruct the landscapes surrounding them. The Beach, which becomes a landscape of confinement for the children, is one of freedom for the tourists, and a landscape of shame for the women. The Interior for the women, once an unlimited space within which their movement was protected by their local legal system, is now a place of confinement to a concrete house.

Acknowledgements

I would like to extend my sincere thanks to the Bedouin of Mzeina in Dahab, Egypt, who unconditionally shared their life with me and made this project possible.

References

Abou Zeid, A. 1966. Honour and shame among the Bedouins of Egypt, in J. Peristiany (ed.) *Honour and Shame.* Chicago: University of Chicago Press.

Lavie, S. 1990. *The Poetics of Military Occupation: Mzeina Allegories of Bedouin Identity under Israeli and Egyptian Rule.* Berkeley: University of California Press.

Lewando-Hundt, G. 1984. The exercise of power by Bedouin women in the Negev, in E. Marx and A. Shumeli (eds) *The Changing Bedouin.* New Jersey: Transaction Press.

Marx, E. 1984. Economic change among pastoral nomads in the Middle East, in
E. Marx, and A. Shumeli (eds) *The Changing Bedouin*. New Jersey: Transaction
Press.

South Sinai Governorate. 1996. South Sinai Information Centre – Statistics.

Wickering, D. 1991. *Experience and Expression: Life among Bedouin Women in
South Sinai*. Cairo: American University Press.

–8–

Whose New Forest? Making Place on the Urban/Rural Fringe

Andrew Garner

The central question explored in this chapter is how people 'make' different places within a small, but highly contested, corner of southern England. The New Forest, like almost everywhere else in England, is a landscape of artifice (Cloke 1994), and in this particular area the artifice of 'natural countryside' is being deployed in increasingly urgent debates over the future of rural landscapes. The arguments, and the array of interest groups, work at many different levels – local, national and European. Part of the engagement and debate occurs in arenas that are far removed from the forest, but much of it occurs 'on the ground'. But 'on the ground' covers a multitude of places. A great deal of landscape-'making' in the New Forest is formed in the techniques and technologies deployed by those responsible for managing the landscape. Management discourse not only takes 'place' in the physical landscape but also in processes of a professionalized technological imagination – at some remove from the teams who do the work. This same metaphor of removal from the landscape – into an office – can be extended to the application of national and international laws, agreements and guidelines, with which managers are compelled to comply.

Whether dealing with the privileged landscapes of the managers or the less privileged ones of the work teams, place is always an embodied experience (Tilley 1999: 177). We tend to over-emphasize the visual, forgetting how powerful soundscapes, smellscapes, and touchscapes can be (Gell 1995; Feld 1996; Porteous 1990; Corbin 1986). Thus, as well as a recognition of discourses that 'image' landscapes through various technical tools, we need to return to the immediately physical, phenomenological landscape made up of experienced places. What follows threads a tentative path between discourse and engagement, between a remote and mythical, and an intimate, lived-in and worked-over New Forest. First the Forest is introduced as not 'out there' but rather something subjectively understood and engaged with; an amalgam of historical contestation and recent tourism pressures. The way in which the Forest is presented to the 'outsider'/ visitor is discussed before examination of contemporary 'insider' politics emerging in one moment of confrontation. That confrontation is described, teasing apart some perceptions of place and situating these within larger social and political contexts.

Historical Roots of Contemporary Discord

The New Forest is an area of approximately 375 square kilometres of mixed woodland and heathland in south-west Hampshire flanked by Southampton and Bournemouth. It occupies a roughly rectangular piece of land between Southampton Water on the east and the River Avon on the west. The New Forest itself dates back to the eleventh century. The modern understanding of a forest generally involves 'a dense growth of tree and underbrush covering a large tract of land' (*Longman Concise Dictionary* 1985). However, originally Forests were places where a sovereign or other lord had a right to keep beasts of the chase. Hence, Forests were places for deer rather than for trees (Rackham 1989: 38), and they might contain large areas of moorland, pasture and other open land.

Tubbs (1986) characterizes many conflicts in the New Forest as a response to the slowly growing importance of silviculture. Crown interest in the New Forest turned increasingly away from deer to its timber and underwood resources (Tubbs 1986: 73) and by 1810 professional silviculturalists operating out of a new Office of Woods were in place. Alongside greater professionalism went a drive for more profit from forestry, leading to the abolition of some common rights. However, the Crown overplayed its hand by provoking the gentry who benefited from higher rents from land with common rights attached. By a series of Acts of the 1870s the battle lines were drawn between the Verderers[2] and the Office of Woods. The Verderers tended to support Commoners'[3] rights while the Office of Woods wanted more timber plantations (Pasmore 1977). A turning point came when a bill for 'disafforestation', effectively privatization, was defeated in 1875 on the strength of a new public concern for diminishing natural heritage. The contours of contemporary landscape contests are set by the Forestry Commission (FC), Verderers Court and Commoners who together mark the poles of a confrontational legal and management landscape. The FC is most closely connected with the everyday management of Crown land within the perambulation. Legally they act as managers on behalf of the owner, the Ministry of Agriculture, Fisheries and Food.

---

2. The Verderers, a name from the original courts that heard cases under Norman Forest law, today have responsibility for management of Commoning and conservation, with powers of veto over Forestry Commission operations in the Open Forest.

3. Commoners are those who occupy land or property to which attaches one or more rights over the Forest. There were originally six rights of common of which pasture and mast are the most important extant rights.

A second focus for conflict lies in the enormous growth in the number of visitors since the early 1950s and the concomitant changes in the significance of the Forest landscape. Essentially, the New Forest has moved from being land that supported a rural agricultural economy to being a major recreational and natural-heritage target for the jaded urbanite. In the process, there have been significant changes in the priorities of the FC, driven increasingly by the heritage and environmental values of a vocal urban population.[4] At the same time there have been considerable social changes in the communities living in and around the forest – gradual erosion of older class certainties, greater mobility and changing economic arrangements as urban incomers move to the rural fringes to commute or retire. This has had a profound effect on the importance and expression of 'local' identity.

Identity is often most clearly expressed through comparison and contrast (Boon 1982) and, furthermore, is very plastic in application. Locals are *not* tourists: 'I was held up by grockles (tourists) queuing for cakes' (interview 22/5/99). Local identity is also a way of claiming authority in terms that the visitors themselves value (for very different reasons) concerning the perceived authenticity of the landscape. Often heard was the statement 'there are only a few real Commoners left'. Degrees of localness of identity and position in relation to 'local people' appeared in and underpinned the discourse of members of other 'user' groups – the Hunt, Ramblers, cyclists, horse-riders, and environmental organizations. While the discourse on who is local and who is an outsider is pervasive, and morally loaded, it is also highly variable, contradictory and contingent in application (see Strathern 1982). Rapport's (1997) reconstruction of the moral universe of an English village dramatically illustrates the contradictory forms of identity and moral indignation by writing about different levels of identity formation – the village, two families, and an individual farmer's wife. Using Boon's (1982) notions of the 'Tribal' and the 'Scribal' he characterizes the dialectic between outsider relativism and local absolutism around land ownership, as the way of understanding the different uses of identity in the village. While the sense of contradictory, context-specific, uses of identity ring true in the New Forest, the dialectic between relativism and absolutism is perhaps less applicable. Absolutism and concomitant moral indignation appear as much in the discourses of, say, environmentalists, who are often identified as 'outsiders', as they do in those of 'locals'.

Selling it to the Tourists – Learning the Lay of the Land

Pictures, maps and brochures are three important ways in which the landscape of the New Forest is constructed for and by many visitors. Images have an important

---

4. The latest Minister's Mandate for the FC (August 1999) has timber production relegated to third place after environmental conservation and heritage preservation.

role to play in the social construction of a sense of place, marking a sense of shared meaning and socially agreed significance. They are also an elusive way of telling significance because they are able to encompass the range of different meanings and discourses that people bring to them: they are not a closed narrative. Yet, these images are an important landmark in the dialectic between discourse and engagement in the physical world of the New Forest. Consequently, there is a moving back and forth between discourse and engagement, while recognizing this is a conceit to draw apart that which is inextricably entwined.

Images

On the cover of the Ordinance Survey map (1996, no. 22) is a 'New Forest pony' grazing a closely cropped lawn in a dappled glade beneath beech and ash trees (Figure 8.1). The trees have all been browsed to a uniform head height allowing glimpses beneath the crown of more distant trees. On the right of the picture bracken encroaches pulling the eye further into the photograph and focusing attention on the pony. Above the pony's back one can catch site of new saplings and other bushy growth. In the foreground a small ditch in the grass runs left to right.

The figure of a pony in woodland is one of the most repeated and popular images of the New Forest. It appears in various formats in tourist brochures, in glossy coffee-table books, in magazines, posters and paintings, and in guidebooks. A pony even appears etched in metal plates on information posts at some FC car parks. Images of ponies, together with those of deer and certain trees – but most particularly ponies – have achieved almost iconic status as signifiers of the landscape of the New Forest, a short-hand way of reading which enables one to imagine the whole area, or rather, *a* whole area. The New Forest pony (and it always is coupled with the regional name) is the icon which provides a separate identity from that of other forests.

The importance of this icon in expressing identity is highlighted because the current image is a replacement for an earlier one showing ponies at Bucklers Hard (Figure 8.2). Some claim it was changed due to a local campaign. The main complaint was that all except one pony were 'coloured outsiders', cross-breeds not as suitable for representing the New Forest as 'proper' indigenous New Forest ponies. While the image of ponies was appropriate they also needed to be 'authentic'. However, one can read off both images a series of ideas about the New Forest – it is peaceful, unique, full of animals and plants, park-like, empty of people and their products – and about the English countryside in general – idyllic, timeless, natural. This is a recursive process: representations of the Forest both form and are formed by interactions with the land. In the highly controlled and carefully bounded landscape of the English rural lowlands, the New Forest is one of the few places where large animals still roam relatively freely. The onus is on

Figure 8.1 'New Forest Pony': cover of the Ordnance Survey map, Outdoor Leisure 22, 1996

individual property owners to keep the animals out of their private gardens. Rounding a corner on one of the New Forest lanes and finding a group of ponies in the shade of a large oak tree carries echoes of a rural past where animals were much more visible in society. For many of the visitors, particularly children, these encounters with ponies are thrilling in themselves and represent both a fulfilment of the images and a measurement of embodied significance.

Maps

Perhaps it is no surprise that this evocative image is on the cover of the popular OS tourist map that provides another culturally important way of imagining the physical landscape. Maps are 'spatial stories' (De Certeau 1984) that claim to represent reality because they describe the land's surface with its physical and human features. They are 'systems of representing and encoding ... cultural

Figure 8.2 'Bucklers Hard': cover of the Ordnance Survey map, Outdoor Leisure 22, 1992

knowledge' (Morphy 1989: 3) or, as Strang puts it: 'they describe cultural values, implicitly or explicitly prioritizing aspects of the land. Specific activities direct reading in a particular way, and different levels of engagement with the landscape also affect the kind of representation that is produced' (1997: 217).

Thus maps are a highly encultured way of representing the landscape and, moreover, one that has considerable power. Here there is a focus on boundaries, areas, heights and distances, giving pictorial elegance to ownership, rights and routes. Here we have another kind of tourist's New Forest.

The current boundary – the forest 'perambulation' – sets the legal boundary of the New Forest and of the area managed by the FC. Within this area, however, are several towns, villages and scattered farms all with private land and further administrated by local and county councils. In addition, large areas of the forest are privately owned, such as Lord Montague's estate running from Beaulieu down to the Solent, various National Trust commons and the Hampshire Wildlife Trust. All of these different ownerships are given form on the map by lines marking the boundaries of specific areas.

While trees have a seminal importance in the landscape, over 53 per cent is open heathland and grassland of various types. In terms of spatial arrangements, it is the difference between 'open forest'[5] – heathland – and the denser, tree-filled space of the forest inclosures that set the tones of landscape engagement. The OS map shows the nodal points of towns and villages (primarily Lyndhurst, Brockenhurst and Beaulieu) with linking routes that provide access to the areas between and the points of entry into these areas. These routes are the constructors of today's landscape views, the visitor equivalent of the landed gentry's stately homes with their carefully arranged pastoral views. The roads have not been routed for a contemporary aesthetic in the same way as a Capability Brown estate, but they have been deliberately moulded to encourage a certain way of approaching the Forest interior. Part of this moulding has to do with the animals that wander freely within the Forest boundary. While main routes such as the A31 and A35 are fenced and are the responsibility of the County Council, smaller lanes are not. Consequently where these intersect each other, cattle grids are in place to stop animals straying out of the Forest and onto the main roads.

Lines on the map translate into experiences of travelling roads and walking paths. Cattle grids were installed in a rolling programme starting in 1962. Today, rumbling over them in a car provides an audible and visible marker of a change in how people are expected to approach the Forest landscape. Speed limits are kept to 40mph or lower, ostensibly to protect animals but also having the effect of forcing a slower viewing of the landscape. More details impose themselves on the visitor. The lanes are narrower and in places the Forest seems to lap right up to the road edges. In many places the tarred area of the road is only one car-width which again forces slower speeds as motorists drop one side onto the narrow gravel verges to pass each other. The FC experimented in a few places with tarring the full width but decided that narrow tarred strips enhanced the 'character' of most of the lanes.

---

5. 'Open Forest' (capitalized) has specific landscape and jural connotations in the NF. Here I simply refer to areas that are treeless plains of grassland or heathland.

Brochures

A leaflet published by the FC, touches on the main parts of another New Forest narrative.

> When about 1079 AD, William I created his 'New' Forest ... the land consisted of relatively infertile woodland and furzy waste, sparsely scattered with farms and homesteads. The act of afforestation in Norman times ... transformed a whole neighbourhood into a royal hunting preserve, placing it under the hated forest law, with all that involved of curtailment of liberty and drastic punishment meted out for any interference with the beasts of the chase or their haunts. Since the unfortunate peasants who dwelt in the Forest were forbidden to enclose their land lest any fence should interfere with the free run of the deer, their domestic animals were allowed by common right to graze and browse throughout the Forest and this grazing, reinforced by that of the deer themselves, severely diminished the ability of the sparse woodlands to perpetuate themselves.

> The dearth of new trees became a serious problem during the middle ages, which saw an enormous increase in the consumption of wood, the principle raw material of the time, and enactments were made to enable large areas in the New Forest to be enclosed for the purpose of establishing woodlands, later to be thrown open when the trees had outgrown the danger by cattle. This process became known as the rolling power of enclosure. The first tree-growing act was passed in 1483 and others followed. The act of 1698 allowed the enclosure of 6000 acres and as the Crown assumed rolling powers, this meant that the area of woodland could increase beyond that, to the detriment of the Commoner's grazing rights (Brief Notes leaflet, New Forest FC, 1988).

In the discourse presented in this brochure and other guides, the Norman imposition of Forest law to protect royal recreation was brutally enforced over a landscape where thanes and churls coexisted in pre-feudal reciprocity – the true Greenwood heart of English liberty. This has considerable echoes in the contemporary Forest landscape. 'Commoners', the visitors are told, in museums, guided walks and conversations with locals, are the inheritors of peasants who protested royal injustice in the Norman Forest. The subtext is that they are the true inheritors of the Forest and the only people to be trusted to look after it properly (cf. Turner 1999). Their interests in depasturing ponies and cattle are in the Forest's best interest too. They, through their animals, create and maintain the Forest landscape in the way it is now and always was, especially by making sure the FC fulfils its responsibilities in maintaining the Open Forest.

Rackham (1990) is suspicious of both the historical documents used to tell this story and the reading that highlights considerable popular opposition to arbitrary and draconian imposition of the Forest laws. In contrast, he presents a conservative picture of deep England emerging through stable, relatively uncontested, historical layers. Schama (1995) paints a more complicated political history of muddied and muddled waters, of deeply resented impositions and old-fashioned greed, where the angriest complaints against the royal Forests came not from common people but from the propertied elite. Whatever the reading, the fact that these are often couched in terms of historical reference and authority shows only that the past is a peculiarly valued place in contemporary Britain. As Bender recently put it, 'we continue to try to create, not *the* past, but *our* past' (1998: 7).

Contesting the Forest: 'Bunny-huggers', Commoners and the Forest with no Trees

This section moves from a mobile and essentially mythic visitor landscape to that of a face-to-face, lived-in and managed place. While the former is *presented* as contested, it is largely *experienced* as highly structured and cohesive. What follows is a description from field-notes of a meeting that took place in May 1999 between various 'interested parties' to consider the proposals for a new conservation plan. Here the day-to-day landscape is literally experienced as contested, and as a site for fervently felt and powerfully expressed emotions. It also becomes an occasion to voice a series of justifications about identity, power and knowledge.

The meeting took place at Puttles Pines a few miles out of Brockenhurst. Puttles Pines are a small straggly group of Scots pines (*Pinus sylvestrus*) huddled around the car park with a long view up a shallow heathland valley. The group, dressed predominately in green Barbours,[6] gathered on the small foot-bridge at the upper end of the valley. In the middle, Joe, the FC 'Life' Ecologist helped by Clare (English Nature and the only female present) were explaining what they planned to do to re-establish a wet mire in the lower part of the valley. Standing around them were three other FC Keepers and a senior Forester, one Verderer, one Agister,[7] two Commoners – one the representative of the Commoners Defence Association – an assistant Ecologist, and two members of a TV crew filming for a documentary being aired at the end of the year. I was introduced as a researcher looking at different perceptions of the Forest. There was laughter as someone commented that I had come to the right place.

---

6. 'Barbours' are a well-known make of green waxed-cotton jackets. Differences of clothes in this setting have some significance given the number of less than complimentary comments by 'locals' about the 'bright' clothes of visitors. The brightly coloured fleeces of both ecologists and the TV crew stood out among the green and dun-coloured jackets of the rest.

7. Agisters are officials of the Verderers' Court whose main responsibility is to ensure that ponies are correctly marked and cared for.

The meeting was called by the Life Partnership staff to discuss the future of this particular part of the Open Forest. The Life Partnership is built around a £5 million budget, half of which comes from the European Union and half from ten partner organizations.[8] The project aims to 'restore and enhance' the New Forest's ancient woodlands, lowland valley mires and heathland, by

> removal of exotic species, repair of erosion damage, encouragement of traditional forest management practices, protection of heathland from encroaching plants and recon-struction of endangered wetland habitats (Life leaflet on Lowland Valley Mires, nd [1998]).

This was an important meeting for them as they needed to persuade the Commoners of the necessity of their work so the Verderers court would not exercise their right of veto over these proposals. Such a blunt statement does little to convey the complexity of politics involved or the degree to which the Life Project cross-cuts other categories of belonging. The Verderers of the New Forest are already members of the Life Partnership. The presence of so many Keepers indicates both their interest in the project and that most are also Commoners. The Life team needed to persuade the FC Keepers as much as anyone else. The presence of the TV camera crew may also have encouraged a certain amount of statement-of-position-for-the-record rather than debate.

Joe started by getting out a clipboard and a map. He referred to this as he described what he planned to do to re-establish the mire system. Essentially, the work consisted of collapsing some of the deeper drainage ditches and filling in the side of the eroded main stream with heather bales. This would slow the through-flow of water and help 'wet up' the surrounding valley. 'Any questions?' he asked.

'How are our ponies going to cross the stream when it's all backed up?' 'Why are you collapsing the ditches – they help take the water away to the stream?' 'What is going to happen to the grassland on either side – next thing we know there won't be any grazing for our stock?' 'Why don't you fill in lower down where it is wet already?'

As Joe fielded the questions it became increasingly clear among those listening that their ideas of what the landscape was for were fundamentally different. Joe temporized and suggested we move further down the valley to look at the erosion of the stream edge. There he explained that the attempts to drain the valley in the past had caused this erosion. 'Yes, and gave us grazing', a Commoner interrupted. One of the Keepers, prodding a collapsing bank with his stick to check the depth,

---

8. These are: English Nature, FC, Hampshire County Council, Hampshire Wildlife Trust, National Trust, New Forest Committee, Ninth Centenary Trust, RSPB, Verderers of the New Forest and Wiltshire Wildlife Trust.

wanted to know why they didn't just leave it alone as it looked like it was already well on the way to re-establishing a bog. Joe referred to his map and started to explain slope angles and drainage rates. One of the Keepers interrupted to ask why they didn't just leave it all alone and save them all a wasted morning. Joe abandoned his notes and asked if they really understood how important valley mires were and then launched into a justification of the project.

> I don't think you understand. We have to do this because of the EU requirement and because this sort of environment is so rare and threatened. There are only 120 valley mire systems in the whole of Europe and 90 of them are found here. There are plants and animals and insects that are only found in these systems. Anyway the mire acts like a big sponge and slowly releases the water over the summer, keeping grass greener and supplying water in a drought. Surely you can see that what we are doing is right? (Joe, Life Project Ecologist, 1999).

Somebody snorted loudly during his outburst. The atmosphere was tense. Clare talked about the statutory requirements under Ramsar and SSSI[9] status to protect this sort of environment. They decided to move on further down the valley to discuss putting bales in at the bottom end that was already quite boggy.

As they spread out to wander I found myself next to one of the Commoners. 'Bloody bunny-huggers!' I nodded.

> You know we are the true original ecologists. We have looked after the countryside for hundreds of years and don't need any university-educated ecologists to tell us what to do. Why not trust us to do what has protected the countryside so far? If it is not one thing it's another with this bloody FC. They are coming on all soft now but they just want us to agree to their plans. This Forest has survived for 900 years without European money and protection for bits of boggy land. They only want to do this because they have to show that they are spending the money. Why don't they spend it on something that they are legally meant to do – like draining and clearing the gorse?[10] Those heather bales – they are just going to fill up with mud and make it dangerous for the ponies. Next thing you know we'll be pulling a dead animal out of here. Why can't they leave well alone? All those plants and bugs have survived so long anyway.

At the final stop, almost directly opposite the pine trees planted to shield the car park, things deteriorated further. Voices got louder and a senior Forester reminded everyone of the 'rules of civilized discussion'. Joe was visibly rattled and suggesting that if they were only going to allow him to put bales in down here

9. The Ramsar Convention of 1993 agreed protection for wetland areas of 'international importance'. A Site of Special Scientific Interest (SSSI) is a National designation that affords some statutory protection.

10. The FC is responsible for draining land under the New Forest Act 1946.

it was hardly worth it. Where was their give and take? No agreement was forthcoming. The group broke into individual conversations and most meandered back to their vehicles to move on to the next site. The TV crew cornered four people to interview, rounding off what for them was a very successful day's filming.

How might a sense of place emerge through this interaction? How are competing landscapes justified? Are the lines of power and influence transparent? Blunt and Rose (1994) writing on the relationship between women and space assert that 'spaces are constituted through struggles of power/knowledge' and that 'different epistemological claims about . . . identity produce different interpretations of space itself' (p. 5). Furthermore, rather than assuming a single imposed structure (patriarchal, in their analysis) on space, they prefer to emphasize a social process. That process, of symbolic encoding and decoding, produces 'a series of homologies between the spatial, symbolic and social orders' (Moore 1988, quoted in Blunt and Rose 1994: 3).

Naming something states what it 'is' and claims ownership of it. In the New Forest, at one level calling a place a 'valley mire system' is obviously different from calling it 'grazing'. At a second level there are the namings that enforce national and worldwide landscape encoding. Here are the reminders of the FC's legal requirement to drain the valley, the subsequent (and not-so-subtle) reminder of the English Nature representative of statutory requirements of environmental protection. These designations themselves immediately include those in the know and exclude others. Here also, the Life project through its capital investment, its staff, and the new coalitions it has spawned represents a new spatial arena. In this arena contemporary environmental notions of nature as threatened by humans on a global scale are written afresh in the valorization of 'endangered habitats' and 'rare species'. Finally, there is the reflexive naming – 'bloody FC', 'obstinate Commoners' – where rehearsal of roles in the landscape is paramount. Embedded in this is a degree of ambivalence as the Life project has opened up the concept of landscape value for an imagined human totality, and a subsequent trying-on-for-size of this new expanded field within the terms of the old power structures.

Secondly, who is making these power/knowledge statements? Using the metaphors of colonial geography of Blunt and Rose (1994), we might imagine the FC as representing a powerful 'colonial' discourse. They have the ability to significantly change the landscape, to 'make' it theirs through direct intervention. But 'the FC' on examination disintegrates. Keepers, Foresters, Ecologists – each have distinctive landscapes, part inherited pattern, part training, part individual interests. Joe was as much talking to the Keepers present as to anyone else. On another occasion a manager asked how they should keep the Keepers 'on message'? The FC attempts to present a cohesive discourse but is itself riven, complex and dynamic – Keepers are often also Commoners. The Commoners themselves claim an identity part historical, part mythical. But they, too, fragment into partial representatives, occasional visitors to the role of Commoner among their other social lives. In other contexts they distinguish between 'real' Commoners and those who are just visitors who have bought land. Some who are vocal, active in consultation panels and at the Verderers Court, are also incomers with time and motivation to spare for debate. Others with commoning rights do not exercise them and maintain a very low profile in debates about the Forest. They also have families with children who either cannot afford to take over farms or do not want to.

Thirdly, there are the technical and professional modes of claiming power/ knowledge. In the introduction it was suggested that a great deal of 'making' the landscape by managers takes 'place' in office environments. A crucial part of this process is the production and use of maps and the measurements on which these are based. The FC has a planning department whose sole aim is producing maps for management interventions. With constant reference to his maps and plans Joe was making claims to an authority and a sense of control not evident in the 'real' world of bitter confrontation. The Commoners and Keepers present were repeatedly drawing his attention away from the maps to *their* landscape. For Joe, power to imagine the morally right universe of a re-established mire was most effectively expressed through the maps and the technical surety of his measurements. The power claimed in this discourse is what Lefebvre (1991) glosses as the 'illusion of transparency', the claim of mimetic representation in maps. As Blunt and Rose explain, 'Transparent space assumes that the world can be seen as it really is and that there can be unmediated access to the truth of objects it sees; it is a space of mimetic representation' (1994: 5).

Furthermore, transparent space tends toward homogeneity, toward a denial of difference and an assumption of authority by removing the possibility of alternative landscapes. Creating what the valley might have been (a boggy piece of land that evolved into a particular environment over hundreds of years of human/animal/ vegetable interaction) measuring what it is, and mapping what it should be elides an imagined future with a 'transparent' present and past. Technical tools obscure the highly specific valuation, the careful selection of significance and the overriding import of proposing a dramatic *change* in the landscape by reference to the past.

Conclusion and Coda: the Interstices of Power

People's ability to talk and act is very context dependent and contingent. In the context of Puttles Pines and armed with his maps and officially sanctioned management role, Joe has some power. In other contexts he may feel more lost. Moreover, Joe's language of landscape transformation masks another, more direct, 'making' of the landscape – that which involves a physical engagement, the moving of things, be it heather bales into streams, earth out of watercourses, trees planted or cut down – all of which is done by the FC work gangs. In the organizational charts of the FC these men are always graphically at the bottom, people without individual identity, 'the recreation work-gang' under a hierarchy of individually named Foresters eventually traced to the Deputy Surveyor. The 'gang' with whom I have spent most time have very different ways of perceiving the landscape. These centre on a close relational description of people they know and places they have worked in. Each 'place' in the Forest is both sedimented memory and taskscape (Ingold 1993). But most specifically, in this case, they have a very ambivalent relationship with the instructions that come from managers.

> We are not paid to think are we? We just do what the Ganger says. It doesn't matter what *we* think about the Forest, we've just got to get on with it (Dan, Forest worker, 1999).

Yet, in other contexts their knowledge and savvy, of tasks and of the environment, is sought after.

Burgess (1995) has shown how forests and woodland are experienced as landscapes of fear by many women. This may be true of the peri-urban woodlands that Burgess has researched, but it did not seem an issue among the women that work for the FC. However, almost all the people I spoke to working in, planning or managing the Forest were men. Women stand out precisely because they are in some respects 'unusual' in the physical, outdoor working world of the men. It is only within the last two years that the FC has changed from an organization where Foresters (all men) sent their writing to a typing pool (all women). While women have made in-roads in the FC, with the exception of one senior post and one active Forester, they are all in high communication roles such as Rangers, administrative staff and receptionists. In traditional forestry roles, such as timber felling and Keepering, the male bias remains unchanged. This is despite the fact that a great deal of the physical work is now done with the aid of machines. Clare, in the Puttles Pines context, did not appear to be reacting in a particularly gendered way but what about in other contexts? Furthermore, judging by the virulence of the comments directed at her behind her back some of the men found her power/role more challenging than Joe's.

At Puttles Pines the landscape becomes a mobile set of signifiers for protagonists to mould, but it also interrupts their flow, is prodded, dissected and discussed. While it may be 'managed' in one way or another, the physical landscape continually escapes and makes mockery of intervention because it is part of a living ecology that is *itself* changing. Here place has been presented as 'a space that is fragmented, multi-dimensional, contradictory, and provisional' (Blunt and Rose 1994: 7), that is tensioned by power and identity. I have attempted to show homologies and contradictions between discourse and engagement, symbols and practice. But in the end has this been successful? It is all too easy to talk about mapping as simply straightforward power/knowledge. Here is a dialectic story of power and the margins, but one that still is patterned by the oppositional discourses of the powerful: the FC, Commoners and Verderers, English Nature and legal definitions, scientific knowledge and heritage. But within these structured relations of hierarchy there is slippage, negotiation and resistance. Understanding the perceptions and politics behind people's experiences of landscape requires attention both to the details of where and how power is exercised and to the silences and asides that suggest other landscapes, other ways of telling and counting significance yet to be addressed.

Acknowledgements

I would like to thank Barbara Bender (UCL) for her critical comments, and Mike Seddon and Bridget Hall at the Forestry Commission for their help and advice. I am grateful to the ESRC, who funded this research.

References

Atkinson, P. 1990. *The Ethnographic Imagination: Textual Constructions of Reality.* London: Routledge.

Barnes, T. and Duncan, J. (eds) 1992. *Writing Worlds: Discourse, Text and Metaphor in the Representation of Landscape.* London: Routledge.

Bender, B. 1998. *Stonehenge: Making Space.* Oxford: Berg.

Blunt, A. and Rose, G. 1994. *Writing Women and Space.* London and New York: Guildford.

Boon, J. 1982. *Other Tribes, Other Scribes.* Cambridge: Cambridge University Press.

Burgess, J. 1995. Growing in confidence: understanding people's perceptions of urban fringe woodlands. Countryside Commission, CCP 457.

Cloke, P. 1994. '(En)culturing political economy: a life in the day of a 'rural geographer', in P. Cloke, M. Doel, D. Matless, M. Phillips and N. Thrift. *Writing the Rural: Five Cultural Geographies.* London: Paul Chapman Publishing.

Corbin, A. 1986. *The Foul and the Fragrant: Odour and the Social Imagination.* London: Picador.

Cosgrove, D. 1990. Landscape studies in geography and cognate fields of the humanities and social sciences. *Landscape Research* **15**(3) 1–6.

de Certeau, M. 1988. *The Practice of Everyday Life.* Berkeley, Los Angeles, London: University of California Press.

Feld, S. 1996. Waterfalls of song: an acoustemology of place resounding in Bosavi, Papua New Guinea, in K. Basso and S. Feld (eds) *Senses of Place.* Albuquerque: University of New Mexico Press.

Geertz, C. 1988. *Works and Lives: The Anthropologist as Author.* Stanford: Stanford University Press.

Gell, A. 1995. The language of the forest: landscape and phonological iconism in Umeda, in E. Hirsch and M. O'Hanlon (eds) *The Anthropology of Landscape.* Oxford: Oxford University Press.

Ingold, T. 1993. The temporality of landscape. *World Archaeology* **26** 152–74.

Lefebvre, H. 1991. *The Production of Space.* D. Nicholson-Smith, trans. Oxford: Blackwell.

Longman Concise Dictionary. 1985. Harlow: Longman UK.

Morphy, H. 1987. *Animals into Art.* London: Unwin Hyman.

Pasmore, A.H. 1977. *Verderers of the New Forest: A history of the New Forest 1877–1977.* Beaulieu: Pioneer Publications.

Porteous, J. 1990. *Landscapes of the Mind: Worlds of Sense and Metaphor.* Toronto: University of Toronto Press.

Probyn, E. 1993. *Sexing the Self: Gendered Positions in Cultural Studies.* London: Routledge.

Rackham, O. 1989. *The Last Forest: the Story of Hatfield Forest.* London: Phoenix.

—— 1990. [1976] *Trees and Woodland in the British Landscape.* London: Phoenix Giant.

Rapport, N. 1997. The Morality of locality: on the absolutism of landownership in an English village, in S. Howell (ed.) *The Ethnography of Moralities.* London: Routledge.

Rival, L. 1998. *The Social Life of Trees.* Oxford: Berg.

Schama, S. 1995. *Landscape and Memory.* London: HarperCollins.

Strang, V. 1997. *Uncommon Ground: Cultural Landscapes and Environmental Values.* Oxford: Berg.

Strathern, M. 1982. The village as an idea: constructs of villageness in Elmdon, Essex, in A.P. Cohen (ed.) *Belonging.* Manchester: Manchester University Press.

Thrift, N. 1996. *Spatial Transformations.* London: Sage.

Tilley, C. 1999. *Metaphor and Material Culture.* Oxford: Blackwell.

Tubbs, C.R. 1986. *The New Forest: A Natural History.* London: Collins.

Turner, M. 1999. *New Forest Voices.* Stroud: Tempus Publishing.

The Political Economy of Landscape: Conflict and Value in a Prehistoric Landscape in the Republic of Ireland – Ways of Telling

Maggie Ronayne

Although all too frequently attempted, we never confront landscape as a self-evident entity; it is always-already-introduced for us:

> *Brú na Bóinne* – the dwelling place of the Boyne – describes an area between the towns of Slane and Drogheda where the river Boyne meanders in dramatic loops and bends (Figure 9.1). Here lies one of the world's most important archaeological landscapes, dominated by the spectacular prehistoric passage tombs of Newgrange, Knowth and Dowth.
>
> The international significance of *Brú na Bóinne* was formally recognized in 1993 when it was designated a World Heritage Site by UNESCO.
>
> Built over 5000 years ago by Neolithic (New Stone Age) farmers, these passage tombs are truly remarkable remnants of a highly evolved society which by the fourth millennium BC had settled widely across much of Western Europe. Both ritual and settlement were centred around these tombs, throughout the Bronze Age, the Iron Age, and Early Christian times, through the Norman invasions and beyond. Looking northwards from the Visitor Centre, the core archaeological landscape of *Brú na Bóinne* comes into view (Figure 9.2). (*Dúchas* – The Heritage Service: 1999).

> One of the most remarkable occurrences in our way hither from Dublin was a large Tumulus or Barrow at a village called New Grange [. . .] the carving of the stones is plainly barbarous [. . .] it remains it should be a place for sacrifice used by the old Irish (Edward Lhuyd 1700, in Herity 1967: 129).

> Among the remains of this ancient cemetery, three mounds stand out conspicuous by their size and importance. [. . .] Of these three the most prominent is Newgrange, which is, indeed, one of the most important prehistoric monuments in the world (R.A.S. Macalister 1939: 1).

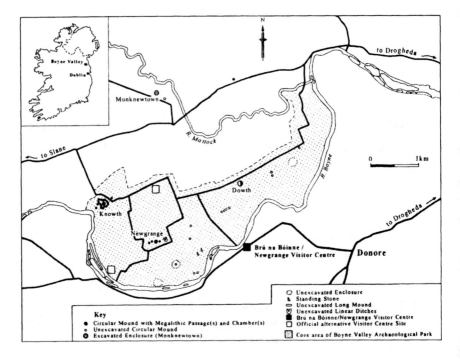

Figure 9.1 Traces of the Neolithic at the Bend of the Boyne (after Shee Twohig 1981, permission of Ordance Survey Ireland; and after Stout 1993, permission of the Geographical Society of Ireland)

The Newgrange excavations of 1962–1975 may be said to have been instigated by the late P.J. Hartnett, Archaeological Officer of *Bord Fáilte Eireann*, the Irish Tourist Board . . . (M.J. O'Kelly 1982: 10).

There can be no doubt [. . .] that Newgrange is older than Stonehenge, older than Avebury, and indeed older by several centuries than the pyramids of Egypt (Colin Renfrew in preface to O'Kelly 1982: 7).

Brú na Bóinne constitutes one of the most spectacular passage tomb cemeteries in Europe and is evidence of a stable society in Ireland in the fourth and third millennia BC (Eogan 1998: 11).

Clearly we have to see the area not just as a series of individual sites but as a landscape in which the tombs are merely the most visible part. [. . .] It has left us a rich inheritance (Cooney 1998: 3).

Figure 9.2 *Brú na Bóinne*/Newgrange: The making of a timeless archaeological landscape (bottom right insert copyright Brady, Shipman and Martin 1996)

The Value of Interpretation

The *Brú na Bóinne* visitor centre opened in June 1997 at a cost of approximately seven million pounds. Owned and operated by the Irish state, it was initially supported by the European Union, but in the end a major part of the funding came from the Irish public purse. With all of the quality conveniences expected and controlling access to the monuments (via suspension bridge and fleet of coaches), it represented a move from a 'honey-pot' to a sustainable landscape approach to heritage management and interpretation (Keane 1997; McManus 1997). Increasingly, this approach is converging with planning and protective legislation relating to archaeological material in the Republic of Ireland. Recent legal activity resulted from a series of highly publicized court cases and public planning inquiries. These cases concerned the rights of the state in relation to the citizen or community in ownership of cultural property and in the building of facilities by the state on archaeological or environmentally sensitive public land.

The first introduction, above, is what the official *Dúchas*[1] information brochure has to say about the heritage landscape at the bend of the Boyne. It is what most tourists read at the visitor centre.[2] The other antiquarian and archaeological introductions legitimate this most recent superlative description. Such work acts to confirm the greatness, antiquity and authentic aesthetic of the 'ancient' landscape. While the material past in this valley was certainly entangled in different sets of social relations over a long span of time, those are now crystallized in the 'value' of these monuments, *as that value is constituted at the present time.* The many introductions to the past of the Boyne valley derive from a series of use values which represent a history of greatness and renown. This renown has been constituted through the diaries of travellers on the Grand Tour, in the notes and letters of antiquarians, the scientific excavations of archaeologists, the actions of the state in promoting tourism and a transnational heritage industry. This kind of fame, a peculiar product of modernity, feeds into the exchange value of the landscape as it is consumed by the quarter of a million tourists who pass through the visitor centre each year. No doubt the hyperbolic eulogizing of the Boyne complex and its timing will be familiar to anyone else who has visited and/or worked at any other 'most important archaeological landscape in the world'. What must be addressed is the relationship between intellectual production of the category of 'landscape' and its socio-economic effects. In doing this, it is as well to have a closer look at the signposts of location and value before our arrival at an understanding of heritage landscape. Rather than assuming the 'economic', the 'cultural' or 'environmental' aspects of landscape as different 'values', these are understood to compose a web of inter-relations within this political economy.[3] Just as it would be reductive to understand the flows of capital through 'heritage attractions' in strictly economistic terms, it is equally problematic to address the

1. *Dúchas*, The Heritage Service is the state organization responsible for the 'built' and 'natural' heritage in the Republic. Although its official role is one of preservation and conservation, its entanglement in amenity-development projects during the 1980s and 1990s clearly demonstrates its function with regard to other interests.

2. The stated purpose of the centre was to achieve 'sustainable' development of this heritage landscape and the entire valley as a resource to be preserved and an amenity to be enjoyed. In particular, the aim was to alleviate what was felt to be inordinate pressure on the monuments, especially Newgrange, from rapidly increasing numbers of visitors. In the year 1997–1998, there was a reduction of 26 per cent from the previous year in the number of visitors going to Newgrange itself, as a direct result of the introduction of a quota system, via the new centre (Keane 1998: 8). Yet as the tourist season in the valley has been extended through substantial marketing of the place as a 'wet-day' facility and in off-peak times as a winter attraction, overall visitor numbers have continued to rise since the centre opened. '*Brú na Bóinne*' is now the most popular of the many 'heritage attractions' in the Republic of Ireland.

3. Cf. Marx's critique of classical political economists, who always began from unexamined assumptions about concepts such as the value form of the commodity (*Capital* vol. I, 1, fn 34).

contestation of landscape as romanticized differences in perception, as part of a process of negotiation somehow separable from socio-economic realities.

Backtrack and Fast-track

The valley of the river Boyne, in the East of Ireland, is considered prime agricultural land with a highly competitive mixed farming regime and a dispersed population. Since the 1970s, it has formed part of a commuter belt for the city of Dublin. This 'rural landscape' is the result of changes throughout the later nineteenth and twentieth centuries, inclu '.ng the migration patterns of workers from rural areas to the cities/other countries and between rural areas, and the provision of farm development schemes by the state since the 1950s (increasingly regulated by the European Union from the 1970s onwards). These schemes led to the enlargement and mechanization of farm holdings, at the expense of smaller farms, in order to increase agricultural production and encourage diversification into agri-businesses (Stout 1993). The latter include farm tourism and regional heritage industries, which developed throughout the state. These changes in relations to land ownership, its value and the scope of working class livelihoods on the land have been understood within a dominant common sense of modernization of 'traditional' practices. In the particular case of ancient monumental renown, it is clear that its perpetuation and/or manipulation, in the process of modernization, are also products of the 'agency' of those who become socio-economically dependent on it. When that renown or the relationship of particular interest groups to it is threatened, when those who cannot claim a part of that renown or have no interest in it are visited by its consequences, forms of dislocation occur which are exhibited in public conflicts over cultural property.

The visitor centre and the monuments in the Boyne valley were the site of a public dispute between and within local and broader interests during the early 1990s. But such battles can be actively and easily forgotten. From 1997 onwards, the history of this conflict has been consigned to the detritus of non-heritage or to the convenient chasm between tradition and (post)modernity. Constant reference to the clear lines of communication set up by the state with those living and working in the valley, the archaeological profession and local authority officials are found in official statements (e.g. Keane 1997: 37; 1998: 8; Brady *et al.* 1996). Clear communication with 'the local community' is emphasized in particular as the key to sustainable projects, despite recurring oral and written claims denying its clarity by individuals and groups in this and other such cases.[4] For instance, a coalition of varied interests in the Boyne valley objected to the particular location of the development (Boyne Valley Trust 1993). A small-scale tourist industry had

---

4. On the difficulties involved in presuming to speak for the subaltern, see Spivak 1988.

developed over the previous decades on the north side of the river, near the monuments, and as the new visitor centre was located on the south side, people involved in this industry felt that they would lose a degree of control over their socio-economic environment. As might be expected, those who gained employment from the new facility, as well as residents on the south side of the river, were more sanguine about its construction. However, all remained in the dark regarding the scope of the development envisaged, located at a key geo-political point for regulation of tourist movement, liberalization of capital flow and maximization of returns from current and future development of the whole valley as an amenity by coalitions of private and state operators. In the conflicting accounts of any such situation, only one, re-enforced explicitly and implicitly by the dominant history of interpretation of the past, is granted legitimacy. Accordingly, it becomes vital to recognize that this particular dispute was not enacted between neatly identifiable groups of locals on either side of a river, although the north/south divide is a form of evidence in a more critical history.

Sign-posting your Landscape

Another way of assessing these relationships is to look at a specific example of commodification in a heritage landscape with a *critical archaeological eye.*

Newgrange, Knowth and Dowth are located on the north bank of the river Boyne, but all tourists must now access the monuments by travelling to the centre on the south side of the river. The process of situating the centre has resulted not merely in a change in the numerical scale of transactions and redistribution of tourist-related income, but in a profound social shift. One sort of evidence for the existence and nature of this change involves the putting up, pulling down and changing direction of signposts in the valley as well as oral and written discourses on these actions:

> It was just overnight and they took the signposts away, coming this way out of Drogheda. So people are diverted back into Drogheda. And they still call it Newgrange [. . .] You just can't move a townland[5] overnight (Boyne valley resident 28/10/1997).

At the time of the opening of the centre, heritage signposts (distinguishable by their brown background and white lettering) appeared on the roads in the area, directing tourists south of the river, in order to find '*Brú na Bóinne*/Newgrange'

---

5. A townland is a small, named unit of land measurement in Ireland; 'places' which will have varied historical origins in any particular instance. The measured demarcation, and invention in many cases, of the boundaries of townlands is the result of the colonial appropriation of land through the science of cartography in the nineteenth century.

Figure 9.3 *Brú na Bóinne* or Newgrange? (photo: M. Ronayne)

(Figure 9.3). The directions on many of the older signposts, including locally made signs, were now incorrect, since they claimed that Newgrange (the monument and its townland location) was still north of the river. So any strategically placed 'incorrect' sign was taken down.

Archaeological and historical work had established a link between this Irish name – in medieval place lore, mythology and inter-dynastic power politics in the region – and the Bend of the Boyne, with a particular correlation between the *Brú* (abode, hall, mansion or castle) and Newgrange (see O'Kelly 1982: 43–48). The aggrandizement of the associated mythology and the Later Iron Age/Early Medieval period in Ireland to the status of the Celtic/Christian Golden Age of the nation, from the nineteenth century onwards, provides the background to this work. Predictably, '*Brú na Bóinne*' is not the value-free translation of 'Newgrange'. Rather, the new link between the nationalized monument, the new centre and the new landscape is a further ideological operation, opening up the 'otherness' of a different language only to flatten it into a conflation of past and present temporalities in the production of a Neolithic celticity. The result of this development is that Newgrange has been dislocated historically and spatially. This operation has been accepted by current scholarship, where heritage, archaeological and other labour will now proceed in a landscape called *'Brú na Bóinne'* (Eogan 1997; papers in Condit 1997; Cooney 2000). This is no mere semantic play, since the slippage between names and places exposed by an archaeology of signposts[6] signals an assertion of dominant forms of ownership of national (pre)history, ostensibly the inheritance of all.

The sliding of names between Newgrange and the centre – manifested in the materiality to the power of naming – also represents a shift in the physical negotiation of the countryside.[7] It signifies a conflict over production reaching far beyond this valley, but most immediately constitutes the collapse of an agency-in-resistance of a local protest, erasure of its brief history and of the histories of the Boyne valley which fed it. The *internationality* of the socio-economic interests involved in the (spatial) constitution of the local is key to this renewed use of identity codings. The last decades of the twentieth century saw an exponential increase in nature and heritage tourism with the emphasis on landscape as a resource. Several recent European Union legal rulings have codified landscape-use over property rights (Prieur 1998). Hardly the promise of common ground, they signal the socio-economic appropriation of the aesthetic properties of land. The point is made clear in one judgement which 'gave priority to the protection of a rural landscape [in the UK] over rights to respect for the home (Article 8 of the European Convention on Human Rights), in the case of a gypsy siting a caravan on his own land' (ibid.). This is also the context in which land in the Boyne valley has become increasingly valuable in terms of its exchange value in the tourist industry. Strict planning controls, being applied to the area from the 1980s onwards (Stout 1993), resulted in a clamp-down on the construction of buildings which would spoil the view of the monuments. Another consequence has been the relative ease with which the state has been able to buy, by compulsory purchase order, land required to maintain this value or develop it as an amenity (at far less than its exchange value in other circumstances).

In the *Boyne Valley Integrated Development Plan* (Brady *et al.* 1996) and other literature on the situation, the centre itself is frequently described as a 'signpost' or a 'gateway', replacing any other directions tourists might want to travel in. Contradictorily enough, this change is presented as facilitating greater choice in

6. In part, signposts are the material culture of tourism; they are also basic to other, related socio-economic processes. The changing relationships which an archaeology of street/road signs and signposts could expose between memory and naming, location and dislocation in modernity is one which would repay further study at an international level. For a South African example, see Hall in press.

7. As Lefebvre (1991: 365) argues, 'spatial contradictions "express" conflicts between socio-political interests and forces: it is only *in* space that such conflicts come effectively into play, and in so doing they become contradictions *of* space'.

the range of attractions and onward journey plans available to the tourist-consumer (Keane 1998; Brady *et al.*, 1996), who is the only agent presented to us in the world of heritage signposts. However, this is a curious kind of agency, in that the presence of 'the visitor' is guaranteed by the creation of demand for heritage tourism rather than any reliance on the volition of the agent. The centre, in a move which is standard in the tourist industry worldwide, is part of a niche-marketing framework, targeting in this case 'the affluent, well-educated tourist' (Brady, *et al.* 1996: 64). Rather than taking 'the visitor' at sociological and statistical face value, it is the set of producer-consumer relationships being formed and regulated that are central. Again, these relationships revolve around location. The predominant reason given for the particular site chosen for the centre is related to the dramatic visual qualities of the landscape at that point. The choice, we are told in a cacophony of planning consultancies, project management, state organizations and academic archaeology, combined several variables: these included conserving the 'rural character' of the area (Keane 1998: 2), being as unobtrusive as possible and creating the best 'original' views of the landscape (Eogan 1997; Keane 1997, 1998; Brady Shipman Martin 1996; Mitchell and Associates 1992). The scopic politics which relates a neolithic 'originality' – a veritable neolithic sublime – to present-day authenticity is re-enforced through scientific, legal and quasi-legal designations and names, such as *Brú na Bóinne* but also 'archaeological landscape', 'prehistoric landscape', 'world heritage site' and 'archaeological park'. The visitor centre and 'the visitor' partake of this encoding of value in the landscape. The centre is disguised as 'original' landscape by means of being partially set into the bedrock of the hill behind it, with grass, wild flowers, and artificial mounds on its roof which have been made to resemble the other small, ancient mounds in the surrounding fields. Tourists, when they are 'hidden' inside the centre, are encouraged by view-finding telescopes, explanatory maps and text panels to gaze out from the viewing platform of the building at the 'prehistoric landscape'. The microcosmic field of vision encompasses all that is distinctively Irish and immediately local in one magnification (Figure 9.2).

This viewing facility acts as a powerful empathic device which treats the present as if it were the past and vice versa, in the same way as it collapses the local into the national and vice versa. While it is clear that tourists can encode and decode these operations in a number of ways and are certainly not 'duped' by them, the powerful effects of such a direction-giving device lie in the materiality of its ideology. This concerns a relationship between the tourist presence as neutral Subject and the guaranteed, genuinely distinctive qualities of people-and-landscape as Object. Both the presence of the tourist in this act and the manufactured *invisibility* of the commodifying process have serious consequences for future preservation of these landscape qualities, offering the prospect of a Becoming Timeless Landscape.

The way in which this has been represented by the state has been through nostalgia for the loss of rural tradition, mediated by suggestions of return to a distinctive rural character. The dislocation of people without physically moving them, and/or the insecurity resulting from a dependency on monuments which 'might close to the public', is the point at which subaltern groups also turn to tradition and distinction. In the 1990s, those who opposed the location of the centre frequently represented themselves in conversation, in testimony and in documents as 'local'. As proof of this, they offered family genealogies on the land, but also knowledge of Newgrange by candle and torchlight, before it was forbidden to climb on top of it. Those placed on the margins can, therefore, 'choose' to identify themselves as living a more authentic life in order to make themselves heard. That many resist shifts in the scale of development and change is only the proof for upwardly mobile class interests, of the existence of a rural timewarp.

Distinction and Dependency

The invention of tradition (Hobsbawm and Ranger 1983), the active and passive contribution of intellectuals, the objectification of those who are traditionalized as 'natural', 'distinctive', 'exotic' or 'Other', the appropriation of tradition by the dominant and the subjugated is well discussed already (e.g. Spiegel 1994). Recent socio-economic changes across the world have not been through a move from traditional rural to modern urban 'mind-set', although processes of modernization, urbanization and alienation are certainly involved. In the Republic, what was traditional was the product of a gradual process of constitution of rural and urban 'underworlds' by the metropolitan centres of colonial and 'post'-colonial regimes, over a couple of centuries. Its most recent manifestation, in the drive towards economic boom since the 1980s, has been in the combination of landscape and technology (Gibbons 1996) or a distinctive Irish sense of place and modernizing 'progress' based on a non-locatable past – a supposedly original, stable society. A strongly maintained image is that of a timeless, un-industrialized Ireland as a survival on the 'Celtic fringe' of Europe, a neo-colonial trope of an empty land, awaiting tourists (O'Connor 1993). As such, it also awaits transnational corporations as a unique place, with modern conveniences yet existing in a temporality 'beyond' the struggle between labour and capital. This distinctiveness no longer needs a *continuous* tradition to legitimate it; rather it frantically and fetishistically juxtaposes fragments of the national past and national mythology. The greater the pace of socio-economic change and the more urbanized the population, the more ancient the distinction discourse on 'Ireland' becomes. In order to signal the temporal and spatial shift, Luke Gibbons (1996) refers to this as neo-traditionalism. Unlike traditionalism, which seeks a continuity with the past in order to legitimate the present, neo-traditionalism nostalgically collapses history (ibid.: 89; cf. Jameson

1991: 18–19) into an aestheticized image of pastness. Hence the ease with which 'the local' may be dislocated from a place in the same moment as the forced identification as local-in-the-world occurs.

Thus, we understand that the value in attributing a unique rural character to others lies in its ability to account for socio-economic inequalities. Hence, the relative success of the dominant in denying the possibility of an agency which could act historically in collective struggle rather than in isolated resistance. Particularly in formerly colonized states (and still-colonized social forces) changes in productive capacity by the ruling class need not be portrayed as replacing or containing 'tradition' in social progress. Rather, it can be intensified as authentic and distinctive neo-tradition (Gibbons 1996: 91). To dominant national and transnational interests, sustaining this kind of development matters a great deal.

Not without irony, David Harvey (1996: 148) remarks that it would be hard not to be in favour of sustaining our planet. However, the crux of the matter is found in an exploration of the interests for which sustainability works. The tourist industry will soon be the world's largest source of employment (Thea Sinclair 1997). In the Republic of Ireland, it accounts for more than one in twelve jobs and netted almost 2.3 billion Irish pounds in 1998 (*Bord Fáilte* 1999: 3). In a trend common to the rest of the world, more impoverished regions of, and social forces in, the Irish state are particularly and sometimes entirely dependent on income from tourism. The seasonal, gendered, 'localized', rural nature of much of the work and accompanying barriers to unionization of the predominantly female labour force are key in this precarious balance. What this also means, of course, is that this industry is likely to be extremely vulnerable to the vicissitudes of the free market, including recurrent recessions in the world economy. However, the carefully tailored brochure of the state tourist board (*Bord Fáilte* 1997: 3) proudly takes the credit for the *productive labour* which goes into the construction and use of, for example, heritage landscapes:

> It would be stretching the point to say that tourism exclusively has provided all of these amenities, but it can equally be argued that without tourism they would be fewer in number, poorer in quality and less accessible to the average citizen.

The danger here is that tourism, its spin-off industries and the mode of production of which it is a part, become reified as an inevitable situation. That is, as the only way in which value can be generated, income (albeit low-waged) earned, facilities provided (for some) or places and the past apprehended-in-travel (for some). As Harvey (1996: 148) argues, sustainability perpetuates an unequal socio-economic order by maintaining the Malthusian argument that limits are natural, rather than social. The scene of huge tourist numbers, demands on heritage workers, the unsightly spoiling of the environment, the threat to the fabric of the monument of

Newgrange have come to justify a certain sequence of events in the Boyne valley as natural and necessary. In other words, as the best answer to the equation of self-evident renown leading to inexplicable demand which leads to pressure on ancient monuments. Of course, heritage workers deserve better than the low pay, inadequate training (apparently two to seven days for seasonal guides employed by the Irish state) and job insecurity which still constitute the predominant conditions within which the past is presented to the public. If the sequence does not begin with a self-explanatory form of value, but rather with one which is historically constituted and contradictory, then that is the point at which to begin to think about how to ameliorate those conditions.

The heritage facilities developed on the basis of a certain renown are part of the creation of a demand to perpetuate both their profitable operation and the continuing commodification of archaeological and heritage labour power. As such, wear and tear of renowned ancient material is the outcome of a series of changing social relations of dependency and exclusion (since those who are excluded also make a place what it is) which are unresolved within current preservation agendas. What is clear is that the commodification involved in heritage, leisure, nature, or whatever else might be set up as a product sets in motion relations of dependency to capital, in which we all participate in one way or another and which grow ever more contradictory and disenfranchising. As an aspect of these social relations, the revolt of the local is not a throwback, nor is it an apolitical form of protest. Yet it is important not to confuse every 'local battle' or the 'choice' of consumers with a collective and emancipatory agency. The point is not that such agency will be made subordinate in all historical circumstances, but rather that the individuating and specifying process of its constitution is such that, in the present social climate, it is all too vulnerable and contained by prior determinants.

Conclusion: Archaeology in the Age of Transnational Capital

The neo-traditionalism exposed by an archaeology of signposts sets up a particular series of relations between (post) modernity and (landscaped) monumentality. It exposes the value of the monuments in the Boyne valley as 'world heritage' or as 'prehistory of the nation' in competition with other unique commodity-pasts such as Stonehenge and the pyramids of Egypt.[8] Any approach based upon sustaining

---

8. This kind of cultural production in capitalism, as Bourdieu (1993) outlines, is based upon the unique use value of the commodity and should not be reduced to 'price' as the key factor. He gives the example of the pricelessness of certain great works of art, their value being premised on a mysterious greatness or creative genius. They may then be sold at auction for several million pounds and still be described as 'priceless'. Of course, it is this unique cultural value which allows them to have an exchange value as commodities.

The Heritage where it is formulated as separate from, but accidentally falling into the world of commodification, fails to take account of the way in which intellectual production of the past is a part of its exchange value in the present. A more dialectical understanding would grasp heritage landscape as constituting relations of dependency across the range between past and present, the particular spatialization of which results in the cutting-off of an objectified entity from more uneven and unequal histories which make any place. While critical debate in the discipline of archaeology has cohered around the need to deal with a range of interests beyond the boundaries of profession, it has also shown that there are a series of hailings for those archaeologists who attempt to make such connections. Hodder's recent discussion of *The Archaeological Process*, for example, attempts to valorize the local (Hodder 1999: 9) in the same moment as he actively objectifies it in a *process* of commodified appropriation in corporate-sponsored fieldwork at Çatalhöyük (cf. Hamilakis 1999). Archaeology in Ireland has served both a colonial and a 'post'-colonial status quo extremely well. The search for the idealized pre-colonial past through the monumentalization of nationality was the pre- and post-independence response to the appropriation of 'barbarous Irish' pasts by intellectual producers of the colonial regime. Latterly, archaeology has served in the nostalgic turn towards a distinctive 'sense of place', in which a suitably iconic, national past is re-colonized as a localized and commodified present.[9] However, it should be clear by now, with regard to the particular situation in the Boyne valley and the general condition of which it is symptomatic, that there are and there always were alternative options. Yet there is an important sense in which the reduction of this issue to short-term solutions – say, changing the content of an exhibit in the centre or the number of approaches to the monuments – misses the more fundamental point. In accepting the 'natural limits' argument, a false optimism is offered with regard to the enormity of the task of opposing the violence imposed by these changing relations of dependency.

The circumstances of an archaeological confrontation with this situation condition any subsequent critical practice. Wherever archaeology produces renown, however spatially and temporally 'remote' the place may be, it has the potential to be exchanged as commodity-past. If the labour of archaeologists and others on landscape is central to its commodification in a heritage spectacle, then archaeological intellectual labour must be directed at tracing the relations which the designations of space as 'landscape' and as 'archaeological' set up. It also requires an engagement with other histories, which this spectacularization hides. The interpretive challenge for a genuinely critical archaeology is in historicizing the culturally dominant in such a way as to establish the kinds of categories which can follow the shifts in a *many-sided past* in relation to the present and direct

9. Recent studies in Irish archaeology have theorized these issues (Ronayne 1997; Tierney 1998).

them towards the future. As a result, the conflictual conditions within which the production of the past take place have epistemological consequences for the interpretation of, for example, a 'prehistoric landscape'. It follows that critical archaeological work will not succeed in public intervention as long as it perpetuates the institutionalization of divisions of labour which reify professional and disciplinary boundaries. In the work which progressive social forces have to do in rediscovering how to live history in an active way – something Jameson (1991) suggests has not presently been achieved – it is important to remember that communal 'local' control of the heritage-as-a-process is not an impossibility. It is simply impossible *in itself*, without reference to a broader transformative struggle.

Acknowledgements

This chapter is the product of work with several interlocutors, though it represents the articulation of a politics with which many of them would disagree. I owe particular thanks to the people who live and work in the Boyne valley and who took the time to contribute to this project. I am indebted to Jayne Gidlow for her work and her company in the field. For insightful comments on the text, I wish to acknowledge Pier Paolo Frassinelli, Barbara Bender and Pedro Paulo Funari. The map is the work of Angela Gallagher (Department of Archaeology, NUI, Galway).

References

Bord Fáilte. 1999. *Tourism Facts 98*. Dublin: *Bord Fáilte*.
—— 1997. *The Fáilte Business*. Dublin: *Bord Fáilte*.
Bourdieu, P. 1993. *The Field of Cultural Production*. Trans. R. Johnson. Cambridge: Cambridge University Press.
Brady, Shipman and Martin. 1996. *Boyne Valley Integrated Development Plan*. Dublin.
Condit, T. and Cooney, G. (eds) 1997. *Brú na Bóinne – Newgrange, Knowth, Dowth and the River Boyne*. Supplement to *Archaeology Ireland* **11**(3). Bray: Wordwell.
Cooney, G. 1997. The *Brú na Bóinne* Inheritance, in T. Condit and G. Cooney (eds) *Brú na Bóinne*. Bray: Wordwell, 3.
—— 2000. *Landscapes of Neolithic Ireland*. London: Routledge.
Dúchas. 1999. *Brú na Bóinne*. Dublin: Department of Arts, Heritage, Gaeltacht and the Islands.
Eogan, G. 1986. *Knowth and the Passage Tombs of Ireland*. London: Thames and Hudson.

—— 1997a. Stonehenge in its wider context, in B. Cunliffe and C. Renfrew (eds) *Science and Stonehenge*. Oxford: Oxford University Press.

—— 1997b. The Passage Tombs of *Brú na Bóinne*, in T. Condit and G. Cooney (eds) *Brú na Bóinne*. Bray: Wordwell. 9–11.

Gibbons, L. 1996. *Transformations in Irish Culture*. Cork: Cork University Press.

Hall, M. (in press). Memory as cultural property: Cape Town's District Six, in R. Layton, P. Stone and J.S. Thomas (eds) *The Conservation and Destruction of Cultural Property*. London: Routledge.

Hamilakis, Y. 1999. La trahison des Archéologues? Archaeological practice as intellectual activity in postmodernity. *Journal of Mediterranean Archaeology* **12**(1) 60–79.

Harvey, D. 1996. *Justice, Nature and the Geography of Difference*. Malden and Oxford: Blackwell.

Herity, M. 1967. From Lhuyd to Coffey: new information from unpublished descriptions of the Boyne Valley tombs. *Studia Hibernica* **7** 127–45.

Hobsbawm, E. and Ranger, T. (eds) 1983. *The Invention of Tradition*. Cambridge: Cambridge University Press.

Hodder, I. 1999. *The Archaeological Process*. Oxford: Blackwell.

Jameson, F. 1991. *Postmodernism or, the Cultural Logic of Late Capitalism*. London and New York: Verso.

—— 1997. The Visitor Centre – Gateway to *Brú na Bóinne*, in T. Condit and G. Cooney (eds) *Brú na Bóinne*. Bray: Wordwell. 36–7.

Keane, E. 1998. *Brú na Bóinne*: Achieving Sustainable Balance in Heritage Landscape Management. Unpublished Conference Paper Delivered at the European Tourism and Environment Workshop.

Lefebvre, H. 1991. *The Production of Space*. Trans. D. Nicholson-Smith. Oxford: Blackwell.

Macalister, R.A.S. 1939. *Newgrange Co. Meath. Brugh na Bóinne*. Dublin: The Stationery Office.

Marx, K. 1970. *Capital. Vol. 1*. London: Lawrence & Wishart.

McManus, R. 1997. Heritage and tourism in Ireland – an unholy alliance? *Irish Geography* **30**(2) 90–8.

Mitchell and Associates. 1992. *Environmental Impact Statement: Park Centre Building for Boyne Valley Archaeological Park*. Dublin: Mitchell and Associates.

O'Connor, B. 1993. Myths and mirrors: tourist images and national identity, in B. O'Connor and M. Cronin (eds) *Tourism in Ireland: A Critical Analysis*. Cork: Cork University Press. 68–85.

O'Kelly, M.J. 1982. *Newgrange. Archaeology, Art and Legend*. London: Thames and Hudson.

Prieur, M. 1998. The landscape in comparative law. *Naturopa* **86** 24–5.

Ronayne, M. 1997. Object lessons: The politics of identity in archaeological discourse. *Assemblage* 2 at http://www.shef.ac.uk/~assem/2/2ronayn.html

Spiegel, A.D. 1994. Struggling with tradition in South Africa: the multivocality of images of the past, in G.C. Bond and A. Gilliam (eds) *Social Construction of the Past.* London: Routledge. 185–202.

Spivak, G.C. 1988. Can the Subaltern speak? In C. Nelson and L. Grossberg (eds) *Marxism and the Interpretation of Culture.* Urbana: University of Illinois Press.

Stout, G. 1993. Grant-aided change in the Boyne Valley Archaeological Park: agricultural grants 1950–1990. *Irish Geography* **26**(1) 79–88.

Thea Sinclair, M. (ed.) 1997. *Gender, Work and Tourism.* London: Routledge.

Tierney, M. 1998. Theory and politics in Early Medieval Irish archaeology, in M.A. Monk and J. Sheehan (eds) *Early Medieval Munster: Archaeology, History and Society.* Cork: Cork University Press. 190–9.

$-10-$

Bringing Contemporary Baggage to Neolithic Landscapes

Gabriel Cooney

Introduction

The image of a Celtic Europe and a Golden Bronze Age being used to buttress the modern European project of unity, explicit in some of the promotional literature for the *I Celti* Exhibition in Venice and for the Year of the Bronze Age in 1995/6, has, rightly, been debated and criticized. In this chapter I want to comment more particularly on the Neolithic period: I want to suggest that some of the images we archaeologists are currently creating are problematic. They may have more to do with the projection of current European identities than with life and landscape as it was experienced several thousand years ago. (For a prescient discussion of the problematics of a 'prehistoric Europe' see Rowlands 1984.) While there is a widespread recognition, in the abstract, that archaeology is a socially reflective practice, there has been limited discussion of the actual impact of contemporary society and discourse on the interpretation of Neolithic landscapes. This is perhaps all the more surprising given that much of the theoretically informed debate within archaeology has focused on the Neolithic. The basis of my critique is the archaeological evidence from Ireland.

A New Neolithic Orthodoxy

There have been a number of recent, important, widely quoted texts written by archaeologists based in Britain concerned with aspects of the European Neolithic (e.g. Bradley 1993; 1997; 1998; Hodder 1990; 1998; Sherratt 1990; 1995a; Thomas 1996a; Tilley 1996; Whittle 1996; 1997a). While the approach taken in these books and papers vary, there are a number of recurring themes: for example, the validity of thinking in terms of structuring principles of life having an impact over very wide areas. A contrast is frequently drawn between central : western Europe, heartland : Atlantic facade (with Ireland being *ultima thule*), core : periphery (e.g. Sherratt 1990). The beginnings of agriculture which was previously taken as the defining characteristic of the Neolithic is now seen to be less important than the changes in social ideas and material culture that took place at this time (Bradley 1998: 160-4). However, there is another general model of the transition which sees agriculture as the major difference between Mesolithic and Neolithic societies (e.g. Rowley-Conwy 1999; Zvelebil 1998, see also Pluccienik 1998).

In effect many of these texts tend to be dominated by a grand narrative, essentialist approach, even when they avowedly concern different regions. Hence, while they celebrate the diversity of Neolithic worlds, mobility of lifestyle is taken to be the central explanatory concept. Take for example Whittle (1996: 355) writing of the Neolithic way of life in Europe: 'While people moved around, the sense of community continued to be maintained, to be reaffirmed by periodic gatherings, gift exchange, sharings of food and drink, joint participation in ritual and an ever-present web of materiality.'

Bradley emphasizes the need to discuss rock art at a regional level (1997: 15) but then generalizes about its context:

> It is clear that throughout Atlantic Europe agriculture was adopted only gradually. For the most part it does not seem to have had a decisive impact until the Later Bronze Age. Before that time settlement sites are difficult to identify and often have an ephemeral character.

Where the issue of regionality is specifically addressed, as by Thomas (1998a), it tends to be seen in terms of a local playing-out of the big picture. Thomas (1998a: 52) suggests that in the case of monument construction in Britain: 'local conflicts of interpretation and struggles were played out through unique improvisations on the basis of available cultural materials'. In this scenario little or no regard is given to the reality of physical differences between regions playing any real role in influencing human activity (Thomas 1999, 228; but see for example Armit and Finlayson 1992; Harding 1997).

These views are often presented as 'radical' or 'controversial', as for example when Bradley (1998: 161) discusses the possibility that the expansion of farming in many different parts of Europe may have been facilitated by ideological change. This persistent presentation of views as radical or controversial brings to mind Glassie's (1991: 260) evocation of the corpses of flayed strawmen. In reality one of the most striking features of this literature is the extent to which the shared views of a number of influential archaeologists now represent a widely and well-articulated orthodoxy about the Neolithic in Western Europe. Thus Bradley, having suggested that the proposed link between the spread of farming and ideological change was controversial, then commented on how frequently this linkage is echoed in recent discussions of the Neolithic period, citing work by Sherratt (1995a), Whittle (1996) and Thomas (1991, 1996a). This might raise the question of how much repetition by how many archaeologists does it take for an idea to be regarded as uncontroversial!

Much of the literature referred to above is written as part of an explicit engagement with postmodernism or with an implicit acceptance that changes in archaeological thinking since the 1980s are part of the wider set of changes in intellectual thought and the nature of society that is labelled as postmodernism (see Hodder 1999: 152; Johnson 1999: 166). It is paradoxical then that one of the central tenets of postmodernism is that it:

> Signals the death of (such) 'metanarratives' whose secretly terroristic function was to ground and legitimate the illusion of a 'universal' human history ... Science and philosophy must jettison their grandiose metaphysical claims and view themselves more modestly as just another set of narratives (Eagleton 1987).

Thus, on the one hand, we have an archaeological perspective which professes to be part of this wider move away from the concept of over-arching explanatory approaches, while, on the other, it produces metanarrative views of the Neolithic. Furthermore, it trails these views as radical and controversial. It should be acknowledged that of the proponents of the 'big picture' approach cited above, Sherratt (e.g. 1995b), explicitly values a 'grand narrative' approach to the past.

There is a further problem with this literature, namely that while postmodernism provides us with a liberating diversity of ways of thinking about the past, there is a danger that the language and terms of postmodernism feed into interpretations of the Neolithic. Postmodernism has to be set in its specific historical context as a response, reaction and/or development of modernity and capitalism (see discussion in Harvey 1990; Eagleton 1996; Lemert 1997). The Neolithic was a very different world. But what is striking is the extent to which we archaeologists have attached the labels that define postmodernism not just to our interpretive approaches to prehistoric societies, but to those prehistoric societies themselves. I would like to suggest that there may be a link between the assumed centrality of mobility in Neolithic societies and the postmodern focus on:

> Proliferation, juxtaposition and disjunction . . . (the preference for) what is positive and multiple, difference over uniformity, flows over unities, mobile arrangements over systems . . . . (the belief) that what is productive is not sedentary but nomadic (Foucault 1984: xiii).

It would seem that, rather than using the postmodern understanding of reflexivity to tack between past and present, postmodernity has anachronistically been exported to prehistory.

The Irish Problem and its Implications

I think one can legitimately question the acceptability of nomadic living arrangement as a widely applicable model of the Neolithic world. While the archaeological
record in some regions, for example southern England, can be read as supporting
an interpretation of mobile, short-stay patterns of residential activity (e.g. Whittle
1997b; Thomas 1999, but see Allen 1997; Evans and O'Connor 1999: 201–9), the
evidence elsewhere, for example from Ireland, suggests more complex interpretations. And yet the Irish evidence has not only been incorporated into this new
orthodoxy, but deployed to support it. For example, Whittle (1996: 243–8) has
used the Boyne Valley (Brú na Bóinne) passage tomb complex to demonstrate the
applicability of his ideas about the meaning of the monuments in western and
northwest Europe. He identifies the variety of ways over time and space that human
activity within and around the monuments could have created a world view focused
on a fusion of the past and present, engendering cohesion, integration and
collectivity of action. The monuments are seen as providing fixed foci in a landscape
with plenty of space and a lack of close control. A very different, local view of
this landscape is presented by archaeologists familiar with it (e.g. Eogan 1991;
Eogan and Roche 1997; Cooney 1991; Cooney and Grogan 1994; Mitchell and
Ryan 1997). As Mitchell and Ryan (1997: 177) state, this view sees the area as a
settled, farmed landscape at the time the tombs were built. Furthermore, in Ireland
there is increasing evidence for Neolithic settlement in the form of rectangular
(and circular) houses (Grogan 1996; Cooney 1999). The Céide Fields, field system
in northwest Mayo has an extensive series of radiocarbon dates correlated with a
palaeoenvironmental sequence, dating farming activity to between 3700 and 3200
BC (Caulfield *et al.* 1998; Molloy and O'Connell 1995). At Céide Fields field walls,
settlement enclosures and tombs appear to be broadly contemporary. But this only
represents some aspects of what is, regionally and chronologically, a very diverse
picture of settlement during the Irish Neolithic (Cooney 2000). This evidence has
provided the basis for an interpretation of Neolithic settlement and society that
might be said to be 'radically' different to the dominant, mobility-based model
proposed for western Europe and particularly for Britain.

However, it is not just the Irish evidence that creates problems for the mobility
model. The interpretation of Neolithic settlement of areas within Britain, such as
Scotland (Kinnes 1985; Sharples 1992; Barclay 1996; 1997), and areas of western
and northern Europe such as southern Scandinavia (e.g. Tilley 1996; Larsson 1998;
Rowley-Conwy 1999) and the Netherlands (e.g. Louwe-Kooijmans 1998), suggests
that there is a more complex picture when the evidence is seen from a local or regional,
rather than a more continental or west European, perspective. For example, Rowley-
Conwy (1999: 44) suggests that the claim that the earlier Neolithic in Denmark
and southern Sweden was nomadic and mainly based on hunting and gathering

disregards the evidence of the sudden change to a terrestrial diet and the shift in settlement away from the coast at the start of the Neolithic. Furthermore, he points out that ard marks suggest permanent fields and the substantial nature of a recently discovered series of residential longhouses does not fit with the belief in nomadism.

We can suggest then that these differences are the result of prehistoric realities, indicating a regionally differentiated Neolithic way of life. So why are regional differences underplayed in more generalized presentations of the west European Neolithic? I think that we need to query the epistemological situation that developed in the course of the last decade of the twentieth century where other patterns of life are seen as variations or aberrations of what has become in effect a normative model. There is a discordance between an archaeological discourse said to be based on the postmodern recognition of the value of multiple interpretive approaches with a reading of the past that privileges a particular, overarching narrative. The idea that we should engage in a continuous, self-reflexive critique has been widely articulated. Geertz (1973) and Wylie (1993), for example, both suggest that we need to 'tack' between the past and/or other people's lifestyles and the present of the archaeologist or anthropologist. Let me attempt such a 'tacking' stratagem in the context of the current popularity of mobility models for the European Neolithic. I shall focus on three issues: nationalism (and imperialism), gender and the concept of landscape and being.

Nationalism and Imperialism

Thomas (1998b), reviewing a critique of the mobility model that I wrote (Cooney 1997), suggested that there was a 'whiff of nationalism' in my approach. The comment initially surprised me since the purpose of the paper had been to argue for a regionally-informed, diversified image of Neolithic landscapes, rather than a uniform, essentialist, mobility-based approach. On the other hand, having written about nationalism and archaeology in Ireland and the way we have underplayed its influence on the development and orientation of archaeological research (Cooney 1995; 1996), the likelihood of its influence acting in a subtle, unconscious way on my views was not to be ignored. After all, as David Clarke (1973) long ago recognized, implicit, unacknowledged bias is the hardest to dislodge.

The views I have expressed about the Irish Neolithic, such as the presence in some areas of stable settlement and an organized sedentary agricultural component, would, I think, find fairly wide agreement among archaeologists in Ireland (e.g. Mallory and Hartwell 1997). Of course in the details of this and other interpretive aspects of the Neolithic there is disagreement. Irish Neolithic landscapes cannot in any way be read as suggesting long strands of continuities between prehistory and the imagined traditional rural landscape of the national imagination (see discussion in Graham and Proudfoot 1993). The dominance of island-wide models of archaeological interpretation in Ireland could be set within a contemporary political and ideological context of continuing concern with the concept of national identity. And, within the Republic of Ireland, linkages can be made between a government apparatus established and maintained with an ethos of national identity in mind, and the centralized nature of state agencies, including those concerned with archaeology (see discussion in Woodman 1992).

We could also, perhaps, suggest that the increasing emphasis on regionalism and regional identities in the past (Cooney and Grogan 1994; Cooney 2000) sits comfortably with post-colonialism in the Republic of Ireland, its current status in the European Union and the sense of marginality felt by both unionists and nationalists in Northern Ireland. The recent emphasis on the Irish Sea as a means of communication rather than a barrier between the islands of Ireland and Britain, and the stress on long-term contacts and shared identity between northeast Ireland and southwest Scotland (e.g. Waddell 1991/2; Cooney 2000), may well have political resonances. They could be seen as reflecting contemporary concerns with the relationships between these islands in the north Atlantic, where Scotland is now being described as Ireland's nearest neighbour (Gillespie 1999).

In Britain, despite the recognition of the relevance of social context (e.g. Shanks and Tilley 1987:18), there appears to have been relatively little written by prehistoric archaeologists about the influence of social milieux on their work. Hodder's (1995) recognition of living in a post-colonial, multi-cultural Britain appears to be one of the few direct comments (see also Bender 1998). There is a recognition of the political import of archaeology, but a relative silence on how social context implicitly lurks behind archaeological writing (but see for example Champion 1991; 1996). Trigger's (1984) important paper recognizing the distinctions between nationalist, colonialist and imperialist modes of archaeological thought is frequently quoted in relation to nationalism. Indeed it served as a catalyst for a more detailed examination of the links between nationalism and archaeology (Atkinson *et al.* 1996; Díaz-Andreu and Champion 1996; Kohl and Fawcett 1995). But where is the recognition that echoes of empire might continue to haunt modern British society and influence the way members of that society write about the past? Nationalism has been seen as a problem for society (and the practice of archaeology) in Ireland, and in Britain for Scotland and Wales, but not for England. In reality, English nationalism, invoking the rhetoric of Britishness, has for long been the most pervasive ideology on the islands of Ireland and Britain. (Hence the British Isles?) The empire which English nationalists created co-opted elements from the fringes into the imperial enterprise and at the same time merged English with British identity (Champion 1996; Dennell 1996; Lee 1997; Strong 1999).

The journalist Hugo Young (1999) described growing up in an educational system where 'the uniquitous redness of the map, the naturally British order of things' was part of the taken-for-granted world in which he was formed. When 'there had to be something to support ... on the international plane Britain, or England, had to win'. Without a hint of irony he goes on:

> As for our history; it's a wonderment, reaching out from this tiny island, producer of a language and literature and a record of power that the people of pretty well every other nation must regard with awe. Now it would seem extraordinary if the writing of the past by archaeologists, regardless of their political hue, in this social and intellectual climate did not exhibit some influence of this strong sense of identity where empire and colonialism, Britain and England, are all inter-digitated in very complex ways. Edward Said (1993: xxiv) in looking at the relationship between culture and empire, commented that:

> I do not believe that authors are mechanically determined by ideology, class or economic history, but authors are, I also believe, very much in the history of their societies, shaping and shaped by that history and their social experience in different measure.

Said calls for the recognition of the embeddedness of the imperial and colonial world in the canon of English literature, 'almost unnoticeably sustaining the society's consent in overseas history' (Said 1993: 12). This was the literature that informed the education of British archaeologists, just as the literature arising from nationalism from the nineteenth century on has to be seen as a social force acting on Irish archaeological thinking (see O'Sullivan 1998; Tierney 1998). We need to work through these complex connections. Hingley (1996) has traced the connections between the ideas of empire as expressed in the British Empire and the archaeological study of the Roman Empire, forcefully reminding us of the interconnectedness of the past and present.

While the imperial era is over, the meaning of the imperial past still has resonances (Said 1993: 11). Perhaps there is a connection between a social context and educational framework in Britain in which imperial concepts still play a part, and the creation of a prehistoric past in terms of grand narratives. 'Big issues' are assumed to be more important than life lived at the local level. Barclay (2000) argues that the wide application of the mobility model in Britain is part of a implicitly metropolitan, universalist view of the past where little allowance or regard is made for regional difference or identity. As a more general point, and another reflection of a social context that has an imperial tradition, it may be the case that the writing of texts that imply wide geographic expertise has a higher academic standing than those concerned with local or regionally-based studies.

Gender and the House

Another feature of the new Neolithic orthodoxy is a down-playing of domesticity. This appears to owe some of its origins to the reinterpretation of the model of settlement for the Neolithic of southern Britain (Bradley 1987; Thomas 1991). Ritual and ceremony are seen as the central issues, and monuments are seen as fixed foci for mobile people. The microscale of activity in the domestic context is seen as less relevant and more difficult to retrieve because the bases of interpretation are frequently lithic scatters. Where houses do occur they tend to be cast in the same light as monuments, as places to which people came and went from, rather than being the foci of their lives. Even the domestic status of LBK houses has been questioned and they have been interpreted as tethers for radial mobility (Whittle 1996: 160, but see Louwe Kooijmans 1999: 7).

This view discounts the range of evidence for buildings in Ireland and Britain during the Neolithic (Grogan 1996; Simpson 1996; Darvill 1996; Barclay 1996; 1997). One of the striking aspects of current work in Ireland has been the discovery of several new houses (e.g. Cooney 1999; 2000). As we have seen above, Rowley-Conwy (1999) summarized a similar situation in southern Scandinavia. While there are varied interpretations of this evidence, what is clear is that residential buildings are a more widely recurring element than is allowed for in much of the current literature. So, why does the notion that northwest Europe is characterized by ephemeral, dispersed, poor settlement evidence continue to retain currency (e.g. Hodder 1998: 98)?

There may be a number of related processes at work. For example, in general house remains are much less spectacular and visible in northwest Europe than in central Europe and southeast Europe. Therefore they might be regarded as less productive as a focus of research, requiring much input for what might be little return. There has also been a wider swing against environmental, subsistence-dominated studies, as part of the reaction to processual approaches. A related issue is the continuing distinction made between ritual and domestic activity. This has the effect of privileging the former and relegating the latter to a background role (Thomas 1996b). Edmonds (1999) successfully pulls together many threads of Neolithic life, but his view is predicated on an acceptance of people on the move for much of the time.

Tringham (1991: 100–3) has identified the lack of interest in the study of houses and households as part of a gendered downgrading of the domestic sphere. She notes the gendered archaeological practice in which women archaeologists engage with 'domestic' issues, while male archaeologists tend to focus on the 'other' and the 'outside', as expressed in exchange and trade, regional studies or monumental architecture. There are exceptions to this, for example Hodder's programme of work at Catalhöyük in Anatolia (e.g. 1998; 1999) and more generally the prestigious role of tell excavation in southeast Europe. But these could be explained in terms of male archaeologists focusing on what after all are monumental sites. Indeed Hodder's work (e.g. 1990) could be seen as a classic example where the concern is with the big ideas expressed in and through the use of houses, rather than with the ordinariness of daily life created by people's actions in and around houses.

While Irish archaeologists have focused on houses, we have only just begun to recognize the importance of in-depth analyses of gendered activities, and to look at the divide between the ritualized *habitus* of the house and more formalized ritual contexts (e.g. Cooney 2000; Murphy 1996). It seems probable that the 'maleness' of archaeological discourse and practice permeates research on both sides of the Irish Sea.

Many of the writers working on the European Neolithic and setting the research agendas are male. But where is the discussion of this issue; of the problem of male writers perhaps creating an early twenty-first century, European, male world – which is high on display and ritual but says little about who was looking after the kids, getting the water, cooking the food? We can all agree that food was symbolically charged for Mesolithic and Neolithic societies but the bottom line is that people have to eat to live. I would suggest that we need to engage more meaningfully in debate about the domestic world, reintegrating subsistence and symbolism, rather than avoiding housework. If people shifted base in a regular cycle how did they cope with the baggage of their material culture (see Haaland 1997 for a discussion of the link between pottery and sedentism)? These issues need to be addressed in looking at the applicability of the mobility model.

Landscape and Being

A final consideration. A contrast is frequently drawn between two landscape interpretations. In the mobility scenario it is argued that, as in the Mesolithic, Neolithic people perceived territories as trails running through the landscape. Attachment to the land would be based on sites and paths. By contrast, in more sedentary societies the land is bounded; human features are imposed on the landscape which is actively changed (Bradley 1997: 6). The premise that the Neolithic is characterized by mobile rather than settled communities rests on the assumption that an agricultural way of life is only typical of the Bronze Age and later periods (e.g. Barrett 1994). But could there be a reflexive link between the world view of Neolithic mobility projected by archaeologists and the way in which our own postmodern, post-industrial world is increasingly dominated by mobility?

Augé (1995) has talked of the anthropology of non-places, as the distinctions between places are dissolved by ease of physical and electronic communication. Komito (1998) has written about the internet resembling a foraging society. In both internet and foraging societies the ideology is strongly egalitarian. Net groups split and combine as foraging groups do. Loyalty is not just to the group in which they currently live but to the extended kin network which includes people in other groups in other locales. As in many foraging societies, individuals on the net resolve sanctions by leaving. Drawing on Komito's analogy, is there a possibility that the image archaeologists are creating of a mobile Neolithic reflects a restless, modern Western society where a largely urban intellectual community (including archaeologists) of postmodern nomads move between places, forging connections as they go (Bauman 1992: 166)?

I am not trying to oppose this picture of a foraging postmodernity with a romantic image of Ireland as some kind of Celtic traditional and placebound zone. The reality is that Ireland has undergone profound social changes and is at the forefront of the postmodern condition (e.g. Gibbons 1996; O'Toole 1994). None of us can avoid the issue of whether we are in danger of representing the past in terms of the postmodern present. It has become increasingly popular to see the archaeologist as anthropologist, negotiating the archaeological record as an ethnographer might in his or her studies. While the authority of archaeologists and anthropologists to represent societies has been questioned, have we been sufficiently critical of the authorities that inform our recent approaches to the understanding of past engagements with the land? Writing on the debate about the nature of authority in ethnography Sangren (1991: 292) commented that there is now a taken for granted notion that:

> The social and the cultural are explainable with reference to subjects, individuals and experience. In this latter sense much of postmodern thought is every bit as ideological and Western as the forms of scientism and materialism it attempts to subvert.

Much recent work on landscape has focused on the human experience of place and the role of senses and the body in engaging with places. As the quote above suggests, the philosophical sources that are used to underpin this approach, such as the work of Wittgenstein, Heidegger and Foucault, cannot be separated from the social context in which they were written. To paraphrase Eagleton (1996: 116) these after all are just more white, Western males who assumed that their version of humanity should apply to everyone else.

Conclusion

I have argued for a critical examination of the current dominance of a grand narrative, mobility model for the Neolithic in western Europe. I suggest that the postmodern condition itself, the impact of nationalism and imperialism, the downplaying of domesticity and the patterns of mobility of modern life are all factors that influence current perspectives on the Neolithic in western Europe. If we want to pay more than lip service to the notion of multivocality and reflexivity, we need to contextualize the current dominant mobility model, and indeed other interpretations. We cannot assume that any contemporary model represents

---

a neutral, value-free interpretation of what is, after all, a contentious and varied past.

Acknowledgements

My thanks to the editors, Barbara Bender and Margot Winer, for the opportunity to include this chapter in the volume and for their work and patience. The paper benefited from the comments of the participants at the Landscape session at WAC in Cape Town and at a seminar on Colonialism and Ethnicity held in Dublin in November 1999. I would also like to thank Finola O'Carroll, Aidan O'Sullivan and Joanna Brück for their comments and suggestions. The views expressed in the chapter are my own.

References

Allen, M.J. 1997. Environment and land–use: the economic development of the communities who built Stonehenge (an economy to support the stones). *Proceedings of the British Academy* **92** 115–44.

Atkinson, J.A., Banks, I. and O'Sullivan, J. (eds) 1996. *Nationalism and Archaeology.* Glasgow: Cruithne Press.

Armit, I. and Finlayson, B. 1992. Hunter-gatherers transformed: the transition to agriculture in northern and western Europe. *Antiquity* **66** 664–76.

Augé, M. 1995. *Non-Places: Introduction to an Anthropology of Supermodernity.* London: Verso.

Barclay, G.J. 1996. Neolithic Buildings in Scotland, in T. Darvill and J. Thomas (eds) *Neolithic Houses in Northwest Europe and Beyond.* Oxford: Oxbow Monograph 57. 61–75.

—— 1997. The Neolithic, in K. Edwards and I. Ralston (eds) *Scotland: Environment and Archaeology, 8000 BC to AD 1000.* Chichester: Wiley. 63–82.

—— 2000. Between Orkney and Wessex: The Search for the Regional Neolithics of Britain, in A. Ritchie (ed.) *Neolithic Orkney in its European Context.* Cambridge: McDonald Institute Monographs. 275–85.

Barrett, J.C. 1994. *Fragments from Antiquity: An Archaeology of Social Life in Britain. 2900–1200 BC.* Oxford: Blackwell.

Bauman, Z. 1992. *Mortality, Immortality and other Life Strategies.* Stanford: Stanford University Press.

Bender, B. 1998. *Stonehenge: Making Space.* Oxford: Berg.

Bradley, R. 1987. Flint technology and the Character of Neolithic Settlement, in A. Brown and M. Edmonds (eds) *Lithic Analysis and Later British Prehistory.* Oxford: British Archaeological Reports, British Series 162. 67–86.

—— 1993. *Altering the Earth.* Edinburgh: Society of Antiquaries of Scotland Monograph 8.

—— 1997. *Rock Art and the Prehistory of Atlantic Europe.* London: Routledge.

—— 1998. *The Significance of Monuments.* London: Routledge.

Caulfield, S., O'Donnell, R.G., and Mitchell, P.I. 1998. Radiocarbon dating of a Neolithic field system at Céide Fields, County Mayo, Ireland. *Radicarbon* **40** 629–40.

Champion, T. 1991. Theoretical Archaeology in Britain, in I. Hodder (ed.) *Archaeological Theory in Europe: The Last Three Decades.* London: Routledge. 129–60.

—— 1996. Three Nations or One? Britain and the National Use of the Past, in M. Díaz-Andreu and T. Champion (eds) *Nationalism and Archaeology in Europe.* London: UCL Press. 119–45.

Clarke, D.L. 1973. Archaeology: the loss of innocence, *Antiquity* **47** 6–18.

Cooney, G. 1991. Irish Neolithic landscapes and landuse systems: the implications of field systems. *Rural History* **2**(2) 123–39.

—— 1995. Theory and Practice in Irish Archaeology, in P.J. Ucko (ed.) *Theory in Archaeology: A World Perspective.* London: Routledge. 263–77.

—— 1996. Building the Future on the Past: Archaeology and the Construction of National Identity in Ireland, in M. Díaz-Andreu and T.C. Champion (eds) *Nationalism and Archaeology in Europe.* London: UCL Press. 146–63.

—— 1997. Images of Settlement and the Landscape in the Neolithic, in P. Topping (ed.) *Neolithic Landscapes.* Oxford: Oxbow Monograph 86. 23–31.

—— 1999. A boom in Neolithic houses. *Archaeology Ireland* **47** 13–14.

—— 2000. *Landscapes of Neolithic Ireland.* London: Routledge.

—— and Grogan, E. 1994. *Irish Prehistory: A Social Perspective.* Dublin: Wordwell.

Darvill, T. 1996. Neolithic Buildings in England, Wales and the Isle of Man, in T. Darvill and J. Thomas (eds) *Neolithic Houses in Northwest Europe and Beyond.* Oxford: Oxbow Monograph 57. 77–111.

Dennell, R. 1996. Nationalism and Identity in Britain and Europe, in J.A. Atkinson, I. Banks and J. O'Sullivan (eds) *Nationalism and Archaeology.* Glasgow: Cruithne Press. 22–34.

Díaz-Andreu, M. and Champion, T. (eds) 1996. *Nationalism and Archaeology in Europe.* London: UCL Press.

Eagleton, T. 1987. Awakening from modernity. *Times Literary Supplement.* 20 February 1987.

—— 1996. *The Illusions of Postmodernism.* Oxford: Blackwell.

Edmonds, M. 1999. *Ancestral Geographies of the Neolithic: Landscapes, Monuments and Memory.* London: Routledge.

Eogan, G. 1991. Prehistoric and Early Historic culture change at Brugh na Bóinne. *Proceedings of the Royal Irish Academy* **91C** 105–32.

—— and Roche, H. 1997. *Excavations at Knowth 2.* Dublin: Royal Irish Academy.

Evans, J. and O'Connor, T. 1999. *Environmental Archaeology: Principles and Methods.* Stroud: Sutton Publishing.

Foucault, M. 1984. *The Foucault Reader.* ed. P. Rabinow. Harmondsworth: Penguin.

Geertz, C. 1973. *The Interpretation of Cultures.* New York: Basic Books.

Gibbons, L. 1996. *Transformations in Irish Culture.* Cork: Cork University Press.

Gillespie, P. 1999. An overlapping of many shared identities, in Scotland and Ireland, a special report. *The Irish Times.* 30 November 1999.

Glassie, H. 1991. Studying Material Culture Today, in G.L. Pocius (ed.) *Living in a Material World: Canadian and American Approaches to Material Culture.* St Johns, Newfoundland: Memorial University, Institute of Social and Economic Research. 253–66.

Graham, B.J. and Proudfoot, L.J. 1993. A perspective on the nature of Irish Historical Geography, in B.J. Graham and L.J. Proudfoot (eds) *An Historical Geography of Ireland.* London: Academic Press. 1–18.

Grogan, E. 1996. Neolithic Houses in Ireland, in T. Darvill and J. Thomas (eds) *Neolithic Houses in Northwest Europe and Beyond.* Oxford: Oxbow Monograph 57. 41–60.

Haaland, R. 1997. Emergence of sedentism: new ways of living, new ways of symbolizing. *Antiquity* **71** 374–85.

Harding, J. 1997. Interpreting the Neolithic: The monuments of North Yorkshire. *Oxford Journal of Archaeology* **16**(3) 279–95.

Harvey, D. 1990. *The Condition of Postmodernity.* Oxford: Blackwell.

Hingley, R. 1996. The Shared Moral Purposes of Two Empires and the Origin of Romano-British Archaeology, in J.A. Atkinson, I. Banks and J. O'Sullivan (eds) *Nationalism and Archaeology.* Glasgow: Cruithne Press. 135–42.

Hodder, I. 1990. *The Domestication of Europe.* Oxford: Blackwell.

—— 1995. Material Culture in Time, in I. Hodder, M. Shanks, A. Alexandri, V. Buchli, J. Carman, J. Last and G. Lucas (eds) *Interpreting Archaeology: Finding Meaning in the Past.* London: Routledge. 164–8.

—— 1998. The Domus: Some Problems Reconsidered, in M. Edmonds and C. Richards (eds) *Understanding the Neolithic of North-Western Europe.* Glasgow: Cruithne Press. 84–101.

—— 1999. *The Archaeological Process: An Introduction.* Oxford: Blackwell.

Johnson, M. 1999. *Archaeological Theory: An Introduction.* Oxford: Blackwell.

Kinnes, I. 1985. Circumstance not context: the Neolithic of Scotland as seen from outside. *Proceedings of the Society of Antiquaries of Scotland* **115** 15–57.

Kohl, P.L. and Fawcett, C. (eds) 1995. *Nationalism, Politics and the Practice of Archaeology*, Cambridge: Cambridge University Press.

Komito, L. 1998. The net as a foraging community: flexible communities. *The Information Society* **14** 97–106.

Larsson, L. 1998. Neolithic Societies and their Environments in Southern Sweden: A Case Study, in M. Edmonds and C. Richards (eds) *Understanding the Neolithic of North-Western Europe*. Glasgow: Cruithne Press. 428–55.

Lee, J. 1997. Scottish debate helps us to understand English identity. *The Sunday Tribune*. 10 August.

Lemert, C. 1997. *Postmodernism is Not What You Think*. Oxford: Blackwell.

Louwe-Kooijmans, L.P. 1998. Understanding the Mesolithic/Neolithic Frontier in the Lower Rhine Basin, 5300–4300 cal. BC, in M. Edmonds and C. Richards (eds) *Understanding the Neolithic of North-Western Europe*. Glasgow: Cruithne Press. 407–27

—— 1999. *Between Geleen and Banpo: The Agricultural Transformation of Prehistoric society, 9000–4000 BC*. Amsterdam: Stichting Nederlands Museum voor Anthropologie en Praehistorie.

Mallory, J.P. and Hartwell, B. 1997. Down in Prehistory, in Proudfoot, L. (ed.) *Down History and Society*. Dublin: Geography Publications. 1–32.

Mitchell, G.F. and Ryan, M. 1997. *Reading the Irish Landscape*. 3rd edn. Dublin: Town House.

Molloy, K. and and O'Connell, M. 1995. Palaeoecological investigations towards the reconstruction of environment and land-use changes during prehistory at Céide Fields, western Ireland. *Probleme der Küstenforschung im südlichen Nordseegebiet* **23** 187–225.

Murphy, E. 1996. Possible gender divisions at the Mesolithic site of Mount Sandel, Co. Londonderry, Northern Ireland. *Kvinner Arkeologi Norge* **21** 103–24.

O'Sullivan, J. 1998. Nationalists, Archaeologists and the Myth of the Golden Age, in M.A. Monk and J. Sheehan (eds) *Early Medieval Munster: Archaeology, History and Society*. Cork: Cork University Press. 178–89.

O'Toole, F. 1994. *Black Hole, Green Card: The Disappearance of Ireland*. Dublin: New Island Books.

Pluccienik, M. 1998. Deconstructing 'the Neolithic' in the Mesolithic-Neolithic Transition, in M. Edmonds and C. Richards (eds) *Understanding the Neolithic of North-Western Europe*. Glasgow: Cruithne Press. 61–83.

Rowlands, M.J. 1984. Conceptualizing the European Bronze and Early Iron Ages, in J. Bintcliff (ed.) *European Social Evolution: Archaeological Perspectives*. Bradford: University of Bradford. 147–56.

Rowley-Conwy, P. 1999. Economic Prehistory in Southern Scandinavia, in J. Coles, R. Bewley and P. Mellars (eds) *World Prehistory: Studies in Memory of Grahame Clark (Proceedings of the British Academy 99)*. Oxford: Oxford University Press. 125–59.

Said, E.W. 1993. *Culture and Imperialism*. London: Chatto & Windus.

Sangren, P.S. 1991. Rhetoric and the Authority of Ethnography, in S. Silverman (ed.) *Inquiry and Debate in the Human Sciences: Contributions from Current Anthropology 1960–1990*. Chicago: University of Chicago Press. 277–307.

Shanks, M. and Tilley, C. 1987. *Re-Constructing Archaeology: Theory and Practice*. Cambridge: Cambridge University Press.

Sharples, N. 1992. Aspects of Regionalisation in the Scottish Neolithic, in N.M. Sharples and A. Sheridan (eds) *Vessels for the Ancestors*. Edinburgh: Edinburgh University Press. 322–31.

Sherratt, A. 1990. The genesis of megaliths; monumentality, ethnicity and social complexity in Neolithic north-west Europe. *World Archaeology* **22** 147–67.

—— 1995a. Instruments of conversion? The role of megaliths in the Mesolithic/ Neolithic transition in north-west Europe, *Oxford Journal of Archaeology* **14** 245–60.

—— 1995b. Reviving the grand narrative: archaeology and long-term change. *Journal of European Archaeology* **3** 1–32.

Simpson, 1996. The Ballygalley Houses, Co. Antrim, Ireland, in T. Darvill and J. Thomas (eds) *Neolithic Houses in Northwest Europe and Beyond*. Oxford: Oxbow Monograph 57. 123–32.

Strong, R. 1999. *The Spirit of Britain: A Narrative History of the Arts*. London: Hutchinson.

Thomas, J. 1991. *Rethinking the Neolithic*. Cambridge: Cambridge University Press.

—— 1996a. *Time, Culture and Identity*. London: Routledge.

—— 1996b. Neolithic Houses in Mainland Britain and Ireland – a Sceptical View, in T. Darvill and J. Thomas (eds) *Neolithic houses in Northwest Europe and Beyond*. Oxford: Oxbow Monograph 57. 1–12.

—— 1998a. Towards a Regional Geography of the Neolithic, in M. Edmonds and C. Richards (eds) *Understanding the Neolithic of North-Western Europe*. Glasgow: Cruithne Press. 37–60.

—— 1998b. Review of P. Topping (ed.) *Neolithic landscapes*. Oxbow 1997. *Antiquity* **72** 455–6.

—— 1999. *Understanding the Neolithic*. London: Routledge.

Tierney, M. 1998. Theory and Politics in Early Medieval Irish Archaeology, in M.A. Monk and J. Sheehan (eds) *Early Medieval Munster: Archaeology, History and Society*. Cork: Cork University Press. 190–9.

Tilley, C. 1996. *An Ethnography of the Neolithic: Early Prehistoric Societies in Southern Scandinavia*. Cambridge: Cambridge University Press.

Trigger, B. 1984. Alternative archaeologies: nationalist, colonialist, imperialist. *Man* **19** 355–70.

Tringham, R. 1991. Households with Faces: the Challenge of Gender in Prehistoric Architectural Remains, in J. Gero and M. Conkey (eds) *Engendering Archaeology: Women and Prehistory*. Oxford: Blackwell. 93–131.

Waddell, J. 1991/2. The Irish Sea in Prehistory. *Journal of Irish Archaeology* **6** 29–40.

Whittle, A. 1996. *Europe in the Neolithic, the Creation of New Worlds.* Cambridge: Cambridge University Press.

—— 1997a. Moving on and Moving around: Neolithic Settlement Mobility, in P. Topping (ed.) *Neolithic Landscapes.* Oxford: Oxbow. 15–22.

—— 1997b. *Sacred Mound, Holy Rings.* Oxford: Oxbow Monograph 74.

Woodman, P.C. 1992. Filling in the spaces in Irish prehistory. *Antiquity* **66** 295–314.

Wylie, A. 1993. A Proliferation of New Archaeologies: Beyond Objectivism and Relativism, in N. Yoffee and A. Sherratt (eds) *Archaeological Theory: Who Sets the Agenda?* Cambridge: Cambridge University Press. 20–6.

Young, H. 1999. Why I'm glad to be European (Saturday Review, 1–2). *The Guardian.* 2 January 1999.

Zvelebil, M. 1998. What's in a Name: The Mesolithic, the Neolithic, and Social Change at the Mesolithic-Neolithic Transition, in M. Edmonds and C. Richards (eds) *Understanding the Neolithic of North-Western Europe.* Glasgow: Cruithne Press. 1–36.

Comments on Part I: Intersecting Landscapes
Julian Thomas

That landscapes are disputed, struggled over, and understood in different ways has been a central theme in this volume. However, it is clear that the respective authors of many of the chapters conceive of these conflicts in a variety of ways, and this disagreement opens up a consideration of some broader issues. It has become a commonplace that the different academic disciplines make use of the word 'landscape' in a variety of ways. These range from referring to the surface topography of the earth (e.g. Trueman 1971: 18) to denoting a particular mode of representation (Cosgrove and Daniels 1988). Glossing these differences, a distinction is sometimes made between the material and the symbolic, with the result that we are obliged to consider landscape to be either a physical thing or its mental representation. Such a framework is perhaps unhelpful. It may be more enlightening to consider whether the term is being used to describe an objective entity, outside of which human beings stand and observe, or a relational structure, within which they find themselves engaged. In the latter case, landscape can be imagined as an uncompleted process rather than a bounded and static *thing*.

The consequences of distinguishing between landscape-as-entity and landscape-as-relationship are quite profound, especially when we turn to consider the 'contestation' that many of the chapters address. To give an example: Caroline Humphrey (Chapter Three) suggests that the Chinese and the Mongols have very different ideas about the landscapes of Inner Mongolia. The Chinese are interested in barriers surrounding and defending inhabited and farmed territory, and revered places of the ancestral dead, while the Mongols are more concerned with paths, ways, auspicious directions and the dwelling places of powers and spirits. Is it more accurate to say that there is a single physical landscape, which is perceived in different ways by the Chinese and the Mongols, or that the two communities actually inhabit *different landscapes*, which intersect in various ways? For as soon as we argue that people are not mere spectators gazing upon the land, but have an integral and constituent role to play within landscape, their involvement must amount to more than a perception of an already-existing entity. If two groups of people are bound in to distinct sets of relationships with places, resources, forms of labour and plants and animals, their confrontation surely amounts to more than a juxtaposition of representations. On the contrary, two (or more) different worlds are occupying the same physical space, or at least overlapping. This suggests that the conflicts that are described in some of the chapters will not be easily resolved through mutual understanding, since they involve the collision of incommensurate ways of being on earth.

This sense of multiple, distinct yet overlapping landscapes is captured very well in Nicholas Saunders' chapter. The pre-war pastoral landscape, the unstable and shifting landscape of mechanized warfare, the landscape of pilgrimage and the landscape of tourism are all the same place. They occupy different times, and yet they leak into one another: the unexploded ordnance from the First World War still renders the farmland a potential place of death. The complexity of relations between intersecting landscapes is evoked when Saunders describes people standing in one landscape and trying to imagine another. Equally important is the suggestion that just as new landscapes are created by human history, so the experience of occupying those landscapes represents an aspect of subjectification. As Saunders notes, the lived experience of trench warfare brought new kinds of humanity and new sensitivities into being. This underlines the way that far from 'looking in' on the landscape from a distance, people emerge as subjects and are realized through their involvement in landscape.

A similar point is made by Veronica Strang in her study of the Mitchell River catchment (Chapter Four), where each of the groups discussed has a particular relationship with the land, and each has an 'internal culture' which is realized in performance. The MRWCWG provides a forum in which these 'cultures' are rehearsed, and by implication represents a context for the relational construction of identities. The miners, for instance, define themselves in relation to the Aborigines, stressing their own progressiveness and modernity. The particular attachment to landscape appears to represent a strong element contributing to these identities, with those groups that are more embedded in place being less susceptible to change. The more tightly a group is tied in to its own 'world', the less likely they are to accommodate the activities of other groups. This conservatism appears to have been a successful strategy for the Aborigines, but less so for the pastoralists.

My question to Veronica Strang: how far does the existence of the MRWCWG contribute to the boundedness of the identities of the groups concerned, and to what extent do you think that 'social multiplicity' is *exclusively* a feature of modernity? Might we not expect such performed and negotiated group identities to exist in other contexts as well?

Heba Aziz's chapter (Seven) is concerned less with conservatism than with change, but it still touches on the connection between landscape and human identities. Significantly, though, the conflicts that she describes are *internal* to the Bedouin community. Here, the penetration of the southern Sinai by tourism and the modern state has resulted in a division of landscape into the Beach, the Interior and the

Road, contexts that elicit distinct modes of conduct from men, women and children. This suggests that it is possible to slip from one set of relationships to another, and it seems that this shifting between landscape frameworks is what the children have become adept at. Aziz's article demonstrates that if landscapes are relational structures the relations concerned are (among other things) ones of power. It has been through the ways in which they inhabit spaces and move from place to place that the prerogatives and freedoms of children have been generated. By contrast, it has been the set of power relations implied by the code of shame and honour that has contributed to the seclusion of women.

A landscape that was more explicitly invested with power is discussed in Eleanor Casella's chapter (Six). The Ross Factory manifested a spatial mapping of social relations, which were experienced through a series of habitual movements that led to redemption or descent into the solitary cells. In a way very similar to that of Saunders, Casella shows how the inhabitation of an unusual set of spaces contributed to the formation of a disciplined subject: a transformation that was organized through the most blatant of spatial orderings. However, she makes the very Foucauldian point that such systems of subjectification are never total, or completely successful. The landscape of discipline, order, segregation and transformation was undermined and paralleled by a shadowy network of illicit pleasures and recidivism whose epicentre was located in the solitary cells. In attempting to exercise complete disciplinary power over the prisoner, the prison system established the conditions under which it could be resisted.

My question to Eleanor Casella: if the 'black economy' of illicit goods amounted to a 'counter-discourse' that parasitized the disciplinary apparatus of the prison, was it also involved in creating subjects of a particular sort?

While I have been stressing the role of landscape in the construction of human identities, the connection between people and place is often popularly seen in much more essentialist terms. As Roxane Caftanzoglou suggests (in Chapter One), the academic critique of foundationalist identity politics has been elaborated at precisely the same time as new discourses of rootedness, belonging and boundaries have emerged following the collapse of the Soviet empire. Where political claims are vested in nationhood and ethnicity, legitimacy has often come to be based upon authenticity. But authenticity is a notoriously slippery concept, and Caftanzoglou demonstrates how the Anafiots and the Greek state appeal to competing modes of the authentic: the cherished heritage of the heroic past versus a 'traditional' way of life. Again, these conflicts are played out through different ways of inhabiting (or not inhabiting) space, the pristine, unsullied monumentality of the Acropolis as opposed to the vernacular dwelling of the Anafiots. A more genteel form of the same confrontation is found in Andrew Garner's discussion of the New Forest (Chapter Eight), where 'the natural' and 'the local' are deployed in different discourses of authenticity. As in the Mitchell River case, debates between interest groups provide a context in which identities are performed and defined, rather than reconciled, and represent the locations in which different landscapes impact upon one another. Authenticity is here connected with authority, with the ability to make decisions and to identify one landscape as the *real* one. But in much the same way as Casella demonstrates with the Ross Factory, power and authority are never absolute, they are exercised contextually, and are continually under threat of overthrow.

My question to Roxane Caftanzoglou: could you imagine an appeal to authenticity which is not essentialist? Does the Anafiots' case, which relies not on an identity that goes back to time immemorial but on having founded a way of life in a particular place, amount to this?

If the majority of these chapters have effectively argued that we can identify a 'politics of landscape', Maggie Ronayne (in Chapter Nine) goes further, and argues that the academic discourse on landscape itself has political effects. Her concern is that archaeology and the other disciplines can valorize space, rendering it susceptible to the attentions of the tourist industry. While these 'landscapes' are identified on the basis of the importance of their ancient past, their transformation into 'heritage' has consequences for those who live there today. However, no landscape is ever meaning-less, and archaeologists do not go around giving meaning to blank spaces. Rather, they add another aspect to the understanding of places that are already thoroughly significant to their inhabitants. There will generally be multiple forces at work in the definition of the meaning of a locality. The problem is that this 'archaeological' understanding can come to eclipse other histories and meanings, and this is what Ronayne's chapter appears to document.

My question to Maggie Ronayne: how might the archaeological investigation of 'landscape' enrich the understanding of place by both visitors and indigenes without displacing local meanings? Or is the discourse on landscape inherently damaging to local communities?

Another discussion of the way that academic discourse has effects in the present is found in Gabriel Cooney's chapter (Ten). Here it is the influence of contemporary social experiences upon our understanding of the past that is at stake. The contestation of (conceptions of) landscapes is one that takes place in the present and, given that I am one of the protagonists, I will take the opportunity to pursue the debate a little further here. Cooney suggests that recent accounts of the Neolithic period in north-west Europe have come to focus on mobility as a consequence of

the changing life-worlds of the academics who investigate the past. The contemporary influences that he isolates include the postmodern condition, nationalism and
imperialism, a neglect of domestic life in favor of ritual, and the increased mobility
of life in the late twentieth/early twenty-first centuries AD. His insistence that we
should consider the ways in which our own society informs our conception of the
past is welcome, although it may be an overstatement to suggest that these
considerations have been entirely omitted from previous discussions of the
Neolithic.

As Cooney argues, it would be unfortunate if the re-evaluations of the Atlantic
Neolithic that emerged over the last decade of the twentieth century were to congeal
into a new orthodoxy. However, he neglects to point out that these perspectives
themselves developed out of a critique of an older orthodoxy, which was anything
but flexible. Since the time of Gordon Childe (1925) the origin and dispersal of
agriculture has been viewed as one of a number of 'revolutions' in Old World
prehistory. The domestication of plants and animals, beginning in the 'fertile
crescent' of the Near East, rolled inexorably into Europe, bringing about social
transformation and sedentization. The hunting and gathering peoples were displaced
or absorbed, and the foundations were laid for the craft specialization and social
hierarchization of the Bronze Age. This, in the full sense, is a metanarrative. Its
interpretive stranglehold on the Neolithic derived from the insistence that the period
was dominated by a single process: a uniform and universal transformation of the
subsistence base. As a consequence, diversity between regions or within communities was played down. Pieces of evidence from different locations could be mixed
together to build up a picture of 'the Neolithic economy', because it was believed
that there was only one Neolithic economy.

As much as anything, the emphasis on mobile ways of life found in the
archaeological literature of the 1990s (e.g. Barrett 1994; Thomas 1991; Whittle
1996) arose from a desire to break down the uniformity of this established
conception of the Neolithic. It may be that this emphasis was at times overstated,
as a corrective against the *idée fixe* of a universal Neolithic 'package' of mixed
farming and sedentism, but the diversity of possible forms of mobility was
nonetheless explored (Whittle 1997). Moreover, given that it was not underpinned
by any notion of a unified world-historical process, this interest in mobility certainly
does not amount to a metanarrative, which Cooney suggests. Furthermore, the
more recent contributions to the debate have moved away from a single-minded
concern with mobility, stressing diversity in economic and social practice (e.g.
Pollard 1999; Thomas 1999: 32–3). If there is a new orthodoxy, it is at least more
sensitive to the potential for variability.

To be sure, there are areas in north-west Europe where the evidence for Neolithic
sedentism is compelling. While much of this does indeed come from various parts
of Ireland, there are dangers implicit in treating 'prehistoric Ireland' as a bounded

entity characterized by an internally homogeneous set of evidence or a uniform economic regime. Irish archaeologists have effectively demonstrated how such notions can support the image of a 'national' past, defined in contradistinction to Britain (Ronayne 1997; Tierney 1996). In the case of the Neolithic, this has taken the form of a reluctance to recognize that certain types of monuments and artefacts (cursus monuments, henges, impressed wares) occur on both sides of the Irish Sea. In a period when communications by sea may have presented fewer problems than long-distance travel across heavily forested land, we should not expect rigid cultural boundaries to have coincided with coastlines, or modern political borders (Waddell 1992: 29).

Yet as Cooney suggests, while Irish archaeology has been engaged in a debate over the role of nationalist discourses in the construction of the ancient past (Cooney 1995; 1996; Woodman 1995), the influence of myths of national identity on English archaeology has been less readily acknowledged. This may be because it is more deeply embedded and more difficult to recognize. Nonetheless, I think that the role of notions of 'Englishness' in the understanding of the Neolithic has taken a different form from the one that Cooney suggests. David Lowenthal (1994) has argued that while the English lack national costumes and customs, their national identity is vested above all in a particular image of landscape. That is to say, a 'timeless' idyll of villages and fields, country lanes and droveways, wooded hilltops and cottage gardens. This *scenic nationalism* has exerted a powerful influence over British prehistory throughout the past century (see for example Massingham 1926). It has promoted the impression that the English countryside has undergone only changes of scale, not of kind, since the start of the Neolithic. Indeed, it was precisely this vision of changelessness that discussions of Neolithic mobility were intended to challenge.

Quite how much these arguments owe to the nomadic conditions of postmodern society is also open to debate. It has been argued that the increasing speed of travel and telecommunications has brought about an 'annihilation of space through time', or 'time-space compression' (Harvey 1989: 240). Transnational flows of capital and information, and the new forms of migrancy connected with flexible accumulation have certainly changed the social conditions under which we live. But while spatial distance has been virtually eradicated, a parallel process has seen the increasing specificity of space, greater attachment to locations, and the growth of locality-bound identity-politics mentioned above (ibid.: 295). One manifestation of this tendency has been an increasing emphasis on the significance and elaboration of the home. In Britain, this has taken the form of a growing interest in interior decoration and gardening, manifested in the growth of garden centres, DIY stores, popular magazines and TV 'makeover' programmes. Under these conditions, it is difficult to argue that interpretations of the past that postulate the *absence* of a stable domestic focus amount to a reflection of contemporary social trends.

The chapters in this book have demonstrated that in the various ways in which human communities inhabit their worlds, they generate conflicts that are more fundamental than mere differences of perception. Landscapes are made up of clusters of connections between people and places, and being embedded in these relations makes us the people we are. I have argued that the contestation to which the title of this volume refers arises from the intersection of multiple landscapes within the same social space. We might expect that such intersections would have occurred in the past just as they do in the present.

References

Barrett, J.C. 1994. *Fragments From Antiquity: An Archaeology of Social Life in Britain, 2900–1200 BC*. Oxford: Blackwell.

Childe, V.G. 1925. *The Dawn of European Civilisation*. London: Kegan Paul.

Cooney, G. 1995. Theory and Practice in Irish Archaeology, in P.J. Ucko (ed.) *Theory in Archaeology: A World Perspective*. London: Routledge. 263–77.

—— 1996. Building the future on the past: archaeology and the construction of national identity in Ireland, in M. Diaz-Andreu and T.C. Champion (eds) *Nationalism and Archaeology in Europe*. London: UCL Press. 146–63.

Cosgrove, D. and Daniels, S. (eds) 1988. *The Iconography of Landscape*. Cambridge: Cambridge University Press.

Harvey, D. 1989. *The Condition of Postmodernity*. Oxford: Blackwell.

Lowenthal, D. 1994. European and English landscapes as national symbols, in D. Hooson (ed.) *Geography and National Identity*. Oxford: Blackwell. 15–38.

Massingham, H.J. 1926. *Downland Man*. London: Jonathan Cape.

Pollard, J. 1999. 'These places have their moments': thoughts on settlement practices in the British Neolithic, in J. Brück and M. Goodman (eds) *Making Places in the Ancient World*. London: University College London Press. 76–93.

Ronayne, M. 1997. Object lessons: the politics of identity in archaeological discourse. *Assemblage 2* at http://www.shef.ac.uk/~assem/2/2ronayn.html

Thomas, J.S. 1991. *Rethinking the Neolithic*. Cambridge: Cambridge University Press.

—— 1999. *Understanding the Neolithic*. London: Routledge.

Tierney, M. 1996. The nation, nationalism and national identity, in J.A. Atkinson, I. Banks and J. O'Sullivan (eds) *Nationalism and Archaeology*. Glasgow: Cruithne Press. 12–21.

Trueman, A.E. 1971. *Geology and Scenery in England and Wales*. Harmondsworth: Penguin.

Waddell, J. 1992. The Irish Sea in prehistory. *Journal of Irish Archaeology* **6** 29–40.

Whittle, A.W.R. 1996. *Europe in the Neolithic: The Creation of New Worlds*. Cambridge: Cambridge University Press.

—— 1997. Moving on and moving around: Neolithic settlement mobility, in P. Topping (ed.) *Neolithic Landscapes*. Oxford: Oxbow. 14–22.

Woodman, P.C. 1995. Who possesses Tara? Politics in archaeology in Ireland, in P.J. Ucko (ed.) *Theory in Archaeology: A World Perspective*. London: Routledge. 278–97.

Responses to Julian Thomas's Comments

Veronica Strang replies

Negotiating the River: Cultural Tributaries in Far North Queensland

My question to Veronica Strang: how far does the existence of the MRWCWG contribute to the boundedness of the identities of the groups concerned, and to what extent do you think that 'social multiplicity' is exclusively a feature of modernity? Might we not expect such performed and negotiated group identities to exist in other contexts as well?

Along the Mitchell River the activities of the inhabitants intersect in various ways: for example at the local rodeo, in providing accommodation for tourists, or in forms of land use and management. There are numerous opportunities for interaction and representation, but in relation to these small 'provincial theatres' the MRWCMG is a 'Broadway' setting. Unusually, it brings the whole range of local groups together and requires direct negotiation between all of them. It also creates a very public space, encouraging the participants to offer highly stylized and 'compressed' representations of identity. Recursively, this appears to contribute to the 'boundedness' of these identities.

Each group contains some opportunities for 'social multiplicity', but the parameters differ radically. To some degree this is defined by educational and economic opportunities. However, much appears to depend upon the extent to which group identity is concretized and continually reaffirmed through long-term physical interaction with the land. There is an important issue of scale here too: such 'rootedness' serves to localize identity within readily definable communities. Whatever roles people take on within the Aboriginal groups, even when they move elsewhere, their social and spiritual location in the land continues to provide the foundations of personal and collective identity. Conversely, mainstream professional groups, with their more emphemeral activities, high geographic mobility and vast 'imagined communities', have a more fluid social landscape.

One cannot say that 'social multiplicity' is exclusively a feature of modernity, as this suggests an artificial divide between urban mainstream Australia and its land-based groups, but it may be reasonable to suggest that those who do not have continuous involvement with a stabilizing physical landscape are more mobile literally and socially. By detaching people from the land, and greatly enlarging the parameters of opportunity, modernity may therefore be said to provide ideal conditions for social multiplicity.

Eleanor Casella replies

Landscapes of Punishment and Resistance: A Female Convict Settlement in Tasmania, Australia.

My question to Eleanor Casella: if the 'black economy' of illicit goods amounted to a 'counter-discourse' that parasitized the disciplinary apparatus of the prison, was it also involved in creating subjects of a particular sort?

Within all prisons, inmate identity is constructed through three points of reference – that of the dominant institutional boundaries, that of the individual agent, and that of the counter-culture of inmate society. The 'black economy' operating within the Female Factories of Van Diemen's Land both reflected and created the underground world of 'rough culture', as this alternate discourse has been termed (Daniels 1993). The 'counter-culture' of the black economy fabricated inmate subjects through both positive and negative forces.

Atop the inmate hierarchy were the 'Flash Mob,' who identified their elevated status by wearing bright handkerchiefs, earrings and rings (Damousi 1997: 91). In their testimony before a Parliamentary Committee of Inquiry, female convict informers described the coercive and sometimes forceful means by which members of the Flash Mob obtained and transported luxuries throughout the prisons. These 'greatest blackguards' attempted to manipulate the black economy through threats of violence, pay-offs, reciprocal relations of honour and obligation, and delicate networks of collusion with lower-ranking members of the prison staff (AOT CSO 22/50). Archival sources also describe in lurid detail the links between the black-market economy and the sexualized inmate subjects – 'trade' with convicts incorporated both sexual and economic exchange (Casella 2000b). The Flash Mob was believed to lure more innocent inmates into 'unnatural acts' and casual prostitution through promises of illicit luxuries.

Nonetheless, this Factory counter-culture also helped create the convict subject through positive forms of discourse. Besides providing a focal point for individual acts of rebellion, the black economy linked women together into a mutually dependent network, one that often turned to collective acts of resistance. Recent studies have examined the tenacious bonds of friendship, obligation and camaraderie that underlay many of the famous disturbances, uprisings, and riots breathlessly reported in contemporary newspapers (Damousi 1997; Daniels 1998; Frost 1999). Archival sources indicate that transient same-sex relationships also formed within the Factories. Accompanied by romantic exchanges of food, tobacco or jewelry, these illicit sexual liaisons not only alleviated the misery of both loneliness and deprivation, but also fuelled significant nodes of the internal black economy (Casella 2000a; Daniels 1993; Damousi 1997).

Ultimately, the black-market economy functioned as an alternative disciplinary force. By linking the inmates into perpetually shifting networks of friendship, hatred, alliance, threat, obligation, desire and fear, the black-market economy challenged the dominant discourse of institutional discipline and penal reformation.

Roxane Caftanzoglou replies

The Shadow of the Sacred Rock: Contrasting Discourses of Place under the Acropolis.

> *My question to Roxane Caftanzoglou: could you imagine an appeal to authenticity which is not essentialist? Does the Anafiots' case, which relies not on an identity that goes back to time immemorial but on having founded a way of life in a particular place, amount to this?*

If we are to subject both kinds of discourses – whether 'hegemonic' or 'subaltern' – to the same analysis (something which academic honesty I think demands), any discourse that builds on concepts such as 'tradition' or 'authenticity' will be recognized as 'essentialist'. This is something that many scholars working on nationalism, national and cultural identity, ethnic, religious or cultural minorities are familiar with.

But to recognize a discourse as 'essentialist' means little. What is interesting – (I would refer to D. Fuss's book *Essentially Speaking* if there was enough time and space, as well as to Fischer's recent article (1999) in *Current Anthropology* on essentialism and constructivism) is not to label a discourse as essentialist but to work out how it emerges as a strategy, what motivates disempowered social groups to invoke 'essentialist' concepts and build 'discourses of defence' on them, as part of their interaction with agencies or centres of power and authority.

I would not claim that the Anafiots' discourse relies solely on having founded a way of life in a particular place *as opposed to* relying on an identity going back in time. Maybe it has not been made clear in my chapter but time is very much a part of their narratives, though they certainly do not claim to have been there since 'times immemorial'. The way of life they claim as 'theirs' is one that is positively valued by the dominant rhetoric but the stress is on its 'betrayal' by metropolitan society, and conversely on its sustaining and upholding by them through successive generations.

Maggie Ronayne replies

The Political Economy of Landscape: Conflict and Value in a Prehistoric Landscape in the Republic of Ireland.

My question to Maggie Ronayne: how might the archaeological investigation of 'landscape' enrich the understanding of place by both visitors and indigenes without displacing local meanings? Or is the discourse on landscape inherently damaging to local communities?

The web of meanings in which any discourse, including those on landscape, is caught is contextual, rather than 'inherent' to it. Furthermore, it would be granting archaeologists far too much importance to suggest that it is they who give value to places in a historical and social void. My argument was rather that archaeology is always already situated in a broader scenario: all-pervasive commodification is the key marker of our contemporary world at large and archaeology is inescapably part of that process. The point is whether archaeology should serve the status quo or become part of an organic, transformative practice going beyond the *profession* of archaeology itself (certainly, a more difficult thing to do than to state).

So, if I may, I will rewrite Julian Thomas's question. Asking me to outline an archaeological investigation of landscape which can be enriching for all sides is, in effect, asking me to presuppose a form of interaction between 'visitors' and 'indigenes' which doesn't involve the unequal socio-economic relations of contemporary transnational capitalism. Should we move from a critique of these relations – and this is my position – or, for instance, do we take for granted and fix the objectifying and fully reified dichotomy visitors (tourists)/local hosts?

The 'critique of political economy' seems to be at best an embarrassing aside for most academics dealing with the politics of landscape. Conversely, I am not suggesting that we abandon 'landscape', but that we engage in a form of interpretative praxis which rather than operating *as though it were in* a different or imaginary time-space, goes all the way through the many sides of the reality in which landscapes are embedded in the present. As such, it should be an eminently dialectical model of investigation: moving from how things are to how we wish them to be.

References

Archives of Tasmania (AOT). CSO 22/50. Colonial Secretary's Office. 1841–1843 Committee of Inquiry into Female Convict Discipline.

Casella, E. 2000a. Bulldaggers and Gentle Ladies: archaeological approaches to female homosexuality in Convict Era Australia, in R. Schmidt and B. Voss (eds) *Archaeologies of Sexuality.* London: Routledge 143–159.

—— 2000b. 'Doing Trade': a sexual economy of the 19th century Australian female convict prisons. *World Archaeology* **32**(2) 209–221.

Damousi, J. 1997. *Depraved and Disorderly.* Cambridge: Cambridge University Press.

Daniels, K. 1993. The Flash Mob: Rebellion, Rough Culture and Sexuality in the female factories of Van Diemen's Land. *Australian Feminist Studies* **18** 133–50.

—— 1998. *Convict Women.* Sydney: Allen & Unwin.

Frost, L. 1999. 'Singing and dancing and making a noise': spaces for women who speak. Hobart: University of Tasmania. Occasional Paper no. 52.

Part II
Landscapes of Movement and Exile

–11–

Landscape and Commerce:
Creating Contexts for the Exercise of Power

Penelope Harvey

The Southern Peruvian Andes is a region where the mountainous landscape memorializes centuries of political history. This chapter sets out to explore how Andean peoples, aware of historical process and of their own social disadvantage in wider national and global contexts, have over time reproduced a sense of the powerful agency of the land and of the mountains. In recent years there have been several influential publications within Anthropology on the subject of 'landscape' (Bender 1993; Hirsch and O'Hanlon 1995; Ingold 1993; Tilley 1994). The aim of all these studies has been to show that habitual Western understandings of landscape are limited by that central paradigm of Western philosophy which insists on a categorical polarization of nature and culture such that agency resides with human beings while the natural world is passively acted upon. This approach renders humanity external to the landscape. Thus we tend to discuss the relationship between human beings and landscape in terms of human capacity to view, survey and map the territories in which they live, imposing meanings on particular landforms or determining land use through the activities done to or on the land. In this extreme culturalist view, human agency imposes meanings on a landscape from the outside. Furthermore, the point of view creates landscape as an object of human attention, just as human action shapes this object for particular ends, but 'landscape' itself has no agency in this process (Viveiros de Castro 1998). One of the alternatives to the culturalist approach to landscape is to emphasize the importance of 'lived environment', and to highlight the historicity of landscape (Ingold 1993). The focus of this approach reflects a concern with the mutually constitutive relationships between persons and the environments in which they live and work.

My worry with much of the current anthropological critique of Western 'landscape' thinking is that attempts to break away from the constraints of dominant Western epistemologies force people into positing alternative, non-Western ways of thinking which tend to the ahistorical and erase the political struggles that characterize the passage of time in so many parts of the world.[1] In places where landscapes are so obviously the sites of political and cultural confrontation an appeal to 'tradition' or cultural otherness is clearly inadequate. To ask why ideas about the animate landscape endure in the Andes involves thinking about how such ideas are made meaningful over time in changing circumstances. It is possible to demonstrate an enduring sense of continuity while refusing to accept a passive, survivalist understanding of tradition. Inspired by Anna Tsing's work on Indonesia (Tsing 1995) I look at the relationship between tradition (in this case the pervasive and enduring sense of an animate landscape) and marginality in people's understanding and experience of power. To refocus on power allows room to think about both history and contestation.

The sense of landscape as the locus of enduring and historically charged agency is familiar to Andean people. One of the most salient generalizations that can be made about this diverse region concerns the regular attention that people pay to the animate forces of the earth and of the mountains. Indeed, the relationship between humans and these forces is a continuous source of anxiety and stimulates the incessant ritual activity that characterizes so much of what is generally seen as the cultural distinctiveness of this region. Whenever people drink alcohol, for example, drops are sprinkled on the earth and flicked into the air in the direction of the mountains. Similarly whenever people chew *coca* they take the three best-formed leaves and wave them in the air, quietly muttering the names of local mountain spirits (*Apus* and *Awkis*) and of the earth spirits (*Pachamama* and the *Tirakuna*).[2] For many Andean people the landscape self-evidently has agency (intentionality and the capacity for autonomous action) and must be actively engaged if that agency is to be directed favourably towards human endeavour. In this respect it is important to understand that the personhood of hills and pathways is not a metaphorical extension of human attributes. Personhood is literal. The reading of the signs that the landscape affords is less like the reading of a map and more akin to how one might try to interpret the feelings of others by looking at facial expressions and bodily postures. It is in this respect that pathways, animal droppings, and the remains of burnt offerings are scrutinized, for humans need to understand the motivations and moods of the non-human beings who live alongside them.

The anxiety associated with these practices is rooted in the disturbing knowledge that the relationship between humans and the 'spirit' world is weighted against the humans. These spirits are human-like and able to enter into productive mutually beneficial relationships in which each side sustains the needs of the other through

1. See Wilmsen (1989) for a critique of the notion that hunter-gatherer peoples live beyond the purview of state systems. His argument is that the particular marginal locations of such peoples is a direct consequence of state expansion.

2. Allen (1988) gives a compelling ethnographic account of these practices. See also Abercrombie (1997), Harvey (1994), and Gose (1996).

exchanges of food, drink, music, talk – the stuff of human sociality. However, spirits are also capricious and destructive, powerful and thus able to destroy life as well as sustain it. In their relationships with the spirit world, people are thus constantly engaged in both drawing the spirit beings into social relationships and in attempting to ascertain the extent to which any particular manifestation of the spirit world is amenable to such attention. People thus pay considerable attention to the corporeal nature of spiritual beings. To know whether a being that you meet on a path at night is capable of human-like sociality you need to know what and how its eats, how it relates to others, what it is made of inside. Feeding, drinking and sex are the principal modes of interaction with the animate forces of the landscape (not the spiritual contemplation encouraged in the Christian relationship between deity and human subject). The relationship between humans and these forces is physical, sacrificial, a manifestation of unequal yet mutual dependency.[3] Knowledge and understandings of these beings ultimately comes through continual close engagement, and the shamanic experts are people whose experience has given them the opportunity for particularly close relationships. Knowledge of the land and its agency is thus not primarily the result of contemplative activity but of active engagement. The animate landscape provides an alternative source of power to that of the urban-based state apparatus. However, the relationship is not one of direct opposition, and the historicity of the landscape also entails an entanglement with the agency of the state that dates back to Inka times.

In the fifteenth century the Inkas elaborated common understandings of the charged, animate environment into a powerful spatial logic of empire, which subjugated groups were forced to embody in both ritual and mundane activities. The capital city of Cusco was the pivotal centre point, the 'belly button' of a hierarchically ordered, symmetrical world. The empire was divided into two moieties, and each moiety in turn divided and further subdivided to produce a nested administrative structure that could incorporate a distant place through a single unifying spatial logic. Connections between the centre of empire and the outlying regions were further reinforced through the tracing of sacred sight lines, known as the 'ceque system' (Zuidema 1964, 1982). Subjugated peoples were required to make ritual journeys that established powerful symbolic and material connections between centre and periphery. And just as the Inkas annexed and extended existing symbolic geographies (Sallnow 1987), so the Spaniards continued the process in the colonial period. They recognized the importance

3. Andeanists have written extensively on the ways in which human beings feed the dead in return for rain (see for example Allen 1988; Gose 1994; Harris 1982). The living and the dead are connected in a cycle of hydraulic exchanges whereby human beings seek to release the potential for growth entailed in dried substance (the earth, foodstuffs, animal dung) in a process of rehydration, enabled by their own offerings of alcohol and blood which sustain the rain-giving capacities (the potent liquidity) of spiritual beings.

and power of the connections that the Inkas had established and attempted to reconfigure the landscape once more, planting crosses on hilltops, and using materials from Inka sites to build Christian places of worship.

In these processes human beings cannot simply be characterized as external agents of change, for persons and their environments have been mutually constitutive over time. The tyranny of both the Inka and the Spanish colonial state appeared in the ways that people were forced to live and move in ways that confirmed their subordinate status. The historicity of the landscape is thus politically charged. Yet landscape exceeds political control. The *Pachamama*, *Tirakuna*, *Apus*, and *Awkis* embody a connection between the present day and a distant past and manifest a capacity for autonomy from state power, and at times active resistance to the exercise of such power in particular localities.

The details of my ethnography refer to the town of Ocongate, a district capital, with a population of around 1500 people, situated in the province of Quispicanchis, in the Department of Cusco, Southern Peru. The town lies on a road that is itself an important landmark in the region. Migrant labour moves between the highland city of Cusco and the forested lowlands of Madre de Dios where workers are always needed for lumber and gold extraction. The local landscape is dominated by the powerful snow-mountain of Ausangate, a peak revered for many hundred years throughout Southern Peru. Less renowned, but no less important locally is the ruined 'settlement' of Cupi (most probably a pre-Inka burial site) where ancestral bodies have been found, mummified, alongside artefacts discarded by the beings from pre-human times.

The economy of this region is mixed. Most people are engaged to some extent in agriculture, particularly the production of maize and potatoes, and in animal herding; cows and sheep in the lower valleys, llamas and alpacas in the high tundra pastures known as the *puna*. There is also much commercial activity and many leave Ocongate to work in Cusco or Madre de Dios. This mixed economy presents a dilemma for those who simply assert a passive model of enduring tradition. The classic Andeanist literature documents the relationship between people and the landscape in terms of traditional agricultural and herding activities. However in Ocongate it is clear that the move to commerce has not displaced these relationships.

On 1 August the *Pachamama* earth force is celebrated. People ask for good fortune in the future by making libations and burning offerings (*despachos*) to feed the earth. The *despachos* offered on 1 August are treated as equivalent to the offerings made on behalf of animals on their special days, but the objects of attention and of libation are not animals but material goods, even money. Women libate the money in the tills of shops or in the secret cranny of a store room. They make miniatures of objects that they would like to possess (Figure 11.1). The process of fashioning these models from the wet clay of the river banks

Figure 11.1 Chewing coca beside the clay miniatures of two-storey houses, a record player with loud speaker and a motor bike

constitutes a request for specific material goods. They also libate the miniatures (as they would animals) to enhance their reproductive capacity. Those with the skill to do so attempt to read the future by casting *coca* leaves. Others leave smooth patches of sand and interpret the animal prints that appear overnight or they read the shapes that emerge when molten lead is thrown into a cup of water. It was the observation of these rituals that alerted me to the huge range of activities that people conceptualize as occurring through connection to the land. As libations are made to the earth they not only request that the fertility of the soil be activated for the coming growing season, but also seek protection and good fortune for all activities that take place on the earth: agriculture, business and travel. This focus on the earth is one that links members of a family: those who stay and work the fields, those who travel on 90-day contracts into the rain forest, those who move from valley to *puna* in the meat and wool trade, those who stay in the village tending shops or stalls in the market place. These rituals bring together agricultural and commercial activity and also reveal how both movement through the landscape and located activity (such as house building, agriculture or shop-based commerce) require attention to the land.

There are two key points to draw out here. The first refers back to the remarkable continuity of this understanding of the agency of landscape in the Andean region. Even if we limit ourselves to the changes of the last 50 years it is clear that such continuities coexist with major social and cultural changes in people's lives. This area has seen the building of a major road and a huge rise in out-migration and through-migration; people have lived through the demise of the local *haciendas*, the formation of co-operatives and the parcelization of land to communities and individuals; the establishment of primary schools throughout the district and the growing strength and use of the secondary school have made it possible for all young people to imagine themselves as working in the professions either locally or in the city.

In 1997 I returned to Ocongate after nine years' absence to find electricity, an improved road, a new primary and secondary school, a refurbished plaza and new town hall. There had been further moves from agriculture to commerce as the mainstay of economic activity and some joked that Ocongate should be renamed Hongkongate. There was more open access to political office and a growing interest both regionally and locally in a local pilgrimage site, the shrine of the Señor de Qoyllorrit'i (Christ of the Snow Star). However, the land and the mountains continued to operate as tangible forces in people's lives. When I remarked on the visible changes, I was told that 'nothing changes, people still get drunk'. For my friends and *compadres* it was important to let me know that they continued to maintain strong relationships with the mountains and the earth. You cannot drink well in this place without drawing these beings into your drinking circles: they must be offered drink, and drunkenness implies the possibilities for continuities of substance between human drinkers and spiritual forces (Harvey 1994).

The changes that people did remark on and show me on return visits often concerned properties that others had extended, fields that had been taken over, buildings that had gone up. The ownership of land is an important way in which landscapes change, for ownership requires either visible evidence of on-going work or fences, walls and surveillance. Such changes affect the movement of others, where paths lead, which terrain they run over, where animals can graze, where herders have to watch with care to avoid trouble, even fines, from straying animals. Ownership is manifestly related to the exercise of power, but ownership in and of itself is no guarantee of productivity. Indeed the problem with closing off your land is that productivity is entirely dependent on relationships with others and walls and fences manifest severed relationships. Gudeman and Rivera (1990) have claimed that in the Andes land is a store of wealth whose productivity is activated by God, as if all you need to do to ensure productivity is make an offering. This folk cosmology of increase is not an adequate description of peasant production. In the Ocongate region the productivity of land is dependent on the ability of the owner to bring others to that land to invest their labour and their goodwill. One of the main reasons for which there are no longer large profitable land-holdings in this region is that there is a scarcity of agricultural labour. People who need cash prefer to work in timber or gold extraction or in the construction industry. Smaller landholdings are maintained through networks of labour exchanges and through regular offerings to hill spirits and earth powers. Small businesses are run in the same way; even maintaining a house requires similar relations to human and non-human neighbours. In this respect it is important to understand that there is as much preoccupation about wresting productivity from land, herds, businesses or houses as there is in securing such assets as possessions. Ritual activity and labour recruitment are intimately connected. In agricultural contexts there is a marked distinction between the open sociality required for productivity (characterized by large work parties, and the exchange of food between persons and with the spirit beings) and the closure that marks the transition to harvest and storage of the product (Gose 1996; Harris 1982). These contexts are far less easy to distinguish in most commercial activity. Most of what commonly passes for 'mestizo' business relations are conducted under the same dynamic; it is just that those involved are always simultaneously 'planting' and 'harvesting', seeking to extend the relationships and networks that bring them the goods which they then need to hold and guard as property.

I spent some time on my last visit to Ocongate travelling up and down the main road with some friends who control the Cuzqueno beer franchise in the region and was able to observe quite closely how this particular business works in practice. While it is clear that the family who run this business make good money from those they sell to, I was not convinced that Bourdieu's characterization of the 'violence of credit'[4] was entirely appropriate for it leaves out of account how those who are being sold the goods have considerable leverage in the credit business. Bourdieu's point was that those who have the economic power to lend money and goods are also in a position to demand an advantageous return on

---

4. Bourdieu's account is important for the focus he gives to the ways in which power is exercised through the manipulation of symbolic capital. However, the lines of power are clearly drawn in his account. My intention here is to show that these traders are in fact less powerful than they might appear when it comes to controlling those to whom they have extended goods or credit.

their investment and thus control those to whom they lend. However, this particular discourse of power/domination obscures the problematic character of class relations in the Andes. Traders with whom I was staying were clear that the success of the beer trade was dependent on gold prices. This is because when the price of gold was high, the migrant workers came home with good money and spent it on beer. When the price was low the money was spent on other things or perhaps did not appear at all. Whatever the debt, it would not be paid in these circumstances. There is a clear awareness that success in this kind of commerce depends on forces beyond the control of any of those involved. The business is also very labour-intensive as finding people to get them to pay their debts is a time-consuming affair. The trader has to calculate when his clients will have the money to pay and cannot call in his debts to suit himself. Even when clients are located, a trader might have to negotiate only a part repayment of the debt. The traders appreciate how difficult it is for their clients to make money. For only 2–4 soles profit per case[5] the small shop keeper has to put up with all the hassle of drunken customers and carry the risks for broken or damaged bottles.

In many ways the trader is dependent on the 'good will' of his clients. It is not a business for somebody who needs cash-flow. The fact of owing money does not in itself constitute an obligation to repay and the 'best customers' are those who have a clearly established and on-going relationship to the traders – that is, kin, *compadres* and *ahijados* (god-children). The down-side of this strategy is that while the relationship is more stable and the trader thus has more possibilities for the collection of his debt, the relationship is also more complex in terms of mutual obligation and responsibility. Many an alcohol business has foundered on a trader's inability to avoid giving away his entire stock to kin and *compadres*. Thus these traders find themselves in a situation where they are constantly going out, making relationships, maintaining contact with people, looking for ways not simply to extend their client base, but to make sure that they know where people are, what their personal circumstances are, whether they are travelling, planning any kind of celebration, and whether they are likely to have ready cash. The sociality required for successful trading is as demanding as that required for completing the agricultural cycle. However, these traders simultaneously live in very enclosed and demarcated spaces. The sociality is on their terms and they are not readily available for visits or for demands to be made on them. The house of the trading family that I have been discussing was a veritable fortress, which I kept finding myself locked into in error. If the family had gone out on business I had to wait for someone to come and let me out. The compound was secure in ways that agricultural compounds never are. The yards of peasant houses always have easy ways in and out for animals while traders' dwellings are as secure as they can make them with high walls and padlocked gates.

---

5. The equivalent of about thirty pence.

As I observed these traders in action I began to understand more about the intense relationship that these same people have with the shrine of the Señor de Qoyllorrit'i. This shrine is a very important landmark in this region drawing tens of thousands of pilgrims to the area for the Corpus Christi festival. The festival is the most significant trading opportunity that most people from the town of Ocongate experience during the year and as many as can take advantage to sell food, drinks and other goods to people both in the village square and at the shrine itself. However, these same people are distressed by their consequent inability to take part in the pilgrimage itself and it is because of this that the September festival of Exaltación has grown considerably over the past decade. Groups of dancers and musicians converge on the shrine to 'greet' the Christ figure and to enact a series of rituals which attend simultaneously to Christian and to the landscape powers.

The shrine, high up on the snowline is also a place where trading games are played. All manner of objects are bought and sold in 'play' transactions that encompass agriculture and pastoralism, higher education, trade in transport and electronic goods and even straightforward financial speculation. Perhaps the most significant difference between these games and the offerings/requests that are made of the Earth forces on 1 August is that the games at the shrine are played between strangers. They mimic the ways in which trading connections are built up within the pilgrimage/commerce frame of the wider event. My interest in this relationship between commerce and agriculture has less to do with the fact that pilgrimage shrines are frequently the sites of intense commercial activity than with the ways in which the ritualized performance of trade to ensure future prosperity gives us some clear insights into how commerce is intimately connected to the land. Commercial activity involves people in movements across the land and in relationships to the forces of that landscape.

For both humans and landscape forces, power manifests itself in the ability to act, and such agency requires relationships between persons. These relationships constitute both the possibility and the limits of power. Even the all-encompassing power of the spirits and landowners is fragile in this dependency. Spirits need feeding. Local elites and the landowning classes from the past needed labour and clients to constitute their power in the locality. Traders need relationships of both trust and respect with clients. The Christian powers do not escape such dependencies either. The Señor de Qoyllorrit'i needs pilgrims and dancers (Sallnow 1987). When this Christ figure originally appeared in the region and his image miraculously formed on the rock around which his chapel was built, he would 'escape' the location and wander in the surrounding countryside. Only when he was assured that dancers would come from the *puna* highlands and from the indigenous tribes of the rainforest was he prepared to stay put in one place. The fragility of powerful beings, the landlords, the traders, the Christian deities, and the animate forces of the landscape is of course relative and is obscured by the huge emphasis on power as the ability to act and to make others move on your behalf. When it suits them, their agency is very dramatically demonstrated in ways that reinforce awareness of their power over others. But the difference between the human powerful and the forces of the landscape is one of degree not kind. In previous decades and in the living memory of many people the landlords of the region exercised this kind of power. The powerful require relationships with those who have less power, but they are also able to call the tune. The danger inherent in power is that the powerful will force the relationship if necessary precisely because there is no autonomous capacity for productivity. Where reciprocity is not forthcoming the powerful can steal with impunity (Skar 1995).

But there is another dimension to power that emerges in the relationship between location and movement. In one sense this relationship is obvious. If power is located, others will have to move to have access to that power. Named locales (or persons) are linked by paths along which others move to attend to them. Ausangate the powerful Apu stands in one place and dominates a whole region. The Christ figure at Qoyllorrit'i, the image of his body etched in the rock, has become the focal point for numerous pathways that pilgrims tread from their diverse points of origin. The landlords of the great *haciendas* lived in mansions that marked their status and their centrality as they sought to control both production and markets in the region. Even today the fortress houses of the traders, located adjacent to the town square, demand that they be treated as the focal point for commerce in the locality. The services that support the public life of the village – police, judges, town administration, schools and medical facilities – are ranged around them and constitute the residences as central in the locality. This relationship between location and movement is thus also about the ability to manifest fixity and to draw people into relationships with you that marks your place as central and defines the marginality of others. This dynamic is one of the ways in which people's everyday actions are constitutive of the powers that surround them. People make offerings to the hill spirits and travel to visit the Christ figure to keep these powers productive and in place. They bring them things and people from different regions so that they do not have to travel themselves to find what they need. The relationship with the Señor de Qoyllorrit'i is very explicitly negotiated in these terms. He requires the presence of dancers from the rainforest and from the high *puna*. If they do not come he himself will leave his located shrine. But the hill spirits and the earth also require things that are not readily available in the locality. The *despacho* has to contain items that are brought from far away, vegetable matter from Amazonia, sweets, silver paper, and most importantly *coca* and alcohol. These relationships thus require a degree of movement and it becomes clear that who moves is crucial in this whole process.

The issue of how people move through the landscape is another area which has seen much change in recent decades. In the times of the *hacienda* the use of horses and later bicycles was reserved as a mark of status and those deemed unworthy of such means of transport would be subjected to abuse by the land-lord's henchmen who jealously guarded these privileges for themselves. In more recent years the acquisition of motor transport has been one of the main ways in which rich alpaca herders or returned migrant workers have demonstrated their economic wealth and challenged the stereotypical association between *puna* dwellers and traditional lifestyles. Women are also beginning to make similar challenges. On my latest return visit I discovered that one of my *comadres* had acquired a pick-up which she was using as a taxi service between the town centre and the village several miles up the road where she lived. The fact that she owned the pick-up was less remarkable than the fact that she drove it, complaining loud and hard to anyone who would listen that she should have been born a man. She said she had a man's character and a man's capacity for work. Her husband muttered that he wished she *had* been born a woman. Modes of transport have strong gender and ethnic connotations, which the marginalized enjoy subverting as and when they can. The attraction of owning a motor vehicle is its inherent claim to status and the possibilities afforded for circumventing the control of trade by wealthy townspeople. This latter point is the more significant, for differences in status are marked in many ways and my *comadre*'s old pick-up is not regarded as equivalent to the huge new Volvo truck that my trader friends use for trips to Puerto Maldo-nado. Particular forms of transport are significant for the kinds of networks that they enable you to build up, the kinds of trade and the levels of trade in which you can become involved. The successful traders can move goods in bulk, can occupy the positions of wholesalers and can command huge distribution networks.

As I have suggested, the powerful have always been those with the ability to move things around – the Inkas magically moved stones with the crack of a whip; they commanded armies of people to transport the goods they required and to build the monuments that then demonstrated their power. In more recent times landlords built huge houses and filled them with European goods. They 'worked' massive landholdings because of their ability to move people around and to transport the goods to the most profitable market places. The local elites of most recent times have a more ambiguous position. These are people whose family wealth was built up through the *coca* and alcohol trade of the early decades of this century. The movements of the traders were balanced by building up landholdings in particular locations, usually by seizing land from less powerful neighbours. Today's elite traders are the children of the men who made large profits in the semi-clandestine business of moving these valued goods from one region of the country to another. They continue this business in the still semi-clandestine domain of Amazonian trade, sometimes transporting fuel, beer and passengers, at other times using connections and guile to bring out protected hardwoods, gold and other contraband items.

Figure 11.2 Market day in the main square of Ocongate

However this tension between movement and locatedness reveals the limits to power. The fragility of local elites is manifest not only in their dependence on local relationships but also in their need to travel to other more central centres of power to manifest their difference from those around them. The necessity of association with the location that is their seat of power also undermines their status in the wider social realm that they move in. They are caught in their own marginalizing logics. If marginalities and exclusion are defined by those who have the capacity to show themselves to be at the centre, there is a problem for local elites whose centrality depends to some extent on their capacity to move long distances, a capacity that reinforces the fear that their centre is in fact someone else's margin. The problem is clearly demonstrated by their need to send their children away from the town to be educated. By doing so they also reveal that the place where they have built up their sense of power and influence lacks what constitutes power in more central locations. The landscapes that enable the exercise of power in one context do not extend beyond these territories. For the landscape encapsulates local understandings and experience of power and therefore does not travel.

In the Ocongate region, many people are intensely engaged with the animate forces of the landscape. They make offerings to protect their families and their possessions and they look to these forces to ensure fertility, increase, and productivity. The land is central to their daily lives, whether their livelihoods are focused on agriculture, commerce or migrant labour. As the circumstances of their lives and the possibilities for securing livelihoods in particular ways change over time, the contexts and the manner in which the forces of the landscape are called into their lives also change. However, there are continuities, most particularly the ways in which relationships to the animate powers of the landscape articulate alternative axes from those of the geo-political maps that designate their place as marginal and backward. The affirmation of creative, on-going relationships to powerful landscape forces does not simply articulate alternative moral geographies, for capitalist commerce can benefit from such relationships alongside more traditional subsistence farming and herding practice, and the morality of spiritual beings is not in any way exemplary. It is rather the temporal and spatial qualities of landscape that come to the fore. The historicity of the landscape resides in its capacity both to endure and to register change and conflict. That capacity is crucially located. As such the powers of the landscape can both constitute the context (background) for contemporary action and also emerge as the achievement of contemporary peoples. They have managed to keep alive a relationship that stands as testimony to their own abilities to articulate an alternative to those centralizing logics of a state that depict such regions as homogeneous and marginal, rather than as complex, differentiated sites where people consciously engage with their peripheral status.

Acknowledgements

An early version of this chapter was given in April 1998 at the Kay Pacha symposium (on Earth, Land, Water and Culture in the Andes), organized by Penny Dransart and Bill Sillar at the University of Wales, Lampeter. Many thanks to them and to the other contributors for helping me to think more about these issues, and to Barbara Bender for her encouragement to develop the topic in such stimulating company at the Word Archaeological Congress held in Cape Town in January 1999. Participants at the workshop on Landscape, Modernity and Exclusion organized by anthropologists and geographers from the University of Hull in September 1999 kept the available material growing far beyond the confines of what I am able to present here.

References

Abercrombie, T. 1997. *Pathways of Memory and Power: Ethnography and History Among an Andean People.* Madison: University of Wisconsin Press.

Allen, C. 1988. *The Hold Life Has: Coca and Cultural Identity in an Andean Community.* Washington: Smithsonian Institution Press.

Bender, B. (ed.) 1993. *Landscape: Politics and Perspectives.* Oxford: Berg.

Bourdieu, P. 1977. *Outline of a Theory of Practice.* Cambridge: Cambridge University Press.

Gose, P. 1986. Sacrifice and the commodity form in the Andes. *Man* **21**(2) 296–310.

—— 1996. *Deathly Waters and Hungry Mountains: Agrarian Ritual and Class Formation in an Andean Town.* Toronto: University of Toronto Press.

Gudeman, S. and Rivera, A. 1990. *Conversations in Colombia: The Domestic Economy in Life and Text.* Cambridge: Cambridge University Press.

Harris, O. 1982. The dead and the devils among the Bolivian Laymi, in M. Bloch and J. Parry (eds) *Death and the Regeneration of Life.* Cambridge: Cambridge University Press. 45–73.

Harvey, P. 1994. Gender, community and confrontation: power relations in drunkenness in Ocongate, in M. McDonald (ed.) *Gender, Drink and Drugs.* Oxford: Berg. 209–33.

Hirsch, E. and O'Hanlon, M. (eds) 1995. *The Anthropology of Landscape: Perspectives on Place and Space.* Oxford: Oxford University Press.

Ingold, T. 1993. The temporality of the landscape. *World Archaeology* **25**(2) 152–74.

Orlove, B. 1993. Putting race in its place: order in colonial and postcolonial Peruvian geography. *Social Research* **60** 2.

Sallnow, M. 1987. *Pilgrims of the Andes: Regional Cults in Cusco.* Washington DC: Smithsonian Institution Press.

Skar, S. 1995. Appropriating pawns: Andean dominance and the manipulation of things. *The Journal of the Royal Anthropological Institute* **4**(1) 787–804.

Tilley, C. 1994. *A Phenomenology of Landscape: Places, Paths and Monuments.* Oxford: Berg.

Tsing, A. 1995. *In the Realm of the Diamond Queen.* Berkeley: University of California Press.

Viveiros de Castro, E. 1998. Cosmological deixis and Amerindian perpectivism. *The Journal of the Royal Anthropological Institute* **4**(3) 469–88.

Wilmsen, E. 1989. *Land Filled with Flies: A Political Economy of the Kalahari.* Chicago: University of Chicago Press.

Zuidema, R.T. 1964. *The Ceque System of Cusco.* Leiden: E.J. Brill.

—— 1982. Bureaucracy and systematic knowledge in Andean civilization, in G. A. Collier, R.L. Rosaldo and J. Wirth (eds) *The Inca and Aztec States 1400–1800: Anthropology and History.* New York: Academic Press.

–12–

Pilgrimage and Politics in the Desert of Rajasthan

Marzia Balzani

This chapter examines the mutual transformations of ritual and landscape in the desert region of Rajasthan in contemporary north-west India. These transformations are understood in relation to the social and religious history of the area; the equally important mythical understandings of the region; recent political transformations which have taken place in India; the violence of communalism serving to divide Hindu from Muslim; environmental concerns; and the modern reworking of the caste system.

Between 5 and 14 September 1986 the Rathor Rajput Maharaja of Jodhpur (hereafter H.H. Jodhpur) undertook a ritual pilgrimage (*padyatra*) from the temple of Chamunda Mataji (his *isht devta* – chosen goddess) in the fort in Jodhpur to the temple of a deified hero, Ramdevji, in Ramdeora village (Jaisalmer district) 171 kilometres west of Jodhpur across the drought-stricken desert regions of Rajasthan. As H.H. Jodhpur walked from one sacred site to another, he walked back through multiple and selective histories. He went from being an ordinary citizen of democratic India, with no right to claim the aristocratic title of his forebears (with the 1971 Deregulation of Princes Act the former rulers of India lost both titles and privy purses), to a Maharaja of imperial times touring his land and its people. He also entered a semi-mythical time when men who were later deified performed their miracles and disseminated their teachings. As he approached his temple destination the gap between the present and the time of Ramdevji closed. The impetus for the pilgrimage was, however, firmly located in present hardships brought about by a long-term drought affecting Rajasthan which the government of India and the state government of Rajasthan had done little to alleviate. With hindsight, it is also possible to suggest that the pilgrimage was not simply a journey which took H.H. Jodhpur back through time, but also one which influenced his decision to enter national politics, a decision some have argued he took after the experiences and meetings which took place on the pilgrimage.

Pilgrimage always involves a displacement of persons through a landscape, and this landscape is often portrayed as dangerous, physically, politically and spiritually. Every pilgrim entrusts him- or herself to the forces of nature and to the friendly disposition of the gods. The undertaking of a pilgrimage such as the one described here in response to drought is commonplace in South Asia. What is out of the ordinary in this particular case is the choice, by a Hindu Rajput of royal standing, of a pilgrimage site with strong historical associations with untouchables and Muslims and that at a time of year when the majority of the pilgrims at the shrine were likely to be untouchables.

In what follows I suggest that this pilgrimage to a peripheral desert site can also be read as a return, via the democratic process, to the political centre of Delhi, a centre with which H.H. Jodhpur's ancestors have mythical and historical connections. In the 1989 general elections H.H. Jodhpur was asked, by individuals, caste groups and the media, which of the two main candidates standing from Jodhpur he supported. Although he attempted to remain neutral at the start of the campaign, it soon became clear to most that H.H. Jodhpur favoured the Rajput candidate for the Bharatiya Janata Party (BJP), a party associated with Hindu fundamentalism and communalism. The BJP candidate, Jaswant Singh, stayed at the Palace during the campaign and had H.H. Jodhpur's legal advisor as his election agent. H.H. Jodhpur's palace staff helped to organize and run Jaswant Singh's campaign. In 1991 H.H. Jodhpur stood for election as an independent member of parliament and was elected unopposed. In 1994 he became the chairman of the Rajasthan Tourism Development Corporation.

The 1986 pilgrimage can also be seen as part of a more widespread effort to reinvent the traditional role of maharaja (with the office and title by then legally abolished) as a way of recapturing political power on the regional and national levels, in part by indirectly influencing tourism. (H.H. Jodhpur owns the two main tourist attractions in Jodhpur – the fort and Umaid Bhavan Palace Hotel.) The very form of the pilgrimage – the procession with H.H. Jodhpur at its head and a lengthy retinue of high-ranking Rajputs, staff, cars and caravans, video crew and newspaper reporters – served to reinforce (if not helped to create) the ideas of what a maharaja should be like and what a maharaja should do. In some way the deliberately recreated 'spectacle'[1] of 'kingly walk-about' both pre-exists and draws on popular images of romantic and chivalrous Rajputs.

The issues outlined above are here disentangled by focusing on one ethnographic example and, by exploring this in as much detail as space permits, drawing from it some understanding of what it was to be Rajasthani at the end of the twentieth century. I follow Basso in conceiving the ethnographer's task as one of determining what ethnographic acts involve, 'why they are performed, how they are accomplished, what they are intended to achieve . . . , and to disclose their importance by relating them to larger ideas about the world and its inhabitants'. In this way a

---

1. On the (political) potential of such spectacle and drama see Kapur 1985: 57–74; Seneviratne 1977: 65–75.

great deal can be discovered from 'instructive statements about places and their role in human affairs [and] through the close contextualization of a handful of telling events' (1996: 57).

The landscape of Rajasthan is here understood as the outcome of centuries of human habitation, wars and colonization. For its traditional inhabitants it is also the product of a mythico-religious understanding of the land and its people in which the well-being of both can be affected by the behaviour and moral standing of the man who rules over them. The landscape is socially produced insofar as it is centred in relation to human agency. As Tilley writes,

> [a] centred and meaningful space involves specific sets of linkages between the physical space of the non-humanly created world, somatic states of the body, the mental space of cognition and representation and the space of movement, encounter and interaction between persons and between persons and the human and non-human environment (Tilley 1994: 10).

Social space is, therefore,

> constituted by differential densities of human experience, attachment and involvement. It is above all contextually constituted, providing particular settings for involvement and the creation of meanings (ibid.: 11).

The place

Situated in the north-west, Rajasthan is the second largest Indian state. Both its climate and geography are sharply divided by the Aravalli range of mountains. To the north and west the land is mostly desert while to the south and east it is fertile. Rajasthan was ruled, in part from AD 1000 and completely by AD 1500, by Rajput kings who carved out for themselves territories of varying size and wealth. The various Rajput lineages independently and under both Mughal and British empires ruled the land until the independence of India in 1947.

Jodhpur district forms a part of western Rajasthan and is now part of the state

> which comprises the principal arid region . . . of India' (Ramakrishna 1994: 7). The rainfall is irregular and '[c]limatological studies find abnormal rainfall (droughts and floods . . .) common; it seems as if "normal" rainfall exists more as a normative construct than in reality. Monsoon failures occur during 40% of years, and "normal" rainfall during the monsoon occurs only during 26% of the weeks when it is expected (Henderson 1994: 3).

Drought conditions ranging from mild to severe in the Jodhpur region occur in 58 out of every 100 years (Ramakrishna 1994: 9). Droughts often lead to famines which are classified by Rajasthanis 'according to their intensity: *ankal* or grain famine; *jalkal* or scarcity of water; *tinkal* or fodder famine; and *trikal*, when grain, water and fodder are all scarce' (Erskine 1909: 125). A recent period of extended drought in Rajasthan continued into 1987 and was part of a greater and devastating drought which affected 21 states across India (Badhwar *et al.* 1987: 8ff).

Despite various irrigation projects over the past decades only 22 per cent of Rajasthan's net cultivated land is under irrigation; this compares to a national average of 31 per cent in 1980–81 (Koshteh 1995: 5). The irrigation canals themselves do not solve all the water problems of the state as corruption and greed means that water does not always reach those who may need or have a right to it (Leaf 1992: *passim*) and the supply of water which can turn desert to agricultural land may itself cause long-term damage to the environment through desertification, salinization and over-exploitation of the fragile natural resource base (Rosin 1994: 42). The human cost includes the loss of a semi-nomadic lifestyle for many of the indigenous inhabitants of the state, the influx of settlers with different languages and of social customs from other parts of India and the loss of land for those who have neither the financial means nor the know-how to adapt to a completely sedentary way of life (Rosin 1994: 47–48; Koshteh 1995: 56–81).

Different rulers of Jodhpur have responded to famine with different levels of practical aid. About the famine of 1868–69 Erskine writes: 'the Maharaja, beyond placing a lakh [100,000] of rupees at the disposal of the Public Works Department in 1869, did nothing' (1909: 125). In the droughts and famines that followed, the railways were used to bring in fodder and food; also, often at the ruler's expense, people who had fled the state were transported back. Land revenues were remitted and import duties on grains as well as regular cesses abolished. All of this represented significant losses to the revenue of the Jodhpur State. Many of the relief projects were clearly intended to improve and expand existing water resources and transport infrastructure to aid the movement of essential supplies; others such as the building in 1929 of the royal Umaid Bhavan Palace, now also an international luxury hotel, appear, in this respect, somewhat anomalous. In 1947, Maharaja Hanwant Singh of Jodhpur was guaranteed a liberal supply of grain for famine relief before he would agree to sign the Instrument of Accession taking his state into the Indian Union (Mankekar 1974: 110–11).

Since independence the elected government has taken over almost all of the relief work (Agarwal 1979: 133–5). The former rulers no longer have the means, either financial or bureaucratic, to undertake major famine relief projects. Land reforms in Rajasthan have changed patterns of land ownership and altered landlord–tenant relations, which means that those who traditionally provided funds for charitable works in time of famine now no longer feel the same obligations or have the means to do so (Rosin 1978: 475–88). Nevertheless, there are still some relatively small-scale projects which are undertaken by private individuals, including H.H. Jodhpur.

The Pilgrimage

According to the palace archive, the idea for the 1986 pilgrimage began in 1984 when H.H. Jodhpur was visiting the village of Kolu and saw pilgrims on their way to Ramdeora. He then decided to visit the holy place on foot himself. Although H.H. Jodhpur went on this pilgrimage in his capacity as a private citizen it is hard to think of many private citizens who take along with them a retinue of approximately eighty people, including cooks, secretaries, speech-writers, journalists and a video crew. The pilgrimage required considerable organization and was planned by a series of committees including the ceremony committee for religious matters, a sanitation and water committee, publicity and medical committees.

Since this was a public event the way in which H.H. Jodhpur was portrayed was crucial. One document in the pilgrimage file is particularly revealing for the ways in which H.H. Jodhpur was constructed for the pilgrimage. It lists eleven points 'to ponder' – the first calls for: 'A note detailing brief details of landmarks and achievements of Ramdevji together with the contemporary rulers of the region and the History.' It is clear that any positive links that can be found between Ramdevji and kings are to be drawn out and made explicit – this is reinforced by point 11 which simply states: '"charismatic" announcements, tour undertaken for Rains'.

The overlap of interests between Ramdevji and H.H. Jodhpur and the reinforcing of the similarities between the two went hand-in-hand with a conscious archaizing trend designed to produce a simple and accessible monarchy.[2] The flag of the former princely State of Jodhpur[3] was used, as were traditional utensils. This because 'the atmosphere must be old times and traditional. To relive in past'. 'To relive in [a suitable] past' included the use of 'Humarists [sic] Storey Tellers [sic] . . . Kavi [poets], . . . folk dance and singers to create atmosphere of gaiety but pious. Culture and traditions.'

As H.H. Jodhpur stepped out of Jodhpur city he not only left the town to enter the rural landscape, he also stepped from the secular commodified world where the landscape of Rajasthan serves as the expendable space of nuclear tests into 'a qualitatively different landscape invested with mythological understanding and ritual knowledges intimately linked with bodily routines and practices' (Tilley 1994: 22). The trappings of modernity were rendered invisible to create a nostalgic image of a golden-age ruler who was accessible to his people and understood them to

---

2. Cf. Mayer 1982.

3. The privilege of flying personal standards ended in 1971 with the de-recognition of the princes but the Jodhpur royal household continues to fly a similar flag to that of the former state with the addition of a kite in the centre which represents the goddess Chamunda and so, apparently, transforms the flag from a political into a religious symbol.

the point of dressing like them, speaking their language and using the same form of locomotion across the land. The air-conditioned caravan which H.H. Jodhpur retired to between periods of walking and meeting people was invisible in the public representation of the pilgrimage.

Each day's walk covered between 13 and 19 kilometres, and was broken up by brief halts at prearranged villages where H.H. Jodhpur met local people and no doubt gave 'charismatic announcements'. Each halt was carefully organized with palace staff responsible for making sure that local dignitaries were in place to meet H.H. Jodhpur. H.H. Jodhpur himself was given information, in advance, about the place, its people and its problems. All this information, collected for a religious pilgrimage, could only benefit H.H. Jodhpur if and when he chose either to support a political candidate or enter politics as a candidate for election himself.

The very public nature of this pilgrimage, with press releases, speeches, interviews and police guards for crowd control, served as a clear barometer of H.H. Jodhpur's appeal and relationship with the people and connection to the land. Indeed, the archive includes poems of support and requests from both groups and individuals for H.H. Jodhpur to take particular routes to pass near them because such proximity would make possible the blessing which the *darsan* or viewing of a deity or king confers on those fortunate enough to behold such a sight. When H.H. Jodhpur began the pilgrimage at the temple of the goddess at the fort he sought her blessing and *darsan*. In this way the levels of the divine and the regal were integrated into the practice of the present. H.H. Jodhpur, enhanced by his *darsan* at the fort, became the mediator between the divine and the human worlds. He was then the one whose *darsan* was sought during the pilgrimage by the various groups which make up the state for '[i]n his person, partly through his participation in ritual observances, the king symbolize[s] abundance and prosperity and [is] an auspicious sight (*darshan*), properly fitted out, for his subjects to view' (Price 1989: 563). When H.H. Jodhpur walked through the former state of Jodhpur he was not only symbolically taking possession of the land of his ancestors, but also giving as many of 'his' people as possible the opportunity to have an auspicious *darsan* of him and so re-establish a pre-independence form of contact between ruler and ruled.

I was told that as H.H. Jodhpur walked the last kilometres of his pilgrimage a few clouds gathered over the drought-stricken Ramdeora and as he approached the temple a light shower fell. In 1988 the rains in Jodhpur were good and H.H. Jodhpur paid a brief return visit by car to Ramdeora to complete the vow made in 1986 that he would return to worship when the rains came. The car journey attracted hardly any media attention and did not in any way parallel the significance of the pilgrimage taken on foot. Where walking and experiencing a pilgrimage on foot, taking in the land as it unfolds in a very human time frame, is deeply meaningful and somehow a 'real' pilgrimage experience, a pilgrimage by car, swift and sensible, may be considered almost devoid of genuine contact with the land and people which inspired the pilgrimage in the first place. Tilley, following De Certeau, describes 'an art of walking which is simultaneously an art of thinking and an art of practice or operating in the world'. Movement through space constructs 'spatial stories', forms of narrative understanding. This involves a continuous presencing of previous experiences in present contexts (Tilley 1994: 28). This way of understanding the multiple values of walking through the landscape appears to go some considerable way towards understanding the force of the decision of H.H. Jodhpur to walk across the land of his ancestors.

Some of the complex meanings and ramifications of the pilgrimage undertaken by H.H. Jodhpur can only be grasped when various aspects of the events are placed in appropriate contexts. This involves in particular some understanding of the nature of the Ramdevji cult: the ways in which both Ramdevji and H.H. Jodhpur are figures of god-kings and the ways in which these reverberate in the contemporary context.

The Historical Background to Ramdevji and his Shrine

Both Ramdevji and H.H. Jodhpur are Rajputs and their histories inevitably intertwine (Tod 1920: 104, 299, 843). Ramdevji is considered by many to be a deified Rajput aristocrat, technically of a lower social status than H.H. Jodhpur. H.H. Jodhpur on pilgrimage was, then, on the one hand on his way to fulfil a vow and receive the blessings of a god, and on the other hand paying a visit to a social, albeit deified, inferior. This deified Rajput is worshipped mostly by untouchables and Muslims and his temple was built within a Muslim cemetery (Khan 1993: 31). He is reputed to have had low-caste women disciples and to have performed miracles for the good of all irrespective of gender, caste or creed.

There is, however, according to Khan (1997), another Ramdevji. This second Ramdevji has been reconstructed from oral traditions and is not a tolerant Hindu but an Ismaili Pir (Muslim saint) whose followers, in order to avoid persecution, may have concealed their true faith. The untouchable female disciple of myth who is now used to provide evidence of Ramdevji's ideology of caste and gender equality was, according to Khan, Ramdevji's partner in tantric rites which his Rajput wife refused to take part in (1994: 447).

Whatever the historical truth of Ramdevji, the current popular Ramdevji is a Hindu not a Muslim, a Rajput of royal descent and a champion of communal harmony. However anachronistic such notions of religious, caste and gender equality may be, it is to this last Ramdevji that H.H. Jodhpur made his pilgrimage. The shrine of Ramdevji thus serves as a material 'vehicle for the active recon-struction of remembrance, lending that inherently fluid process an aura of stability' (Thomas 1993: 32).

Ramdevji and the God-king

Beyond the directly royal links outlined above, Ramdevji, by his behaviour and in his concerns, manifests the true nature of the ideal king. Like an ideal king, he deals in the well-being and preservation of those in his domain – irrespective of caste, creed or gender. Preservation is not limited to the right to worship as one chooses and to live in peace; it is more actively the right to enough water and food to live on.

In India, from ancient times, rulers have been considered as uniquely 'in touch' with nature. The earth is a goddess, and Prthu, the first anointed and model king, her husband, compelled her to become fertile again during a famine (Stutley and Stutley 1977: 234–5). All kings are considered to be husbands of the earth (Hara 1973; Dumont 1980: 298; Inden 1978: 45; Hocart 1969: 104–5). As such it is their duty to ensure, by participating in or providing for sacrifices, that the earth is fertilized by rain. Rainwater, which the rule of a good king provides at the right time in the agricultural cycle, is crucial to the right functioning of the world, for 'all society and decency depend on rain' (Derrett 1959: 110). A ' bad king by neglecting his duty is a disaster for his country: rain ceases, the crops fail, creatures perish, in short the harmony with the unseen is disturbed' (Gonda 1959: 174).

Water and drought are central to the myths and histories of Ramdevji and the rulers of Jodhpur. The site of Ramdevji's shrine is in the desert area – where the annual rainfall is measured in millimetres and where Ramdevji is said to have constructed a water tank. He also repaired an old well whose waters are considered curative (Gupta 1966: 82). In Jodhpur itself the recurrent droughts are, in myth, explained by events surrounding the foundation of the Jodhpur fort. When a holy man was forced to move to make way for the construction of the fort he responded by cursing the fort to have only unpalatable water and for the state to suffer from droughts every few years (Tod 1920: 949). Here we have the common connection made between a good ruler and a plentiful water supply and a bad ruler and drought. The transformation of empty land into a place of habitation and a political centre requires not just naming and building but also to be in accord with the powers of nature in the form of the spiritual forces pre-existing on the land. When the king errs, the whole state suffers.

H.H. Jodhpur himself gave the following as the motive for his pilgrimage: 'For peace among the disturbed villagers, for rain, for moral support I vowed that I would walk on foot to Ramdeora and pray to Ramdeoji Baba to give courage and strength to our people in these hard times' (UBP 1986).[4] In a more secular vein there are the charitable trusts set up by H.H. Jodhpur which do some work in the

4. Cf. Cadène 1991.

area of drought relief and in one interview given by H.H. Jodhpur during the pilgrimage itself, two and a half pages of a six-page interview transcript are taken up with environmental issues, mainly dealing with tree-planting schemes to prevent further desertification and to attract water, ways of reclaiming sand dunes that would not further degrade the environment, and ways in which the state government has failed to carry through to completion a lift canal project for Jodhpur.

Ramdevji and the Trans-caste State

Politics in India has always involved castes and the caste system. Here too, the shrine of Ramdevji has a special significance. Traditionally attracting mainly rural untouchables and Muslims, Ramdevji's cult, in a time of increasing communal tension, has become more and more popular with higher castes for a variety of reasons and now has an urban following spread throughout India (Binford 1976: 125n; Bharati 1963: 142; Pinney 1995: 92, 110n34). It should also be noted that in visiting Ramdevji's shrine H.H. Jodhpur was also recalling a particular debt the Jodhpur rulers owe to the Meghwals (untouchables) of Rajasthan. It is said that a Meghwal offered himself for the sacrifice necessary at the founding of the fort, thus guaranteeing the security of the fort and the state of Jodhpur.

When H.H. Jodhpur goes to worship at the deified Rajput's *samadhi* (resting place) he is not directly calling on the support of the Muslims of the state (though rulers do in Rajasthan traditionally have the support of Muslims), but it is impossible nowadays for local people to dissociate the shrine of Ramdevji from ideas of tolerance towards Muslims. Ramdevji is worshipped by low-caste Muslims as well as Hindus, and prominent among the tales of Ramdevji's life are those in which Muslim *pirs* (saints) from Mecca visit him and are convinced of Ramdevji's saintliness by the miracles he performs for them (Binford 1976: 138–9). Since partition fewer and fewer Muslims actually attend the fair at Ramdeora and so H.H. Jodhpur made the pilgrimage to a Hindu god/Muslim *pir* precisely when many Muslims have ceased to go themselves.

Traditional Rajput rulers themselves very often owed their position to the continued support and goodwill of Mughal emperors, and many of Rajasthan's pre-independence prime ministers and state officials were Muslims. Rajput customs are often a syncretic mixture of Hindu and Muslim practices. There were important marriages arranged between the rulers of Jodhpur and the Mughals (Ziegler 1978: 222, 229, 230, 238) which made the sister's sons (*bhanej*) of such unions Muslims, and the potential of overlapping categories allowed for the inclusion of Muslims into the medieval Rajput hierarchy.

The traditions generally represent the Rajput *jati* (caste) as being divided into two categories: Muslim (or Turk) and Hindu. This category of 'Muslim' within the Rajput *jati* did not include all Muslims, but only those who were warriors and who possessed sovereignty and power equal to or greater than the Hindu Rajput. The Jodhpur fort actually contains a shrine to a Muslim warrior and a half-finished and little-known seventeenth-century mosque (Tillotson 1987: 136). The origins of these are too complicated to go into here. The Muslim Emperor in particular held a position of high rank and esteem, and the traditions often equate him with Ram, the pre-eminent culture hero and god of the Hindu Rajput (Ziegler 1978: 235). Contemporary clear-cut distinctions between Muslim and Hindu are therefore belied by a long and complex history and the current public statements of tolerance by the Jodhpur royal household towards Muslims are as much a result of a long tradition of association with Muslims as they are of modern liberal ethics and humanistic politics.

At a time when the maharajas of India no longer have political power by virtue of high birth it is possible for those among them who so choose to be able to assert a 'traditional' capacity to bridge the Hindu/Muslim, urban/rural and clean caste/untouchable divide. This 'traditional' right of mediation is achieved by evoking (Moore 1978) and foregrounding those aspects of 'tradition' such as the ruler being responsible for all those in his state irrespective of caste, or which may serve current purposes and needs (cf. Freitag 1989: 208; Ramusack 1978: 159).

H.H. Jodhpur, for those who support him, is just such a traditional symbol of unity. He himself recalls being taught in childhood that as maharaja he had no caste because he had to treat all people as the same and be responsible for all who called on him in his territory. Ram Rajya is a term frequently heard in the context of the contemporary evocation of the golden age of the rule of just kings and it is probably as well to remember that in Rajasthan '[i]n 1952 in India's first democratic election campaign, the party of landowners called itself the Ram Rajya Parishad: a title evocative of that Golden Age, the Regime of God, when those whom he meant to rule, those born to rule, ruled' (Stern and Kamal 1974: 282). This was a deeply conservative party (Tinker-Walker 1956:228). Religion and politics are never completely separated and when H.H. Jodhpur, no matter what his consciously stated intentions were, undertook the pilgrimage to Ramdeora at a time when the idea of Ram Raj was again in the air, the connection between religion and politics could not but be reinforced. Despite such conservative associations, H.H. Jodhpur's pilgrimage was a complex undertaking in which he could appear both traditional and modern, regal and in touch with the masses, politically correct and historically justified. All this stands out even more sharply when contrasted with the events at Ayodhya where pilgrimage has been used to divide Hindu from Muslim and clean caste Hindu from untouchable, and also with pilgrimages which have been *explicitly* used as a means of gaining electoral advantage over ruling and other political parties.

Conclusion

H.H. Jodhpur is not a constitutional monarch and it is only recently that many of the ceremonies and rituals of the court in Jodhpur have been revived or begun for the first time. Part of the reason why so much energy and thought goes into these rituals is precisely that political power and land has been taken away and what remains for the descendants of the princes of India is their traditional ritual role. Shorn of the guarantee of political pre-eminence and economic power, former rulers may develop and expand their role as the only traditional unifying figure in the state, as symbolic protector of all and not just one caste group or religious community. This can be done in the name of tradition, religion and cultural values without ever explicitly entering the domain of public politics.

Other important factors leading to the decision to undertake the pilgrimage were the drought and the perceived inability of the government to deal quickly and decisively to prevent crisis (Mathur and Jayal 1993). This led to increasing disillusionment with the power of elected government to act when required for the good of the people, and resulted in a general nostalgic yearning on the part of some for past days of regal power. The tales of mythical kings such as Vikramaditya gave way during the course of my fieldwork to more strident stories of Ram Rajya. Environmental crisis, disillusionment with the local and national government, ancient traditions, religious practice, folk knowledge and an increasingly ritually confident and active H.H. Jodhpur all combined to produce a context in which the pilgrimage by a former ruler across a desert landscape in a time of severe drought and hardship for those on the land not only served as a spiritual journey for H.H. Jodhpur himself but acted as a physical and visible reminder of what the ideal rule of just kings was once (in memory and myth) like. In this way the pilgrimage served as a critique and protest against the inaction of the government of the day as well as a reminder of the possibilities for communal harmony which belief (if not fact) located in the time when there were Maharajas of Jodhpur and the desert fed the people who understood its ways and behaved accordingly.

This chapter has described and attempted to unravel some of the complexities of a contemporary, primarily Rajput, cultural landscape where culture can be conceptualized as the agent working on the natural medium of the land in order to produce a meaningful world which lies 'beyond science' (Hirsch 1995: 9). Clearly, the landscape portrayed here from the perspective of a Rajput elite is not the same in all respects as that of an untouchable and would be quite different again from the Rajasthan landscape as understood by an international tourist. However, when one gives way to

> thoughts of membership in social groups, of participation in activities that transcend the concerns of particular people, of close involvements with whole communities and

their enduring historical traditions . . . a sense of place may gather unto itself a potent religious force. Fueled by sentiments of inclusion, belonging, and connectedness to the past, sense of place roots individuals in the social and cultural soils from which they have sprung together, holding them there in the grip of a shared identity, a localised version of selfhood (Basso 1996: 85).

For all that, there is no ideology-free space or place, and for some the land works better than for others.

Acknowledgements

I wish to acknowledge the support of the British Academy in sponsoring my attendance at the WAC conference where the first version of this chapter was delivered.

References

Manuscript

UBP = manuscripts held in the offices at Umaid Bhavan Palace, Jodhpur.
UBP 1986 *Padyatra.*

Published sources

Agarwal, B.D. 1979. *Rajasthan District Gazetteers: Jodhpur.* Jaipur: Mahavir Printing Press.
Badhwar, I., Rahman, M., Pratap, A., Mahurkar, U., Pillai, S., Ahmed, F. and Midha, T. 1987. The devastating drought. *India Today.* 15 September. 8–20.
Basso, K.H. 1996. Wisdom sits in places: notes on a Western Apache landscape, in S. Feld and K.H. Basso (eds) *Senses of Place.* Santa Fe, New Mexico: School of American Research Press. 53–90.
Bharati, A. 1963. Pilgrimage in the Indian tradition. *History of Religions* 3(1) 135–67.
Binford, M.R. 1976. Mixing in the color of Ram of Ranuja, in B.L. Smith (ed.) *Hinduism: New Essays in the History of Religions.* Leiden: E.J. Brill. 120–42.
Cadène, P. 1991. State and society in Rajasamand, a small Indian town in South Rajasthan, in J. Pouchepadass and H. Stern (eds) *Purusartha 13, De la Royauté*

à L'Etat dans le Monde Indien, Paris: Editions de l'Ecole des Hautes Etudes en Sciences Sociales.

Derrett, J.D.M. 1959. Bhu-Bharana, Bhu-Palana, Bhu-Bhojana: an Indian conundrum. *Bulletin of the School of Oriental and African Studies* 22 108–23.

Dumont, L. 1980 [1962]. The conception of kingship in ancient India. *Homo Hierarchicus*. Chicago: University of Chicago Press. 287–313.

Erskine, K.D. 1909. *Rajputana Gazetteers Vol. III A. The Western Rajputana States Residency and the Bikaner Agency*. Allahabad: Pioneer Press.

Freitag, S.B. 1989. State and community: symbolic popular protest in Banaras's public arenas, in S.B. Freitag (ed.) *Culture and Power in Banaras: Community, Performance, and Environment, 1800–1980*. Berkeley: University of California Press. 203–28.

Gonda, J. 1959. The sacred character of ancient Indian kingship. *Numen*, Supplement 4. Leiden: E.J. Brill. 172–80.

Gupta, C.S. 1966. *Census of India, 1961*, vol. 14, Rajasthan, Part 7-B, Fairs and Festivals.

Hara, M. 1973. The king as husband of the earth. *Asiatische Studien* 27(2) 97–114.

Henderson, C. 1994. Famines and droughts in Western Rajasthan: desert cultivators and periodic resource stress, in K. Schomer, J. Erdman, D. Lodrick, and L. Rudolph (eds) *The Idea of Rajasthan: explorations in regional identity*. New Delhi: Manohar. 1–29.

Hirsch, E. 1995. Landscape: between place and space, in E. Hirsch and M. O'Hanlon (eds) *The Anthropology of Landscape: Perspectives on Place and Space*. Oxford: Oxford University Press. 1–30.

Hocart, A.M. 1969 [1927]. *Kingship*. Oxford: Oxford University Press.

Inden, R. 1978. Ritual, authority and cyclic time in Hindu kingship, in J.F. Richards (ed.) *Kingship and Authority in South Asia*. Madison: University of Wisconsin. 28–73.

Kapur, A. 1985. Actors, pilgrims, kings and gods: the Ramlila at Ramnagar, *Contributions to Indian Sociology* 19(1) 57–74.

Khan, D.-S. 1993. L'Origine Ismaélienne du culte Hindoue de Ramdeo Pir, *Revue de l'histoire des religions*. 27–47.

—— 1994. Deux rites Tantriques dans une communauté d'Intouchables au Rajasthan. *Revue de l'histoire des religions*. 443–62.

—— 1997. *Conversions and Shifting Identities: Ramdev Pir and the Ismailis in Rajasthan*. Delhi: Manohar.

Koshteh, K. 1995. *Greening the Desert: Agro-Economic Impact of Indira Gandhi Canal of Rajasthan*. Delhi: Renaissance Publishing House.

Leaf, M.J. 1992. Irrigation and authority in Rajasthan. *Ethnology* 31 115–32.

Mankekar, D.R. 1974. *Accession to Extinction: The Story of the Indian Princes*. Delhi: Vikas.

Mathur, K. and Jayal, N.G. 1993. Parliamentary response to drought 1987. *The Indian Journal of Political Science* **54**(3–4) 352–68.

Mayer, A.M. 1982. Perceptions of princely rule: perspectives from a biography, in T.N. Madan (ed.) *Way of Life: Householder, King, Renouncer.* Delhi: Vikas. 127–54.

Moore, T. 1978. *Evocation.* Birmingham University. Unpublished manuscript.

Pinney, C. 1995. Moral topophilia: the significations of landscape in Indian oleographs, in E. Hirsch and M. O'Hanlon (eds) *The Anthropology of Landscape: Perspectives on Place and Space.* Oxford: Oxford University Press. 78–113.

Price, P. 1989. Kingly Models in Indian political behaviour. *Asian Survey* **29**(6) 559–72.

Ramakrishna, Y.S. 1994. Droughts in the Indian arid zone, in R.P. Singh and S. Singh (eds) *Sustainable Development of the Indian Arid Zone: a Research Perspective.* Jodhpur: Scientific Publishers. 7–13.

Ramusack, B.N. 1978. *The Princes of India in the Twilight of Empire: Dissolution of a Patron-Client System 1914–1939.* Cincinnati: Ohio University Press.

Rosin, R.T. 1978. Peasant adaptation as process in land reform: a case study, in S. Vatuk (ed.) *American Studies in the Anthropology of India.* New Delhi: Manohar 460–95.

Rosin, R.T. 1994. Locality and frontier: securing livelihood in the Aravalli zone of central Rajasthan, in K. Schomer, J. Erdman, D. Lodrick and L. Rudolph (eds) *The Idea of Rajasthan: Explorations in Regional Identity.* Delhi: Manohar. 30–63.

Seneviratne, H.L. 1977. Politics and pageantry: universalisation of ritual in Sri Lanka. *Man* **12** 65–75.

Stern, R.W. and Kamal, K.L. 1974. Class, status and party in Rajasthan. *Journal of Commonwealth and Comparative Politics* **12**(3) 276–96.

Stutley, M. and Stutley, J. 1977. *Dictionary of Hinduism: Its Mythology, Folklore and Development 1500 BC–AD 1500.* London: RKP.

Thomas, J. 1993. The politics of vision and the archaeologies of landscape, in B. Bender (ed.) *Landscape: Politics and Perspectives.* Oxford: Berg. 19–48.

Tilley, C. 1994. *A Phenomenology of Landscape: Places, Paths and Monuments.* Oxford: Berg.

Tillotson, G.H.R. 1987. *The Rajput Palaces: The Development of an Architectural Style 1450–1750.* New Haven: Yale.

Tinker-Walker, I. 1956. Rajasthan, in S.V. Kogekar and R.L. Park (eds) *Reports on the Indian General Elections 1951–52.* Bombay: Popular Books Depot 222–34.

Tod, J. 1920 [1832]. *Annals and Antiquities of Rajasthan.* London: Oxford University Press.

Ziegler, N.P. 1978. Some notes on Rajput loyalties during the Mughal Period, in J.F. Richards (ed.) *Kingship and Authority in South Asia.* Madison: University of Wisconsin. 215–51.

-13-

Landscapes of Separation: Reflections on the Symbolism of By-pass Roads in Palestine

Tom Selwyn

It is my assessment that we need to separate from the Palestinians. Simply separate ourselves, physically – us here and them there. And I say this as I sit in my . . . living room 50 meters from the Green Line . . . (Israeli Prime Minister Ehud Barak). (Ha'aretz Newspaper 19.5.00)

Preliminary note

This chapter was completed in March 2000 while this note was written at the time when page proofs were corrected in October 2000. As it stands in its March form, however, the chapter bears directly on the tumultuous and terrible events presently unfolding in the area. Apart from the road construction itself (contemplation of which yields its own distinctive perspective on the lineage of the crisis) links are drawn between the uneven economic development which has characterized the region since 1948 and the notions of separation which the chapter explores. One underlying assumption is that any lasting peace in the area would need to be built on a dual strategy. A first part would be a programme of economic development leading to both Israelis and Palestinians having parity of access to land and resources in the region (enabling the latter, for the first time, to become equal partners in a peace-making process). A second would consist of a systematic effort to imagine a future of co-existence based on the re-membering of a Mediterranean history of joint Arab/Jewish formation over many centuries. If a reader were to come away from the chapter wondering what alternatives there are to this dual approach, apart from the apocalyptic ones which some espouse, then the chapter would have served its purpose.

Introduction

This chapter reflects on regimes of separation and movement regulation in occupied Palestine, and on the landscapes that support these regimes. Its particular focus is upon the network of by-pass roads bisecting the West Bank, which connect up

Israel with the Israeli settlements in that territory, and the prime interest is in the symbolic function of these roads. The argument is that they tell a particular kind of narrative about the relationship between Israelis and Palestinians, a narrative which speaks of the inevitability of separation between the two peoples just at a moment when the region is moving through what is presently known as a 'peace process'. A basic purpose of the chapter is to stimulate reflection on the implications of, on the one hand, the erection of boundaries and strictures of movement in Israel/Palestine and, on the other, the possibilities and conditions of their dissolution.

The interpretation unfolds against a roughly sketched backdrop of regional and Jewish pasts, partly empirical and partly provocative conjecture, as a way of imagining alternative futures. It tries to loosen the sense of relentless persecution that links 'peace' with separation. Although this persecution-centred posture is not shared by all Israelis, it is shared by a majority, among whom are even some members of the Israeli Left. In challenging it, therefore, the intention is to move closer to a position from which to consider how landscapes of mixing and reconciliation might look.

The chapter, and in particular the section entitled 'Separation and Uneven Development', draws extensively on Yaacov Garb's as yet unpublished work on questions of occupation and the management of mobility in the West Bank and Gaza. Garb chronicles the pervasiveness of movement-related phenomena in the history of Israel's occupation of the Palestinian territories, as part of his broader attempt to understand the relationship of mobility and its management to power and political life. He describes the increasingly ornate and at time surreal technologies of identification, boundary-making, and mobility-management necessary to support the kind of large-scale separation increasingly proposed by Israel as the basis of a 'peace agreement'. When taken to its logical conclusion, the coupled repression of Palestinian autonomy and movement which Garb describes points to something like the subjugated separation that threatens to emerge if the Oslo 'Peace Process' becomes what Benvenisti has termed 'the Peace of the Generals'.

The chapter also builds upon two closely linked aspects of the symbolic geography of Israel/Palestine which I have explored elsewhere (1995, 1996). The first is an anthropological concern with the Israeli landscape as one of the symbolic ingredients of nationalist mythology, while the second is a more practical interest in the present and future of tourism in Palestine. Taken together these complementary concerns have led to a developing interest in the relationship between ideas of nationalist and cosmopolitan cultural heritage in the region.

Inscriptions on the Landscape

In October 1998 in the UK, the *Guardian* newspaper reported that in 1995 Israeli and Palestinian negotiators had signed a document known as 'Military Order 50' which, as the article explained, 'shows a network of by-pass roads linking the Jewish settlements and slicing the West Bank into Salami-like pieces'. This was closely followed in Israel by a report in *Ha'aretz* (19.11.98) about plans to build a new bypass road around the El Aroub refugee camp south of Bethlehem. The present road skirting the camp, it was explained, was the site of a Hamas ambush in 1996 when two Israeli doctors had been killed. The article continued:

> The property which would be expropriated to make way for the road is . . . the finest agricultural land (belonging to the Palestinian village of Beit Umar) . . . and the road would also disrupt the operation of El Aroub's agricultural school.

Pursuing the theme of bypass roads and the disruption caused by them, the UK *Observer* newspaper (29.11.98) described by-pass road-building south of Hebron:

> Across the geometric furrows . . . of ploughed earth . . . a monstrous yellow bulldozer is making its way lazily down the valley. Accompanied by soldiers, it is pushing the earth in its path, making way for one of the costliest roads in the world.

By-pass roads in the Occupied Territories have been, as these reports indicate, the subject of widespread interest in local and foreign press. This is not difficult to understand as they are potent expressions of struggle in a bitterly contested landscape.

Figure 13.1 Slicing through hills in the West Bank

Figure 13.2 Road building through farmland

As noted already, the roads we are concerned with are highways which connect Israel to the 200 or so Israeli settlements in the West Bank. They are wide, without any sharp bends, and by-pass Palestinian towns, villages and refugee camps. They have a minimal relationship to the network of Palestinians roads (which tend to wind their way around hills and through the centres of populated areas). Sometimes, as in the case of the road under a suburb of Bethlehem, the roads go through tunnels while some sections, on the northern edge of Jerusalem for example, are perched on flyovers.

The roads have a dual function. One is to enable Israeli settlers and their visitors to reach the West Bank settlements without having to go through Palestinian towns, thereby keeping ordinary Palestinians out of sight. Another is to serve as security conduits. Like the Hausmann-like boulevards in Jerusalem itself, by-pass roads were built with military security in mind.

From Israel's point of view, roads built in the captured territories serve to bolster its control of the West Bank, ease movement of Israeli forces and settlers, and enhance the territorial contiguity of the occupied areas with Israel proper. From the Palestinian point of view, the roads negate the possibility of autonomous control, restrict movement to precisely the bounds set by Israel, and fragment the territories beyond recognition.

The West Bank settlements themselves are built as if they were fortresses on the crests of hills, surrounded by fences and surveillance equipment. Linked as they are to the arteries of roads described, they look out over a landscape of continuing conquest sculpted by the appliances of occupation and underpinned by principles of avoidance. This is a landscape of separation in which technologies of recognition and visualization (video cameras along fences, checkpoint apparatuses with the capacity to read the retinas of Palestinians in a fraction of a second, for example) vie ironically for spatial dominance with modes of keeping the local population invisible.

Routes in Imagination and Memory

Remembering that roads have been woven into the symbolic textures of various cultures (the cult film *Easy Rider* is just one example) we may ask what does this landscape of separation, this asphalt text, tell us about contemporary Israel/Palestine?

Being concerned with fantasies of separation and in line with the *modus operandi* here of working with the lightest of ethnographic brush strokes, we may approach the question by picking out some moments of Israeli historical imagination associated with roads and/or, more generically, routes. The aim here is to trace a structure of nationalist thinking which seems comparable to that made familiar from other geographical contexts by authors such as Kedouri (1960) and Smith (1991). As they have pointed out, nationalist myths frequently have a tripartite structure. The starting point is an imagined 'golden age'. The middle section is marked by national tragedy and subjugation. The final part celebrates a resurgent nation triumphant in the face of adversity.

The routes out of Egypt celebrated each year at the Passover meal, and the roads, marked at the festivals of *Succot* and *Shavuot*, that the pilgrims took to the Jerusalem Temple in the Roman period, seem attended by connotations of freedom and community. The routes which criss-crossed the historical Mediterranean world come with associations of cities, trade and cosmopolitanism. Braudel (1973) writes of these and tells of a world in which Jews maintained networks of relations across the region, enabling them to occupy significant roles in cultural, scientific, kinship and economic life there. Before 1492 (see below) this world is spoken of in Israel as a historical golden age (Barnavi 1992). From then on, however, the theme of expulsion becomes more insistent until the routes of the Holocaust – the roads of dispossession, railroads of deportation, routes of despair, defeat, and death – seem emblematic of the darkest period of all.

From early in the last century in Palestine roads played a seminal role in the mythologies surrounding the early Jewish settlement there, being linked to the heroic establishment of territorial facts on the ground through the rapid erection of tower and stockade settlements. Road building was accompanied by a whole culture of songs and stories about the brigades which forged the transport infrastructure that made possible the establishment of the state itself.

Finally, as already described, there are the roads of the West Bank, which carry their own sets of connotations. They have become synonymous with the establishment, maintenance and management of deepening occupation and have contributed to a bizarrely doubled inhabitation of the Territories by what is imagined to be two peoples or two societies. Despite being packed into the same physical space, the two societies live in markedly different worlds, which, if Israelis had their way, would intersect as little as possible. Palestinian villages are (compared with Israeli settlements) on the whole, poor. They are linked with one another by networks of back roads and (oddly) the occasional segment of by-pass road. Israelis live in the settlements, nowadays surrounded by fences and encircling patrol roads, that are connected by high quality highways to one another and to Israel itself. They have some of the most spacious (and cheapest) houses in Israel, with the workplaces, shopping malls, and theatres of Jerusalem and Tel Aviv only a short car-ride away.

Understanding the complex tapestry of Israeli imaginings about roads is clearly way beyond the scope of this chapter and the making of these references, and the drawing of preliminary implications from them, falls far short of the rigorous social and symbolic analysis which would be needed effectively to discuss the cultural function of roads in Israel. Nevertheless the references do provide some scattered starting points for the sort of speculative counterpoint (to more established historiographies) which this chapter is attempting to chart.

The more conventional nationalist narrative, such as some of those described by Kedouri (1960) and Smith (1991), could start with the mythic golden age in which Biblical routes are linked to senses of freedom and a sense of being a People. The roads of the medieval Mediterranean carry that sense into a more proximate history in which the routes of the region which articulated Jewish life across the region were imagined as the communication highways of the world. However, the expulsion of Jews and Muslims from reunified Spain in 1492 is often referred to in Israel as a determining moment when the dangers of such communication came to be learnt. The terrible dénouement to this line of thought comes from ideas about Holocaust transportation, which forced roads into a symbolic world filled with death and defeat and the closing down of all communication with others. But the story starts again with a new beginning in which the weakness and extreme vulnerability of individuals and communities in Europe are thought of as being heroically translated into the seemingly invincible strength of a nation state built on an extremely effective infrastructure of roads. We can trace the tripartite structure to which we drew attention above: mytho/historical golden age(s) followed by tragedy followed, in turn, by rebirth. Looked at this way it appears to be a classic tale of triumphant nationalism.

In the present context, though, the concern is with one of the implications of the latest chapter of the story, for the most recent entry of roads into this mythic architecture has been the West Bank highways described here. The message here seems pretty clear. In the world today 'peace' must be linked to the 'security' of occupation, military dominion, and separation. After all, asks the voice of conventional Israeli narrative, was not all that communication, and the cosmopolitan life it made possible, swept away to be replaced by mass destruction?

A moment's thought, however, reveals that this is only one out of a number of possible narratives which could be composed out of the raw material about roads in Jewish historical imaginings and that there is nothing logically inevitable about the ending as we have it so far. In order to explore a little further why the story has taken the form it has done, and in order then to enable a thought or two about possible alternative endings, we need to take a step back.

Building a History of Jewish Separation

There is a caricatured history many contemporary Israelis tend to teach themselves. It has been the staple of popular conceptions about Israel abroad and is a part of a more general frame into which our particular road narratives are located. Its hallmark is an enforced but ultimately protective separation of the Jews from a persecuting alien world. This story gives us a wandering people, shunned, persecuted and separated in walled-off ghettos, beyond the Pale of Settlement or, most starkly, in concentration camps. The uniqueness and vitality of Jewish culture and the very survival of the Jewish people are conceptually linked with the notion of a flame which has been kept alight despite, and in large measure because of, this harsh environment.

This account of historical separation has many manifestations in Israel today, where it pervades much of the thinking about the present and the future. For example, in her fine analysis of the Museum of the Diaspora in Tel-Aviv, Golden (1996) draws our attention to the section of the exhibition devoted to Jewish life in Spain in the Middle Ages. Following descriptions of the Spanish Golden Age there is a display entitled Eclipse. This documents the gradual taking-over of Spain by the Christians, and the ultimate expulsion of the Jews in 1492. At the point where the signing of the documents to expel the Jews is depicted, the explanatory text reads 'with a stroke of a pen, a 1000 years of Jewish life in Spain came to an end'. Golden comments: 'In this very statement, the exhibition appears to question the worth of those thousand years. Look, we are told, all that glory came to nothing.'

The notion of cultural eclipse and the vulnerability which follows is the subject of an essay by Don and Lea Handelman (1991). At first glance the object of their analysis seems quite removed from Golden's museum. In fact, one might suggest, museums and memorials in this particular case are complementary. The Handelmans are also concerned with ideas about the inevitability of expulsions and separations, and the marking of these by memorials to the violent death which often accompanied them. Such memorials, they argue, have supplied some of the building blocks of Israeli nationalism. As they observe, individuals may die but 'their lives are given up in order that something of greater worth may be received or preserved'. In our present context this approximates to a view that nothing but the state can be trusted to provide the necessary security and well-being.

The other part of this line of thought is that the security and cultural renewal promised by the state depends, precisely, upon the enshrinement of the idea of cultural separation between peoples in the history it teaches its citizens. Or, to put this another way, the fear expressed in the Diaspora Museum, and by implication in the memorials, is that cultural mixing will be followed by cultural eclipse and death. Only the nation can redeem that death and it is this thought which also leads on to a sense that national identity requires the complete separation of nations.

Tragically, it is these notions which are reshaping the region's future in the image of a (mis)remembered past.

In large measure, the dominant élite who came to Palestine before the establishment of the State of Israel, and the many more who gathered in the wake of the Holocaust, sensed themselves as implanted on a narrow strip of safe territory, amidst a threatening sea of hostile others. Despite more than a millennium-long history of joint formation, and the fact that in some ways historical cultural affinities between Jew and Arab have far outweighed the differences, it has been all too easy to transpose Arabs into the role of what a Kleinian might call 'the persecuting other'.

One finds resonances of this imagination of separation on the largest macro-historical scale in the writings of ideologues such as Samuel Huntingdon (e.g. 1997). According to this presently lionized best-selling US political scientist, the world in general is moving towards cultural disengagement and global apartheid.

Separation and Uneven Development

Although the 1948 war created a fairly sharp border between Israel and its Arab neighbours, it was hard to maintain for long. The border was, in fact, highly permeable for years. Formulations, such as those by Jabotinsky, of an 'iron wall' between Israel and the Arab states remained largely rhetorical.

After 1967, when the West Bank and Gaza fell into Israeli hands, the question of the boundary between Israel and a largely Arab population became real. Initially a sharp border was reinstated through Military Order 1 in Gaza and Military Order 5 in the West Bank, declaring the Occupied Territories closed military zones, legally obstructing all ingoing and outgoing traffic. However Moshe Dayan, who was Defence Minister until 1973 and the primary architect of policies of occupation, insisted on open bridges between the Territories and Jordan, and on a permeable boundary between the Territories and Israel (Kimmeding and Migdal 1993). Thus separation soon gave way to an opening of borders under a series of increasingly permissive General Entry Permits, allowing entry to classes of people (rather than individuals) to travel without individual permission. In 1972 the Israeli military lifted all restrictions on movement (Roy 1995). Closure of this border remained only as a formal legal potential.

In the two decades after 1967, the combination of open borders and military occupation by a developed of an undeveloped country led to a very one-sided entwinement of the two entities. The inhabitants of the Territories were, at once, a pool of cheap labour, the second largest market for Israeli goods, and a source of resources. By 1987 about 120,000–180,000 workers commuted daily or weekly to employment in Israel. This represents between one- and two-thirds of the Palestinian labour force; movement of goods and people was on strictly unequal terms, with Palestinian independence and control of resources strictly curtailed. Flows across the borders served Israeli purposes as the Territories grew increasingly dependent on the Israeli economy.

It was in the context of the uneven development taking place either side of the borders, and the growth of its visibility, that the *intifada* broke out in December 1987.

Many of the expressions of Palestinian resistance and Israeli response to it involved mobility and regulation of movement, both sides in differing ways and contexts attempting to hinder and/or promote movement within the Territories. From an early response of attempting to restore mobility, Israel moved into a period of increasing restrictions. In 1988, for example, Palestinians convicted of security offences were issued a green identity card, rather than the regular orange one, and in 1989 Palestinians wanting to visit Gaza were issued a magnetic identity card. The general restrictions on Palestinian movement increased through the 1990s. Open borders and free movement came to be associated in Israel with feelings of terror and vulnerability.

From summer 1992 border closures became more extended. Bombings were followed by checkpoint installations, suicide attacks by the reassertion of the Green Line and, in 1994, the fencing in of the entire Gaza Strip, a precedent in the international history of territorial engineering that has gone surprisingly unremarked. Procedures for entering and leaving the Strip became stricter, movement between Gaza and the West Bank became more difficult, and the social and economic gulf between the two parts of the emerging state of Palestine deepened, despite international agreements to prevent that from taking place.

In the period before and after the coming to power of Netanyahu, modes of separation were progressively ratcheted up. There were partial closures, total closures, internal closures (which prevented movement between villages and towns, even within the Territories), and curfews banning movement outside houses during certain hours, sometimes for weeks on end. The management of mobility had reached all the way to the level of the household.

And yet there was, and remains, something strange and incomplete about this chronology of events as presented here. The fact was that even during the strictest closure, determined Palestinians could in fact still cross over the bulk of the long and mostly unguarded border between the Territories and Israel. Everyone knew this, knows it now, and recognizes the absurdity of the idea of a border which really prevents entries and crossings. But we can say that one effect of the fences was (as it is) to stir the imagination towards ever more elaborate notions of the 'persecuting other' and the desirability of permanent separation.

From here on mobility became a commodity and a source of political control and economic value. Its withdrawal could be used as a punishment, its granting a potent enticement to co-operation (a valuable perk for Palestinian VIPs, or a tempting lever for recruitment to collaboration with Israeli Security Services). An elaborate permit system grew up, with its accompanying brokers. At the same time Israel began to import foreign workers from abroad to replace Palestinians whose arrival had begun to become tenuous and costly.

At the end of the 1990s, Israel pushed to accelerate the Final Status talks that were intended to culminate the preceding decade over which the separation preparations had taken place and Palestinians had been softened up. In these talks, an energetic Barak, heading a robust Israel that had refined its techniques of direct and indirect domination, would meet a frail, ill Arafat, representing an exhausted people that had been physically and socially divided. Decades of attrition, fragmentation, and dependency had laid the ground for the ironic situation in which the longed-for separateness of the emerging Palestine would clinch its subservience rather than snapping the constraints of domination. Now that it had consolidated the settlements and corridors it had strategically extended throughout the territories, Israel saw itself as having little to lose from cordoning itself off from, and nominally granting independence to, what remained.

Notions of separation are prominent even among the Left. Yizhak Rabin talked explicitly about separation from the Palestinians and of a quite literal security fence between Israel and the Territories. Separation was seen by some as strengthening the Palestinian cause by reaffirming, albeit by closure, the borders of an emerging political entity. These borders had been blurred over the decades in which the Territories had been occupied. 'Get Gaza out of Tel Aviv' became one popular slogan on the Left, and more recently, *Shalom Ulehipared* (roughly: peace/goodbye and to part) another.

In late 1999 and early 2000, surrealistic visions of landscape/social engineering for separation surfaced extensively, no longer as the wishful fantasies of a fringe, but as serious proposals by the Barak government, with broad public support.

During that time, Barak scarcely made any speech on national policies without reiterating the necessity for separation. In a revival of the plans by Moshe Shahal, the public security minister in Rabin's government, Barak proposed a security fence along the final settlement border, like the contemporary one encircling Gaza. The estimated cost was a million dollars per kilometre, the same rule-of-thumb cost for a major modern highway. This guarded and patrolled barrier would be perforated only at designated passage points. Gaza and the West Bank were to be linked by fifteen to eighteen safe passage points, allowing highly supervised passage along constrained corridors.

'Good fences', Barak has said, 'make good neighbours.'

Routes of Reconciliation?

In the short term, the kind of separation imagined by Israel's senior political establishment, ideologically in tune with powerful political and academic voices abroad and apparently supported by a majority of the Israeli public, may be a possibility in the same way that the massive social experiment of the occupation itself was possible. But in the medium or long term it is, of course, a practical impossibility. Ideas of a fence along some resurrected Green Line, of an elevated highway from Gaza to the West Bank are the stuff of fantasy on a grand and tragic scale. Besides, 'fencing off' seems out-of-step in a supposedly globalizing world (until we notice that what is really happening here – as elswhere – is a globalizing towards the West which coincides with the erection of barriers to the East).

How might it be possible, then, to think about routes of reconciliation?

If it is right to suggest that the present and future of the region is being shaped in the image of a (mis)remembered past, a project involving a future based on engagement rather than disengagement would thus need to begin with an attempt at re-remembering.

The work of the historian and critic Ammiel Alcalay (1993; 1996) suggests that such a project as this might begin by remembering that as well as the dispossession of Palestinians in the process of state building, the formation of Israel and its aftermath also involved the subjugation of entire seams of experience and historical memory possessed by Jews from the Arab world. For Alcalay (1993), re-thinking our way into this tradition would provide a starting point from which imaginings of different futures might be possible.

Alcalay's own writings, together with that of the Arab Jewish writers for whose voices he has provided a space, as well as the work of such authors as Benjamin Arbel (1996), Ron Barkai (1996) and Amitav Ghosh (1992), make up an emerging historiography which has come systematically to challenge the kind of remembered histories we have sketched here, the ones which, when they are assembled, make up what Rabbi Louis Jacobs (personal communication) has termed the 'lachrymose version' of Jewish history.

Alcalay writes with the angry poignancy of one deeply engaged with the absurdities of ideas such as separation, observing that the writers assembled in his recently edited volume of new Israeli writing

> . . . have done everything in their power to use the materials of the personal and collective past and present to create new memories of the future, alternatives to versions of history that reject a multiplicity of identities, that banish different parts of the self and others to separate realms where there can be no intimacy or ambivalence, love or jealousy, respect or common destiny; where the full range of complex emotions, conscious and subconscious traces inherited through a long life lived together will simply be shelved in the name of some impersonal and polite forms of 'co-operation' or, perhaps even worse, just deemed unimaginable. Any relationship to Israeli culture must include a relationship to the Middle East and its diverse cultures that is informed by knowledge and the sympathy of a shared life (1996: xii).

He draws on the memories of such writers as Naim Kattan to argue that

> Far from being an unobtrusive, silenced, or submissive minority, the Jewish presence and way of life were not simply tolerated but were always acknowledged and recognised as part of the texture of the Levant (Kattan 1980).

and quotes a poem by Bracha Serri:

> Jerusalem on high and Sa'ana down below
>
> are one. One is my city.
> The same openness/the same majesty . . . I longed
> to kiss 'these strangers', 'our enemies',
> to whisper my thanks
> that they exist
> as in days gone by never to return. (Serri 1982).

For his part Arbel (1996) has assembled an impressive collection of portraits by contemporary historians of individual Jews in the historical Mediterranean who have in common lives which interconnected and integrated (sometimes intimately) with Muslim and Christian neighbours.

In brief, there is an emerging wealth of accounts of and reflections on historical and more recent experiences about the relationship between Jews and Arabs, Hebrew and Arabic, in the Mediterranean which seems strangely at odds with the history supposedly excavated by the bulldozers in the West Bank. The sense of cultural flow is placed against an even larger canvass by Ghosh (1992) whose ethnographic work in Egypt manages to encompass South Asia, the Middle East, Africa and Europe, underscoring a view of a world composed of trade, community, kinship and other links and movements within which the idea of the kind of complete separation described here simply has no place.

Alkalay (1996) quotes Sami Chetnit's suggestion that efforts to re-remember the history of the Mediterranean need not only Israelis and Palestinians to be there but also Europeans – not just Jews and Muslims but also Christians. The point is that the inner and outer identities of each of the three are fashioned within a triangular relationship to the others. A poem of his recounts a conversation between himself and a 'friendly American Jew'. Here are three lines:

Excuse me for asking but I just have to ask you, are you Jewish or Arab?
I'm an Arab Jew.
You're Funny. How can you say 'Arab Jew' when all the Arabs want to do is to destroy the Jews?
And how can you say 'European Jew' when the Europeans have already destroyed the Jews?

Conclusions

Our asphalt text tells of the inevitability of separation between two peoples and a 'lasting peace' which comes from the 'security' (to pick up on some familiar rhetoric) promised by by-pass roads and all the technologies of surveillance and 'defence' with which they are associated. The story unfolds against a canvas of ideas in which Jewish identity seems inexorably bound to a malevolence of 'terrifying others' both in the region and in the diaspora (spectres which are routinely conjoined in the imagination).

Being clear-eyed about the early, middle and late twentieth-century political and economic conditions – in which this narrative, of which our roads act as a mnemonic, was constructed – could serve as a starting point in a project designed to find a way out.

Only the very briefest reference to what these might have been is possible here, but we might remember that the drive to establish the state of Israel took place at a time when the West was actively engaged in hastening the demise of the Ottoman Empire and that in this context it was ideologically and symbolically congenial to brand anything remotely 'Turkish' (such as Palestinian peasants working for Turkish landlords) as dark and slightly barbaric. With their new styles of European-ized agriculture, early Jewish settlers in Palestine appeared in Europe and America as fortuitous allies in this ideological effort (Selwyn 1995).

As to the local re-emergence of notions of separation, we have argued that we should emphasize the consequences of the uneven development of the region and the de-development of Palestinian lands. It was against this background that the *intafada* broke out. But instead of interpreting it in these prosaic terms and taking appropriate remedial action, such as a thoroughgoing programme of regional development, the option of a politics of separation was chosen.

There was another group, the *Misrahi*, drafted into the economic and political crucible in which this ideological edifice was being formed. They too were regarded as a bit backward – so, although like Palestinians they were enlisted into the workforce – it was hardly surprising that their different stories were largely ignored (in the light of which the emergence of the *Shas* party over the last two decades of the twentieth century appears deeply politically ironic). After all, ideas of a common Arab/Jewish formation over more than a thousand years of Mediterranean history could deal a fatal blow to the popular support for the 'Peace of the Generals'.

An imagined future would need to be based not so much on the structures of 'defence' establishments (fence building is, among other things, good business for some) but of a determined effort to allow new/old memories of shared pasts to flood back. This might make it possible to comprehend the shared present as a prelude to the *embarras de richesse* that shared futures could bring.

A project like this might begin by drawing attention to, to coin a phrase, some 'facts on the ground' or, as Braudel (1981) might have put it 'structures of everyday life' in the social economy of contemporary Israel/Palestine. Examples here might well begin with the early morning stream of Palestinian construction and other workers crossing the checkpoints each morning for daily work in Israel, and might continue with such features of the regional economic and cultural landscape as a tourist/pilgrim economy based on a near-total interdependence of Israel and Palestine. In turn, such recognition might assist acknowledgement of other day-to-day practices at present conceptually locked out of sight behind the fortress-like walls of the rhetoric of separation. There is, for example, the growing reputation throughout parts of Israel/Palestine of a jazz club in Ramallah as one of the cooler venues in the Middle-East. There are also the West Jerusalem shopping malls and coffee bars, much favoured meeting places for young Palestinians. There is the growing trend among young Palestinian women to purchase, specifically for pre-nuptial 'shower parties', the latest fashions from the smarter clothing shops of Jerusalem and Tel Aviv. And then there are the Palestinian-owned engineering workshops near the Green Line in which Palestinian metal workers repair, for Israeli clients, by hand and with a skill difficult to find elswhere, Israeli-owned fork-lift trucks: the very same which are used in the construction of by-pass roads.

Reflection on such quotidian activities as these could lead to the imagining of a future in which the notion of separation comes to occupy an altogether less compelling presence than it does today.

Acknowledgements

Apart from the 'Contested Landscapes' session of the WAC in Cape Town in January 1999, earlier versions of this chapter were also read at the 'Landscape, Modernity and Exclusion' conference organized by the Anthropology Department of the University of Hull, in Dubrovnik, in July 1999, and at the departmental seminar at the School of Oriental and African Studies in the Autumn term of 1999. Thanks are due to the participants in these seminars and discussions. While stressing that all the errors are entirely my own, I would also like to thank the following: Michael Safier, Christiane Nasser, Ghassan Andoni, Jad Isaac and Norma Hazboun. I would like to make a special acknowledgement to Yaacov Garb, without whom this chapter would not have emerged. Finally I would like to thank Barbara Bender for her incisive comments on earlier drafts.

References

Alkalay, A. 1993. *After Jews and Arabs: Remaking Levantine Culture*. Minneapolis: University of Minnesota Press.
—— (ed.) 1996. *Keys to the Garden*. San Francisco: City Light Books.
Arbel, B. (ed.) 1996. *Intercultural Contacts in the Medieval Mediterranean*. London: Frank Cass.
Barkai, R. 1996. Between East and West: a Jewish doctor in Spain, in Arbel, B. (ed.) *Intercultural Contacts in the Medieval Mediterranean*. London: Frank Cass.
Barnavi, E. 1992. *A Historical Atlas of the Jewish People*. New York: Schoken.
Braudel, F. 1973. *The Mediterranean and the Mediterranean World in the Age of Philip II*. London: Collins.
—— 1981. *The Structures of Everyday Life: The Limits of the Possible*. London: Collins.
Ghosh, A. 1992. *In an Antique Land*. Delhi: Ravi Dayal.
Golden, D. 1996. The Museum of the Diaspora tells a story, in Selwyn, T. (ed.) *The Tourist Image: Myths and Myth Making in Tourism*. Chichester: Wiley.
Handelman, D. and Handelman, L. 1991. The presence of the dead: memorials of national death in Israel. *Suomen Antropologi* 4 3–17.
Huntingdon, S. 1997. *The Clash of Civilizations and the Remaking of the World Order*. London and New York: Touchstone Books.
Kattan, N. 1980. *Farewell Babylon*. New York: Taplinger.

Kedouri, E. 1960. *Nationalism.* London: Hutchinson.

Kimmerling, B. and Migdal, J. 1993. *Palestinians: The Making of a People.* Cambridge, Mass.: Harvard University Press.

Roy, S. 1995. *The Gaza Strip: The Political Economy of De-Development.* Washington: Institute of Palestine Studies.

Selwyn, T. 1995. Landscapes of liberation and imprisonment, in E. Hirsch and M. O'Hanlon (eds), *The Anthropology of Landscape: Perspectives on Place and Space.* Oxford University Press.

—— 1996. Atmospheric notes from the fields: reflections on myth-collecting tours, in T. Selwyn (ed.) *The Tourist Image: Myths and Mythmaking in Tourism.* Chichester: John Wiley.

Serri, B. 1982. *Seventy Wandering Poems.* Jerusalem: Bracha Serri.

Smith, A.D. 1991. *National Identity.* Harmondsworth: Penguin.

Newspapers

Guardian. 22.10.98.
Ha'aretz. 19.11.98.
—— 08.06.99.
—— 22.10.99.
—— 22.11.99.
—— 09.12.99.
—— 19.05.00.
Observer. 29.11.98.

–14–

Rites of Passage: Travel and the Materiality of vision at the Cape of Good Hope
Jessica Dubow

Looking to the figure of the nineteenth-century newcomer to the Cape Colony, this chapter sets about charting the process of spatial re-emplacement. My aim is to understand the travelling body as a matter of various perceptual and practical competencies: to focus on the drifting mass of the subject's sensory surfaces as well as on the meanings of the physical world that surround it. More acutely, I look to the appeals and intentions that come to connect that sensory surface to its world of surrounding meanings. My key terms are those of the body, travel, and the practice of perception. My context is the inaugural sights and scenes of a Cape colonial landscape.

I start off with the figure of the traveller borne by ship from Europe and on the lookout for the celebrated promontory of the Cape of Good Hope. After months at sea, and with bodies long poised in anticipation, the cry is raised: 'Land at last!' 'The cry of land', remembered the settler Robert Godlonton of his arrival in 1820, 'causes every heart to vibrate with quicker action, while every eye is strained to catch a glimpse of the shores of that country . . . to which he is bound.' (Godlonton 1984: vii). 'Land of Last', however, might not just signal the termination of the outward-bound journey. More than this, its status as opening exclamation also initiates the journal. Indeed, with the exaggerated optimism that the sight of the Cape invokes and with the recording of sights, scenes and occurrences that hasten on the apostrophe, the traveller regains a certain descriptive and story-telling capacity. Relieved from the protracted tedium of the sea-voyage, sight of land signifies an ending which is also a textual beginning. As such, seaborne arrival carries with it a profound epistemological function. It raises the question of where the journey begins. At the point of origin? In the moment of disembarkation? Or en route itself? It provokes an enquiry into the relationship of travel to the possibility of its narration; of the journey to the journal.

An extensive literature has built up around such and similar problematics. Beginning with Aristotle's prescription for a 'well-constructed plot' – namely that it follow the logic of a beginning, middle and end; moving through Claude Lévi-Strauss's *Tristes Tropiques* – a classic text *about* travel that simultaneously interrogates what it *means* to write; and including in its sway the very different work of Walter Benjamin, Michel de Certeau, James Clifford, Paul Carter (among others), the triangulation of travel, territory and text continues to be an issue of vigorous theoretical analysis.

Such questions will not concern us here, except inasmuch as the journals of sea-voyagers to the Cape exhibit a characteristic which runs off this generalized concern. That is to say, for the most part nothing seems to have immediately preceded the moment of arrival. At sea, the old Aristotelian injunction, it seems, undergoes a structural revision. For while the journals of travellers to the Cape often include vivid accounts of the scene of departure – final farewells, emotive displays of anxiety and trepidation, and not a little pre-emptive nostalgia – shipboard experience itself registers as a narrative lapse. As the physical port of origin fades from sight and with destination still only a matter of imaginative speculation, a gap appears where an event might have been. 'Do not those who are departing' asks the Cape traveller Adulphe Delegorgue, 'enter as it were into a field of death? For what is there at sea if not the total absence of all that the land offers? Here all is contrary . . . the weary soul must find its rest in the billowing waves, a kind of watery hell, a sort of oblivion into which it sinks' (Delegorgue 1990: 5).

Amidst the sea's spatial invariance, then, the apprehension of a breach, an impotence. Amidst its limitlessness, its lacunae, there is nothing to maintain the laws of thought or the principles of effective action. 'No words can describe', 'nothing particular has occurred', 'language can convey but little' all become familiar refrains of shipboard writing (see a similar point in Goldsworthy 1996). 'Sometimes dolphins are caught', remembers Delegorgue, 'which distinguishes those days from the rest. Sometimes the appearance of a bird is hailed by the watchman who calls it twenty times by name . . . May this serve to give you some conception of the boredom of life at sea, a boredom which is not of the ordinary sort' (Ibid.: 6).

If the absence of the quotidian event and the breakdown of that subjective unity born of territorial loss – Delagorgue's extra-ordinary boredom – is what character- izes the sea voyage and makes it unnarratable, it is also what renders it unvisualiz- able. Except for the vanishing horizon, the visible line of the deck rail and, at times, the contours of a distant coastline or passing ship, there is nothing to stake out the region one is in. Within the blue constant of sea and sky there is no environing marker which might align the eye. Within its free uncertainty there is no injunction of geometrics to orient the body or grant the meaning of progress to its movement. Indeed, other than the feverish projections of an anticipatory mind there is nothing, no discernible object, for the sea-body to extend or *intend* towards. 'Not a sail in sight, or a peak to break the complete circle of the horizon' is how one traveller to the Cape in 1890 describes that sense of a body encompassed, but not delimited (Finch 1890: 19). Accordingly, perception and movement at sea finds neither recourse in Euclidean lucidity nor determination by system and structure. Rather, lawless and liminal, the sea is inhabited by the subject's autonomous evaluation; a space discerned by intuition and the responsive symptom. Thus, here, the body gives over to the fluidity of wave and fog, to the palpability of wind and swell, to the chance fluctuations of climate. Indeed, one could say that like the figure of the Romantic artist J.M.W. Turner, who famously strapped himself to the mast of a ship the better to observe the swarm of a storm and so transform line into a translucent mass of colour, hue and matter, to be 'at sea' is to be in communion with random empirical forces. It is to enter into the pure capacity of the immediate. For Deleuze and Guattari, one travels at sea less *efficiently* than *intensely*. Seemingly endless and divested of any gridded dimension, experience here becomes a matter of 'intense *Spatium* instead of *Extensio*'. (Deleuze and Guattari 1992: 479).

'While on board, we knew that it was no use troubling ourselves about the future', writes John Finch of his passage to the Cape in 1890. 'For a time at least we had to turn our attention to *other grooves*' (Finch 1890: 19). Finch's words are significant. For being *in* the groove – in the immediate middle term between two terms, in the intensity of the linking passage itself – temporality for the sea-journeyer has no relevance. Or rather, with the collapse of any markers that might speak of a quantitative extension, movement refuses the cultural – one could say, colonial – virtue of thinking futurity. Indeed, with no end in sight to resolve the caesura, the sea becomes that space which tests the limits of narrative teleology. Here identity and experience struggle for representational structure: 'No words can describe.' And whence the cry of 'Land at Last': the end of the unnarratable interval, the apprehension of a ground that makes the journey's destination the journal's point of departure. But more than this. For if we understand the sea as non-narratological it becomes, too, a non-visual space; or, more correctly, is a space in which the eye has a non-optical function (Deleuze and Guattari 1992: 492–500). Thus immured within the sensorium of wave, wind and fog in a space where sea and sky share the same substance, there is nothing – no centralizing perspective – to tidy the flux of phenomena or authorize the rules of visual cognition. The sight of land, then, not only empirically closes off the voyage. It might also disclose the very terms of optical thought in restoring that network of lines, limits and dimensions that in the West – ever since the Renaissance – have been valued as the constitutive dynamics of human sight. In this sense, arrival on a foreign shore might not merely be a *founding* event. It might also be a moment of a *founding perception*: an inaugural moment in time and history that is also, for the travelling body, a reinsertion into the self-referential domain of the visual.

Accordingly, we might approach the opening journal entries of travellers to the Cape in a slightly different way. For arrival at the shores of Table Bay represents not only a relief from the visual incoherence of the 'senseless deck' (Burchell

Figure 14.1 Thomas Baines: 1847 *Southeaster in Table Bay*

1953: 10). More than this, the topography of the Cape, I suggest, presents an object lesson in optical rhetoricity: a natural landscape that 'descries out of the ocean . . . *opening full to view*' (Ibid.: 11). The phrase should give us pause. For in manner both elemental and ontological Table Mountain does indeed qualify space as visual. After one has been tacking down the Western littoral of Africa the mountain presents the broad middle mass of its northern side to the ship coming in from Europe. In a very literal sense, then, the newcomer finds himself settled in a centrist position with the space before him suddenly made capable, by convention, of appealing to perspectival view. 'Like the uplifting of a curtain on some drop scene', is how one newcomer describes the sense of a natural environment that suddenly accedes to specular perception. Indeed, one could say that Table Mountain seems to attract the very meaning of a re-presentation: a *Vorstellung* in Heidegger's terms, a 'setting down in front of.'

It is perhaps for this reason – of an object defined by reference to the viewing body – that descriptions of Table Mountain unfailingly dominate the opening lines of travellers' journals. There is no newcomer who does not feel compelled to talk of its impossibly flat horizontal top and precipitous front. Nor one who fails to be reassured when that veil of cloud that frequently obscures the mountain during the Cape's south-easter gales lifts to reveal the mathematics of its natural form.

Indeed, as it 'descries out of the ocean' Table Mountain, I suggest, marks a translation from the sea into the propertied qualities of sight. More acutely, conversion from the realm of the unvisualizable and unnarratable to that of the representational proposition can be evidenced in the properties of the mountain itself. With its play in granite of architectonic horizontals and verticals it stands as the exemplar of the measure and measurable quality. Rising to a height of 3,500 feet and backing the bowl-like settlement of the town itself, the Mountain orientates an optical field of which it is the focus and, crucially, the self-articulation. Accordingly, the sheer dimensional relation of ascent to summit allows the traveller to transcend the amorphous and contemplate the object in its very structure. To the 'bliss of sensation' is now added the 'power of intellection' (Barthes 1979: 11), a natural form that is not only sensually experienced but that, like a concrete abstraction, performs the idea of culture. And so, the tableau of Table Mountain as a gain of tabulation: a sight that reduces a foreign space to the geometry of conditional entrance.

If the eventual sighting of Cape signals the voyager's reinsertion into a cognitive gauge, it also provokes an unexpected discontinuity. Unused to time which takes a regular and habitual course, and a space which shows up regular and habitual contrasts, seaborne arrival appears as a moment of disconcerting acceleration. William Layton Sammons puts it this way:

> As the newcomer travels by water and not by land he pounces as it were suddenly upon the place, and all its beauties, faults or blemishes crowd upon him at once . . . For by land the newcomer embraces the scenery *by degrees*, every mile initiating him into some new feature and thus he is prepared for every variation until he reaches his destiny. But not so by sea; for then his thoughts and sights are . . . concentrated for the most part to clouds and water; sunshine and gloom; stars and moon (Sammons 1873: 78).

Embracing the new country *by degrees*. The phrase is evocative. For if after the initial dazzlement of his sense impressions, Sammons' induction into alien surrounds relates to a modified spatio-temporal order of things, it serves to complicate the customary idea of arrival as inaugural event. Indeed, contrary to the positivism that sees a foreign landscape spring into perceptual being at the instant of first sighting, Sammons' comments propose reality to be a burgeoning rite of practical passage; a gradual, tactile process of inducement and initiation. As such, land-travel does not merely repair the shock of seaborne arrival. More importantly, it rejoins the body to an incremental mobility and reaffirms the sentience of space.

It is to these ideas that we now turn. Looking specifically at the idea of travelling the Cape's routes by ox-wagon and on foot, I am concerned with how the subject's engagement in slowed time and circumspect space provides a certain 'pedestrian' perceptual practice. Moreover, it is a practice that has a specific relevance to colonial spatial inhabitation. For the wagon and walk, I suggest, are the means of both a way-finding and a place-learning; a digression through space that is also a subjective ingression in place.

Early nineteenth-century British South Africa inherited from its Dutch administration little in the way of a road system outside the immediate enclave of the Cape Peninsula. As established as the Colony was by this time it remained a country, in the opinion of one commentator, almost 'destitute of the means of locomotion' (Anonymous 1862: 20). 'One must find one's way into the interior of Africa without guide posts or sign-posts' (Hattersley 1969: 107) writes another. While nearer to the capital farmers travelled in light carts or rode on horseback, the general means of conveyance remained that of the ox-wagon. Fashioned from well-seasoned wood and purposely dislocated to maximize its structural elasticity, it was the ox-wagon that seemed to answer best to the perils of the uneven route. 'This great machine', remarks Delegorgue, 'must be made to travel across country where roads do not exist. It will be required to climb steep mountains and descend slopes crumbling with loose stones, it must twist and turn and recover itself across river-beds and hills of shifting sand' (Ibid.: 17). Despite its suitability to a Cape topography, however, the ox-wagon appeared to the average British newcomer less as a novelty than an anachronism. Indeed, with its lumbering and laborious movement, the wagon not only presented a ready analogy with the long-held myth of Africa as the 'Old World'; a space, as Hegel famously saw it, of non- or ahistorical time.

More specifically, as a means of conveyance directly associated with the figure of the *boer* it also heightened the stigmatized perception of the Cape's previous colonial tenancy as a period of indolence and underdevelopment. It is precisely the idea of an impeded modernity that the geologist and engineer, Andrew Geddes Bain, emphasizes in a letter to *The South African Commercial Advertiser* in 1825.

> The principal part of the road in the Colony consists of the original tracks of the first colonists who, in their several peregrinations, were only guided by chance, and of course, where a bush or a stone lay in their way they rode around them. The first who followed took the same track, and so they have remained ever since, presenting all over the face of the country so many serpentine wanderings that they look more like river courses than public roads (Bain 1949: 206).

On one level such a report registers as an unsurprising condemnation of the Colony's inadequate structures of spatial efficiency. That is to say, its failure to replace the randomness of the route with the ideality and power of the straight road: an ideality and power, as recent critique insists, allied to that impulse for Euclidean reason that partners the socio-political conquest of space. However, we may also brush Bain's report – and its customary critique – against the grain. In

Figure 14.2 Thomas Baines: 1847 *The Curlew off Cape Point*

so doing we may approach colonial space less as an accomplice of modernity than as a victim of its rationalizations. Beneath the ideology and rhetoric of spatial ordering, in other words, we may discern the traces of an anterior, and alternative, understanding of colonial landscape. That it is essentially *topological*. Importantly, I use the word here not in its scientific designation but in the sense that Maurice Merleau-Ponty understands it: of space as a matter of proximate envelopment; or, as Deleuze and Guattari (1988) argue, of space given as a direct reflection of *where it is;* as a function of the *place it is in.* Thus to talk of the Cape as a landscape beaten out by the footfall of travellers inflecting the patterns of the land as they went, or as traversed by the wagon at each linking turn of its wheel, is to see it hold to the palpable and the particular; to the intimate and immediate. And with this, I suggest, the colonial traveller becomes less a subject moving ahead between points than a body restoring itself to a world it *topologically* works itself into.

With this in mind, Bain's complaints of a landscape historically waylaid by the 'serpentine wandering' might represent less the failure of any geographic stratagem than the necessary mastery of the local spatial operation. Indeed, what so many spatial irregularities may reveal is rather the victory and logic of what Michel de Certeau (1988) would call the tactical initiative. That is to say, a victory given by the body's practical response to its ground and a logic which, evinced by the path that needs veer round a bush or the route that bends to accommodate an obstructing stone, reveals the minute material act of passing by.

In many ways, then, to travel the rough colonial route is to return to the space of the sea. It is to re-engage the empiricism of the sensory and recover the immediacy of linking passage itself. Or, more subtly, one could say that with the movement of the wagon over rough ground the experiential begins to show through the representational, the latter temporarily articulating itself as a pre-formulated activity. For William Guybon Atherstone travelling by ox-wagon – 'this ship of the South African wilds' – the colonial route seems to partake of all the qualities of the sea-voyage. Of his travels through the eastern Cape in 1870, he writes:

> A pleasant prospect for us truly . . . to be condemned to sit on this box . . . for thirty consecutive hours – without moving, I was going to say; but I mean of course the very opposite, with the *maximum* of incessant oscillation, like a bottle shaken violently into froth and foam (Atherstone 1978: 81).

Atherstone's experience bears out my understanding of wagon travel as intuitive symptomatic response. For here the sensation of 'incessant oscillation' is a manifestation of the vehicle's inherent structural elasticity. Likewise, the 'maximum' occurs as a consequence of a replete *spatium*. Moreover, this is a symptom held within the travelling body itself. 'Like a bottle shaken violently into froth and foam', Atherstone takes on and shares the jarring tremors of the conveyance, his body doubling the very movement of wagon over ground. With traveller and conveyance made one, with both absorbed in the self-same intensity, Atherstone feels his mind pressed dangerously close to the materiality of its object. Traversing a particularly rutted pathway he writes: 'You try to think, but your thoughts get so beaten up, jolted and jostled together, you can't recognise one as your own. They become split up and mingled with dreams' (Ibid.: 82). Another traveller, Atherstone reports, talks of the wagon effecting a 'giddy brain and quivering nerves'. On fording a river, yet another complains of having 'a headache in the stomach' (Ibid.). On the basis of such descriptions one could see the novelty of wagon travel as producing a form of psychosomatic pathology. That is to say, the experience of a space that so thwarts intellection, and so exceeds the bounds of the rational that mental unease becomes borne in the body itself: the cognitive shock of an alien landscape transferred and transformed as felt bodily symptom. A spatial nausea.

More positively, however, I suggest that such diagnoses find their compensation in a certain primacy of perception: an experience of the somatic and sensuous evoked precisely by the disorder of dissolving thought. What the wagon over rough ground establishes, then, is not merely an agitation of mind but a phenomenal contiguity between traveller and space travelled. What it presents is not just a body jolted into distress by its means of conveyance, but a subject *co-localized* in the lie of the land. In this sense, the topological route might be taken not merely as the indicator of a particular spatial modality. It might also be taken to define a particular mode of colonial subjectivity: that is, a particular corporeal commitment to territory.

To say that the topological nature of colonial space allows for a certain proximal intensity is also to prompt an alternative understanding of its visual perception. For insofar as the rough route can be seen to determine a somatic immersion in space – and thus a particular way of occupying a foreign landscape – it also comes to institute a specific visual modality. And what it institutes, I suggest, is a close and motile mode of seeing. Taken in at a footpace or at each turn of the wagon wheel, it is a form of seeing that redraws the eye into the specificities of the physical environment as into the physical body of the seer. What is introduced, then, is a form of colonial landscape perception that restores proximate over distancing sensuousness and reinserts the eye into the natural mobility of its setting. Put another way, it counters the canonical perspective of an 'imperial gaze' that projects to regulate the far-distant with one that reacts to the detours of the present. It foreshortens the totality of the legible field with a view of things as they fold in and out of the path of observation. And indeed it is this mode of peripatetic vision that John Keats Lord advises in his travel guide *At Home in the Wilderness* of 1871. Thus the novice traveller to the Cape

> [M]ust train his eye until his sight equals in delicacy of perception the touch of the blind . . . The disturbance of insects, the switch of a tail, the flap of an ear, the gleam of an eye, a displaced stone, or a broken twig . . . are not matters to be lightly passed by. Indeed, he must educate his ears too. The voices of birds, the hum and buzz of insects, the sough of the breeze and the roar of the torrent must be to the cultivated hearing of the dweller in the wilderness as understandable as different musical notes are to the ears of a practiced musician; and to some extent he must be a musician and ventriloquist of a certain kind himself (Lord 1871: 4).

Clearly, then, our nineteenth-century European traveller is not merely the pupil of the contemporary science of a Linnaeus, or of an earlier Euclid. Neither is he the ideal Enlightenment individual who, undivided within itself, is simultaneously wholly divided from an external environment. Rather, in the coincidence between ear and eye, foot and ground, as in the relation between the *adaptive* body and its *adoptive* organs, Lord's traveller occupies a space less laid out in predictive certainty than disclosed in sensory activity. What observation represents here is not the citation of what is seen but how the eye is itself ambient, negotiating the subject's proximal presence in space.

Thus far, I have suggested a number of interrelated ideas: the route as spatial digression and subjective ingression and colonial space as it presupposes a motile body. Ox-wagon travel, however, may refer us to an even more rudimentary experience of spatial orientation: walking. Indeed, while the wagon was the chief form of transport in the Colony, more often than not the distinctive characteristics of Cape topography made it essential to discern the proposed route on foot. 'It was necessary', Delegorgue recalls, 'to explore the way in advance, to make great detours in order to reach practicable fords, to skirt mountains, or where the paths are too narrow, to cut through the woods, to fill gullies' (1990).

For this traveller then, the digressionary walk was essential to the success of the journey. Indeed, I suggest that in a country where the smoothness of the line still remained the privilege of the map rather than of the way itself, walking is the prerequisite of its localized knowledge. The Gnostic aspect of the digressionary walk has an application, of course, much broader than a colonial one. It stands as one of the central metaphors of a Western metaphysics with the correlation of knowledge and mobility located at the heart of Enlightenment and Romantic discourse. It is a figure no less representative of that moment than that of Jean Jacques Rousseau's *Emile* (1762) in which is dedicated an entire chapter to exploring the contiguity between ambulation and the learning process. For Rousseau, the instructive value of the walk involves the way that slowed time and expanded space allow for the pleasure and power of observational curiosity. Indeed, in words that foreshadow contemporary phenomenological thought Rousseau proclaims that he cannot

> imagine a reader still so prejudiced by custom as to suppose us in a well-closed post-chaise, progressing without seeing or observing anything, making worthless for ourselves the interval between departure and arrival, and by the speed of our progress wasting time in order to save it. Therefore, we travel not like messengers but like travellers. We do not think about departure and arrival but also the interval separating them. The trip itself is a pleasure to us (Ibid.: 411).

If the space of travel for Rousseau is properly that of what I'd like to call the Absolute en Route,[1] then its knowledge is dependent, both materially and philosophically, on the procedures of 'legwork'. The lesson continues:

> Do I notice a river? I walk along it. A thick wood? I go beneath its shade. A grotto? I visit it. A quarry? I examine its minerals. It is hard for me to understand how a philosopher can resolve to travel in any other way . . . When one wants to travel, one has to go on foot (Ibid.).

1. The extended version of this chapter examines the relationship between the Rousseauian walk and a Deleuzian phenomenology.

Figure 14.3 Thomas Baines: 1852 *Klaas Smit's Drift – Waggon broke down, crossing the drift*

That such pedestrian pedagogy is underwritten by an Enlightenment episteme is not in question here. Rousseau's Everyman pupil is a truth-seeking mobile observer; his affective detour through sensation ultimately enabling of an intellectualist consciousness. The Rousseauian meander, in short, intends its telos. Like the contemporary practice of the European gentleman undertaking the Grand Tour and that of the naturalist as colonial emissary, it is premised on the idea of an ultimate return: the conversion of travel into truth, of ideality discovered by indirection, reason by way of wandering.

Abstractive certainties notwithstanding, Rousseauian knowledge presupposes the walking body; it depends, I suggest, on what Deleuze and Guattari have called 'an extraordinary fine topology' (1992: 382). Possessed of such powers, walking can be seen as a significant trope within the literature of colonial travel instruction. In *Shifts and Expedients of Cape Life, Travel and Exploration* (1861), a manual designed for expectant emigrants to the Cape, the authors W.B. Lord and Thomas Baines display a clear Rousseauian concern with the distinction between the two poles of spatial knowledge. On the one hand, knowledge as gained through accumulated sensory experience; on the other, of knowledge as refracted through the double glaze of its scientific, or formalized redescription. For Rousseau, as suggested, to know only of the latter – the written word, the cartographic sign –

would be to commit a fundamental epistemological error. '[W]ithout the idea of represented things', he writes, 'the representative signs are nothing.' One must not read, one must see (Ibid.: 827).

It is in a manner close to this spirit, I suggest, that Lord and Baines contend that '[m]any highly-accomplished travellers to the Cape fail to obtain much reliable information beyond the limit of their own observation'. For these instructors it is a myopia resulting from the fact that such travellers 'do not sufficiently allow for the great difference in the manner of expressing a geographical idea between an educated European observer and an untutored savage'. And yet, they acknowledge, 'it would not be too much to say that the latter has often enough a thoroughly practical idea of the district he actually knows'(Ibid.: 758).

In very clear terms, then, Lord and Baines point to the shortcomings of transposing the map onto the face of the Colony. Here, in fact, the key to obtaining geographical guidance is not the map at all. Or, not merely the map. Rather, knowledge of the colony relies on the traveller's ability to imagine space beyond its graphic trail. It depends on an engagement between the body and the precise material features of its surrounding world.

This kind of acknowledgement, of course, carries with it another and more implicit one. That wherever Europeans went they did so in the footsteps of others who went before. That to be effectively mobile in the colony meant making use of the local guide and following his tracks; it meant mimicking the terms of another knowledge and modifying one's own. For Lord and Baines, it is precisely an awareness of the native's perceptual and practical competency in his surrounds that the European apprehends and so confronts what – with astonishing theoretical canniness – they call 'the limits of the geographical idea' (Ibid.). After cautioning against the map as sole orientational authority, our travel instructors issue their second warning. It refers us to a related field of symbolic negotiation: speech. Thus, in all dealings with natives there is no use in saying

'Let us come to the point at once'. It is far better, indeed it is absolutely necessary, to delay judiciously, as there is always an implied contest between visitors. Do not disturb your informant's train of thought, but try to accommodate your own to it. Let him tell you as minutely and as tediously as he pleases how he has travelled; how long he has walked with the rising sun on his right or left; how much he turned either way; where he has halted for rest or refreshment; whether he has crossed rivers on foot or in canoes (Ibid.).

This passage is remarkable. And it is remarkable, I suggest, because of the implication that the polarization between the spatial act and its narration is itself a function of a predominantly representationalist theory of language. For, at issue here is not merely the notion of foreign travel as it entails a failed semiology. It is not merely the proposition – and implicit Rousseauian fear – that to know only about the designative function of a sign, a place-name or a compass point, is an empty effort unless attachable by experience to that to which it refers. Nor does the passage merely concern the formal 'discrepancy' between question and answer or the failure of communication across difference. Rather, the passage invokes a far more evocative idea. That is, that geographic *expression* functions as more than a symbolic supplement to geographic *experience*; that to narrate the walk is not merely to translate pedestrian movement into the field of language or to displace an itinerary into a topic of discourse. Rather, following de Certeau's thesis of spatial practice, one could say that the 'alphabet of spatial indication' is what constitutes the walk; that the act of narration is what makes the journey: not retroactively but 'before or during the time the feet perform it' (de Certeau 1988: 115–16).

Put another way, to walk is to deploy a contiguous concrete grammar. We talk when we walk of a 'here' and a 'there', a 'near' or 'far', a 'front' or 'behind.' Such directions, however, are not pre-positional points on a compass. They form, as de Certeau argues, a framework of enunciation given with the sensuous reflexes of the ambulatory body. Thus to speak – as our instructor's native guide does – of the changing trajectory of the sun, or of the sudden fact of a river to be crossed, is to constitute the vectors and arrests of actual, physical movement. Likewise, to narrate the route 'minutely' or 'tediously' is to see linguistic formation as itself coincident with the rates and pacings of the pedestrian process. The style of speech of the 'untutored savage' parallels the style of a particular spatial operation. In this sense, not to 'come to the point at once' is to express the length and time variables of the circuitous route; to pause syntactically is to enact the journeyer's halt. To the order of words is subtended the order of space, to language the lie of the land.

Out of this we may extrapolate a larger theoretical point. That to place the body at the centre of spatial analysis is to counter that alienating tendency which in reducing meaning to a sign excludes it from the materiality of practice. Moreover, if the condition of spatial alienation, as this chapter has proposed, is what has to be overcome in establishing the self within a foreign landscape, then the activity of walking might be seen as a kind of colonial desideratum. It is, in short, the search for a space where structures of representational may re-engage with the existential immediacy of the act. It is the search for a space where the experience of the body situated in relation to the object world also constitutes the structures of its expression.

This chapter began with the sea voyage. It proposed that immersed within a space where points of origination and destination become invisible and where departure implies the possibility of no return, Western subjectivity struggles for its referential and unitary point of view. The moment of arrival, it then appeared, reinserted the sea body back into the cast of visual and narrative convention as back into a field of spatial orientation. Here gaining the tableau of Table Mountain meant regaining the tools of abstract tabulation. Our various journeys by wagon and on foot, however, introduced the possibility of an alternative interpretation. Thus the inert outside observer I replaced with the wagon traveller and walker: figures for whom spatial perception does not issue from the fashioning of representational systems, but rather involves a conversion to a body at close range with the ground and cohering with it. In broad terms then, to the figure of the sea-voyager – that body suspended in the breach between territory and text – I have proposed the perceptual conditions of a nascent colonial one. Or, more quietly, the sentient subject who might make sense of a new country step-by-step.

Acknowledgements

The images are reproduced courtesy of MuseumAfrica, Johannesburg and the State Library, Cape Town.

References

Anonymous. 1862. The post-cart, in *Cape of Good Hope Literary Magazine*. **IX**(61) January. 20.

Atherstone, W.G. 1978. From Grahamstown to the Gouph, in *Selected Articles from Cape Monthly Magazine*. Cape Town: Van Riebeeck Society.

Bain, A.G. 1949. *The Journal of Andrew Geddes Bain*. Cape Town: The Van Riebeeck Press.

Barthes, R. 1979. *The Eiffel Tower*. New York: Hill and Wang.

Benjamin, W. 1979. *One-Way Street and Other Essays*. Trans. E. Jephcott and K. Shorter. London and New York: Verso.

Burchell, W. 1953. Rpt 1822–24 edn. *Travels in the Interior of Southern Africa*. London: Batchworth Press.

Carter, P. 1987. *The Road to Botany Bay: An Exploration of Landscape and History*. London and Boston: Faber & Faber.

—— 1992. *Living in a New Country: History, Travelling and Language*. London and Boston: Faber & Faber.

Clifford, J. 1992. Travelling cultures, in L. Grossberg, C. Nelson and P. Treicher (eds) *Cultural Studies*. New York and London: Routledge. 96–116.

de Certeau, M. 1988. *The Practice of Everyday Life*. Berkeley, Los Angeles and London: University of California Press.

Delegorgue, A. 1990. *Travels in Southern Africa*. Pietermaritzberg and Durban: University of Natal Press.

Deleuze, G. and Guattari, F. 1988. *A Thousand Plateaus: Capitalism and Schizo-phrenia*. London: Athlone Press.

Finch, J. 1890. *To South Africa and Back*. London: Ward, Lock and Co.

Godlonton, R. 1844. *Memorials of the British Settlers of South Africa*. Grahams-town: Richard, Glanville & Co.

Goldsworthy, K. 1996. The voyage south: writing immigration, in K. Darien-Smith, L. Gunner and S. Nuttal (eds) *Text, Theory and Space: Land, Literature and History in Southern Africa and Australia*. London and New York: Routledge.

Hattersley, A.F. 1969. *An Illustrated Social History of South Africa*. Cape Town: Balkema.

Hegel, G.W.F. 1991. *The Philosophy of History*. Trans. J. Sibree. Buffalo, New York: Prometheus Books.

Lévi Strauss, C. 1992. *Tristes Tropiques*. New York: Penguin.

Lord, J.K. 1867. *At Home in the Wilderness*. London: Robert Hardwicke.

Lord, W.B. and Baines, T. 1871. *Shifts and Expedients of Cape Life, Travel and Exploration*. London: Horace Cox.

Rousseau, J.-J. 1991. *Emile*. London: Penguin Classics.

Sammons, W.L. 1873. Localities. the old familiar faces – and places, in *Cape Monthly Magazine* **IX**(3) 78.

Landscapes, Fear and Land Loss on the Nineteenth-Century South African Colonial Frontier

Margot Winer

Introduction

The conflict on the expanding Eastern Frontier[1] of the colonial Cape in the late eighteenth and early nineteenth century represents a critical moment in South African history.[2] It was here that Europeans and Bantu-speakers initially came into sustained contact as competitive occupants of the region.[3] As first Dutch and then later English settlers pushed the frontier eastwards, they met expanding groups of Xhosa farmers moving from the north-east (Peires 1989). The frontier zone, running along the Fish River, was the locus of extensive and sometimes violent cultural and material exchange between colonizers and unwillingly colonized. This is the site of the Hundred Years War, the longest series of wars (1779–1870) in the history of the colonial conquest of Africa (Saunders, 1976). Even in times of relative peace, as Robert Ross writes, 'the threat of war, the experience of war and the recovery from war dominated the minds and lives of most of the frontier's inhabitants' (1999:1).

Significant changes took place in the Eastern Cape, beginning in 1820, as the frontier of this remote British colony was transformed by the arrival of nearly five thousand predominantly English settlers who were sent as part of a Government-

---

1. It must be acknowledged that the concept of the 'frontier' is a historical construction that is problematic, but further discussion is beyond the scope of this chapter. Martin Legassick's (1980) examination of the notion of the frontier in South African historiography is an important starting point, as is Lamar and Thompson's 1981 comparative volume. Timothy Keegan (1997) reviews the term's significance and meaning comprehensively.

2. Historical background to South Africa and the importance of the frontier region in shaping South Africa can be found in Elphick and Gilomee (1989), Ross (2000), Thompson (1996) and Worden (2000).

3. Historian Robert Ross points out that it could 'with equal justice be seen as the Western frontier of Xhosaland' (1999: 1).

sponsored emigrant scheme to create a buffer zone and to reduce military deployment in this contested region.

I have chosen the highly visible transformations of the cultural landscape[4] of a small British settler village for analysis because this material culture (vernacular building in particular) became one of the prime physical symbols of a heavily mythologized history of Anglo-South Africa used to produce a politically expedient version of the past. It is important to gain a better understanding of the colonial past and its role in producing and maintaining the white South African consciousness that dominated until recently. Through the recording and analysis of the colonial transformation of existing cultural landscapes – the reworking of the physical terrain sometimes under conditions of terror and isolation – this chapter throws light on the complexities and contradictions[5] of this period of European–indigenous confrontation.

Archaeology can play an important role in 'making alternative histories' (Schmidt and Patterson: 1995) when the analysis of both indigenous and colonial material culture is used in the reinterpretation of South African history since the mid-seventeenth-century arrival of the Dutch and the subsequent late eighteenth-century transition to British domination (Winer 1994; Schrire 1990 and 1995; Hall 1992 for example). Some productive questions we can ask as archaeologists about this period concern the collision of what Braudel (1992) came to call an emerging capitalist world system – the so-called Modern World – with indigenous subsistence economies on the landscape of what was to become known as the Cape.[6] It must be highlighted that this process was subtle and never one-sided: 'Colonisation always provokes struggles – albeit tragically uneven ones – over power and meaning on the frontier of empire' write Jean and John Comaroff, who continue, 'It is a process often much too complex to be captured in simple equations of domination and resistance; or for that matter, by grand models of the politics of imperialism or the economics of the modern world system' (1991: 5).

Archaeology reveals the social and economic consequences of the shift from a pre-industrial to a capitalist economy in South Africa. The changing nature of society on the Eastern Cape frontier from the late eighteenth into the nineteenth century is not a simple one. This was not a rigid, impermeable frontier on which narrow racial paradigms were played out. The practical, logical *modus vivendi*

4. Theoretical influences in this interpretation are drawn from diverse sources: Carter (1988), Coetzee (1988), Cosgrove and Daniels (1988), Harley (1988), Mitchell (1994), Ranger (1999), Schama (1996), Bender (1993), and Upton (1988).

5. Monica Wilson, for example, describes this ambivalent interaction in 'Co-operation and Conflict: The Eastern Cape Frontier' (1969).

6. As Europe spilled out over its borders the same theme was played out in societies in every corner of the globe. The set of powerful forces described by Eric Wolf (1982) in *Europe and the People without History* could not be successfully rejected.

bred of proximity, intimacy, familiarity and mutual convenience was co-operation and conflict simultaneously (Mostert 1992). This existing Dutch pattern shaped British interaction, so that by the time of the en masse arrival of the five thousand ill-advised,[7] misguided and insufficiently prepared settlers in 1820 the frontier was a ruinously governed, ill-structured relic of the VOC (Dutch East India Company) albeit under British direction and command (ibid.).

In spite of the fluidity and negotiation of the frontier, contact was to become a collision of catastrophic proportions. In Southern African archaeology we use the terms 'hunters', 'herders' and 'farmers' – descriptive terms of economic activities – to label groups of indigenous people – among them the San or Bushmen (Smith *et al.* 2000), Khoikhoi (Boonzaier 1998) and Xhosa (Peires 1981). For all the differences between the Dutch and later the British colonial economies and those of local pre-literate indigenous people, in one critical way they had the same basic need – vast tracts of land on which to carry out their hunting, herding and farming. Both Dutch and later English frontier economies depended in part on subsistence- or commercial-scale livestock management, exploitation of local hunting resources, and agriculture.[8]

The archaeology of this period of contact is a story of loss that had at its centre the perpetually expanding and permeable colonial frontiers. Those very things, hunting and herding and farming by which certain indigenous groups are defined, were done better, or more forcefully, or with a shorter-term view, by the newcomers who appropriated, not always easily or without loss, the best for themselves. So, as we look at the Eastern Cape in the nineteenth century we see that land and stock are the core of this story; as archaeologists we can address the nature of this resistance and subsequent dispossession in a way that complements the work of historians addressing these same issues from other starting points (Marks 1972; Comaroff 1985; Crais 1992 for example).

Early nineteenth-century British colonial settlement on the Eastern Cape frontier left a rich legacy of material and documentary sources. The nature and effects of this collision of many worlds is written in the minutiae, the material remains of social acts, hidden in archaeological sites on the frontier, the military trading forts and Xhosa kraals, the fortified colonial farmsteads and the Company Gardens in administrative centers. Wolf's 'chains of causes and effects' (1982) are mirrored in the evidence in the sites for the trade and exchange of livestock and raw materials for manufactured goods, or of labour and land for protection and allies.

---

7. W. Burchell's (1819) *Hints on Emigration to the Cape of Good Hope* were at least based on first-hand knowledge of the Colony. Much advice in the popular press was not – an example is James Griffin's (1819) *The Real Facts Disclosed* . . .

8. The reason for early European presence at the Cape was trade in livestock and the simplest of farms – a vegetable garden to supply passing ships.

Salem Village

The sample area for this study is Salem, a characteristic settler village in the Albany District established in 1820 during the British-government-sponsored emigration programme. This case study is based on a larger research project[9] examining the transformation of both the landscape (fields, roads, paths, hedges, village layout, manipulation of vistas and so on), and vernacular architecture (domestic, agricultural, and religious/communal) and household goods (excavated artefacts) of Salem. The shaping of the material world was not understood only in terms of terrain modification or building on the frontier, for the textual and visual representations of landscape (landscape paintings, travel and scientific illustrations, cartography, poetry, adventurer's tales and even pantomime) that were familiar to many through popular media in Britain helped shape attitudes and thus the cultural landscape prior to arrival (see Winer 1995).

The village of Salem (meaning 'peace') was built by a joint-stock party[10] of predominantly urban families. One hundred adult men and their families from the Great Queen St Chapel in London, under the nominal leadership of Hezekiah Sephton and accompanied by Reverend William Shaw[11] as minister, arrived in Albany District and established a village on forty-seven square kilometres of government-granted land south-west of Grahamstown on the confluence of the Assegaaibos and Mantjieskraal Streams (Winer 1994). Though the land was perceived as vacant, the entire region west of the Kieskamma River had been Xhosa pastoral land, recently cleared[12] by government decree (Crais 1991). Salem soon became well known for the quality of its schools, the vigor of its missionaries and the bowling skills of its cricketers.

There is more to it than this. In Salem it has been productive to concentrate on divisions within the colonizing population – divisions of power, class, ethnicity and gender that resulted in the conflicts and negotiations that Frederick Cooper and Ann Stoler (1997) have termed the tensions of empire. It is important to recognize how new discourses and practices of inclusion and exclusion were contested and worked out and to examine the complexity and fluidity of colonial society, the way these tensions played out across racial lines, between rulers and

9. This more comprehensive work was carried out by the Eastern Cape Historical Archaeology Project (1988–1991), which comprised the late historical archaeologist James Deetz (University of California, Berkeley/University of Virginia), historian Patricia Scott (Rhodes University/University of Virginia) and myself, with the assistance of both North American and South African students.

10. D. Nash (1982) and H. Hockly (1957) provide useful descriptive background to the structure of emigrant parties.

11. See Shaw (1860).

12. This clearing of native inhabitants from land can be seen to foreshadow the later policy of 'forced removals' of 'surplus people' of the Apartheid era.

the uneasily ruled, to see how the indentured servant becomes a merchant while his master starves, how the slave become a Dutch widow of substance, the hunter becomes a herder of sheep and the Xhosa chief, who chose his allies badly, is incarcerated on Robben Island. It is this plasticity of identity – a notion we have learned much about from anthropologists – that is difficult to capture, but by drawing on the material culture of sites in combination with written sources we do often catch a glimpse.

Architectural Changes: Phases of Colonial Domestic Building

The changing frontier society from 1820 to 1860 is embodied in the surviving built environment. I have made use of Dell Upton's definition of vernacular architecture as 'the visual embodiment of a social process, in which available architectural ideas from many sources . . . are shaped into buildings answering the special requirements of a social class, an economic group or a local or ethnic community' (1985).

Vernacular buildings of the first forty years of settlement can be grouped into four distinct chronological and stylistic phases.[13] Shifting social, economic and political contexts not only shaped new construction and remodelling – these new contexts were in turn affected by the way the frontier villages and towns looked and were structured.[14]

The phases (see Table 15.1) are termed the Architecture of Coping (huts and other small, early impermanent housing solutions after first land grants), the Architecture of Identity (the first permanent one- and two-room dwellings that expressed the desire for 'proper' housing made from familiar materials), Architecture of Affluence (larger, more fashionable houses and additions to many older houses that resulted from the growing prosperity experienced by some settlers through increased military contracts, commerce and wool production) and the Architecture of Fear (defensive measures and fortifications against Xhosa attack).

Architecture of Coping: 1820–1823

The ephemeral architecture of earliest colonial settlement in contexts worldwide has received little attention except for Carson *et al.* (1988) on the impermanent architecture in the Southern American colonies. On this South African frontier, documentary sources suggest that there was a reliance on folk building traditions from England as well as extensive borrowing from Dutch and local building

---

13. This four-phase model builds on Ronald Lewcock's three phases of early British colonial building patterns (1963).

14. M. Winer and J. Deetz (1990) traces these architectural changes, but Winer (1994) places the phases more fully in context.

FOUR PHASES: 1820–1860	CHARACTERISTICS
1820–1823 **Architecture of Coping**	Impermanence, borrowing of Dutch and indigenous forms and construction methods. Use of innovative materials.
1823–1832 **Architecture of Identity**	Greater permanence, more conventional materials, beginning of characteristic E. Cape style. Incorporation of Georgian forms. Most houses have only one or two rooms.
1832–1860 **Architecture of Affluence**	More formality in house forms, greater display of prosperity and use of imported materials, increased disparity in house size in village. Decrease in room size as house size increases. Incorporation of Georgian forms in both new and modified houses.
1835+ recurring **Architecture of Fear**	Defensive features incorporated into older forms, new domestic buildings fortified with gun slits, blank walls and enclosed cattle pens. Brush and thorny plants used as barriers.

Figure 15.1 Four phases of colonial domestic architecture in Salem

traditions to produce single-room or other small-scale impermanent houses. No known houses from this period survive on the frontier, though numerous similar thatched, mud brick or wattle-and-daub dwellings are found from later Xhosa and Khoikhoi settlements.

This early period of settlement was characterized by settler inexperience, crop failure, severe labour shortages that hampered intensive agriculture (settlers being forbidden to hire Khoikhoi servants or hold slaves) and inconsistent government policy. Xhosa reactions to large-scale land loss took the form of cattle rustling and tense stand-offs over symbolic resources such as red clay for body marking.

Architecture of Identity: 1823–1832

In spite of the shortcomings described above, some settlers rapidly became successful in their adaptation to the environment and to local subsistence methods. It was impossible to farm intensively on the poor soil, and settlers were advised to rely on livestock rather than agriculture – something the Dutch had learned decades before in their emulation of indigenous herding practices. By the beginning of this period only 50 per cent of Salem residents remained on the land as others with artisan skills moved to town. The village became more closely tied to the market economy.

Increasing cross-frontier trade was making inroads into Xhosa lifeways as the colonial demand for stock depleted herds. Into these trade paths, following the mercantile thrust of the post-Waterloo industrial society, came Evangelical Protestant expansionism. Missionary activity both followed those trade routes and facilitated that trade. Salem during this phase sent both traders and missionaries into Xhosa country.

Architecture of Affluence: 1832–1860

By the early 1830s affluence and rising class differences[15] from wool exports and large-scale commercial animal husbandry forced land consolidations and new land purchases for additional grazing. The permanence and inevitability of colonial occupation was apparent. Ties to the outside mercantile world are strengthened by the newly affluent class.

Buildings in the second and third phases provide important clues to understanding the 'tensions of empire' that resulted from conflict and diversity within this rapidly changing society. It was during the Architectures of Identity and Affluence that some of the settlers who had kept hold of their land built more substantial houses and then improved on those houses or built larger, more formal dwellings as prosperity increased. This prosperity was differentially distributed within the community and thus created conflicts that are made visible in the variability within the Salem houses of the period.

Builders selectively drew on elements from the Georgian architectural style and combined them with older, often more economical and less self-conscious building styles. This vernacular pattern, far from being a simple exercise in colonial domination resulting in the perfect recreation of *home,* of English forms, involved far-reaching changes in the way the settlers perceived their world. There is a changing consciousness, a *creation* of an English frontier form rather than the simple *re-creation* of English forms. I suggest that the houses, particularly in the move to incorporate more urban styles and formal Georgian facades, were used to make a political statement about settler success and the unifying forces of British identity both to villagers and to a wider audience of Cape Town officials and visitors.

The realities of this period of transition on the frontier made multiple but simultaneous messages, aimed at different audiences, an effective means of communication suited to the shifting colonial social interactions between settlers, colonial powers, missionaries, Boers, and various indigenous people.

Expression through material culture, specifically the manipulation of the physical landscape and the building and furnishing of houses, was one of the few effective avenues available to the British settlers who found themselves increasingly

---

15. See Bonner *et al.* 1990 on the larger context of these changes.

voiceless and ignored. The polysemic messages played out in the material world had their roots in the nature of the settlement: a settler was simultaneously high- and low-status, powerful and powerless. On one level, the settlers had been marginalized by colonial officials in charge of the ill-conceived settlement plan. Grievances, both written and oral, went unanswered. Settlers felt they suffered from severe restrictions on mobility during the early years of settlement – they were required to request and carry a pass when leaving their allotments. There were constraints on types of jobs practiced and no settler was allowed to leave his land to practice his craft in the towns until 1823. Rations and imported materials were often in short supply. There was little freedom of expression – printing presses were confiscated when the settlers arrived and any form of political meeting restricted. They had no representation in a politically unstable colony with an administration that had difficulty even agreeing on the most basic policy affecting the settlers. Reductions in the military presence on the frontier made the settlers vulnerable to cattle raiding and other challenges by African people whose land they had been deeded. Ultimately, ill-informed and idealistic, many of the settlers were unprepared for the rigours of frontier life.

In this uneven relationship, material culture was the one way to 'talk back'. On a second level, material culture offered a medium to 'talk down' to the indigenous people. As willing, if somewhat uninformed, participants in a colonial endeavour that brutally alienated the indigenous communities and appropriated their lands, the settlers continually needed to assert their position of dominance, both as rightful occupants and as the first 'real owners' of the land. Indigenous voices, although muted by force, were still present in this dialogue.

Landscapes of Fear (a recurring nightmare)

It is necessary now to backtrack to the first few years of the Architecture of Affluence to examine the Architecture of Fear. For many of the settlers who had been in the Eastern Cape for almost a decade-and-a-half a growing feeling of permanence emerged. Economic prospects increased as the money brought in by wool farming was redistributed. Apart from the now normal cattle raiding and minor clashes, relations with the Xhosa had been stable and by 1834 many in the Albany District had become complacent.

This fourth phase emerged as a reaction to escalating security needs on the frontier. The now-entrenched English became increasingly unnerved by the intensification of raids, massacres and counter-raids by the disenfranchised and betrayed Xhosa people. Taken unawares after almost fifteen years of relative calm in the region, the settlers had few means of protecting property when the Sixth Frontier War erupted just before Christmas in 1834. In hindsight, this lack of preparation was clear.

> While the government established additional posts, and provides a more suitable force than formerly for the defense of the Frontier, it is not unreasonable to expect, and self-interest must assuredly dictate, that the colonists will also *assist* to defend their own property by fortifying their houses in a simple manner. They will thus lessen the probability of another Irruption, by shewing the savages that they are not slumbering, as hitherto, in fancied security, but are prepared to repel treacherous and unprovoked aggressions (Smith 1835).

Constructed or modified after the end of this war, the Architecture of Fear shows heavy fortification, walled farmyard areas and other defensive features borrowed in an eclectic manner from various sources.

The intensity of the Sixth Frontier War (1834/5), the English settlers' first experience with the widespread violence of frontier warfare, affected the way in which they thought about their position on the border. In the space of a few months across the colony more than 325 farmsteads were reported sacked and burned, 261 as pillaged, 42,615 cattle, 5,115 trained oxen, 1,772 horses and more than 112,000 of sheep and goats were killed or raided and driven back across the frontier by fifteen thousand Xhosa warriors (Webb 1975).

The indefensible thatched cottages the settlers had built for themselves, despite warnings by officials wary of the losses suffered in 1819, offered little protection to their occupants.

> On the occasion of the late Kafir Irruption, it appears that the settlers on the Eastern Frontier were completely taken by surprise — none of them having ever made any preparations for defending their dwellings against sudden incursion of an active enemy. Yet such precautions are ever necessary in countries so situated, and were accordingly observed, at no distant date by the British settlers in America, and also by the Dutch Farmers in South Africa (Smith 1835).

Unable to hold their ground, settlers in Salem sought refuge in the church. Here brush kraals were hastily erected in the churchyard and part of the village for a communal cattle pen.

In contrast to other settler settlements, Salem came through the war with only minor property damage and little loss of life or livestock. Losses elsewhere in Albany were much greater. Many rural settlers were left destitute in what had become a prosperous area and were forced to establish themselves again – to rebuild their houses, replant burned crops and build up their cattle and sheep herds.

The war touched both small and large property-holders – even those who had previously had the power and prestige to buy protection. It appears that many of the more substantial and ostentatious houses in the region were burned by the Xhosa to prevent them being used by the military.

Everyone was aware that few proper precautions had been taken to protect property and life. Methods of building and 'retro-fitting' domestic and farm architecture to discourage arson and attacks were explored and discussed by both settlers and officials. Of particular interest is a government report published as a supplement to the *Graham's Town Journal* a month before the end of the war: 'On the means of defending farm houses', which the editor recommended with the following commentary (No. 191): 'It is just as easy to erect a dwelling capable of being defended as it is to construct it in such a way as to tempt ... the commission of outrage.' This document provided suggestions for 'easy, cheap, and effective methods of defending Farm Houses against Savages and other Robbers, ... most earnestly recommended by the Governor and Commander in Chief to the attention of all of the Frontier Farmers' (Smith 1835). Even latrines were fortified, and walls, usually seen only as symbolic perimeter markers or barriers to livestock, were modified by deep ditches on the outsides to create fortifications. It is probable that all surviving buildings in Salem were renovated in some way to increase security. A small handful of farmers built new, heavily fortified farmsteads in which the dwelling house, outbuildings and livestock areas were protected within high loopholed walls.

The Landscape is a Palimpsest

These fortified English houses on increasingly tamed and controlled agricultural landscapes crisscrossed by walls and wagon tracks inform us not only of the changes in the village but changes further afield – for these changes are concomitant with erosion of authority and social disruption in the Xhosa kraals and 'great places' (households of the political elite) across the Fish River. In other words the business of the settlers – farming, herding, sometimes hunting or trading (that is, the subsistence processes and commercial resource exploitation) – is mirrored archaeologically and allows us to begin to unravel the story of contact and the changing balance of power.

In Salem the landscape is a palimpsest, a colonial layering superimposed on that of local pastoralists, herders and hunters. The San painted cave in one Salem ravine became a curiosity visited by travelling artists and Sunday walking parties in the absence of those who painted there. Grazing land and springs now fattened imported merino sheep that made many so rich they could buy up the land of failed settlers. Khoi labourers now herded cattle that they did not own. Imported tea in Staffordshire cups was served by servants more used to serving soured milk. The permeability of the frontier – the trade (Beck 1987), the skirmishes and 'irruptions' (Mostert 1992), the loss of traditional land (Bergh and Visagie 1985), native peasant involvement in producing for colonial markets (Bundy 1979), the appropriation of Xhosa and Khoikhoi labour (Cock 1990) and the missionary inroads into African belief systems (Elphick and Davenport 1997) – are all seen in the way the landscape was shaped and written about.

It is in this context that we must understand the Xhosa's well-planned and devastating attack on villages, forts and towns across the frontier. The Sixth Frontier war was not merely a skirmish but a strategic last-ditch effort to win back control. Land was lost, the rules of war ignored, promises broken, treaties disregarded and chiefs disrespected. It was by the mid-1830s with this confrontation that we can recognize changing Xhosa attitudes to the colonial authorities and settlers.

Noel Mostert (1992) recounts a telling interaction between a Xhosa chief Tyali and Lt.-Gen. Harry Smith who had travelled with missionary William Chalmers deep into the Amatolas to retrieve raided colonial cattle. Tyali defiantly told them 'If the Governor wants his cattle HE must come and get them'. Tyali said he would order his people to 'slaughter and eat the cattle, slaughter and eat, slaughter and eat'. He himself had no desire for the conventional diet of corn and milk – only meat. As Xhosa traditionally maintain herd or grow herd size and slaughter only on ceremonial occasions, this can be read as a graphic, contemptuous and bloodthirsty rejection of colonial demands.

By the late 1850s, though, it was clear that the Xhosa nation was weakened and in despair after 70 years of disastrous wars and British betrayal that had cost them almost all of their ancestral lands. They were susceptible from within to the millenarian movement and regeneration prophecies that resulted in the Great Cattle Killing Movement of 1856–7 (Peires 1989). And that, as Noel Mostert writes, was the 'tragedy of the Xhosa People' (1992).

But not the end of resistance, for it is from here on the former frontier that generations of black leaders have come (Steve Biko and Nelson Mandela as two examples). Neither was it the end of landscapes of fear. I would argue that this Architecture of Fear is a recurring trope in the South African material world. The walls topped with broken glass and razor wire, electric fences and 'armed response' signs that mark suburban houses and rural farms alike, the night-time chorus of barking dogs – all tell us something about a struggle that is not yet over (Judin and Vladislavic 1999).

Conclusions

The revelation of the ways in which a position of colonial power was created and maintained through material expression allows a closer understanding of the historical background to the creation of the present-day independent South African state. The roots of current obstacles to democratization in contemporary post-apartheid South Africa can be ascribed to specific legacies of colonialism.[16]

16. See for example Mamdani (1996).

Images of the past play an important role in the creation of meaning in the present. Some within a politically compromised society such as South Africa continue to rely on a mythology that justifies colonial occupation of a resistant land and affirms their role in the creation of the modern state. They buy into a production of identity that rests on the feeling of achievement and cohesion at having carved a 'civilized' place out of the wilds of Africa. As critical archaeologists and historians have stated, the ways in which South Africa's past is written, or rewritten, have profound implications for the politics of the present.

Acknowledgements

As always I owe a debt of enormous gratitude to James Deetz for shaping my view of the past, and to the people of Salem, Xhosa and settler alike, who made me so welcome in their landscapes. Thanks also to Barbara Bender, Robert Ross and Justin Hyland. This research was funded in part by the US National Endowment for the Humanities, Wenner-Gren Foundation for Anthropological Research, and St. Mary's College Alumni Faculty Fellowship.

References

Beck, R. 1987. The Legalization and Development of Trade on the Cape Frontier, 1817–1830. Doctoral Thesis, Indiana University Department of History.

Bender, B. (ed.) 1993. *Landscape: Politics and Perspectives*. Oxford: Berg.

Bergh, J.S. and Visagie, J.C. 1985. *The Eastern Cape Frontier Zone 1660–1980: A Cartographic Guide for Historical Research*. Durban: Butterworths.

Bonner, P., Hofmeyer, I., James, D. and Lodge, T. (eds) 1990. *Holding Their Ground: Class, Locality and Culture in 19th and 20th Century South Africa (History Workshop, No. 4)* Johannesburg: Ravan Press of South Africa.

Boonzaier, E., Malherbe, C. Smith, A. and Berens, P. 1998. *The Cape Herders: A History of the Khoikhoi of Southern Africa*. Athens: Ohio University Press.

Braudel, F. 1992. *The Structures of Everyday Life. The Limits of the Possible (Civilization and Capitalism: 15th–18th Century)*. Berkeley: University of California Press.

Brink, Y. 1992. Places of Discourse and Dialogue: A Study of the Material Culture of the Cape During the Rule of the Dutch East India Company, 1652–1795. Doctoral Dissertation, University of Cape Town.

Brown, J., Manning, P., Shapiro, K. and Wiener, J. (eds) 1991. *History from South Africa: Alternative Visions and Practices (Critical Perspectives on the Past)*. Philadelphia: Temple University Press.

Bryer, L. in collaboration with Hunt, K. 1987. *The 1820 Settlers*. Heritage Series: 19th Century. Cape Town: Nelson.

Bundy, C. 1979. *The Rise and Fall of the South African Peasantry*. London: Heinemann.

Burchell, W. 1819. *Hints on Emigration to the Cape of Good Hope*. London: Hatchard.

Carson, C., Barka, N., Kelso, W., Stone, G.W. and Upton, D. 1988. Impermanent Architecture in the Southern American Colonies, in R.B. St George (ed.) *Material Life in America, 1600–1860*. Boston: Northeastern University Press.

Carter, P. 1988. *The Road to Botany Bay: an Exploration of Landscape and History*. New York: Knopf.

Cock, J. 1990. Domestic Service and Education for Domesticity: The Incorporation of Xhosa Women in Colonial Society, in C. Walker (ed.) *Women and Gender in Southern Africa to 1945*. Cape Town/London: David Philip/James Currey.

Coetzee, J.M. 1988. *White Writing: On the Culture of Letters in South Africa*. New Haven: Yale University Press.

Comaroff, J. 1985. *Body of Power, Spirit of Resistance: The Culture and History of a South African People*. Chicago: University of Chicago Press.

Comaroff, J. and Comaroff, J. 1991. *Of Revelation and Revolution: Christianity, Colonialism, and Consciousness in South Africa*. Volume 1. Chicago: University of Chicago Press.

Cooper, F. and Stoler, A. (eds) 1997. *Tensions of Empire: Colonial Cultures in a Bourgeois World.* Berkeley: University of California Press.

Cosgrove, D. and Daniels, S. (eds) 1988. *The Iconography of Landscape*. Cambridge: Cambridge University Press.

Crais, C. 1991. The Vacant Land: the mythology of British expansion in the Eastern Cape, South Africa. *Journal of Social History* **25**(2) 255–76.

—— 1992. *White Supremacy and Black Resistance in Pre-Industrial South Africa: The Making of the Colonial Order in the Eastern Cape, 1770–1865*. (African Studies) Cambridge: Cambridge University Press.

Elphick R. and Davenport, R. 1997. *Christianity in South Africa: A Political, Social and Cultural History*. Cape Town: David Philip.

Elphick, R. and Gilomee, H. (eds) 1989. *The Shaping of South African Society, 1652–1840*. Middletown, Connecticut: Wesleyan University Press.

Griffin, J. 1819. *The Real Facts Disclosed, or the Only Real Guide to the Cape: A Correct Statement of the Advantages and Disadvantages Attendant on Immigration to the New Colony*. London: Duncombe.

Hall, M. 1992. Small Things and the Mobile, Conflictual Fusion of Power, Fear and Desire, in A. Yentsch and M. Beaudry (eds) *The Art and Mystery of Historical Archaeology*. Ann Arbor: CRC Press.

Harley, J.B. 1988. Maps, Knowledge and Power, in D. Cosgrove and S. Daniels (eds) *The Iconography of Landscape*. Cambridge: Cambridge University Press.

Hockly, H. 1957. *The Story of the British Settlers of 1820 in South Africa*. Cape Town: Juta.

Judin, H. and Vladislavic, I. 1999. *Blank – Architecture, Apartheid and After*. Cape Town: David Philip.

Keegan, T. 1997. *Colonial South Africa and the Origins of the Racial Order*. Charlottesville: University of Virginia Press.

Lamar, H. and Thompson, L. (eds) 1981. *The Frontier in History: North America and South Africa Compared*. New Haven: Yale University Press.

Legassick, M. 1980. The Frontier Tradition in South African Historiography, in Marx, S. and Atmore, A. (eds) *Economy and Society in Pre-Industrial South Africa*. London: Longman.

Lewcock, R. 1963. *Early Nineteenth Century Architecture in South Africa: A Study on the Interaction of Two Cultures, 1795–1837*. Cape Town: Balkema.

Mamdani, M. 1996. *Citizen and Subject: Contemporary Africa and the Legacy of Late Colonialism* (Princeton Studies in Culture/Power/History). London: James Currey.

Marks, S. 1972. Khoisan resistance to the Dutch in the seventeenth and eighteenth Centuries. *Journal of African History* **13** 55–80.

Mitchell, W.J.T. (ed.) 1994. *Landscape and Power*. Chicago: University of Chicago Press.

Mostert, N. 1992. *Frontiers: The Epic of South Africa's Creation and the Tragedy of the Xhosa People*. New York: Knopf.

Nash, M.D. 1982. *Bailie's Party of 1820 Settlers: A Collective Experience in Emigration*. Cape Town: Balkema.

Peires, J.B. 1981. *The House of Phalo: A History of the Xhosa People in the Days of their Independence*. New History of Southern Africa, Johannesburg: Ravan Press.

—— 1989. *The Dead will Arise: Nongqawuse and the Great Cattle-Killing Movement of 1856–7*. Bloomington: Indiana University Press.

Ranger, T. 1999. *Voices from the Rocks: Nature, Culture and History in the Matopos Hills of Zimbabwe*. Bloomington: University of Indiana Press.

Ross, R. 1999. The Kat River Settlement in the Frontier Wars, 1835–1853: Hintsa's War, the War of the Axe and Mlanjeni's War. Conference paper, Siegburg.

—— 2000. *A Concise History of South Africa*. (Cambridge Concise Histories) Cambridge: University of Cambridge Press.

Saunders, C. 1976. The Hundred Years War; Some Reflections on African Resistance on the Cape-Xhosa Frontier, in D. Chanaiwa (ed.) *Profiles of Self-Determination*. Northridge: California State University Press.

Schama, S. 1996. *Landscape and Memory*. London: HarperCollins.

Schmidt, P. and Patterson, T. (eds) 1995. *The Making of Alternative Histories: The Practice of Archaeology in Non-Western Settings.* Santa Fe: School of American Research Press.

Schrire, C. 1990. Excavating archives at Oudepost-1. *Social Dynamics (Journal of the Center for African Studies, University of Cape Town)* **16** 11–21.

—— 1995. *Digging through Darkness: Chronicles of an Archaeologist.* Charlottesville: University of Virginia Press.

Shaw, W. 1860. *The Story of My Mission in South-Eastern Africa: Comprising some Account of the European Colonists; with Extended Notices of the Kaffir and other Native Tribes.* London: Hamilton, Adams and Co.

Smith, A., Malherbe, C., Guenther, M. and Berens, P., 2000. *The Bushmen of Southern Africa: A Foraging Society in Transition.* Athens: Ohio University Press.

Smith, W.H. 1835. On the Means of Defending Farmhouses. *Graham's Town Journal.* No. 191. 20 August.

Thompson, L. 1996. *A History of South Africa.* New Haven: Yale University Press.

Upton, D. 1985. The Power of Things: Recent Studies in American Vernacular Architecture, in T.J. Schlereth (ed.) *Material Culture: A Research Guide.* Lawrence: University Press of Kansas.

—— 1988. White and Black Landscapes in Eighteenth-Century Virginia, in R.B. St George (ed.) *Material Life in America, 1600–1860.* Boston: Northeastern University Press.

Webb, A.C.M. 1975. The Agricultural Development of the 1820 Settlement Down to 1845. Unpublished Masters thesis, Department of History, Rhodes University.

Wilson, M. 1969. Co-operation and Conflict: The Eastern Cape Frontier, in M. Wilson and L. Thompson (eds) *The Oxford History of South Africa, Vol. 1. South Africa to 1870.* Oxford: Oxford University Press.

Winer, M. 1994. Landscapes of Power: British Material Culture of the Eastern Cape Frontier, South Africa: 1820–1860. Doctoral dissertation. Department of Anthropology, University of California at Berkeley.

Winer, M. and Deetz, J. 1990. The transformation of British culture in the Eastern Cape, 1820–1860. *Social Dynamics (Journal of the Centre for African Studies, University of Cape Town)* **16**(1) 55–75.

—— 1995. The painted poetic landscape: reading power in nineteenth century textual and visual representations of the Eastern Cape frontier. *Kroeber Anthropological Society Papers* (79).

Wolf, E. 1982. *Europe and the People without History.* Berkeley: University of California Press.

Worden, N. 2000. *The Making of Modern South Africa: Conquest, Segregation and Apartheid.* (Historical Association Studies) London: Blackwell.

–16–

Places of Longing and Belonging: Memories of the Group Area Proclamation of a South African Fishing Village
Anna Bohlin

In a contribution to a recent volume focusing on personal and public memory in contemporary South Africa, historians Gary Minkley and Ciraj Rassool ask for social histories '. . . that do not easily romanticize and essentialize the past through a simple dichotomy between apartheid and resistance' (Minkley and Rassool 1998: 95). They further suggest that

> There is a growing realization that [. . .] apartheid did not always produce resistance, and that resistance was not always occasioned by apartheid. Rather, alongside difference and inequality lie more subtle forms of economic, cultural, and intellectual exchange integrally tied to the layers in which past and present are negotiated through memory, tradition, and history (Minkley and Rassool 1998: 94).

Memories of the proclamation in 1967 of the fishing village of Kalk Bay, situated on the False Bay coast of the Cape peninsula, as a 'white group area' provide insights into precisely such a complex and manifold history. While the more overt and readily observable consequences of forced removals under the Group Area Act (GAA) in South Africa have been explored through extensive media coverage, museum exhibitions and popular and academic literature, less is known about how the GAA subtly, and silently, affected communities in ways that cannot easily be fitted into generalized tropes of struggle and resistance. In Kalk Bay, around one-sixth of the so-called coloured residents were forced to move and resettle elsewhere as a result of the GAA proclamation, while the majority managed to remain.[1] Today, some thirty years later, the proclamation and its effects are remembered and imagined in ways that are intrinsically bound up with local experiences of

---

1. Whenever racial categories are used in the context of this chapter they should be understood as essentially contested terms that nevertheless continue to play a significant role in social and political discourses in South Africa.

place and landscape, and simultaneously involve resistance, silence and denial. Unlike for example District Six, near the Cape Town city centre, where a giant scarred landscape still bears witness to the eradication of the neighbourhood under the GAA, the landscape of Kalk Bay remains intact, and the harbour and the fishing boats, symbols of the fishing families who managed to remain, visually dominate the scenery.[2]

When I began to interview people in Kalk Bay in 1997, I was told that the GAA proclamation of Kalk Bay was 'pretty much a non-event' there and that nobody, or very few people, had actually been forced to move due to it. The reduction in size of the community since the time of the proclamation was explained as a result of a spontaneous and voluntary process of emigration of people to less overcrowded areas. Subsequently, interviewing people who had indeed been forced to move from Kalk Bay because of the GAA, I found that for them the proclamation remains a painfully remembered, indeed a pivotal life event, which is regarded as having had a profound effect not only on their own lives, but on the whole Kalk Bay community. The experience of concurrently conducting interviews with current and former residents without having recourse to a formal historical record, since none exists for the relevant time period, was a profound lesson in the creative and socially constructed, and constructing, nature of memory. I often left an interview with the feeling of finally having arrived at a 'balanced' and more 'accurate' view of what had transpired during and after the GAA proclamation, only to have that understanding turned on its head in a subsequent interview.

The process of remembering is a profoundly social activity in which the past is invoked to construe, reproduce, or alter one's relationship with the world (Fentress and Wickham 1992; Middleton and Edwards 1994). Any account of the past must be understood as being in part a 'social portrait', expressing ideas and sentiments concerning identity, morality and cosmology (Tonkin 1992: 1). As is well known to anthropologists, landscapes provide ideal contexts for the process of remembering, since they allow for a simultaneous movement through time and space (Cosgrove and Daniels 1988; Bender 1993; Hirsch 1995; Lovell 1998). Bearing witness of past activities, landscapes are concretized and collapsed 'taskscapes' (Ingold 1993) which serve as aides-mémoires, providing frameworks through which people perceive and engage with the present and the future (Halbwachs 1992 [1950]). Rather than being merely a mental category, 'a substanceless void to be filled by cognitive intuition', the concrete spatiality of social life is the outcome of a dynamic and open-ended process in which spatial and social forms dialectically intertwine and transform one another (Soja 1989: 17).

---

2. See Jeppie (1990) and Bohlin (1998) for discussions of the mnemonic and symbolic aspects of the empty landscape of District Six.

As the case of Kalk Bay reminds us, socially produced spatiality is never permanently fixed, but always remains open to, on the one hand, contestations in the present and, on the other, further transformations in the future. Focusing on the ambiguity and open-ended nature of lived-in as well as imagined landscapes, this chapter explores how notions of place and belonging have shaped narratives of the GAA in Kalk Bay. Another theme that is explored concerns the different kinds of physical, temporal and symbolic landscapes that are construed and engaged with, with regard to both those who were forced to move from the village and those who succeeded in staying.

The Group Area Proclamation of Kalk Bay

Founded as a whaling station in the eighteenth century, Kalk Bay is one of the few remaining communities in South Africa where fishermen still use hand-lines to catch fish from boats. Its name can be traced back to 1687, when the area was named after the lime kilns that were set up by European settlers on the beach to produce lime (in Afrikaans: *kalk*) from seashells. Geographically, the community has well-defined boundaries, cradled between the sea and the mountain. Through-out history various groups of people have settled down in Kalk Bay as fishermen, including Khoisan people, freed slaves and seamen, notably from south-east Asia, who deserted ships in the nearby naval Simon's Town (Whisson 1972; Quinlan 1980; Kirkaldy 1996). Today, members of the fishing community are either Christians (Roman Catholics and Anglicans) or Muslims. Some of the white residents are also fishermen, but most are employed outside of Kalk Bay.[3] A majority of them belong to the Anglican Church or the Dutch Reformed Church.

As historian Alan Kirkaldy has pointed out, it would be a mistake to view the GAA proclamation of Kalk Bay as a sudden, disruptive force which destroyed a previously harmonious and undivided community (Kirkaldy 1996: xix). Economic and social segregation had been a feature of village life in Kalk Bay since the onset of colonialism, and during the late nineteenth and early twentieth centuries conflicts of interests grew between the fishing- and the non-fishing communities. White residents generally belonged to a social and economic elite, employing women from the economically disadvantaged fishing community as domestic aides. Social and racial segregation became increasingly formalized around the turn of the century (Kirkaldy 1996: 83), and throughout the twentieth century fishermen and their families were gradually forced out of Kalk Bay as a result of shortage of accommodation. However, there also existed a relatively high level of residential

---

3. Hereafter I will use the term 'fishing community' when referring to people who under apartheid were classified as 'coloured' (white fishermen and their families were not directly affected by the GAA and therefore are not included in this category).

and social integration, reflected not least in the broad support offered by the white residents during the protests against the GAA declaration (Ritchken 1965; Cape Argus 1967).

In 1964 an announcement in the press stated that the Group Area Development Board (GADB) was to start investigations into the racial zoning of the area. Despite vocal protests, Kalk Bay was declared a white group area in 1967. As a result of the objections, however, those who lived in the Fishermen's flats, built by the Cape Town City Council for the fishermen in the 1940s, were given a period of respite of fifteen years. All other 'disqualified' people, living outside the flats, were given one year to leave. In 1982, the government, in an unusual course of action, decided to rescind the previous proclamation of Kalk Bay. A new coloured group area was suggested in its place, but the plan was later abandoned.

Reconstructing the precise effect of the proclamation in Kalk Bay is not easy, since the historical documentation is scanty. Nine families, comprising around thirty-five individuals, were forced to sell their properties after they received letters stating that they were disqualified as owners and had to sell to members of the right population group. Of the tenants, interviews with former landlords and tenants suggest that fourteen families, a total of seventy-five individuals, were evicted because of the proclamation, but there exists no written record of the exact number. In other words, altogether twenty-three families – a total of some 120 individuals – left the village because of the GAA. This amounts to roughly one-quarter of the original community at the time of the proclamation (see Whisson and Kaplinsky 1969: 10).[4]

A Sound and Healthy Place: Landscape and Identity

> I am often asked, why are you so different? And I usually say to them, I come from Kalk Bay. That's why I am different (Skipper, living in Kalk Bay).

During the decades of apartheid, when one community after the other was declared as a white group area throughout the Cape peninsula, 'the Cape Flats' was the area to which people were forced to move. As a consequence, the Cape Flats became understood as a space associated with displacement, hardship and suffering. The flatness of the place, its strong winds and the constant whirl of fine sand edging its way into all corners of the houses, are a few of the sources of grievance among residents often mentioned alongside high levels of crime and violence, as

---

4. Quinlan (1980: 39), White (1992: 4) and Kirkaldy (1996: xvii) all quote a larger number and suggest that the fishing community was reduced to less than half its size because of the GAA. This estimation, however, includes those who left Kalk Bay for other reasons than direct pressure from the GAA, such as marriage, lack of housing, eviction by private landlords etc.

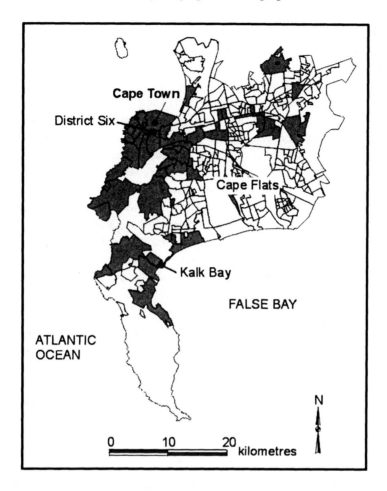

Figure 16.1 Map of the Cape Peninsula. The shaded fields indicate areas with mixed populations that were declared white under the Group Area Act (after list compiled by Delport 1991)

well as increased distances to work and health-care facilities.[5] On a more fundamental level, this space also became regarded as the epitome of the system of an externally imposed classification: of being defined by others.

For people in Kalk Bay one way of attempting to reject such imposed definitions was to define themselves and their community against a stereotypical image of the Cape Flats and its residents. Kalk Bay came to be regarded as a place that can provide what the Cape Flats cannot – a unique history, beautiful surroundings,

5. See Western (1996: Ch 9).

opportunities for economic autonomy via the income from the sea, as well as possibilities for integration between people of highly varied social and economic backgrounds.

Still today, a frequent assertion among people in Kalk Bay is that Kalk Bayers are different from 'people up the line', referring primarily to those living in the Cape Flats. Central in the construction of this difference is the notion of Kalk Bay as a 'healthy' landscape. The proximity to the sea, the mountains and the beaches, as well as the small scale of Kalk Bay, are features described as contributing to the healthy character of Kalk Bay, and by implication, also its residents. 'In Kalk Bay we don't need any social workers,' a Kalk Bay resident told me, 'because we have the mountains.' He described how potentially wayward youth are 'improved' by spending time in the mountains where they are able to acquire valuable knowledge about the various paths, caves, plants and berries on the mountainside, information which can be used to obtain pocket money, for example by selling flowers. The beaches are described as a similar space of socialization and regeneration, providing opportunities for constructive and healthy outdoor activities. The most significant source of images of Kalk Bay as a healthy place, however, is the sea. Providing a scenic space for various forms of recreation, this 'pool of health' also spills out into the less wholesome areas of the Cape Flats, as described by a retired fisherman:

> I feel very proud of the fact that ever since we started fishing here, and I think it must be over two hundred years, we've been the source of supply of a very very healthy commodity to our own people on the Cape Flats at a very cheap price. That I feel very proud of.

The image of Kalk Bay as a healthy landscape also has a deeper level of signification. As Swanson has pointed out, in discourses promoting racial segregation in South Africa metaphors of health, contamination and disease were frequently used to express racial relations and hierarchies. Serving not merely as a biological fact, 'disease' also became a social metaphor that was used by various institutions to justify the expulsion in particular of black African communities from white neighbourhoods (Swanson 1977: 408; Field 1996: 168–72). By construing Kalk Bay as a desirable landscape, intrinsically linked to the activities of the fishermen, the fishing community has created an unassailable argument concerning their legitimate existence in the village. While the perceived threats to the fishermen's livelihood are of a mainly commercial character today (such as plans to create a yachting marina and a new commercial 'waterfront'), the same imagery continues to be used in efforts to protect the status quo.

The sea, furthermore, is linked to the construction of a specific Kalk Bay identity. Providing an 'honest' source of income, it allows the young to escape the troubles

Figure 16.2 The fisherman's flats overlooking Kalk Bay

such as the notorious gangs and the drug commerce that prevail in the Cape Flats. Working on the sea, with its hazardous conditions, is seen as promoting commendable qualities such as honesty, endurance and discipline. A man who left Mitchells Plain in the Cape Flats, where he was born, to stay with his grandparents in the fishermen's flats, said the following:

> There's no gangsterism here in Kalk Bay, it's a humble place. I wonder what I'd turned out if I had stayed in Mitchells Plain? Job opportunities there are not so wonderful. I mean what else do you have to do to get money? You have to steal, you have to do this, you have to do that. Here, you can go fishing, earn an honest living, so it's cool. You don't have to do any naughty things.

Another implication of life on the sea is its incompatibility with the restrictions imposed by apartheid. 'The sea is in our blood' is a popular phrase that serves as a playful reminder of the shared humanity of those who work together on the boats, contrasting the superficial emphasis on skin colour in the rhetoric of apartheid. On the sea, which is conceptualized as a primordial force eliciting from people qualities that are common to all human beings, the divisiveness of apartheid is exposed as being a shallow construction of little consequence. 'There is no apartheid here, ou pellie (old friend), the fish don't mind who catches them', a fisherman said (Moskovitz 1982). In this discourse, the fluidity of the sea is metaphorically brought into the sphere of social relations, and a collective, idealized identity is constructed that draws on, and is negotiated through, images of land- and seascapes.

To be able to partake in this unique, collective Kalk Bay identity provides people with a constructive self-image and sense of belonging in a context where such sentiments often have been fundamentally threatened or destroyed. Crucially, however, in this discourse, the GAA proclamation and its consequences for those who had to move are virtually omitted. The construction of an idealized Kalk Bay identity presupposes the image of Kalk Bay as an intact, resilient and unbroken community, an image which by its very nature excludes the possibility of recognizing the experiences of those who were forced to move.

Paradoxically, those who were forced to leave Kalk Bay express a sense of belonging to Kalk Bay by adopting a very similar discourse, in which a streamlined landscape, devoid of conflicts and contradictions, is conceptualized. For them, however, the landscape of Kalk Bay, imagined in this way, becomes a medium of commentary on the place to which they have been forced to belong, providing the means for a conceptualization of a clear-cut border between their own identity and the perceived chaos and lawlessness of the surroundings. As for people who still live in Kalk Bay, this mythical landscape is a vital element in processes of identity formation, helping to form 'the narrative threads that provide a sense of continuity when fragmentary experiences threaten' (Field 1996: 115). A woman who was forced to move from Kalk Bay to the Cape Flats contrasts the two places in the following way:

> We had everything in Kalk Bay, we had the mountain, we ran wild, we never knew about sickness, because everything was so clear, and clean. Coming to this place when it rained, the water stayed on the soil, I mean for three years we couldn't even go out with our daughter on account of being sick!

Inside this woman's house in the Cape Flats, as in most of the houses belonging to people who were forced to move, this idealized landscape is symbolically present. Various kinds of memorabilia, such a model of a fishing boat, photographs of the harbour from the turn of the century, books or tourist brochures illustrated with quaint Kalk Bay scenes, sometimes depicting the house left behind, are some of the objects that conjure up a 'memory room' (Swiderski 1995), enabling this landscape to be visited.

While those who remained in Kalk Bay construe a mythical notion of Kalk Bay in the present, as being an intact social landscape that is not affected by the forced removals, the ones who moved continue to live with the very consequences of this rupture. For them, the Kalk Bay of the present is damaged. A common theme is that Kalk Bay has changed and 'is not the same', and that 'new' people, who 'do not belong' have moved into the village since the GAA proclamation, corrupting the very essence of what Kalk Bay once was. There is a perception that if only the old Kalk Bayers, born and bred in Kalk Bay, were able to move back to the village, it could then become restored to what it used to be. The 'real' and 'authentic' Kalk Bay is in other words primarily a landscape of the past. This can be compared to how former residents of the GAA-affected community of Winder-mere, near Cape Town, used images of a past Windermere to construct hopeful images for the future South Africa (Field 1996: 128). Related to the perceived temporal distance to the idealized landscape of the past is the frequently mentioned physical distance to the Kalk Bay of the present. Although most of the people who moved would be able to reach Kalk Bay by car in around fifteen minutes, they speak of it as being remote. The spatial gap between their new life on the Cape Flats and the old one in Kalk Bay is conflated with the temporal gap between the present and the past.[6]

Yet, there are certain features of the landscape in Kalk Bay that are perceived as not having changed, and these are the churches. A majority of those who were forced to move continue, despite the geographical and emotional distance, to come

---

6. Some do not own a car, however, and for them the journey can take as long as two hours.

to Kalk Bay every Sunday and worship with their old congregations.[7] Whatever else Kalk Bay may be perceived to have become, the churches serve as physical embodiments of the streamlined and idealized landscape of belonging – inside there are no 'street people' (one of the frequent complaints about the deterioration of Kalk Bay is the intrusion of vagrants), no racial tensions, and, importantly, no divisions between those who still live in Kalk Bay and those who have moved. People often point out that the churches were built by the early generations of fishermen and their families, with 'white and coloured people, rich and poor', working together, using stones from the Kalk Bay mountains. As such, the church materializes a spirit of communal enterprise and symbolizes the overcoming of social and racial divisions, while providing a concrete and manifest expression of rootedness in Kalk Bay. Similarly, outside the church, the weathered gravestones proclaim the names of deceased family members and serve as solid and tangible symbols of belonging. The churches provide a space where those currently dispersed in the Cape Flats are able to partake in, and reinforce, the notion of a rooted, collective identity that has a shared origin and a common purpose. Perhaps the most telling sign of a sense of entitlement to this landscape is the fact that many of them have chosen to be buried there when they die.

Making Sense of the Past: Landscapes of Ambiguity

The historian Uma Mesthrie has described how, in Black River, a suburb outside Cape Town, people who managed to stay despite being declared 'disqualified' residents under the GAA proclamation of the village were regarded with suspicion by those who were forced to move (Mesthrie 1997: 33–5). Similar confusion exists among former residents of Kalk Bay. Many express a sense of bewilderment as to how certain people managed to remain, and speculations, ranging from suggestions that some of those who stayed may in fact have been classified as white, to ideas concerning their possible connections with authorities and influential individuals, serve as attempts to make sense of the perceived inconsistency of the application of the GAA.[8] The GAA is interpreted as a power that has the capacity to distinguish between people not only on the basis of racial belonging and place of residence,

---

7. Muslim families who were forced to move are for practical reasons unable to attend the mosque in Kalk Bay for their prayers five times a day. On special occasions, however, they too return to worship in the mosque in Kalk Bay, which is still in use.

8. Exactly how people managed to stay outside the flats is unclear. One family evaded being evicted by not registering the original owner's death for eighteen years, thereby avoiding the inevitable eviction that took place once the original owner of a property died. Others were advised by lawyers to simply refuse to sell their properties. It is possible that Kalk Bay remained an area where strict implementation of the GAA was not prioritised by the authorities given the involvement in the matter by a local Member of Parliament.

but also on the basis of occupation, property ownership and religion. In such speculations the landscape plays a crucial role, serving as a source of semantic material that is used in the construction of arguments explaining how and why the GAA affected individuals differently.

One of the socially and symbolically most significant topographical features of the built environment in Kalk Bay is constituted by the fishermen's flats. Occupying a prominent position high on the mountainside, the flats are sheltered from the southwester and allow the fishermen quick access to the boats should weather conditions change. Until a few years ago, a family was allowed to reside in the flats only under the condition that at least one member of the family was a fisherman. Although this condition for tenancy was recently abolished, it firmly established this space as morally, historically and economically belonging to the fishermen. Such is the extent to which the flats are associated with the fishermen that in a report on Kalk Bay one resident felt inclined to warn that 'we must always bear in mind that the Fishing Community is scattered throughout Kalk Bay, and not just in the Council Flats' (White 1992: 7).

When I asked people who were forced to move why residents in Kalk Bay deny that anybody had to leave because of the GAA, a common response was that this collective 'amnesia' is related to the existence of the fishermen's flats. The fact that the flats are still there, they argue, signalling with their prominent position the continued presence in Kalk Bay of the fishing community, has prevented people from remembering the existence of coloured families living outside this area. In fact, this was the line of argument adopted by a white resident in Kalk Bay who told me that 'anybody who says that Kalk Bay was affected by the group areas is telling a lie' and explicitly referred to the presence of the fishermen's flats as evidence for his assertion. Although only a small percentage of the fishermen actually remain in Kalk Bay today, the presence of the fishermen's flats, as well as that of the harbour, which constitutes another noticeable and tangible representation of the fishing character of Kalk Bay, creates the impression of a lively and well-preserved fishing community. Few features in the landscape remind visitors and residents of the fact that the vast majority of the fishermen commute to the harbour from the Cape Flats. In a publication by the Kalk Bay Historical Association a fisherman asks 'is it not time to stop thinking that the harbour belongs only to a few (fishermen) who reside here?' (Stibbe and Moss 1999: 119).

The 'fishing theme', furthermore, which is reinforced in the selection of maritime books, postcards and objects sold in antique shops in the main road, and by the wall murals and decorations in the local cafes and restaurants, has affected the way in which the GAA proclamation is imagined. The area around the flats was excluded in the proclamation, thus making it possible for the occupants in this area to remain. The popular interpretation, however, is that the residents in the flats were allowed to stay because they were fishermen. The fact that many families living outside the fishermen's flats also managed to remain is understood in the same terms: only those who were not fishermen, or did not own a boat, were made to leave. In attempts to explain the perceived contradictions of the GAA application, the fishermen's flats serve as a conceptual model in which a certain kind of belonging to the landscape, manifested through the activity of fishing, and concretized in the form of ownership of a boat, is construed as a criterion for being allowed to stay.

While the fishermen's flats indisputably express the fishing community's presence in Kalk Bay, the images invoked by *die dam* are more ambiguous. Demolished in the 1950s, the wash house, or *die dam*, where coloured women used to do the laundry for the white residents as well as for the nearby hotels, was located in the heart of Kalk Bay, where water used to be piped down from the mountain. The surrounding area was one of the few places outside the fishermen's flats where coloured families used to live. Today most of the old cottages are demolished, while others are renovated in a 'gentrification process' similar to that described by Western, referring to Mowbray, another suburb of Cape Town that was affected by the GAA (1996: 185–96). While the buildings around *die dam* contain few reminders of the past, the fact that no new buildings have been erected on the empty space contributes to keeping the memory of the wash house alive. The mosque, situated at one side of the small park that now covers the ground where the wash house used to stand, further defines this space as one in which coloured people once lived and worked.

Indeed, many residents in Kalk Bay spontaneously reminisce about *die dam*, and, specifically, about the friendly relations that are understood to have existed between the white and coloured residents, exemplified by the interaction in connection with the laundry dealings. It is noteworthy that in such reminiscences questions concerning what happened to the people that lived and worked around *die dam* are absent. A white woman, living near die dam, spontaneously spoke at length about the area, the surrounding buildings, and the coloured occupants that used to live there. Yet, her initial response to my question about the GAA was that she was under the impression that Kalk Bay was one of the few places in the country where people did not have to move. Subsequently in the interview, speaking about her domestic aide who was forced to move from Kalk Bay, she said that she was in fact aware that people had to move under the GAA, but had not spontaneously remembered it. There are doubtless many and complex factors involved in this woman's 'forgetting' of the GAA. Without further going into these issues here, it is clear that although *die dam* invokes certain very specific memories of the past, it does so primarily in the form of nostalgia. It has become a landscape of the past which can be momentarily pondered upon, but the memories that are invoked by it are not juxtaposed or cross-referenced with the fact that most of the people inhabiting this landscape are now gone. Although *die dam* has the potential to offer a focal point for contrasting narratives of the past, and provide a space in which they could be confronted, it seems that the selective and contextual nature of remembering precludes the exploration of such differences and contradictions.

Conclusion

To some extent Kalk Bay can be seen as a community in which the implementation of apartheid was successful. The community which was once relatively integrated residentially – if socially and economically stratified – is today divided spatially and socially, with more or less clearly demarcated 'white' and 'coloured' areas. Most importantly, the boundaries of these areas are perceived as 'natural' in the sense that they are not understood as having been reinforced by apartheid. The sea, meanwhile, has remained a landscape in and of itself, where strict apartheid could never be implemented. Yet, ironically, the very symbols of this maritime landscape, the fishermen's flats and the harbour, have by virtue of their conspicuous and imposing presence in Kalk Bay contributed to the erosion of the memory of those who lived outside these areas and who were forced to move. In fact, many people in Kalk Bay today are not even aware that Kalk Bay was ever proclaimed a white Group Area. Newspaper articles, if they mention the GAA proclamation, reinforce the image of Kalk Bay as a place where the GAA removals were 'successfully fought off' (Cape Times 17 May 1999). Given that the proclamation, when issued, was hotly debated in the media as well as at a number of well-attended meetings that took place in Kalk Bay during the years of protests, the contemporary awareness of this recent history has faded remarkably quickly.

We have seen how conflicting narratives surrounding the GAA reflect notions of place and belonging that have grown out of perceptions of the landscape – both as a metaphor and as a concrete, tangible experience. For those who live in Kalk Bay the landscape has served as an aide-mémoire, albeit in a negative sense – certain features of the landscape have contributed to the forgetting of a certain aspect of the past. For those who were forced to move, on the other hand, the Kalk Bay of today is imagined to be dramatically different from the Kalk Bay they left. Although both groups share the notion of a mythical and idealized landscape – the embodiment of health, peace and egalitarian values – they locate this landscape in different times. In both instances, however, the creation of such imagined landscapes helps to explain inconsistencies and pain in ways that, to borrow Tonkin's words, 'create a moral order which redeems the sufferings [. . .] from senseless chaos' (1992: 44).

Acknowledgements

Fieldwork was carried out in 1997 and 1998, and was made possible by the Swedish Council for research in the Humanities and Social Sciences. My thanks go to Royden Yates, Åsa Boholm, Barbara Bender, Margot Winer and staff and students at the Department of Anthropology, University of Cape Town, for their helpful comments on drafts of this chapter.

References

Bender, B. (ed.) 1993. *Landscape: Politics and Perspectives*. Oxford: Berg.

Bohlin, A. 1998. The Politics of Locality: Remembering District Six in Cape Town, in N. Lovell (ed.) *Locality and Belonging*. London: Routledge.

Cape Argus. 1967. It may be a slow road to a brighter Kalk Bay. 15 July.

Cape Times. 1999. One city many cultures. Cape Town. 17 May.

Cosgrove, D. and Daniels, S. (eds) 1988. *The Iconography of Landscape: Essays on the Symbolic Representation, Design and Use of Past Environments*. Cambridge: Cambridge University Press.

Delport, P. 1991. *'Res Claimant – The Earth Cries Out': Background and Pictorial Guide to the Holy Cross Mural*. Cape Town: Hirt and Carter.

Fentress, J. and Wickham, C. 1992. *Social Memory*. Cambridge: Blackwell.

Field, S. 1996. The power of exclusion: moving memories from Windermere to the Cape Flats 1920s–1990s. Unpublished PhD thesis. Department of Sociology, University of Essex.

Halbwachs, M. 1992 [1950]. *On Collective Memory*. Chicago: University of Chicago Press.

Hirsch, E. and O'Hanlon, M. (eds) 1995. *The Anthropology of Landscape: Perspectives on Place and Space*. Oxford: Oxford University Press.

Ingold, T. 1993. The temporality of the landscape. *World Archaeology* 25(2) 152–74.

Jeppie, S. and Soudien, C. (eds) 1990. *The Struggle for District Six: Past and Present*. Cape Town: Buchu Books.

Kirkaldy, A. 1996. *'The sea is in our blood': Community and Craft in Kalk Bay c.1880–1939*. Pretoria: The Government Printer.

Lovell, N. (ed.) 1998. *Locality and Belonging*. London: Routledge.

Mesthrie, U. 1997. *Remembering Removals: the Story of Black River, Rondebosch*. Cape Town: University of the Western Cape.

Middleton, D. and Edwards, D. 1994. Introduction. *Collective Remembering*. D. Middleton and D. Edwards (eds). London: Sage Publications Ltd.

Minkley, G. and Rassool, C. 1998. Orality, Memory, and Social History in South Africa, in S. Nuttall and C. Coetzee (eds) *Negotiating the Past: The Making of Memory in South Africa*. Cape Town: Oxford University Press.

Moskovitz, S. 1982. Steering by the star of the sea. *Odyssey* 6 (2) April/ May.

Quinlan, T. 1980. Line fishing in Kalk Bay: an account of a marginal livelihood in a developing industrial environment. BA Honours thesis. Department of Social Anthropology. University of Cape Town.

Ritchken, M. 1965. The fisherfolk of Kalk Bay. *The Black Sash*. **9** 2–3.

Soja, E. 1989. *Postmodern Geographies: The Reassertion of Space in Critical Theory*. London: Verso.

Stibbe, G. and Moss, I. 1999. *A Traditional Way of Life: the History of the Kalk Bay Fishermen*. Goodwood, Cape Town: National Book Printers.

Swanson, M. 1977. The sanitation syndrome: bubonic plague and urban native policy in the Cape Colony, 1900–1909. *Journal of African History* **18**(3).

Swiderski, R. 1995. Mau Mau and Memory Rooms: Placing a Social Emotion, in M.C. Teski and J.J. Climo (eds) *The Labyrinth of Memory: Ethnographic Journeys*. Westport, CT: Bergin and Garvey.

Tonkin, E. 1992. *Narrating Our Pasts: The Social Construction of Oral History*. Cambridge: Cambridge University Press.

Western, J. 1996. *Outcast Cape Town*. Berkeley: University of California Press.

Whisson, M.G. 1972. *The Fairest Cape? An Account of the Coloured People in the District of Simonstown*. Johannesburg: South African Institute of Race Relations.

—— and Kaplinsky, R.M. 1969. *Suspended Sentence: A Study of the Kalk Bay Fishermen*. Johannesburg: South African Institute of Race Relations.

White, A.L.B. 1992. *KB90: Towards a better understanding of Kalk Bay and its needs*. Cape Town: South African Library.

–17–

Homes and Exiles:
Owambo Women's Literature
Margie Orford and Heike Becker

While I was in exile I remembered home through things I had known. Now that I am in Namibia all that I knew of Namibia, of home, has changed. I am finding myself lost in my own country . . . If I am lost, if my past is lost amongst historical events over which I have no control, *who then shall make or remake my history*? (Namhila 1997)

How does a woman, faced with dramatic change, map her own historical and geographical space? In this chapter we have drawn together some previously isolated texts by women who originate from Owambo, central northern Namibia. We want to create a literary archipelago that links their shared experiences over time and space. We focus on Owambo literature as a discrete entity, not in order to 're-bantustan' the diverse people of Namibia, but rather as a way of looking at the artistic articulations of a unique historical and social experience in expressive oral and written texts.

The Historical Background to these Stories

People have occupied Namibia, a dry and sparsely populated land, for many thousands of years – its wealth of rock art is testimony to very ancient patterns of settlement and documentation. As the oral history of the various Owambo polities attests, the ancestors of its present-day inhabitants have occupied the area for many generations (Williams 1991). Starting in the late eighteenth century various groups of people moved into central and southern Namibia from the Cape Province, and over the following centuries there has been intense competition over scarce resources. In addition, the arrival of missionaries and traders in central Namibia, starting at the beginning of the nineteenth century, increasingly impacted on social structures. Northern Namibia remained only marginally affected by these developments but was subject to informal colonial penetration, especially in the form of traders from Angola. Finnish missionaries entered Owambo in 1870 followed by German Lutheran missionaries in the early 1890s.

German colonial rule over Namibia, tenuously established in 1884, was consolidated only in 1907 after a period of intense and prolonged conflict (Sylvester, Wallace and Hayes 1998). The German colonial period ended in 1915 with the arrival of South African troops. Northern Namibia was only formally colonized after the South Africans took over and Namibia remained under South African rule until Independence in 1990.

When South Africa took over in 1915, resident colonial officials were based in Owambo for the first time. However, the colonial administration of the northern territories was run on a shoestring, with never more than a handful of resident officials, who administered as a unique brand of indirect rule. Crucial to the system of indirect rule was the continued application of 'ordinary native law and custom', as the administration perceived it, and the official recognition of indigenous rulers. However, if the administration deemed fit, this was combined with political and military intervention (U.G. No 33/1925, quoted in Olivier 1961: 195).

The colonial freezing and reinvention of 'native law and custom' greatly affected gender relations in Owambo. The selective use of ostensibly traditional law was exemplified in the efforts of colonial officials to prevent the migration of women out of Ovamboland, as the area was officially called during the colonial era. Women's mobility was seen as highly threatening to the 'traditional' order. It was prohibited on the grounds that it contravened 'traditional laws and customs'. Oral history suggests that the colonial construction of gender did indeed build on, but was also modified by, pre-colonial gender practices, representations, and conflicts (Becker 1998a: 18). The colonial construction of gender further essentialized gender images by isolating the category of 'women' from other social categories with which they had been intertwined in earlier representations. Women's place was increasingly restricted to the domestic and traditional spheres of society, whereas men were to enter the public sphere, predominantly as migrant labourers.

The colonial administration and senior Owambo men shared the redefinition of 'traditional' gender attributes while they were often at loggerheads with the Christian missions as the third player in the field of colonial sexual politics. The missions redefined gender in the interface of tradition and Christianity, following the historically specific patterns of the patriarchal European societies of that time (Becker 1997: 175). In both the official colonial and the mission-colonial construction of gender Owambo women were silenced and rendered invisible.

Ellen Namhila's question *who then shall make or remake my history?* is particularly vexed, not only because of the severe social dislocations caused by war, but also because of the insistently claimed absence of women's writing or orality in most of the colonial ethnography. The construction of the invariably powerless and mute Owambo woman has survived as a commonly-held belief in present-day Namibia, and it is clear from historical evidence and from oral and written literature that women's experience in Owambo has been shaped by this oppressive gendered construction of their place in society. Even so, women have been neither passive nor silent: this gendered construction has been constantly re-represented, reshaped and challenged (Becker 1997: 177). In exploring the textured literature available it is possible to counter popularly held views about women's subordination, and the often unrecognized role Owambo women have played, and continue to play, in the structuring of culture and society can be brought to the fore. It is a way of reasserting women's cultural centrality and rediscovering the legacies passed from mother to daughter.

Owambo is the westernmost part of the central African matrilineal belt. Structural-functional anthropology (Richards 1950: 246) made much of the apparent contradiction of matrilineal descent and male authority in these societies with the assumption that matriliny did not entail greater authority for women, but merely meant that authority flowed through the mother's brother rather than the father. More recent approaches towards the relationship between matrilineal kinship and gender hold that matrilineal forms of organization and ideology tend to give greater social and political space to women. Considerable scope for women's authority is found in matrilineally organized groups, although the particular meshing with male authority varies (Peters 1997: 133–4). In Owambo, elements of matriliny have been under pressure through socio-economic changes since at least the 1940s (Hayes 1992) but the 'matrilineal inheritance' of culture and representation by women seems to have been hidden and marginalized, rather than abandoned.

Text and Story

Owambo women have written prolifically, primarily in English, in the years since Independence. These texts are 'the cultural daughters' of the older, oral texts, told and recorded in Oshiwambo[1] discussed below.[2] And alongside the texts, oral literature continues to be produced and reproduced. As the subject matter changes to suit particular circumstances and performances, so we can trace changes in social structuring over time.

Our sketch of the 'matrilineal inheritance' of texts, oral and written, evokes a self-authored history of the experiences of women in Owambo. Literary works are presented here in an attempt to trace, to reconstruct and re-present Owambo women's experiences as an acknowledged literary canon. They show how women have positioned themselves in language vis-à-vis the silencing discourses of patriarchy and colonialism and how they have reclaimed the position of speaking subject for themselves. The role of explanation and healing manifest in these texts

---

1. Oshiwmabo is the collective name that has been applied to the various linked languages spoken.
2. The presentation of different genres of Owambo songs follows Zinke (1993).

is important in the face of often rapid and violent social change. It has also been in these moments of rupture that women artists have carved out new spaces for women to occupy.

The rich oral literature of the Owambo includes prose narratives such as tales, myths and legends as well as epic and lyric poetry. Most of the poetry is performed in singing at various occasions (Zinke 1993). There is the lullaby, *okulolola okaana*; but most genres are sung by groups of people. The generic term *oshiimbo* (song) implies several performers, such as the *oshiimbo shefundula* (initiation/wedding song), the *oshiimbo shoihanangolo* (the song of the 'ashbrides', young women during the transitional period following the initiation), the *oudano,* but also the more mundane hoeing song, *oshiimbo sheendina* or *okulina*, and the threshing song, *okuxua*. However, the dividing line between sung and spoken poetry is rather blurred. The *oshitewo*, poem or recital, may also include elements of singing, although it is clearly perceived as a different genre. There has been a grievous lack of research in all these areas, which is only now being addressed.

The presentation of ritual leadership, political power, and the performance and transmission of oral history and traditions as exclusively male domains is one of the persistent features of the colonial ethnography of Owambo. However, it appears that these presentations tell us more about their authors than about the real gender attributes of Owambo cultural elements. Recent research has shown that before the onset of colonialism female rulers were no exception in at least some of the Owambo polities (see e.g. Becker 1998a). And, whereas earlier representations by missionaries and colonial officials depicted the rituals as male-led, women were, and still are, central as ritual leaders, particularly in the female initiation ceremonies. Female initiation, known as *efundula, ohango* or *olufuko* in the Owambo languages, constitutes the central ritual in Owambo culture (see Becker 1998b).

It also appears that both women and men were, and still are, performers and composers of songs, poetry and prose narratives, including those related to the transmission of history. The performance of oral traditions emerges as non-gendered; anyone with language and performance skills could take it up. There were also no fixed prescriptions of specific genres as either 'female' or 'male'. The only exception were those that were performed within a culturally clearly gendered context, such the songs of the 'ashbrides' or those of the herd boys. Men and women equally authored and performed prose or epic 'historical narratives', whereas 'fiction', for example the telling of tales, was largely, but not exclusively, the domain of women.[3]

3. Interviews with Jason Amukutuwa, 13.5.1999, Elim and Shekumtaamba Nambala, 17.5.1999, Oniipa.

The Literature of Colonialism and Exile

Much Owambo poetry refers to current affairs or historical occurrences. Many songs and poems revolve around historical persons and events. This is apparent in the long epic poem *Song of Chief Iipumbu* (in Dammann and Tirronen 1975), which was performed in OshiNdonga by Loide Shikongo (*c.* 1886–1961), and recorded on 23.12.1953 at Onandjokwe. The poem directly addresses the controversial Iipumbu, the son of Shilongo, the *omukwaniilwa* (king) of the Kwambi from 1908 to 1932. Shikongo also praises five of her sons in the poem.

Iipumbu's stubbornness and resistance against the colonial government led to a stand-off with the administration. Apart from Iipumbu's struggles with the colonial administration, he was also opposed to the efforts of the missionaries in Uukwambi. Much of the conflict arose from his treatment of both the missionaries and their converts. Iipumbu is said to have forced young Christian women to participate in the *ohango* female initiation rituals. A particular issue of contest were his alleged violent sexual advances towards young Kwambi women.

In 1932 the conflict with both the mission and the administration climaxed when he directed his attentions towards Neekulu yaShivute, a baptismal candidate, who according to some sources was his illegitimate biological daughter (Hayes 1992: 261). Other sources deny this fact, but it is agreed that Neekulu was his social daughter, as her mother was a sister to one of Iipumbu's wives.[4] His marriage to her was thus prohibited. Neekulu fled to the missionary at Elim who hid her and smuggled her out of Uukwambi. Iipumbu sent his men to fetch her from the mission, where they fired into the air. This act of violence towards the white missionaries finally brought about the military intervention by the administration and Iipumbu's deposal. He died in exile in 1959.

It emerges from most oral sources that the Christian community in Uukwambi, and probably the majority of the population there, welcomed his deposal at that time. Over the ensuing decades, however, Iipumbu emerged as a hero of the anti-colonial struggle. There are many praise songs which celebrate his staunch resistance against colonial rule. However, especially among the older generation of Christian believers Iipumbu is regarded as an anti-Christian villain even today. Shikongo was a committed Christian. In this poem, she advises Iipumbu to take stock and act wisely for his people.

> Wait a minute; let me to tell you
> Let me come and tell you
> You, Iipumbu, Get up!

---

4. Interviews with Jason Amukutuwa, 13.5.1999, Elim and Shekumtambaa Nambala, 17.5.1999, Oniipa.

> Get up and see the circumcision of men
> Get up and see the circumcision of men
> Look at the horrors being done in the sky
> Get up and see the aeroplane
> Nelomba, the plane, is moving up in the sky
> The big-legged ones have settled like manna
> The big-legged ones have settled over the oshana
> It's you they have been told about
> You, it's you they have been told about
> You, Iipumbu get up . . .
> You brought it on yourself
> You brought it on yourself.[5] (Shikongo in Daymond *et al.* forthcoming 2002)

Loide Shikongo is unequivocal about her right to warn and criticize Iipumbu about the recklessness of the action that led to the attacks. This rare poem places both the author and the conflict she describes at the centre – the invaders simply materialize from some unnamed periphery. She maps a political arena that locates the agency of power, control and change firmly within Owambo. The right to comment is unquestionably within the female realm at this time. This was to change, as will be seen in other texts.

Women's mobility, as well as their productive and reproductive capacity, was fiercely contested during the colonial period. Although male migrant labour was actively recruited in Owambo during both the German and the South African colonial periods, women were required to stay at home. A few women did manage to find work outside Owambo, but the administration and Owambo male elders who 'shared a discourse of responsible patriarchy' (Hayes 1992: 288) effectively prevented such movement, and every effort was made to keep the Owambo 'tribalized' (Hayes 1996).

The fact that women's mobility was seen as highly threatening to the 'traditional order' is borne out in several oral and written texts. For women, the ideological journey to Christianity marked an exile from the 'home', or traditional ideology of the time. It was a journey that offered no return. This is clear in an interview conducted with Selma Amutana[6] on the early Christianization process in Ondonga:

> Let me make myself clear. When it comes to me, I think these men did not come here as runaway children because men had choices. It was their choice to come here and be educated. They did not break the relationship with their families, unlike runaway girls.

---

5. Translated by Nepeti Nicanor.

6. Selma Amutana, transcribed by Kamau, interviewed by Meredith McKittrick and Fanuel Shingenge, 21 July, 1997, Ondando Ondonga.

The literary mapping of real landscapes that remained inaccessible to most women is an important feature of women's poetry, particularly in the *Oudano*. The *Oudano*[7] are group songs, performed by moonlight, by young unmarried women. In these songs, social relations, problems and journeys – imaginary and real – are mapped in choral compositions. Nevertheless, the primary map seems to be the mapping of the female body, through symbol and words. Louisa Hamukoshi described her transition from girlhood to womanhood with the beautiful image of the lost eggshell beads, which circle the waists of maidens and thus map the contours of the virgin female body:

Mothers and fathers, goodbye, I am going
Sisters and brothers, I have wedded
I am dispossessed of the eggshell beads
Now I have womanhood beads
I dislike the womanhood beads
It darkens my heart
I like the eggshell beads
That whiten the waist[8]

In another song the journey made by men, who might come back with gifts or with sufficient money to marry, is mapped in a round sung by several women. These songs draw a landscape that they were not permitted to experience directly:

Child, I ask you the way to Oranjemund
I ask for the way to Grootfontein

The way which leads to the Union
Where is the way that leads to Otjiwerongo?

Child, when you walk, do not be in a hurry
Where we are going it is too far . . .

I have discovered that months are many
There is October

In the Police Zone, they write January
June and April

---

7. Ongoing research: Betty Hango-Rummukainen of the National Museum of Namibia.
8. *Oudano* songs translated by Betty Hango-Rammukainen, ongoing research.

I have discovered that Tsumeb is near
I went there in the daytime. . .[9]

But it was a landscape that would soon be braved as the situation in Owambo grew increasingly repressive. The novel, *Marrying Apartheid* by Ndeutala Hishongwa (1986), explores the implications and reasons that prompted a woman to move. It is a unique text as it locates the struggle against apartheid directly within and on the body of the female protagonist. Hishongwa writes of the restrictions of 'traditional' patriarchy, which are compounded and corrupted by the violence of apartheid. The increasing domestic violence the heroine Tanga suffers at her collaborator-husband's hands is a gendered metaphor for the violence suffered by Namibia. Tanga flees her marital home but still finds no lasting relief.

After having been the 'spoken to' and the 'spoken for', Tanga's husband asks her to return as her absence creates great social embarrassment for him – the removal of mother and wife nullifies the social meaning of the home. The truce does not last and he beats her again, almost to death. She is thus forced to go against the grain of what she perceives to be tradition: to defy patriarchal authority and to move to Walvis Bay. Her journey is in fact the journey of the male migrant workers mapped out in the *Oudano* song. Tanga moves out of Owambo and into the then hostile south only when the gendered construction of her own social milieu becomes intolerably hostile to her. This is represented as a brutal and unwanted internal exile, described in terms that are similar of the descriptions of the external exile so many Namibians were forced to choose.

This is the first literary depiction of an Owambo woman taking possession of a previously masculine landscape by physically moving through it, thus mapping it as her own. Her destination, the harbour town of Walvis Bay, symbolized employment and some measure of independence for Owambo men. Her journey claims a similar, ambivalent, independence for a woman. Tanga speaks little in this novel, but her moment of healing, of constructing a new identity, is a verbal moment. She says of her brutal husband, who was badly injured in a guerrilla attack:

> 'I knew that such a thing could happen to him one day. I told him many times but he did not want to listen to me. I am now here because of him. Our children had gone into exile, he made me a woman without a kitchen. I married nothing else, but Apartheid! Oh! I forgive him now but I cannot forget. Let God the Almighty preserve his life,' Tanga said with eyes full of tears (Hishongwa 1986: 69).

Although by this time, the mid-1980s, Tanga is far more diffident than Loide Shikongo was in her exhortation, there are interesting parallels to the *Song of Chief Iipumbu*. Tanga, although very unsure of her right to speak, also warns her

---

9. *Oudano* songs translated by Betty Hango-Rammukainen, ongoing research.

husband, claiming an understanding of the situation that her husband does not have. Her concerns for her own children in the novel mirror the more formalized praise that Shikongo uses. There is a parallel frustration: both women know what is damaged and corrupted, both warn and advise, but are unable to change obdurate masculine behaviour by direct means. One solution is to flee.

Oral and written literature by Owambo women has been a continuation of the processes of explanation and challenge through which the emergence of political agency takes place. In written texts new selves and identities are created which counter the devastating effects of exile and war. Hishongwa's disturbing and violent book depicts the gathering violence wreaked on one woman – the force of it nearly destroys her. However, through language – Tanga speaking and Hishongwa writing – new solutions are woven. Tanga finds a new matrilineal home where she is offered 'one of the bedrooms occupied by the girls' (Hishongwa: 69).

This book also marks another transition – another kind of exile. Hishongwa writes in English rather than her mother tongue for a variety of complex but familiar reasons. She wrote the novel while she was in exile where, along with many other writers, she was exiled from her own languages. Another book – *Wir Kinder Namibias* (1984) – a unique autobiography by Magdalena and Erastus Shamena who wrote alternate chapters, has been published only in Finnish and German – languages which are accessible to few Namibians.

The chapters by Magdalena Shamena provide a poignant and unique insight into the struggles faced by a woman whose husband was imprisoned in Pretoria by the South African regime. It describes the personal devastation of another kind of internal exile – imprisonment – as well as the circumstances which led the Shamenas to decide that, after brutally suppressed internal protest, exile was the only possibility in the face the increasing violence in Namibia. When her husband Erastus Shamena is arrested, Magdalena resists Owambo male authority and the authority of the army by expressing unequivocally her conviction that she is entitled to travel in order to find her husband.

Erastus was said to be in prison but for months I had not had any news from him . . . One of Erastus' colleagues, Hosea Namupala, went to South Africa and brought back the news that those that had been arrested would be put on trial . . . Immediately I went to see Johanna Shoombe . . .

'Listen, Johanna, I'm planning to go and see Dr Olivier. He is the highest-ranking white official here. I'm going to ask him whether I can go to Pretoria to listen to the proceedings. Everywhere on this earth wives are allowed to attend their husbands' cases. Why shouldn't I be allowed to do it?'

We discussed practical things, such as money. All would work out if only we got permission to travel. Johanna seemed to be excited, too. But then she mentioned our plans to some pastors and teachers at the training college.

These men tried to talk us out of it: 'These days the boers don't even shy back from beating women. Let's not do this thing, please.'

I would not even listen . . . The men thought I was stubborn but didn't put any more pressure on me (Magdalena and Erastus Shamena 1984).

Magdalena Shamena eventually wrote a letter of protest to the Secretary-General of the United Nations in 1973. Her appeal for relief on the behalf of Namibian women led to increased repression and she finally fled into exile a few months after her husband in order to avoid arrest by the South African administration.

The Literature of Return

Literature by Owambo women since independence has expressed the harrowing experiences of the past, the difficulties inherent in negotiating the present, and hopes for the future. Many of the pieces that have been anthologized attempt to heal by naming the traumas witnessed or experienced by the authors. These stories are the return maps to a whole and healed self.

Kaleni Hiyalwa's short story, *The baby's baby*, is about Shekupe, an orphaned thirteen-year-old girl, and her unguided journey into the world of sexuality (Orford and Nicanor 1996). This story explores her situation with great gentleness but it is clear that her tragedy results from her being alone, outside the containment of maternal control. Sister Mary comments on how the effects of war have ruptured the patriarchal order: 'Shekupe was a victim of love and war. When she delivered her baby, what would the name of her child be? A fatherless baby though the father lived. A baby's baby' (Kaleni Hiyalwa in Orford and Nicanor 1996: 67). But a strong matrilineal element comes into play when Shekupe and her unborn baby are adopted and mothered by Sister Mary. The form of the Oudano is also presented as an important aspect of the culture of home that the girls keep alive by dancing the 'traditional moonlight dance'. It makes the alien and strange place that is exile a home. There is an additional matrilineal element present in the imagery of '. . . *the eggshells/ That whiten the waist.*' The pain of their loss maps the journey from girlhood to womanhood.

On their way, Shekupe thought bitterly of her pregnancy. 'Look at me, dear girl. I should have been proud of myself. Now I have broken ondjeva – beads worn exclusively by girls around their waists. I should have kept to myself'. (Kaleni Hiyalwa in Orford and Nicanor, 1996: 56).

Ellen Namhila's autobiography, *The Price of Freedom* (1997), was seen by many readers as an affirmation of the experiences of exile. These experiences were perceived by many to have been silenced by the euphoria of return and the pressure to forget the journeys of the past.

Hearing people talk about going back home was like waking from a wonderful dream
... [but] ... a lot had happened to me and to Namibia since I had left. I would not just
be able to continue from where I had left off and pretend that I had never been away.
(Namhila 1997: 148)

Namhila initiates ways for Owambo (and of course other) women to deal with the
huge changes which resulted from their journeys. Paradoxically the return home
has been another form of exile: for many women the equality they desired and
expected from Independence has not materialized. Writers like Ellen Namhila deal
with a female experience that appropriates the centre for itself, thus expanding
the cultural space allocated to women. Namhila's book, full of contradictions and
surprises, retrospectively creates order and weaves a contemporary meaning out
of journeys that were often chaotic, and rarely embarked on by choice.

Woven in among the written texts the rich nurturing stream of oral literature
flows strongly. A celebratory performance of the renowned oral poet, Mekulu
Mukwahongo Ester Kamati, welcomed the long lost children of exile on their
return with an oratory and rhetorical force reminiscent of that of Loide Shikongo.

Children of Namibia

You returned
Calves with no horns
Left in the kraal
Howling like hyenas
Faces and mouths pointed northwards
Welcome friends
You returned gracefully

Children of Namibia
Like a joke, we see you
Like a dream we look at you
Your faces were not visible in this land
Your shadows were seen in death

Our cry as parents
Has resulted in jubilation
Though not all returned
We say thank God
For bringing along a nation.[10]

10. Translated by Kaleni Hiyalwa and Ndeshi Immanuel. *Mekulu Mukwahongo Ester Kamati
1997*, oral performance filmed for the series Stories of Tenderness and Power, OnLand Productions.

It has taken some time for women writers to reclaim their matrilineal inheritance. *In Meekulu's Children* an author returns to her birthplace for the first time (Hiyalwa 2000). Kaleni Hiyalwa, who was exiled for many years, has written a novel that returns 'home' as a way of laying the ghosts of exile to rest finally. The novel, set in a small village in Owambo, renders with great compassion the lives of those who stayed at home. It is the story of a young girl, Ketya, orphaned by a vicious South African army attack on her homestead in which her parents were murdered and her siblings scattered. Ketya and her Mekulu (grandmother) endure the bitter years of deprivation and violence that follow, its only softness their love for each other. Eventually Ketya is reunited with her brother and sister when they are repatriated in 1989. The returnees never again see Mekulu but Ketya keeps her spirit alive with the stories and hope that sustained her during the long years of separation. The ending of this novel marks a 'coming home' both literally and metaphorically, as the matrilineal home offers the possibility of healing and a reconstitution of a female-headed family.

> 'Rest in peace Mekulu,' I heard Kamati say. He threw a handful of sand into the grave – the eternal home where his grandmother would lie forever.
> 'We are home Mekulu. We will fulfil your wish,' said Estela . . .
> There was a long silence.
> 'Where is our home?' Estela and Kamati asked me anxiously. 'Is it near?'
> 'Oh, yes – just look over there!' I responded, pointing to Mekulu's homestead (Hiyalwa 2000).

Acknowledgements

Betty Hango's collection and translation of the Oudano songs and her comments on early drafts were of great value. This research is part of the ongoing Women Writing Africa project of the Feminist Press of the City University of New York.

References

Becker, H. 1997. Voreheliche Sexualität und Traditionelles Recht in Nordnamibia. *Peripherie* **65/66**.
—— 1998a. *Gender, Power and Traditional Authority: Four Namibian Case Studies*. Report prepared for Swedish International Development Agency, Windhoek CASS.

—— 1998b. *Efendula past and present. Female initiation, gender and customary law in northern Namibia.* Paper presented at 'Gender, Sexuality and Law' Conference. Keele University, 19–21 June 1998.

Dammann, E. and Tirronen, T. 1975. *Ndonga-Anthologie.* Berlin: Verlag von Dietrich Reimer.

Daymond, M., Driver, D., Molema, L., Meintjes, S., Musengezi, C., Orford, M., and Rasebotsa, N., Forthcoming 2002. *Women Writing Africa, Southern Volume.* New York: Feminist Press of the City University of New York.

Hahn, C.H.L. 1928. The Ovambo, in C.H.L. Hahn, H. Vedder and L. Fourie. *The Native Tribes of South Western Africa.* Cape Town: Cape Times Ltd.

Hayes, P. 1992. A History of the Ovambo of Namibia, *c.* 1880–1935. Cambridge (PhD thesis).

—— 1996. 'Cocky' Hahn and the 'Black Venus': the making of a Native Commissioner in South West Africa, 1915–1946. *Gender and History* **8**(3).

——, Silvester, J., Wallace, M. and Hartmann, W. 1998. *Namibia under South African Rule: Mobility and Containment, 1915–1946.* Oxford: James Currey.

Hillebrecht, W. 1990. *'Do not have papers in your box. . .' The Sources of Namibian History* (Ms).

Hishongwa, N. 1986. *Marrying Apartheid.* Abbottsford, Victoria: Imprenta.

Hiyalwa, K. 2000. *Meekulu's Children.* Windhoek: New Namibia Books.

Namhila, E. 1997. *The Price of Freedom.* Windhoek: New Namibia Books.

Olivier, M.J. 1961. *Inboorlingsbeleid en administrasie in die mandaatgebied van Suidwes-Afrika.* PhD thesis. Stellenbosch: University of Stellenbosch.

Orford, M. and Nicanor, N. (eds) 1996. *Coming on Strong: Writing by Namibian Women,* Windhoek: New Namibia Books.

Peters, P. 1997. Revisiting the puzzle of matriliny in south-central Africa. Introduction. *Critique of Anthropology* **17**(2).

Richards, A. 1950. Some Types of Family Structure amongst the Central Bantu, in: A.R. Radcliffe Brown and D. Forde (eds) *African Systems of Kinship and Marriage.* London: Oxford University Press.

Sandelowsky, B. 1971. The Iron Age in South West Africa and Damara pot making. *Africa Studies* **30**.

Shamena, M. and Shamena, E. 1984. *Wir Kinder Namibias.* Erlangen: Verlag der Evan-Lutherischen Mission.

Sister Namibia Collective, 1994. *A New Initiation Song: Writings by women in Namibia.* Windhoek: Sister Namibia.

Sylvester, J., Wallace, M. and Hayes, P. 1998. Introduction, in Hayes *et al. Namibia under South African Rule: Mobility and Containment 1915–1946.* Oxford: James Currey.

Vedder, H. 1991. *Die Geschichte Sudwestafrikas bis zum Tode Maherero 1890.* Windhoek: Wissenschaftliche Gemeinschaft.

Williams, F. 1991. *Pre-colonial Communities of Southwestern Africa: A history of Owambo Kingdoms 1600–1921*, Windhoek: National Archives of Namibia.

Zinke, S. 1993. *Neue Gesange der Ovambo. Musikethnologie Analysen zu namibischen Liederen.* PhD thesis. Berlin: Humboldt-Universität.

Egypt: Constructed Exiles of the Imagination
Beverley Butler

Because exile, unlike nationalism, is fundamentally a discontinuous state of being. Exiles are cut off from their roots, their land, their past . . . Exiles feel, therefore, an urgent need to reconstitute their broken lives, usually by choosing to see themselves as part of a triumphant ideology or restored people. The crucial thing is that a state of exile free from this triumphant ideology – designed to reassemble an exile's broken history into a new whole – is virtually unbearable, and virtually impossible in today's world. (Said 1984: 163)

Not the least curious thing about Egypt, a country with so much 'past', is that the stranger finds no historical continuity . . . the innocent exile coming back to the cradle of civilisation is taken aback. (Robin Fedden quoted in Lagoudis Pinchin 1977: 24)

Exile, like landscape, is a highly relative and contextual term. It can be emotional, political, intellectual, aesthetic, imaginary and, as Said reminds us, as an experience of violent dispossession 'virtually unbearable' (Said 1984: 163). In this chapter I focus on selected dynamics of exile and landscape in order to explore powerful narratives of belonging and exclusion in which Egypt is constructed as an exile of the imagination.

To date, critics have reflected upon the enduring potency of the Egyptian landscape – the 'lure of Egypt' – as the site for the construction of 'mythical pasts and imagined homelands' (Howe 1998: 122–38). There is also a growing awareness of the ways in which the Egyptian monumental heritage, in particular the Pyramids and the Sphinx, and the narratives of Exodus and of Egypt as the 'cradle of civilization' have been pressed into the service of many of these projects. Most critics emphasize Egypt's attraction as part of quests for deep roots and ancient origins. The seductiveness of Egypt has not only had a sustained resonance for the colonial imagination (for example, Orientalists, Egyptologists), the post-colonial imagination (Afrocentrists), the post-modern imagination (deconstruction-ists) but has also become embedded in tourist mythologizing (cf. Selwyn 1996).

By way of contrast, what interests me is the heightened significance these desires give to the dynamic of 'exile' and to the enactment of a return – usually symbolic – to Egypt. I move between two landscapes – Alexandria and Old Heliopolis –

capable of pulling out different contexts in which 'Egypt' is understood as synonymous with the conditions of exile. I draw out the ways in which modern writers (poets and scholars) assert an attachment to, or identification with, Egypt's ancient grand narratives, including narrations of its monumental heritage and ancient Egyptian cultures, as a means to align with a 'triumphant ideology'.

What emerges is 'Egypt' as a template or 'resource' for memory work. Its narratives are remembered and reinscribed in order to work through feelings of wounding, trauma, humiliation and alienation in order to reclaim a sense of healing, regeneration and wholeness, and to affect liberation from current oppressions which threaten the disintegration of self and self-group. In the extreme, this 'liberation' has included calls for retribution. My conclusions highlight the partial nature of these projects and explores their relationship to alternative experiences of exile.

The Landscape of Alexandria: West 'writes' East

> Alexandria, which is our birthplace, has mapped out this circle for all western language: to write was to return, to come back to the beginning to grasp again the first instance; it is to witness anew the dawn. (Foucault quoted in Errera 1997: 138)

> The wartime writers in Egypt . . . – all had intimations of an historical breakpoint they were living through; their exile was a time of transition as well as a foreign place, a crisis moment as well as an accidental homeland they had to struggle against, appropriate, and invent in poetry and fiction. (Bowden 1995: 24)

The landscape of Alexandria evokes a host of histories and mythologies. These have exerted a powerful hold on the western imagination, as part of, but distinct from the rest of Egypt (Green 1996: 3). In order to explore some specific dynamics of exile and landscape in its Alexandrian context I turn to the Personal Landscape Group, a network of European writers who were exiled in Egypt during the Second World War (Bowden 1995). Many of the writers were evacuated from Greece following the Nazi invasion of April 1941. Egypt offered a refuge or 'accidental homeland' for these 'castaways' (op cit:15). The group, who during the war years published a quarterly magazine *Personal Landscape*, sought to explore what they termed the 'interior' or 'personal landscapes' created by the experience of exile (op cit: 45–53). They saw exile as a condition which inevitably involved an exploration of self: in particular of the pain, wounding and trauma involved in the act of separation upon which exile is premised. The group saw the act of writing – or the narration of exile – as a resistance or 'refusal . . . to be overwhelmed by the experience of exile' and as an artistic or intellectual creation of a second exile – one made in an attempt to escape the realities, limitations and humiliations of enforced exile (ibid.: 47).

The key contributors to the *Personal Landscape* journal were Robin Fedden, Bernhard Spencer, Keith Douglas, Terence Tiller and Lawrence Durrell. Durrell, perhaps the best known of the writers, saw Alexandria as the only possible place to survive an Egyptian exile (op cit: 159–209). His decision to narrate his exile in Alexandria connected him and his fellow exiles with a previous generation of modern writers – colonial cosmopolitan inhabitants of early twentieth-century Alexandria – including Constantine Cavafy (1863–1933) and E.M. Forster (stationed in Alexandria during the 1914–18 war as a Red Cross volunteer) (see Lagoudis-Pinchin 1977). These writers had previously narrated Alexandria as a landscape of the imagination by identifying intellectual roots, constructing literary lineages and poetic pathways which attached them to what they claimed as their ancient self-group: the ancient colonial-cosmopolitan culture of Alexandria, itself often understood as a culture of 'exiles' (Alexandre-Garner 1997: 163).

This elite poetics of Alexandria, initiated as a form of revivalism, re-inscribed Alexandria's literary identity almost exclusively with reference to the city's ancient origins and through the lens of a privileged Western genealogy. This trajectory stages Hellenistic Alexandria as 'Golden-Age' founded upon the city's characteriza-tion in terms of the New Athens; the meeting point of the world/of east and west; the 'birthplace' of cosmopolitanism and universalism; the site of Hellenistic colonial creativity and intellectual inquiry (Green 1996: 3–29). The ancient city is likewise narrated in terms of: the heroics of Alexander the Great (who founded the city in 331 BC); the glamour and seductions of Cleopatra; the fame of Pharos (the lighthouse which was one of the wonders of the ancient world) and the glory of the Mouseion/library (the fascination here usually centres around its ambitious project to collect all the texts in the then known world and the mythologies of its destruction).

Modern Alexandria, meanwhile, with its relative poverty of ancient material culture, has been distinguished as a site of nostalgia and loss (Lagoudis-Pinchin 1977: 34–82). Durrell gave depth to this latter image by dubbing the modern city the 'Capital of Memory'. Durrell envisaged his 'return to Alexandria' as a means to engage in a form of memory work which would mitigate the conditions of exile and connect him with his ultimate lost object, not in this case ancient Alexandria but 'Greece' (Bowden 1995: 51). The ancient Alexandria Mouseion/Library, an object of the imagination lacking material traces, was to be recovered in memory and text and invested as a pivotal point in a wider landscape of healing (Errera 1997: 138). The archive, understood in its ancient context as a repository of Greek memory for generations of 'Greeks' (Hellenes) who had left behind their 'homeland' to settle in Alexandria, was reimagined as serving a similar function for the modern Alexandrian exiles. Thus, the Mouseion/Library was raised as a shelter for the western self in a foreign land and as an archive for intellectual-aesthetic supply. This literary exploration and excavation of Alexandria was thus endowed with the means to reclaim links with a familiar Greek landscape and to offer continuity and repetition at a time of what was felt to be overwhelming discontinuity and rupture.

The Personal Landscape Group's emotional and psychological investment in Greece was both historical and contemporary. In terms of historic Greece the work of Cavafy (privileged by the group as their honorary 'artist in exile') provided the inspiration for a series of neo-classical and Hellenistic poetic themes, many of which were manifestations of the story of 'eternal Ithaka': the voyager/the traveller always seeking a lost homeland (Bowden 1995: 50). If Alexandria was the 'resource' from which to access the lost homeland, historical Greece, when depicted in the group's work, was invested as the desired place of return/arrival. Greece was idealized as an eternal landscape of unity and wholeness: the fountainhead of democracy and the home of the artist self.

The investment in contemporary Greece was intense during the period of the poets' exile. The wounded exiled writers empathized with Greece, itself now a wounded culture as a result of occupation by Fascist forces (op cit: 48). This identification also enabled the writers to share a common imagined homeland which hid the diversity of origins and of writing styles. Many of the writers met in Greece (Fedden and Durrell were first introduced in Athens when the former was Cultural Attaché and the latter resident in Corfu) and shared the trauma of a flight from the 1941 invasion (op cit: 48–9). Greece, then, was not a literal birthplace, but rather the Personal Landscape Group's assertion of a wider western claim to collective Greek origins which transcended individual autobiography. Fedden, for example, was born in France to Anglo-French parents, and Durrell in India. As Olivia Manning, a fellow exile and contributor to the group's journal, outlines, this Egyptian captivity becomes a complex mode of exile with seemingly contradictory loyalties and attachments: 'We faced the sea / Knowing until the day of our return we would be / Exiles from a country not our own' (op cit: 46).

Such attachment to Greece, however, meant the rejection of any intellectual and artistic engagement with Egypt. The writers joined with E.M. Forster in reiterating the ancient separation of Alexandria ad Aegyptum (Alexandria by, not in, Egypt) (Green 1996: 6). When Egypt did feature as literary subject it was in terms of the negative aspects of exile, in particular experiences and feelings of alienation, humiliation, wounding and impotency (Bowden 1995: 46–70). Egypt, both ancient and modern, was thus characterized unsympathetically. The Pharaonic landscape which seized the imagination of travellers and inspired an Egyptomania in many other Western scholars and poets (together with a certain claim to a 'White Egypt' as Western origin (Howe 1998)) failed to stir the emotion of the exiles. These writers felt themselves to be in Fedden's words 'latecomers on the scene'; 'mere spectators' (quoted in Bowden 1995: 46). Their curiosity for a foreign landscape was thus blocked by contemporary loss and nostalgia for home. Poetic images of modern Egypt as a site of degeneration and imprisonment were frequent: the desert in particular, become a literary device symbolizing the estrangement, placelessness and disintegration of self experienced by the poets in exile. Fedden's *White Country* makes these sentiments clear: 'We do not know the landscapes anymore, / Cannot tell what people we once were / Like ghosts we wonder in our tracks'.

One connection which the group did make with the traditional Western investment in Egypt is its problematic association with death. The act of a 'return to Egypt', in contrast to aspirations of rebirth and revival synonymous with a return to Alexandria and to Greece, is explored by the writers in order to pursue a deeper anxiety surrounding the theme of death. The poets picked up on what they considered to be a trace of an earlier memory. They become the 'innocent exiles' returning to the cradle of civilization, an act which ultimately confronts them with the grave (Lagoudis-Pinchin 1977: 24). The close proximity of the Alamein campaigns (which became the focus of world attention in July and November 1942) provoked further anxieties. One member of the group, Keith Douglas, wounded in the Alamein campaigns, took the experiences of the battlefield as his literary subject pursuing an anti-war sentiment in the style of Wilfred Owen (Bowden 1995: 66–93).

The theme of death was also used to narrate the decline and ultimate death of European control and privilege in Egypt, an experience symptomatic of a more general post-Second World War wounding to Western omnipotence through decolonization. As Bowden comments: 'If theirs [The Personal Landscape Group's] tone is frequently elegiac, that now seems percipient of them for their world had not survived. Theirs is a tale, intentionally or not, of the end of empire. One history blots out the other' (Bowden 1995: 24).

A final acknowledgement of the end of western control in Egypt comes with Independence in 1952, and is powerfully symbolized with the 'loss' of the Suez canal in 1956. The 'dispersal' of Alexandria's cosmopolitan community – the 'khawaga'/ the 'foreigners' quickly followed (Brown and Taieb 1996: 9). Memories and narrations of the city, however, did survive, most powerfully in Durrell's most famous novel *The Alexandrian Quartet*, the 'final and elaborate poem of exile', written after his return to Greece (Bowden 1998: 193).

The Heliopolitan Landscape: 'Writing Back'

> For us, the return to Egypt in every domain is the necessary condition to reconcile African civilization with history . . . it will play the same role in rethinking and renewing of African culture that Ancient Greece and Rome plays in the culture of the 'West'. (Diop 1992: 149)

On the spot occupied by this obelisk there formerly stood a temple dedicated to the sun
... Nothing, save this one solitary obelisk remains of this important city in which
Egyptians and Hebrews were united for many centuries in brotherhood. (Wilson 1885:
61)

Old Heliopolis is situated in what are now modern Cairo's Ains Shams and
Matirraya suburbs. Like Alexandria, this landscape has been subject to a wealth
of images and mythologies: Heliopolis as the place of creation (where the 'benben'
mound emerged from primeval chaos); the centre for the sun cult; the setting for
the Exodus and the Holy Family's flight into Egypt. 'Mary's Tree' is located nearby
– reputedly one of the places where the Holy Family took refuge from Herod's
persecution. The area is currently a heritage site managed by the Supreme Council
of Antiquities.

Another bond with Alexandria is the poverty of archaeological remains. Some
of the ancient heritage from this site has been famously exiled in New York and
London. Only one obelisk – that of Usertsen I Pharaoh of the 12th Dynasty, also
known as Plato's column, the oldest of all known obelisks – still stands at the
original site (ibid.). This landscape, and Plato's column (Figure 18.1) in particular,
form the centrepiece for another, and very different narrative of exile. One in which
Egypt becomes an extension of the African landscape, of an African genealogy.
One which posits the reversal of the routes/roots of culture (cf. Gilroy 1993; Clifford
1997). At stake here is the privileging of an earlier Egyptian origin over that of a
Greek origin: more specifically a Black African, rather than a White European
origin (Howe 1998).

I turn to the work of the Senegalese historian and political activist Cheikh Anta
Diop (1923–1986). In his latter years Diop became Professor of Egyptology and
Prehistory at Dakar University but has been more affectionately characterized by
his supporters as the Black Pharaoh or Pharaoh of African Studies. Diop, writing
in the 1950s and 1960s, asserted a connection between contemporary sub-Saharan
Black African culture and the ancient Egyptian Pharaonic culture which he
understood to be a Black African civilization (Diop 1992). He saw his work as
inextricably linked to contemporary political agendas of decolonialism in Africa,
in particular narratives of unity and revivalism as expressed in Pan-Africanism.
Diop advocated a 'return to Egypt' as an essential part of this project, as a way of
reconnecting with lost origins and deep roots, and allowing Africa to gain a sense
of forward development.

Unlike for the European writers previously mentioned this 'return' did not
symbolize death for Diop but was an act which would bring about the renewal,
rebirth and regeneration of African culture. The death of African culture, Diop
believed, was enacted by Western scholars who strategically exiled Africa from
its place in world history (op cit: 149). The reclamation or repossession of this

Figure 18.1 'Plato's Obelisk', 'Old' Heliopolis, Ains Shams/Matirraya, Cairo

heritage took the form of a symbolic return. Diop's thesis asserts that everything starts in Egypt – Egypt is thus positioned as the distant, forgotten or repressed mother of science and culture of the West: a teacher to Greece in its infancy – a culture Diop believed owed everything to its encounter with Egypt (op cit: 163).

A specific link between this thesis and the ancient Heliopolitan landscape is the academy or centre of learning which once stood at the Heliopolis site: another object of the imagination lacking material traces. For Diop and others, this prominent centre of science and religion which was in existence before the Alexandrian Mouseion/Library was pivotal in proving that the flow of universal knowledge came from Egypt to the rest of the world (op cit: 299). Diop and other authors list those ancient scholars including Plato (hence the name of the obelisk), Strabo, Solon, Pythagoras, Thales, Eudoxus to name a few, who they claim either visited or were initiated at Heliopolis. The thesis continues that these philosophers came to ancient Heliopolis to 'learn' wisdom from Black African culture: an historical 'fact', they argue, that Herodotus and other ancient authors took as common knowledge (op cit: 300).

For Diop and others Old Heliopolis is re-invested as the place for the regeneration of contemporary African culture – in terms of both the African continent and the African Diaspora. Diop stated that Black African memory was traumatized not only by racist Western scholars exiling Africa from world culture, history and philosophy but also as a result of the historical experience of slavery (op cit: 113). He believed that the psychological impact of this 'exile' and its associated trauma needed to be addressed: to lose one's history was to lose one's soul and to risk a disintegration of self and self-group. An alternative mode of memory-work was advocated via attachments and identifications made between modern Black African culture and ancient Egyptian Pharaonic culture. Part of the training of initiates at Heliopolis involved the practice of the 'strengthening of the soul'; Diop felt that this was an apt prescription for the contemporary African (op cit: 299–300). Heliopolis was thus privileged by Diop as the place for internal psychic restoration and, as he understood it, memory recovery.

The central tenets of Diop's work continue to be reworked and revived by other authors in new cultural and political contexts. The landscape of ancient Egypt has thus sustained a privileged place in what have become known as Afrocentrist theses (Howe 1998). The publication of Martin Bernal's *Black Athena* (1987) provoked both academic and popular profiling of the issues, and this time attachments to ancient Pharaonic culture found a renewed resonance for many within the African American community, with Egypt emerging as a significant feature in US culture wars (Howe 1998: 7). However, this identification with Egypt has also led to an extreme form of Afrocentrism which has gathered increasing criticism. Critics suggest that authors simply invert the traditional Western model in order to make claims for a superior African origin, without problematizing the pseudo-scientific, essentialist and transhistorical notions of 'race' on which the thesis resides (op cit: 215–75). As Howe comments, 'Black Athena is just as wrong as White Egypt' (op cit: 9). Perhaps to offer an antidote, Egypt has also provided a point of inspiration for the recent articulation of a thesis of 'travelling cultures' which privileges and intellectualizes the fluidity of routes over the obstinacies and fixities of roots (see Clifford 1997 on Ghosh).

The potency of ancient Egypt persists in other domains of intellectual discourse; for example, 'Egypt' has been reworked by deconstructionists as part of critiques of what Derrida refers to as the 'White Mythologies' (1982). These interventions are understood as attempts to resist or destabilize the dominance, the ethnocentrisms and exclusive qualities of Western – or 'Greek' – metaphysics and its associated discourse of origins. This deconstructionist critique of the 'Greek' metaphysical subject built upon the work of intellectuals such as Levinas, who had earlier sought to articulate the metaphysical position of 'Jew', thus challenging the essentialism of the 'Greek' position (Bennington 1992). The possible stagings of the 'Egyptian' has subsequently featured in the texts of authors such as Derrida and Bennington (ibid.). Much of their critical commentary is informed by the work of Freud who, having in his earlier work focused on Greek mythologies, began in his closing years to develop a deeper interest in Egypt and in Egyptian mythology (Cororan 1991). Freud's work, which interestingly has connections with the landscape of

Heliopolis in the figures of Akhenaten (the 'creator' of Monotheism) and Moses, raised the possibility of positioning oneself 'as Egyptian'. Egypt is understood as that 'inbetween' site of 'deconstruction' capable of connecting with the heritages of Thoth the god of death and of writing. 'Egypt' in this sense emerges as the pharmarkon, the 'poison-cure' invested with the means to probe the margins, to destabilize and to enact an intellectual exile from the tyrannies of the 'White Mythologies' (Bennington 1992: 104).

Afrocentrist and deconstructionist narrations of Egypt could themselves be problematized as political and intellectual neo-colonizations of Egypt, and indeed, issues of ownership and appropriation of Egypt's grand narratives have not gone unchallenged. The Exodus, for example, is another narrative connected with this site which has engaged empathetic identification and generated contestation. The Exodus as a 'triumphant ideology' describing the initial oppressions and eventual liberation from Egyptian captivity is a narrative which offers a story of a restored people and thus of a way back to a homeland when external forces threaten to enact the death or destruction of self and self community. The experiences of the Holocaust and of African Slavery have found particular identification with Exodus. However, the politics of empathy here have not gone unproblematized; for example, Gilroy critiques the competing African and Jewish claims to narration (Gilroy 1993). The latter's purchase as the 'proverbial people of exile' is often expressed as a more authentic alignment, based on shared religious identity with the ancient self group, and this identification intensifies conflict, in particular with Zionist fundamentalist interpretations of Exodus which have not only transformed the Egyptian landscape into a faultline for ideological conflict but have been used to legitimate modern exile and dispossessions from Palestine (Said 1984: 164).

Egypt 'writes' Egypt: the Repossession of National Origins and Revivalism

> Is my identity Mediterranean? Some people say Egypt is not an African country but is in fact linked not only geographically but also culturally to the Mediterranean basin. Am I a woman whose past and future are linked to Black Africa? Or am I a White Egyptian whose land is bathed by the Mediterranean Sea like Italy, and Greece and France and Spain? Does this make North Africa a part of Europe rather than the continent from which it draws its name? Does the Sahara Desert decide my culture for me? (Saadawi 1998: 127)

Said articulates an Hegelian 'Master and Servant' dialectic to the concept of nation and exile, one which supposes 'nationals' to have an immunity to the condition of exile (Said 1984: 162). However, the narrations of the Egyptian landscape rehearsed in this chapter assert an empathy with ancient Egyptian cultures but afford little or no recognition of modern Egypt or of the Egyptian people's own attachments to 'their' 'national' ancient pasts. Nawal El Saadawi, an Egyptian author, doctor and founder member of the Arab Woman's Solidarity Association has dramatized some of the fragmentation and fracture affected by current contestation over the Egyptian landscape which often perpetuates a sense of detachment or exiling of Egypt's modern, predominantly Arab-Muslim Egyptian from such discourse (Saadawi 1998: 127). As she and other writers illustrate, the project of repossessing Egypt and (again, typically separately) Alexandria from Western colonial appropriation, has been a theme running through Egyptian national literature.

The process of constructing Egyptian cultural identity has, as Gershoni has shown, oscillated between 'two competing 'imagined national communities': on the one hand a territorial Egyptian based on a distinctive historical heritage of the Nile Valley, and on the other a supra-Egyptian Islamic heritage community based on Egypt's bonds of the Arabic language and Islamic heritage' (Gershoni 1992: 8). The first of these 'imagined communities' predominated in the period immediately before and during the British occupation of Egypt and has subsequently been characterized as the 'awakening of [national] memory' (Hassan 1998: 204). Appeals were made to an Egyptian national 'rebirth' and 'renaissance' based upon concept of an 'eternal Egypt', for the 'return of the Egyptian soul', and for an 'awakening sense of Egyptian nationalism grounded in Pharaonic history' (op cit: 205–6). This vision of Egyptian intellectuals included a return to the Hellenistic past; for example, Taha Hussein's *The Future of Culture in Egypt* (1936) promotes an identity for Egypt rooted in its Mediterranean context. Hussein saw this reclamation of heritage as part of repossession of the key cultural agencies, previously dominated by Europeans, for the Egyptian nation.

Following Egypt's independence in 1952 a revolution also occurred in terms of the characterization of national identity. The Nasser and Sadat eras have been described as a time of dramatic 'fashioning of political identity' premised upon a 'denial of memory' (op cit: 207). Thus the political discourse 'that centred on Pharaonic Egypt was replaced with a discourse that placed Egypt within the folds of Arab nationalism' (ibid.). Interestingly, in post-1950s literature Alexandria is positioned as an abandoned, declining, colonial backdrop, and a place of 'self-exile' for dissident Egyptian writers and intellectuals. Once again, the city is understood as distinct from the Egyptian landscape (Kararah 1998). Writers today highlight the violent polarization of positions: 'A fundamental internal split exists between modernists, who seek to legitimate Egyptian nationalism by reference to the glory of Egypt within a European context, and Islamists, who revoke nationalism in favour of a transnational religious ideology legitimized by reference to historical times of Islam's golden-age' (Hassan forthcoming: 5).

Saadawi's writings take us further into this critique by not only placing Egypt within a wider global landscape of North–South power relations but also by exploring Egypt's internal political landscape. In terms of the former, this global landscape is, for Saadawi, dominated by the neo-colonialism of the North: complicit here are international agencies (the United Nations, the International Monetary Fund, the World Bank (Saadawi 1998: 13)), Western intellectuals (in particular, postmodernists and deconstructionists) and (international/Western) tourists (op cit: 169–70). She sees these forces combining together in a violent consumption of the Egyptian landscape as part of discourses of development, of intellectual colonization of 'docile bodies' and 'the subaltern' and of the monumental heritage and cultural difference.

In terms of internal conflicts Saadawi alludes to a landscape of terror and violence within Egypt: a hidden network of spaces of detention constructed by a state with an escalating number of human rights violations (MiddleEast Watch 1992). Saadawi, due to her critical writings on Egyptian political culture, has herself met with the violence of the state (being imprisoned under Sadat) and experienced an exile from Egypt, as a result of fundamentalist Islamist threats of assassination: she sees these events as indicative of conflicts surrounding attempts to stage identities and heritages in contemporary Egypt (Saadawi 1998).

Rewriting Egypt: Contemporary Returns

Alexandria is reclaiming the heritage of its heyday. (Mitchell 1998: 110)

. . . it seems that the West is regaining something fundamental to its heritage or even more its very beginnings. (Errera 1997: 129)

In order to draw out some of the implications of these competing and contested Egyptian landscapes I want to return briefly to Alexandria, this time to the contemporary city. The Alexandrian landscape is currently undergoing a metamorphosis described by commentators as a 'revival' or 'renaissance' (Mitchell 1998: 103), the common theme of which is a return to origins: to Alexandria's ancient cultural heritage (Mitchell 1998; Empereur 1998; La Riche 1998). Underwater excavations off the Alexandrian coast at Fort Qait Bay (the site of Pharos), Operation "Cleopatra '96'" in the eastern harbour (the site of the Ptolemies' royal palaces) and six land excavations (including the Necropolis site – Strabo's City of the Dead) are, for the first time, providing dramatic information and evidence of the ancient city. The city is also the site for the recreation of the Museum/Library in an international project, the New Alexandrina or Bibliotheca Alexandrina, a joint venture between UNESCO and the Egyptian Government (www.bibalex.gov.eg).

The return of these artefacts from their underwater exile has created a 'disturbance'. On seeing the thousands of finds strewn on the seabed Jean-Yves Empereur, director of the excavations at the Pharos site, has commented 'At first glance the chaos was incomprehensible' (Empereur quoted in La Riche 1998: 52). In all this messiness our two polarized landscapes – Durrell's 'Greek city' and the landscape of Heliopolis – were among those found merged, mixed and strewn on the seabed. The presence of the latter is a result of the movement of objects from the Heliopolis site to Alexandria during the Ptolemaic period. On a metaphorical level this disturbance is capable of breaking the fixity of exclusive claims to narrate the Egyptian landscape and of opening up the landscape to the new narratives of belonging and exile complicit in current revivalism.

The force of 'cultural revivalism' has been marked by not only disturbance but by contradiction and ambivalence. At the time of writing – the time of excavation and revelation – Alexandria finds itself embroiled in the tensions between the old Romantic neocolonial imagination and new agendas of development, and between religion and secularism. Revivalism as the return of the Western neocolonial imagination certainly has a purchase. Alexandria's ancient heritage is perceived by many as an exclusively Western heritage, with UNESCO and international archaeological teams as 'international brokers', and international tourists envisaged as the key consumers (Mitchell 1998). Memories of the historical colonialisms of the West and of its concomitant violences are also resurfacing in other ways. Excavations have revealed more of the 'unexpected', for example in the form of wreckage from the French flagship *Orion*, which was sunk off the coast at Aboukir during the Battle of the Nile in 1798 (Goddio 1998: 67). Pitching even further into the modern age the discovery of a Second World War Royal Air Force bomber, believed to have been involved in the El-Alamein campaign, was found lying on top of the palace site.

However, some of the fiercest contradictions of this revivalism lie in Egyptian society itself and internal tensions. This return of ancient heritage can be perceived as a provocative act especially at a time when Islamic extremists have expressed their intention to destroy the 'pagan' past and its monuments (Nail 1994: 31). This faultline was made visible with the murder in Luxor in 1997 of 58 tourists and 4 Egyptians by terrorists – the landscape of heritage was transformed into a site of violence and death (Hassan forthcoming). The Mubarak government's use of cultural revivalism to navigate a course between 'Western capitalist influences' and 'religious fundamentalism' is tangible (cf. Saadawi 1997: 5). Alongside the international presence, the support given by many Alexandrian 'intellectuals' to more liberal and inclusive agendas of revivalisms is symptomatic of the complex relationships of ex-colonial contexts and of the inextricable links between cultural discourse and current political aspirations. One final contradiction: in the contemporary revitalization of Alexandria, the previous characterization has been inverted. The discrepancy is now between the wealth of material culture and a relative poverty of histories and mythologies.

Banalities of Exile: Conclusions

> Exile is strangely compelling to think about but terrible to experience. It is the unhealable rift forced between a human being and a native place, between self and its true home: its essential sadness can never be surmounted. And while it is true that literature and history contain heroic, romantic, glorious, even triumphant episodes in an exile's life, these are no more than efforts meant to overcome the crippling sorrow of estrangement. The achievements of exile are permanently undermined by the loss of something left behind for ever. (Said 1984: 159)

Said, Professor of English and Comparative literature at Columbia University, experienced an exile in Egypt when he and his family were displaced from Palestine in 1948. He was also a member of Palestinian parliament in exile from 1977 to 1991. These experiences have given rise to his double status as exile-intellectual (Hovesepian 1992: 5). From this positioning Said sought to problematize the aesthetic and literary understandings of exile. These writings, he claimed, 'banalize its mutilations' and 'obscure what is truly horrendous' about exile, that which cannot be made 'aesthetically or humanistically comprehensible' (Said 1984: 160). Said reiterated that exile in its twentieth-century context was 'irredeemably secular, unbearably historical; that it [was] produced by human beings for other human beings'.

In this chapter I have concentrated upon landscape as a literary construct and as a touchpoint for a wealth of histories and mythologies. But these need always to be set alongside the 'undocumented people' (Said 1984: 161), those made mute by their losses; those denied an identity and forced to experience a 'discontinuous state of being' (op cit: 163). This acknowledgement of the 'unsayable' takes us away from the notion of a return to origins as symbolic death or rebirth and nearer to a state of existence 'like death but without death's ultimate mercy' (op cit: 160).

The gulf between manicured heritage spaces and the desperate experiences of rootlessness, fear, violence, the acts of mass deportations and detentions – 'the perilous territory of not-belonging' (op cit: 162) is one that, in a global culture, demands the recognition and responsibility of all.

References

Andre-Garner, C. 1997. The enigma of the quartet, in R. Ilbert, I. Yannakakis and J. Hassoun *Alexandria 1860–1960: The Brief Life of a Cosmopolitan Community.* Place: Pubr. 162–71.

Bennington, G. 1992. Mosaic Fragment: if Derrida were an Egyptian . . . in D. Wood (ed.) *Derrida: A Critical Reader*. Oxford: Blackwell. 97–119.

Bernal, M. 1987. *Black Athena: The Afroasiatic Roots of Classical Culture and the Fabrication of Ancient Greece*. London: Verso.

Bowden, P. 1995. '*Many Histories Deep' The Personal Landscape Poets in Egypt, 1940–45*. London: Associated University Press.

Brown, K. 1996. Alexandria in Egypt. *Mediterranean*. 8/9. France: Diffusion.

Clifford, J. 1997. *Routes: Travel and Translation in the Late Twentieth Century*. Cambridge, Mass.: Harvard University Press.

Cororan, L.H. 1991. Exploring the archaeological metaphor: the Egypt of Freud's imagination. *The Annual of Psychoanalysis* XIX. London: Analytic Press.

Derrida, J. 1982 [1971]. White mythology, in *Margins – of Philosophy*. Trans. A. Bass. Chicago: University of Chicago Press.

—— 1993. Violence and metaphysics: an essay on thought of Emmanuel Levinas, in *Writing and Difference*. Trans. A. Bass. London: Routledge & Kegan Paul.

—— 1996. *Archive Fever: A Freudian Impression*. Trans. E. Prenowitz. Chicago and London: University of Chicago Press.

Diop, C.A, 1992. *Great African Thinkers: Cheikh Anta Diop*. Ed. I. Van Sertima. New Brunswick: State University.

Empereur, J.-Y. 1998. *Alexandria Rediscovered*. London: Berths Museum Press.

Errera, E. 1997. The dream of Alexander and the literary myth, in R. Ilbert, I. Yannakakis and J. Hassoun *Alexandria 1860–1960: The Brief Life of a Cosmopolitan Community*. Place: Pubr. 128–44

Forster, E.M. 1961. *Pharos and Pharillon*. London: Hogarth Press.

Gershoni, I. 1992. Imagining and Reimagining the 'past': the use of history by Egyptian nationalist writers, 1919–1952. *History and Memory* **4**(2) 5–37.

Gilroy, P. 1993. *The Black Atlantic: Modernity and Double Consciousness*. London: Verso.

Goddio 1998. *Alexandria: The Submerged Royal Quarters*. Paris: Periplus.

Hassan, F.A. 1998. Memorabilia: archaeological materiality and national identity in Egypt, in L. Meskeu (ed.) *Archaeology under Fire: Nationalism, Politics and Heritage in the Eastern Mediterranean and the Middle East*. London: Routledge.

—— 2001. Terror at the Temple, in F. Haikal (ed.) *Memorial Volume F. Haikal*. Cairo: Cairo University Press.

Hovespian, N. 1992. Connections with Palestine, in M. Sprinker *Edward Said: A Critical Reader*. Oxford: Blackwell.

Howe, S. 1998. *Afrocentrism: Imagined Pasts and Imagined Homes*. London: Verso.

Keeley, E. 1996. *Cavafy's Alexandria*. Princeton: Princeton University Press.

Lagoudis-Pinchin, J.L. 1977. *Alexandria Still: Forster, Durrell, and Cavafy*. Princeton: Princeton University Press.

La Riche, W. 1998. *Alexandria: The Sunken City*. London: Weidenfeld & Nicolson.

Maehler, H. 1983. Egypt under the last Ptolemies: An inaugural lecture delivered at University College London. *Institute of Classical Studies Bulletin* No. 30. London: Institute of Classical Studies.

Middle East Watch. 1992. *Behind Closed Doors; Torture and Detention in Egypt*. Washington Human Rights.

Mitchell, C. 1998. The renaissance of Alexandria: a new great library revives hopes for a return to Alexandria's intellectual Golden Age. *Highlife*. London: British Airways. January. 106–13.

Raphael-Leff, J. 1990. If Oedipus was an Egyptian. *International Review of Psycho-Analysis*. London: Institute of Psycho-Analysis. **17** 309–35.

Saadawi, N. 1997. *Why Keep Asking Me About My Identity?: The Nawal El Saadawi Reader*. London and New York: Zed Books.

Said, E. 1984. Reflections on exile. *Granta* **13** London: Penguin. 157–72.

Selwyn, T. (ed.) 1996. *The Tourist Image: Myths and Mythmaking in Tourism*. Chichester: John Wiley.

Wilson, E. 1878. *Cleopatra's Needle: with Brief Notes on Egypt and Egyptian Obelisks*. London: Nimmo.

www.bibalex.gov.eg [Bibliotecha Alexandrina Web Site].

Young, R. 1990. *White Mythologies: Writing History and the West*. London: Routledge.

-19-

Migration, Exile and
Landscapes of the Imagination
Andrew Dawson and Mark Johnson

This chapter concerns situations in which migration and exile informs constructions of place and locality. However, the focus of the chapter is not on the migrant or exiled per se: those who see themselves or are seen by others to be living in a state of variously enforced separation from 'home'. Rather we are interested in situations in which the imagining of migration and exile become constitutive parts of the construction and experience of place and landscape. Migration and exile we suggest may be as much about cognitive movement as they are about the actual physical movement of groups and individuals from one locality to another.

Writing on migration and exile has thus far primarily focused on the experiences of those living in exile, i.e. individuals or groups who have either left (or have been forced to leave) their 'home' and/or those who see themselves as living in a state of separation from their 'home'. Thus for instance the structure of a recent edited volume on migration and exile (King, Connell and White 1995) is laid out largely in terms of what might be called the social biography of exile – that is, of leaving, arrival and return. The focus of analysis is the sense of 'betwixt and between', of being between 'here and there' which characterizes the experience of the exiled, and which is seen to incite responses which centre around the idea of return.

Recent writing has, of course, critically problematized the notion of 'return', demonstrating that while the experience of exile may at times lead to the search for 'roots', it also may act to destabilize fixed notions of shared history and ancestry. As White (ibid.: 1–19) suggests, the experience of return never effects a simple recovery of origins. Rather, the experience of exile not only calls into question cultural authenticity, but also disrupts linear narratives of time and place, since each and every place, time and event is reconstituted in a relation in which none is given ontological priority. Leaving and the place one has left is constituted through the process of relocation and return and vice versa. In this way of narrating and experiencing exile, the betwixt and between, is not something which can in any simple way be resolved. Indeed, for some, it is particularly the transient – one might say liminal – quality of exile, of routes over roots which provides important sites of resistance to hegemonic discourses of place-based identity (Clifford 1997; Gilroy 1993a).

Important though these critical interventions have been, the notion of movement and passage celebrated in writing on migration, diaspora and exile still works within a framework in which there are individuals and groups who inhabit movement and passage and those who do not. In this way, writing on exile continues to authorize a particular group of individuals – the exiled, the migrant, etc. – as bearers of a particular kind of existential truth, whether it be the truth of a traumatic nationalism or the truth of the traveller. Indeed, as Malkki (1995: 513) notes, while 'refugees' continue to be viewed as individuals out of place and in crisis, exiles, as well as migrants, nomads, travellers and diasporas (see, for example, Eades 1993; Clifford 1992) have recently become the romantic figures for anthropologists and others who seek to move anthropology away from what are regarded as static views of people and culture confined to and conditioned principally by particular places, towards a view of people and culture as mobile, creolized and hybrid, increasingly inhabiting non-places (Augé 1995).

Studies of this variety constitute an invaluable contribution to the inventory of contemporary issues we must tackle. However, as a recipe for the transformation of anthropology's substantive foci it is absurd (maybe even ethnocentric), a call for nomadology rather than anthropology. As Hammann, *et al.* (1997) have recently pointed out, for example, 98 per cent of the world's population never physically moves to another place on anything like a permanent basis, and the greater proportion of this 98 per cent hardly move at all. Paradoxically, moreover, rather than challenging the static, place-based view of people and culture, the study of movers and variously displaced persons reaffirms a static view of the relationship between people, place and culture, re-creating the division between those who are 'emplaced' and those who are 'out-of-place', the sedentary and the non-sedentary, fixed vs fluid, roots vs routes, isled vs ex-isled.

What we seek to emphasize, above and beyond the actual physical movement of individual subjects, are two things. The first is the physical movement individuals confront in their conditions of physical fixity – the intercultural import-export of goods and ideas (Clifford 1992), the translocal networks Olwig (1993, 1997), and appropriation of cultural otherness (Massey 1991, 1992) through which the specificity of local places and identities are made. The second, however, are individuals' vicarious movements . . . the sense in which people move imaginatively or cognitively in time and space in constructing their identities and experiencing particular places (Rapport and Dawson 1998). Moreover, as the case studies on which we draw demonstrate, while emplacement suggests fixity and roots, it is often achieved through language which metaphorically invokes spatial and temporal movements and relocations. Similarly, the discourse of migration, displacement and exile is as much the property of the seemingly most fixed or rooted individuals as it is of those who live physically transient lives. In sum, we argue that place and identity are rarely made or inhabited in a singular or straightforward manner, but are most often constructed and experienced as a variety of both literal and metaphorical roots and routes (Tilley 1999: 177–84).

Migrant Minds and Places of the Imagination

The former coal-mining town of Ashington, in north-east England, would seem to be a particularly apt context to test out the thesis that emplacement should be treated as an active search involving cognitive movement in time and space, for here is a place whose residents have been characterized in the sociological literature as facing a triple-faceted fixity. Many are socially fixed, working-class with little opportunity for social mobility. Most are spatially fixed (isolated and geographically immobile). Finally, there is a sense in which this increasingly elderly population of residents are temporally fixed. With death nearby, time is running out.

The particular event we wish to focus on is the conflict that emerged in one particular old people's club surrounding the issue of the representation of community.[1] The case is interesting because it demonstrates how competing discourses of fixity and movement, and particularly residency and migration, play out in struggles over the depiction of place and collective identity. At the time of research several clubs were approached by local government who sought the involvement of elderly people in the running and construction of a local museum of mining. Participants from each club were asked to choose one from among them who with others would act as voluntary curator, record local poems, songs and passages of dialect for broadcast in the museum and serve on an advisory body concerned with the design of the museum's displays.

In the event two fairly resolute candidates and groups of backers emerged. A ballot was called by club leaders, and in the days leading up to it a fairly conflictual debate took place. The conflictual nature of the debate was hardly surprising. First, in the eyes of participants the advisory body on which the successful candidate would serve was responsible for nothing less than playing a leading role in the construction of a visual and oral representation of the community. This kind of activity is the very raison d'être of the clubs. Secondly, the debate focused on the issue of the ownership of rights to community definition. Thirdly, the divergent biographies of the respective candidates lent the debate a particularly polarizing set of substantive issues around which claims to ownership of definitional rights were contested. One of the candidates was a former school head teacher, an activist in the local historical movement and a lifelong resident of the town. The other

---

1. This section develops a case study presented elsewhere (Dawson 1998).

was a former miner who in the economic depression of the 1930s had temporarily moved for work to the coalfields of Kent, Canada and America. In terms of class at least, the social profiles of the two groups of supporters reflected broadly those of the two candidates.

The first set of issues were, then, those of class and occupation. The right of community definition accorded to the former miner was represented as stemming from his direct erstwhile involvement in mining. The second key issue was residency. The right of community definition accorded to the former headmaster was represented as stemming both from his unbroken residency in the town and the fact that, as a long-term resident and activist within local historical circles, he had become an expert in the histories, songs, poetry and dialect of the local mining working class.

With change, wrought largely by the demise of mining, the seemingly 'objective' referents of community are steadily disappearing. As such, a sense of community is increasingly obtained at a second remove, through learning rather than direct experience. Moreover, the central images of community are part of a cultural fiction that becomes ever more elaborate as they are celebrated in the burgeoning local history societies, writing groups and the local museum. It is clear that community is being refined as a discourse by a middle class that manipulate images and symbols that have only a condensed historical meaning for them, rather than a more personal historic link. What is important to note is that through his mastery of apparently mining- and working-class-specific cultural forms, the middle-class former head teacher was able to represent himself as more working-class than the working class. Here, then, personal identity is dislocated from the objective referent of class and relocated via the mastery of working-class memorabilia into a privileged relation to a historical place.

The teacher's claims to represent community, in other words, was based not simply on long-term residency but on his rootedness in the particular lifeways and landscape of an imagined historical place. By contrast, the miner's claim to represent community was based not simply on his working-class credentials, but more importantly on his experiences of the larger landscape inhabited by the international working class and of which Ashington was seen to be a part. This was achieved by a critical reappraisal of the idea of the 'local', a critique and argument that resonate with a series of strands of socialist thinking in which the idea of 'local' community was seen as intimately connected with the paternalistic-ally oppressive objectives of pre-nationalization mining companies, whose strategies of control involved the discursive construction of 'local' places and communities (Dawson 1990: 30–8). In other similar thinking, such as that of the internationalism of the Communist Party of Great Britain in the 1930s (a politically formative era for many of the club participants), local community identity is represented as a form of class consciousness.

The point here is that through deployment of the discourse of the international community of the working class the former itinerant miner who had spent much of his life exiled from the local community could represent himself as more of the community than others with histories of permanent residency. Here, then, community identity is effectively dislocated from the objective referent of place. In real terms this consisted of a re-presentation of migration and to an extent temporary economic exile as a rite of passage to emplacement and community membership. Three, often explicitly stated, reasons were given for why this should be so.

First, migration was claimed as an origin(al) experience of belonging. Much was made of the newness of Ashington, a town that simply did not exist before the onset of the mining industry in the eighteenth century. The argument was embellished with subtlety. For example, in commenting on the complexity and cleverness of local language, one supporter of the former miner was able to add the descriptive term 'polyglottal buzz' to that of the 'pitmatic'. The term pitmatic refers to a process whereby mining terminology is developed for metaphorical usage in the description of everyday reality. The term polygottal buzz refers to the multifarious inputs to the language, from the migrant settlers who were the area's first significant population.

Secondly, mirroring an emphasis on spatial segmentation in the way that community is constructed, migration was represented as heightening through lived contrast consciousness of a community whose distinctiveness derives from juxtaposition with the world beyond its boundaries. Thirdly, mirroring socialist internationalism, migration and temporary exile was represented as enabling consciousness of a community of the working class which, because locally suppressed, is realized principally in its international aspect (see also Olwig 1993). Conversely, and somewhat paradoxically given the use of socialist internationalist ideas, through localizing these three discourses, of origins, hybridity and internationalism, migration was represented as a quintessential characteristic of local community and culture. In essence, apart from the fact that it is a working-class coal-mining town, what distinguishes Ashington from the isolated agricultural communities that surround it is that it is a migrant town per se, it has a kind of 'been-to' culture, and, in at least some cases, its people are conscious of its international locatedness.

It is no doubt true that the people depicted in this case study face extreme conditions of social, spatial and temporal fixity. However, it is clear that their competing definitions of community that are constructed through a process of identity location and dislocation, are also engineered through engagement in a kind of movement. At one level people move socially, to working class from the objectively perceived social status of middle class, for example. At another level they move temporally to defining moments of community: to Ashington's moment of inception, to its depression-years era of intermittent wage migration and to the era of the rise of socialist internationalism. Finally, they move spatially, to the southern locus of their exploitation and depreciation, and from local community to international community to internationally located local community. As part of this process, migration and exile are represented often as defining features of community and place.

In essence, while these people face conditions of fixity, they seem like many others to engage cognitively in movement. Furthermore, we may be able to describe fixity and movement as interdependent modalities. There may be a situation where the imagination of other places and times informs images of community constructed in the here and now that people seek to instil in perpetuity, in this case in the bricks, mortar, display cabinets and cassette tapes of a heritage museum, perhaps so as to overcome the crises of discontinuity that impending death threatens: movement gives on to fixity gives on to movement. Here then are home bodies and migrant minds, for whom place is fashioned and remade as a route for, as much as it is the root of, identity.

Romancing Hue: Loving and Leaving Place

While the lives of rural miners in Britain are mistakenly imagined to be both thoroughly fixed and firmly emplaced, precisely the opposite might be said of popular imaginings of the Vietnamese. Indeed, refugees and exiles are a recurrent theme both in Vietnamese history and in imaginings of Vietnam. Exile figures as an important part of the story of anti-colonialist struggle in Vietnam, a badge of honour bestowed by the French on errant emperors and early nationalist thinkers alike. In the more recent past, in terms of Western (particularly Anglo-American) media, after the war itself it was the image of 'boat people' and refugees – individuals who whether through their own or other's choosing set off on perilous journeys – that dominated news stories on Vietnam and the Vietnamese. What the rest of the world initially saw simply as another story of third-world refugees, however, has more recently been variously rewritten in terms of 'exile': of leaving, arrival and return, part of the stories through which immigrant Vietnamese communities living outside of Vietnam narrate their lives (Nam 1993; Dorais, Chan and Indra 1988; and see also Young 1998 for a Western journalist's recent reflections on one Vietnamese family's story of flight into exile).

Within Vietnam itself, there continues to be much discussion about both the original movement of Vietnamese during the war and more recent migrants who together make up the diasporic Viet Kieu (Vietnamese living outside of Vietnam). These discussions raise complex issues linking economics, politics, kinship, gender and personal identities. Our interest here, in particular, is in the way in which exile, or the possibility and imagination of migration and exile and of exiled imaginings – that is to say, discourses of and about the exiled – informs everyday constructions and relationships to place and landscape in the emerging tourist centre and 'world heritage site' of Hue, the former imperial capital and current seat of the people's committee of Thua Thien Hue province in Central Vietnam.

'Hue is more lovely as a reminiscence than as a place to live.' This expression is found in the introduction to the chapter of a book on the traditional arts and crafts of Hue (Thong 1994). Immediately striking is the way in which the book situates Hue as a place in relationship to a sense of nostalgic longing and loss. The author, a history professor at the local university, suggests that this saying encapsulates how many people feel about Hue. People who go away from Hue, he suggested, remembered with fondness the aesthetic beauty of the City and the romance of the perfume river, but most people who live in Hue are actually tormented by the weather, particularly the long rainy season which usually causes extensive flooding. Other individuals, however, interpreted this saying in different ways. On the one hand, some individuals felt that there was a special quality about Hue and people from Hue, which always made people wish to return. On the other hand, many individuals, young people especially, bemoaned the lack of economic opportunities and job possibilities, as well as the all-too-quiet life of a sleepy provincial town where most shops and restaurants closed at 11 o'clock. For these individuals, it was not the weather, but the sense of cultural and economic stagnation which at times made living in Hue difficult to bear.

Hue, both people and place, are, perhaps increasingly, constructed and to a certain extent 'policed' as the living embodiment of a traditional Kinh or Viet cultural aesthetic. Strict zoning regulations have been adopted in order to protect, so far as possible, the 'unique' interplay of natural and man-made features which characterize the Hue landscape. A tightly imposed curfew has been placed on women working in the evening, with most activity in hotels, restaurants, karaokes ending by 11 p.m., in order to protect, so far as possible, 'the modest beauty and charm of the social landscape'. Significantly, this reconstruction of Hue – marked among other things by the renovation and conservation of monuments and the reopening of fine arts training departments, as well as by the growth of private entrepreneurial activity such as hosting 'traditional'-style meals – is being produced as much by discourses originating outside of Hue (among others by Viet Kieu or overseas Vietnamese) as it is by the discourses of State and people living there.

One internet site, 'Hue Net' (www.geocities.com/Tokyo/2579/), compares Hue with other 'ancient capitals in SE Asia' and points to its representativeness as an 'Oriental city'. The authors note how all the monuments are 'in sublime harmony with nature', a harmony which is seen to be mirrored in the 'courteous, mild and quiet' people of Hue. 'Both life and landscape here are poetical, bringing self-confidence and worrilessness to everybody.' The site is apparently maintained by a Viet Kieu. It is not possible to document here the direct material effects or consequences of such apparently naive and nostalgic images or imaginings on

Figure 19.1 Hein and Tuan pose in the 'traditional' Hue restaurant which Hein runs. The clientele is mainly foreign tourists, among them overseas Vietnamese (Viet Khieu). Hein said she had been propositioned by several Viet Khieu men, who reportedly come to Hue in hopes of marrying a 'real' Vietnamese woman.

Hue. More importantly, however, for the purposes of this chapter, is the perception among local people of the impact of overseas Vietnamese on the locality. Young tour guides (both women and men) with whom one talks, for instance, continually commented on overseas Vietnamese men coming back to Hue to find 'real' Vietnamese women – 'Hue women' – as wives. One tour guide mentioned that there had been 10,000 overseas Vietnamese visitors in Hue the previous year, and that he and his friends reckoned Hue was now short 1,000 women as a result. Whether or not their characterization of the Viet Kieu is accurate, what is of interest here is the way in which both for the tour guides and other individuals living in Hue, the Viet Kieu (men especially) are commonly viewed as being motivated by a longing for return, a rediscovery of their Vietnamese roots and the desire for an authentic, if regal, Vietnamese woman: a longing which was set against the presumed loss of Vietnamese identity in the countries within which they were newly settled.

In fact, tour guides and other individuals have a complex relation with exile and the exiled. On the one hand, the longing and desire of the exiled is read and constructed by these individuals as proof of place and evidence of an essential truth of the self; e.g. why would the exiled return unless there were not, in fact, something quintessentially Vietnamese about the place and people? At the same time, this essential truth was always called into question by the fact that many of these same individuals expressed a desire to be and/or to live elsewhere and otherwise, places and lives which were more often than not constructed as being in complete opposition to the dominant visions and viewings of 'Hue'. For example, the same tour guide who said that the Viet Kieu had taken away 1,000 local women, lamented the fact that his family had narrowly missed out on emigrating to the US. More than about the relative desirability of one place over another, however, it was fundamentally about the possibility of different subject positions which enable different versions and relations to place, including home place. The paradox is that it is the imagined longing of the exiled which in part creates the burden of an authentic self which they see themselves as carrying.

In order to further illustrate the complex and often contradictory ways in which both the imagining of exiles and the possibility of migration (in this case to Saigon) inform constructions of place in this particular locality, here is a love story of sorts between two individuals encountered there, Tuan and Hein. Tuan had at that time recently returned to Hue from Saigon where he had spent two years living with his uncle and working as a waiter in a restaurant there. While he was in Saigon, he said, he longed to get back to Hue, though the longing was tempered by the pleasure of living in an urban cosmopolitan centre and of earning a decent wage. He originally came back to Hue, he suggested, only because he had decided to go to University and pursue a degree studying English. On completion of his degree course, his original intention was to return to Saigon to find a job with a multi-national firm whom he had heard paid very good wages for University graduates who were able to speak English. Tuan was being forced to rethink his plans, however, because he had met and fallen in love with Hein.

Hein had completed a degree course in French and worked in the Hue post-office. She also worked in her family's business, a relatively expensive restaurant which prepared and served food in the 'manner of the former royal court'. The restaurant was in fact part of the family home, with guests served on the verandah surrounded by landscaped bonsai gardens. The picture of Hein which Tuan painted was a kind of quintessential Hue individual: he mentioned several times how she loved and served her parents, how she not only was well educated, but also was specially talented in preparing traditional Hue dishes. Indeed, Tuan and Hein recounted how on two separate occasions, foreign visitors – one a French Caucasian, the other French Vietnamese (Viet Kieu) – had unsuccessfully sounded out the possibilities of marrying Hein because of her 'beauty, talent and charm'. The only cloud in this otherwise fairy-tale picture of romance was that unlike Tuan, Hein was apparently fixed on staying in Hue, despite the fact that, as she herself said, Vietnamese gender and kinship protocols specify that women should follow their partners, rather than vice versa.

For Tuan, the question as to whether or not to leave Hue was complicated in a number of ways by Hein's apparent refusal to leave Hue. Leaving Hue for Saigon provided economic opportunities which Tuan clearly thought would enable him to embark on a successful and prosperous career and increase his social standing and prestige. If he stayed in Hue, the potential for increasing his economic and social status would be greatly diminished and he would be continually reminded of his inferior status vis-à-vis his wife and his wife's parents, both of whom were influential and affluent individuals. Tuan's desire to leave Hue, however, was not only about his desire to transcend his present social and economic status, but was also about the possibility of exploring both other places and alternative selves: possibility spaces which Tuan, like many other young people in Hue, does not see as being readily available in the local landscape.

What of Hein, who unlike Tuan, did not give any overt indication of ambivalence with Hue, and certainly no sense of being oppressed by the place which she appears to have chosen for herself. First of all, having chosen to live in Hue, not desiring to move, not having physically moved, does not mean to say that she experiences no movement. Apart from anything else, Hein is in frequent contact with tourists and travellers who pass through her family's restaurant. Hein's mother has also previously worked abroad in Iraq as a doctor. Both her mother's stories of living and working abroad and her day-to-day contact with travellers, from places either physically or conceptually distant, present possibilities for cognitive movement, through whom she might, as with the tour guides, imaginatively explore other possible selves and view home place from a different perspective.

But why in particular does Hein not want to leave Hue with Tuan? One possible answer lies in the fact that the longing and love of Tuan for Hein is akin to, and mirrored in the desiring gaze of Viet Kieu men, for both of whom Hein is the objectification of an essential sense of place and location. Recall for instance that Tuan has experienced the kind of longing for Hue similar to that which he and others attribute to the exiled. His return to Hue is then complicated by the fact that he falls in love with Hein, as do other Viet Kieu men, on their return from exile. Hein thus becomes the site for Tuan's identification of an essential Hue self, a part of his self, of his place and identity which he wishes to take with him, while at the same time he is actively engaged in the process of leaving and re-inventing identity, place and self. For Tuan, that Hein seemingly refuses to leave becomes another instance of the burdensomeness of this part of himself which, as it were, refuses to let him leave. What he cannot or does not wish to see is that the object of his desire is a subject who, like himself, does not wish to be confined or contained, but also has and experiences alternative selves. The crucial difference is that whereas Tuan sees the exploration of alternative selves as necessitating physical relocation, for Hein, the exploration of alternative selves lies in a kind of exiled imagining, an act of self-imposed exile from the categories through which she is continually being constructed as a passive and docile body. By choosing to live in Hue, Hein simultaneously confirms her status as a Hue woman, one located 'at home', and destabilizes the social fictions that keeps her 'in place'. Moreover, while constructed as passive and docile, she incorporates, through the contacts she makes, her own exiled imaginings. In this way a conceptually rooted place of past-presents – the idea of an essential and original Hue – is transvalued in such a way that the actual physical locality can become a route to alternative future-presents. In this case it seems a moot point as to whether or not the would-be physical migrant and exile – Tuan – or the migrant mind and exiled imagination – Hein – is the more rooted or routed.

Conclusion: on Migrant Minds and Ex/isled Imaginings

In this chapter we have essayed the argument that the making of place, like the making of identity, involves both literal and metaphorical movement. While drawing on recent theorists who have emphasized routes over roots, what we have sought to demonstrate is that the exiles search for roots, no less than the unfolding of migrant routes takes place within landscapes of the imagination. As we suggested in the introduction, however, imaginings of exile, no less than the cognitive movement of migrant minds, are never singular and straightforward but often involve contradictory expressions and desires, both literal and cognitive dissonances which are never completely reconciled.

Migration and exile are often written about as a movement away from that which is familiar and self-same, which either leads to nostalgic attempts at recovery or to a liberatory experience from the self. We wish to disrupt this oppositional logic of either roots or routes to posit a more complex relation of both/and, which we suggest might be written as the ex/isled. In particular we think ex/isled is a useful metaphor for rethinking identity processes in general, because it not only evokes the sense of leaving, which is a longing and a carrying with, but also is evocative of destination not yet achieved, and of return never fully realized. Exile points to the possibility of experiencing self and place as 'other', or, more precisely, of the experience of self and place as located in the movement between and in acts of identification with other possible selves and places. Indeed, it is important to reiterate the point often lost in discussions of self and others that in experiencing self as other, we experience the other as self.

Finally, in trying to think through the making of place and identity, we wish to reconceptualize liminality as the awareness or realization of the betwixt and between, in order to get away from its being seen as a temporary stage in the process of movement from one fixed state or place to another. We want to see it as proximal and immanent in all acts of identification, including the construction of and acts of identifications with particular places. That is to say we do not conceptualize liminality in Van Gennep's (1960) or Turner's (1974) sense of discreet phases, states or places, between which lie a temporary and transitional period which is resolved. To do so would simply be to affirm fixed states of being. Indeed, even if one takes a dynamic version of Van Gennep and Turner which sees social life as a continual series of changing states, of lots of little series of beginnings, middles and ends, this still does not capture what we are after. It is true that we are born, we live and we die, for most, though by no means all, in one physical and seemingly familiar location – but living, the place we are at in the present, is a condition of in-betweenness, a crossroads of various real and imagined comings and goings.

Acknowledgements

We would like to thank the following for their comments and contributions to the formulation of the chapter: Barbara Bender, Judith Okely and Nigel Rapport. Research in Vietnam was sponsored by a grant from the British Academy South East Asia section.

References

Augé, M. 1995. *Non-Places: Introduction to an Anthropology of Supermodernity*. London: Verso.

Clifford, J. 1992. Travelling cultures, in L. Grossberg, C. Nelson and P. Treichler (eds) *Cultural Studies*. London: Routledge. 99–116.

—— 1997. *Routes: Travel and Translation in the Late Twentieth Century*. Cambridge, Mass.: Harvard University Press.

Dawson, A. 1990. Ageing and Change in Pit Villages of North East England. Unpublished PhD thesis, University of Essex.

—— 1998. The dislocation of identity: contestations of Home Community in Northern England, in N. Rapport and A. Dawson (eds) 1998. *Migrants of Identity: Perceptions of Home in a World of Movement*. Oxford: Berg.

Dorais, L.J., Chan, K.B. and Indra, D. (eds) 1988. *Ten Years Later: Indochinese Communities in Canada*. Montreal: Canadian Asian Studies Association.

Eades, J. 1987. *Migrants, Workers and the Social Order*. London: Tavistock.

Gilroy, P. 1993. *The Black Atlantic: Modernity and Double Consciousness*. London: Verso.

Hammann, T., Brochmann, G., Tamas, K. and T. Faist (eds) 1997. *International Migration, Immobility and Development: Multidisciplinary Perspectives*. Oxford: Berg.

Johnson, M. 1998. Global desirings and translocal loves: transgendering and same-sex sexualities in the Southern Philippines. *American Ethnologist* **28**(4).

King, R., Connell, J. and White, P. (eds) 1995. *Writing Across Worlds: Literature and Migration*. London: Routledge.

Malkki, L. 1995. Refugees and exile: from refugee studies to the national order of things. *Annual Review of Anthropology* **24** 495–523.

Massey, D. 1991. A global sense of place. *Marxism Today*. June. 24–9.

—— 1992. A place called home? *New Formations: Journal of Culture/Theory/Practice* (The question of home) **17** 133–45.

Nam, Wong Phui. 1993. *Ways of Exile: Poems from the First Decade*. London: Skoob Books.

Olwig, K.F. 1993. *Global Culture, Island Identity: Continuity and Change in the Afro-Caribbean Community of Nevis*. Reading: Harwood Academic Press.

—— 1997. Cultural sites: sustaining home in a deterritorialized world, in K. Hastrup and K.F. Olwig (eds) *Siting Culture: The Shifting Anthropological Object*. London and New York: Routledge.

Rapport, N. and Dawson, A. (eds) 1998. *Migrants of Identity: Perceptions of Home in a World of Movement*. Oxford: Berg.

Thong, N.H. 1994. *Hue, its Traditional Handicrafts and Trade Guilds*. Hue: Thuan Hoa Publishing House.

Tilley, C. 1999. *Metaphor and Material Culture*. Oxford: Blackwell.

Turner, V. 1974. *The Ritual Process: Structure and Anti-Structure*. Harmondsworth: Penguin.

White, P. 1995. Geography, literature and migration, in King, R., Connell, J. and White, P. (eds) *Writing Across Worlds: Literature and Migration*. London: Routledge. 1–19.

Van Gennep, A. 1960. *The Rites of Passage*. London: Routledge & Kegan Paul.

Young, G. 1998. *A Wavering Grace: A Vietnamese Family in War and Peace*. Harmondsworth: Penguin.

–20–

Hunting Down Home: Reflections on Homeland and the Search for Identity in the Scottish Diaspora

Paul Basu

'Hunting Down Home', the title of this chapter, is taken from a semi-autobiographical novel by a Scots-Canadian writer and sometime colleague, Jean McNeil. It is a novel about journeys – some imagined, some painfully real – in which the quest for one kind of home is often the flight from another. Its narrative crosses worlds: from Kodachrome coloured slides of southern Africa – in which occasionally appear glimpses of a mother never known and always dreamed of – to an inescapable cultural memory of an emigration that was also an exile, one which saw the forced eviction of McNeil's ancestors from one homeland, and their founding of another: in this case a Nova Scotia, a new Scotland.

There is nothing settled in McNeil's evocation of home: every place is haunted by another.

> The last thing he sang that Christmas Eve was Sweeney's Gaelic *"Salm an Fhiarainn"*, the Psalm of the Land. He was the soloist; the company the chorus. He sang as if he were a priest leading a congregation on Barra, South Uist, Eriskay, Benbecula; one of those tripping-syllable places from which we had come.
> It was a reedy, piped sound, tribal, minor-keyed, and Middle-Eastern in its wailing. It spoke of a bone-chilling devotion come galloping out of the desert, drifting across the velvet skin of Asia, carrying the historical migration of the Celts on its back (McNeil 1997: 77).

Morag, the protagonist of the novel, escapes from the disintegration of her foster-home and from the cold weight of history into a fantasy of an exotic Africa and a reunion with her mother who deserted her in infancy. The image goes beyond the personal and becomes a metaphor for the migrant's ambivalent search for the motherland which once cast its children adrift.

McNeil's story seems apposite in the context of this volume concerned with landscapes of movement, diaspora and exile. Not only because she is writing from within a diaspora, and part of that Celtic migration, but because she is concerned with connections between people and places: territories from which one might either escape or be forced to leave physically, but perhaps not psychologically. Places of the imagination, then, but places which may also be visited and revisited, reviewed and revised. Places of the past which, like it or not, are places of the present and of the future.

Moving Stories

Recent collections of essays such as those edited by Olwig and Hastrup (1997), Lovell (1998), and Rapport and Dawson (1998) demonstrate a desire to explore ethnographically what has hitherto been a somewhat theoretical discourse on the nature of identity, belonging and territorial rootedness within the complex contexts of globalization. 'An examination of these concepts,' writes Lovell, 'appears especially topical since displacement, dislocation and dispossession have become such common themes in contemporary political experiences and debates' (1998: 1).

The current anthropological discussion is characterized as revolving around two *competing* attitudes: the broadly modern which allies identity with fixity, and the broadly postmodern which asserts the individual's ability to find 'home' in movement. The former attitude is perceived by Rapport and Dawson as being the traditional anthropological model where identity is rooted in a notion of home which may be understood as 'the organization of space over time' (1998: 7). This sense of being 'at home' or 'in place' may be disturbed by the alienating forces of modernization – for example, the ontological uprooting caused by physical migration and displacement – giving rise to what Peter Berger *et al.* (1973) have described as the 'homeless mind':

> This condition is at the same time normative, spiritual and cognitive; the anomy of social movement correlates with personal alienation on the level of consciousness. However, the 'homeless mind' is hard to bear, and there is widespread nostalgia for a condition of being 'at home' in society, with oneself, and with the universe: for homes of the past that were socially homogenous, communal, peaceful, safe and secure (Rapport and Dawson 1998: 31).

While acknowledging that this remains 'a challenging thesis', Rapport and Dawson find it 'steeped in communitarian ideology' and 'ethnographically ungrounded in the present' (1998: 32). Instead they believe the ethnographic evidence supports a view that it is 'in and through movement that human beings continue to make themselves at home' (1998: 33), that individuals are 'at home in personal narratives that move away from any notion of fixity within a common idiom, and their identities derive from telling moving stories of themselves and their world views' (1998: 30).

Perhaps recognizing with Barthes that discourse moves by 'clashes', and that 'a new discourse can only emerge as the paradox which goes against . . . the surrounding or preceding doxa' (Barthes 1993: 388), the writers are being intentionally provocative. Their anthropology is more individualistic than social, their metaphors more rhizomic than rooted, their position more postmodern than modern. But does the ethnographic evidence really support their case? Are they correct in stating that 'home *versus* movement' is an outmoded paradigm that must now be superseded by 'home *as* movement' (Rapport and Dawson 1998: 30)?

Drawing my observations from an on-going research project which explores notions of home and homeland within the Scottish diaspora, I should like to question Rapport and Dawson's assertion. For, in discussing narrative as a mobile resource, they seem to discount the possibility that it may also be used to articulate senses of rootedness. Indeed, they may be correct in doubting the (objective) reality of lost edenic homes evoked in migrant tales – 'We would query the existence of that 'original life-world' of traditional absoluteness and fixity' (1998: 32) – but surely they ignore the (subjective) reality of these putative homes for the people who invoke them. Similarly, they describe contemporary identity as a *search* (1998: 4), but perhaps they do not explore the full range of that metaphor. Is not to search, in part, at least, to seek that which is felt to have been lost?

The 'Homecomings' project[1] is concerned with journeys made by people of Scottish descent from throughout the world to their 'old country'. Some know little of their 'roots' and are content to tread the well-trod tourist trails, but others have encyclopaedic knowledges and have come pursuing their genealogical research, visiting libraries and archive offices, scouring overgrown graveyards for ancestral tombs, making pilgrimages of sorts to the ruins of the houses and villages they left behind. It is easy to find a narrative structure in such quests, but less easy to assert that these 'moving stories' have nothing to do with a desire to find somewhere incontrovertible on which to ground identity.

I want to be able to tell my children where their ancestors came from. I think it gives them a sense of 'belonging' in a world that sometimes moves too fast (i.e. everything is always changing) (New South Wales, Australia).

I have found, after being in the States for a few months [born in Canada], that there is an opinion that the reason a number of people here feel lost and hopeless, is the loss of

1. The Homecomings project is based at the Department of Anthropology, University College London and the Highland Folk Museum, Kingussie, Inverness-shire. A multi-sited ethnographic study of diaspora from the perspective of return migration to homelands in the form of 'roots tourism', the project employs a wide-ranging set of methodologies. The informant statements used in this chapter are garnered from an internet discussion list established for the research. The list may be accessed via the project web site at: http://www.scotweb.org/homecomings.

roots. I have found a great deal of people are realizing this. I have always felt that it is important to know these things and have passed many of the family stories on to my children and plan to write a family history for the benefit of the whole family. I consider myself very lucky in knowing where my roots are (California, USA).

How can I, a USA national, get a passport and/or some form of citizenship with the homeland of my heritage? I shall never feel like a whole being until I can feel and be part of Scotland. Please Scotland give to me some form of simple citizenship, for then I may no longer have to suffer the slings and arrows of mental and physical separation from my true homeland (Louisiana, USA).

Walking through Cawdor village and castle knowing my ancestors also walked there . . . I felt like I came home after several generations' journey (Texas, USA).

It seems, therefore, that we ought to address both the mobile and the static in these narratives of identity, and recognize that, while in certain circumstances home may become deterritorialized, in many cases senses of territorial and social rootedness continue to give people ontological security in a world of perceived movement.

Diaspora and Homeland

Another way of articulating the complicated relationship between movement and rootedness may be to consider the tropes of 'diaspora' and 'homeland'. These are relational terms like 'the global' and 'the local', each constituted in the other such that there can be no diaspora without homeland (actual or imagined), no homeland without dispersal. Indeed, part of the recent redefinition of 'diaspora' (Safran 1991; Cohen 1997) has been not only to recognize the diversity of reasons for population displacement (giving rise to 'labour', 'trade' and 'imperial' diasporas in addition to the archetypal 'victim' diaspora), but also to realize how essential the 'myth' of homeland is in maintaining senses of common identity among such populations.

It is worth reproducing Cohen's tabulated summary to reinforce the point:

Common features of a diaspora (after Cohen 1997: 26)

1 Dispersal from an original homeland, often traumatically, to two or more foreign regions;
2 alternatively, the expansion from a homeland in search of work, in pursuit of trade or to further colonial ambitions;
3 a collective memory and myth about the homeland, including its location, history and achievements;

4   an idealization of the putative ancestral home and a collective commitment
    to its maintenance, restoration, safety and prosperity, even to its creation;
5   the development of a return movement that gains collective approbation;
6   a strong ethnic group consciousness sustained over a long time and based on a
    sense of distinctiveness, a common history and the belief in a common fate;
7   a troubled relationship with host societies, suggesting a lack of acceptance
    at the least or the possibility that another calamity might befall the group;
8   a sense of empathy and solidarity with co-ethnic members in other countries
    of settlement; and
9   the possibility of a distinctive creative, enriching life in host countries with
    a tolerance for pluralism.

There is not the space here to examine Scottish migration in the light of this check-
list; suffice to say it meets the criteria, and is even something of an exemplar. A
sense of 'Scottishness', of belonging to a distinctively Scottish community,
transcends national boundaries and is expressed in many ways, particularly through
the activities of clan societies and their gatherings and games. Certain regions of
the United States, Canada, Australia and New Zealand are ironically described as
being 'more Scottish than Scotland'. Highland language, dance and music traditions
have survived in some Nova Scotian communities, for example, and have recently
been reintroduced to the Scottish Highlands where they had become extinct. The
most powerful emblem, however, bonding people of Scots descent throughout the
world, is an attachment to the homeland and its distinctive landscape and history.
The 'Canadian Boat Song' remains the anthem of many – and not just Canadians
of Hebridean descent:

> From the lone shieling on the misty island
> Mountains divide us, and wastes of seas;
> Yet still the blood is strong, the heart is Highland,
> And we, in dreams, behold the Hebrides.

The Scottish diaspora is exemplary in another way too. For, although Cohen
suggests that dispersal may be *either* forced *or* voluntary (points 1 and 2), it is
evident that the two are more complexly related. Thus, while the trauma of eviction
and exile is often invoked in Scottish emigrant stories and songs (particularly those
relating to the infamous Highland Clearances), the Scots were also prominent
colonists, missionaries, soldiers, politicians and explorers, and therefore compliant
in the British expansionist project. Indeed the Scottish diaspora can be interpreted
in a variety of ways according to the inferences one wishes to invoke: Scots as
exiles banished from ancient homelands, as pioneer settlers civilizing savage places,
as agents of British imperialism, as perpetrators of displacement in the homelands

of others. Such are the apparent incompatibilities which yet seem to cohere in the diasporic identity.

Or, perhaps, it is the fact that they do not cohere so easily that provokes a search for what one Australian informant calls 'a place of uncomplicated belonging':

> I have noticed the similarities between what happened to the Highlanders in the Clearances and what happened to the Australian Aborigines (i.e. a whole load of men in red coats arrive and say, 'get off the land, we want to put sheep here!'). Unfortunately, I'm not sure this made my pioneer ancestors any more sympathetic to the local Aborigines. It seems to have been a case of 'what's done to you, you do to others'. But I do think for us in the diaspora, especially third or fourth generation like me, our idea of 'homeland' is inextricably linked to the place we live in now. And I sometimes wonder if part of the longing for a homeland is a longing for a place of uncomplicated belonging, especially in the current Australian climate, where a lot of conscience examining is going on. It's hard to claim a place here without being aware of who is being displaced by that claim. In a way I feel that in Australia I'm still on trial as far as belonging to the land is concerned. Somehow it has to be earned. The idea of a place where my ancestors belonged for thousands of years is very appealing (Victoria, Australia).

That such a place forms in the imagination – literally as an 'idea' – is significant and supports Rapport and Dawson's argument that 'home' is essentially insub-stantial. But what is equally significant, and what empowers these places in terms of identity construction, is, paradoxically, their very materiality: they may be visited, they may be touched, pieces of them may be held in the hand, put in pockets, retained as keep-sakes. In short, 'home' is given substance in 'home-land'.

Highland Homelands – Landscapes and Narratives

It is to this dual nature of 'home-land', this union of the imaginary and the material, that I would now like to turn, and to consider some of the processes whereby landscapes with which one may be arbitrarily linked acquire more profound personal significances. I propose that the homelands of diasporic Scots may be apprehended through a sequence of epithets, each situated within a distinct theoretical field. Thus, a heuristic journey may be taken in which the Scottish Highlands, for example, may be conceptualized and understood respectively as networks of *sites of memory, sources of identity* and *shrines of self*. In what follows I attempt to navigate a course through various literatures while using photographs and informant quotes to provide some ethnographic counterpoint.

Figure 20.1 'I was very moved during our visit to Culloden. I had a sense that my ancestors were there. (California', USA)

Sites of memory

The network of heritage sites, visitor centres, ruins, battlefields, castles, monuments and so on that make up the Highland 'heritage-landscape' may be examined in terms of the work of Yates (1966), Halbwachs (1971) and Nora (1989), each of whom has been concerned, in different ways, with the manner in which the past has been objectified in place. Thus, whereas 'the document was the quintessential form through which the modern historian remembered the past',

> postmodern historians such as Nora place the document among the countless artefacts in which memory has been materialized. They shift the emphasis from documents themselves to the architectural places of memory in which they and other memorabilia are contained – in archives, museums, commemorative monuments. (Hutton 1993: 151)

As well as these places in which the past is 'intentionally' materialized, we might extend the discussion to include those which have not been explicitly designed to 'house' the past, but which do so implicitly: the abandoned villages and ruined croft houses, for instance, which one often encounters in the Scottish Highlands. After Riegl, we might call them 'unintentional monuments' (see Riegl 1982; Basu 1997 and 2000).

A fascinating inversion takes place in such 'sites of memory' in which the past – the narrativized past of memory, history and myth – becomes externalized in the landscape, endowing the battlefield of Culloden, for example, or the ruins of villages depopulated in the Clearances, with a powerful aura. 'The deserted place "remembers" and grows lonely', writes Kathleen Stewart (1996: 156). It is as if the landscape itself 'holds' the memory of its past and tells its own story separate from the subject who perceives it. Informants often report being moved to tears when visiting such places, or experiencing sensations that they have difficulty in expressing. They talk in terms of 'resonances' and senses of 'déjà vu'.

Thus the 'sense of place' may be experienced as if it were emitted from or dwelt in place itself, an *animus loci*, but such a sense derives from the experiencing subject, or rather from the juxtaposition of subject, place and the specific circumstances of the encounter.

> As vibrantly felt as it is vividly imagined, sense of place asserts itself at varying levels of mental and emotional intensity. Whether lived in memory or experienced on the spot, the strength of its impact is commensurate with the richness of its contents, with the range and diversity of symbolic associations that swim within its reach and move on its course (Basso 1996: 85).

Of course, we do not encounter 'place' naïvely. If we sense it, it is likely that we consciously or unconsciously know something of it already. As the pheno-menologist Edward Casey writes, 'Knowledge of place is not . . . subsequent to perception . . . but it is ingredient in perception itself' (Casey 1996: 18). The landscape is never inert, never a material *tabula rasa* awaiting inscription, but is always already embedded within webs of personal and cultural narratives, memories and associations.

> Standing on the bluff at Lower Killeyan. There were still ruins of the homes my ancestors left in 1856. The view was spectacular. I could sense the past, and knew I was seeing the same sites as they did back into the 1700s, maybe earlier. It put an identity to the places I had been looking at on the map (Wisconsin, USA).

> It was as though, if I'd stepped off the train, I'd be alighting in a different era . . . It made the stories I'd heard throughout my life about my ancestors concrete. I was obstinately of this place! (Nevada, USA).

But, just as the past may be objectified or externalized in the landscape as 'sites of memory', so the sites of memory – and thus the past they embody – become internalized through individual engagement and encounter. Bourdieu character-istically describes this process as the 'dialectic of the internalization of externality and the externalization of internality' (1985: 72). Hutton's discussion of Nora provides some additional insights on the matter in terms of the individualization or personalization of cultural identity:

> Nora points out . . . that this trend towards the exteriorization of memory in its formal representations has also called into being a deepening interiorization. He locates the emergence of this process about the turn of the [nineteenth/twentieth] century in the work of Henri Bergson and particularly Sigmund Freud. The exteriorization of collective memory in public institutions designed to store them is complemented by the deepening interiorization of individual memory. In an age in which the collective identities of traditional society, especially those of family, church, and nation, were disintegrating, the individual felt the need to search his own memory for some surer sense of personal identity (Hutton 1993: 151).

Nora's postmodern history, in which individual memories 'surface at the interstices of broken collective memories', in which 'the individual forges his identity by historicizing his own memory' amid the 'remnants of the collective memories of family, church, and nation' (ibid.), seems particularly apposite in the study of family history – 'ancestor hunting', as it were, among *Les Lieux de mémoire* of the Scottish Highlands – where 'everyone is his own historian' (ibid.).

Figure 20.2 'I certainly saw my visit to the now empty Isle of Pabbay as returning to my native land, and was thrilled about how, once I had established my credentials by quoting my lineage, I was immediately accepted and introduced as a 'Pabbaich''. (Victoria, Australia)

Sources of identity

Through the 'interiorization' of collective memory, the sites of memory thus become 'sources of identity'. Myths of place may be seen as forming a reservoir of 'cultural resources' from which individuals may draw to construct a myth of the self. Both place and person are thus seen as intertwined in narrative: narrative as myth, as history, as memory.

Describing a hermeneutics of self, Kerby suggests that the self 'appears to be inseparable from the narrative or life story it constructs for itself or otherwise inherits' (1991: 6). Kerby goes on to explain how the 'narrating subject' is nevertheless also a 'narrated subject', limited in its auto-creativity by the possibilities of a particular *habitus*:

> ... it should be clear that such narratives are considerably influenced by the social milieu in which the human subject functions. The stories we tell of ourselves are determined not only by how other people narrate us but also by our language and the genres of storytelling inherited from our traditions. Indeed, much of our self-narrating is a matter of becoming conscious of the narratives that we already live with and in . . . It seems true to say that we have already been narrated from a third-person perspective prior to our even gaining the competence for self-narration. Such external narratives will understandably set up expectations and constraints on our personal self-descriptions, and they significantly contribute to the material from which our own narratives are derived. (1991: 6)

A pertinent elaboration of this notion of 'heritage' in narrative may be found in the Scottish moral philosopher, Alasdair MacIntyre, who himself emigrated to the USA in 1970.

> I inherit from the past of my family, my city, my tribe, my nation, a variety of debts, inheritances, rightful expectations and obligations. These constitute the given of my life, my moral starting point . . . the story of my life is always embedded in the story of those communities from which I derive my identity . . . What I am, therefore, is in key part what I inherit, a specific past that is present to some degree in my present. I find myself part of a history and that is generally to say, . . . whether I recognize it or not, one of the bearers of a tradition (1984: 220–21).

This discussion of narrative, landscape and identity is central to Rapport and Dawson's argument that home, in the postmodern world, is to be found in movement. They emphasize the ability of individuals to transcend the structures of cultural discourse and invent themselves anew. 'At the base of every language-act resides "a personal lexicon"', they write, citing Steiner, '"a private thesaurus" constituted by the unique linguistic "association-net" of personal consciousness:

by the fact that each individual's understanding of language and the world is different' (Rapport and Dawson 1998: 29). It is in the movement of narrative – the perpetual reinvention of the story of the self – that home is found, they assert, but perhaps they overestimate the inventiveness of the individual, or underestimate the resilience of the cultural story against such 'migrations of identity'.

Indeed, it is the absence of choice that is striking in many informant statements, particularly those implying a kind of genetic predestination:

> For me, being Scottish is not a choice, it's in the blood. It is something which has no name, but yet lingers there within me (Washington, USA).

> It's not something tangible I can put my finger on that draws me to Scotland. I guess I would have to say I feel it's like a homecoming, like I belong there. Feels like it's in my blood, so to speak . . . I guess it is really, if I think about it (Ontario, Canada).

> Why shouldn't you feel the blood of your ancestors stirring within you? I took my son, born in Canada, to my homeland in 1995 and I watched in utter amazement as he felt his 'roots'. At one point, standing on the esplanade of Edinburgh Castle and looking towards Arthur's Seat he put his hand on his heart and said, 'Mum, I feel it right here!' Nothing to do with me . . . but something stirred within him (Ontario, Canada).

Similarly, in a wonderful passage, the Canadian writer Hugh MacLennan records how his father had no need to journey to Scotland to know that he was of *Scotch* descent, it was a 'home' (and a story) he could not escape even if he wanted to.

> Whenever I stop to think about it, the knowledge that I am three-quarters Scotch, and Highland at that, seems like a kind of doom from which I am too Scotch even to think of praying for deliverance. I can thank my father for this last-ditch neurosis. He was entirely Scotch; he was a living specimen of a most curious heritage. In spite of his medical knowledge, which was large; in spite of his quick, nervous vitality and tireless energy, he was never able to lay to rest the beasties which went bump in his mind at three o'clock in the morning. It mattered nothing that he was a third-generation Canadian who had never seen the Highlands before he visited them on leave in the First World War. He never needed to go there to understand whence he came or what he was. He was neither Scot nor yet was he Scottish; he never used these genteel appellations which are now supposed to be *de rigueur*. He was simply Scotch. All the perplexity and doggedness of the race was in him, its loneliness, tenderness and affection, its deceptive vitality, its quick flashes of violence, its dog-whistle sensitivity to sounds to which Anglo-Saxons are stone deaf, its incapacity to tell its heart to foreigners save in terms which foreigners do not comprehend, its resigned indifference to whether they comprehend or not. 'It's not easy being Scotch,' he told me once. To which I suppose another Scotchman might say: 'It wasn't meant to be'. (MacLennan 1961: 1–2).

It is interesting to note that, while MacLennan's father had no need to travel to the Highlands to know who he was, it seems that MacLennan himself did. His essay *Scotsman's Return* (1961), records an uneasy journey where home is found at last . . . in Canada.

Hedging his bets between modernity and postmodernity, Giddens' discussion of the 'trajectory of the self' is situated in a 'late modernity' which, while recognizing the rootedness of the self in the past, acknowledges that the past may be revised to suit an anticipated future. Giddens notes that 'the reflexive construction of self-identity depends as much on preparing for the future as on interpreting the past', but that 'the "reworking" of past events is certainly always important in this process' (1991: 85). In the 'post-traditional' late modern age, the existential dilemmas of 'What to do? How to act? Who to be?' (1991: 70) are part of a project of the self in which 'We are, not what we are, but what we make of ourselves' (1991: 75). The project is, above all, a moral one, as Taylor stresses in *Sources of the Self*:

> My self-definition is understood as an answer to the question Who I am. And this question finds its original sense in the interchange of speakers. I define who I am by defining where I speak from, in the family tree, in social space, in the geography of social statuses and functions, in my intimate relations with the ones I love, and also crucially in the space of moral and spiritual orientation within which my most important defining relations are lived out (Taylor 1989: 35).

Such moral tellings of the self may be grounded in place. Thus, according to Basso, for the Western Apache – or at least for his key informant, Dudley Patterson – 'Wisdom sits in places',

> . . . It's like water that never dries up. You need to drink water to stay alive, don't you? Well, you also need to drink from places. You must remember everything about them. You must learn their names. You must remember what happened at them long ago. You must think about it. Then your mind will become smoother and smoother. Then you will be able to see danger before it happens . . . You will be wise (Patterson quoted in Basso 1996: 70).

Basso describes how Apache men and women come to acquire wisdom and 'an unshakeable sense of self' through their knowledge of their landscape, in their perception of a 'moral reality' beyond the 'visible reality' of place: an 'interior landscape', a landscape of the 'moral imagination' (1996: 86). What wisdom might sit in the heritage-landscape of the Scottish Highlands, what moral realities might be perceptible beyond the visible?

Shrines of self

Figure 20.3 Relics

There are two senses in which the search for the self among the sites of memory and sources of identity may be considered a sacred act, akin to pilgrimage. The first is associated with the perceived homologies between tourism and pilgrimage. Graburn, on a trajectory from the anthropology of tourism to the anthropology of pilgrimage, has described tourism as a 'sacred journey' (1989). Graburn's argument is based on a Turnerian notion of structure (secular) versus anti-structure (sacred), thus 'the touristic journey lies in the nonordinary sphere of existence, the goal is symbolically sacred and morally on a higher plane than the regards of the ordinary workaday world' (1989: 28). The quest of such journeys is seen as 'symbolically equivalent' (1989: 22) to that of pilgrimage in 'traditional' societies, while the acquisition of souvenirs such as exposed rolls of film, postcards and other mementoes is seen as analogous to collecting fragments of the 'real cross' or other relics, a way of reconstructing the sacred in the secular world of home.

On the reverse trajectory from the anthropology of pilgrimage to the anthropology of tourism, collections of essays edited by Reader and Walter (1993), Morinis (1992), and Coleman and Elsner (1995) not only recognize that the sacred-pilgrimage and secular-tourism dichotomy is probably a very recent one, that pilgrimage could at once be considered both sacred and secular (Chaucer's

Canterbury Tales attests to this), but they are also aware that in 'non-traditional' societies, the definition of the sacred becomes even more problematic (Anthony Smith's 'sacred spaces' of the nation, for example (1991)).

The second sense in which the practice of journeying to ancestral lands in search of ancestral connections may be considered akin to pilgrimage, is in regarding the *self* as being the object of a quest. Western individualism is thus epitomized by a preoccupation with the self: knowing oneself, understanding oneself, improving oneself, discovering 'the truth' about oneself, testing oneself. This quasi-sacredness of the self is further evinced in the popularity of psychoanalysis, of 'self-help' therapies of one kind or another, of alternative religions and new age philosophies, and, not least, in the practice of ancestor hunting. Each provides a solution to the problem of *where* to find oneself.

It is not adequate to merely dismiss this preoccupation with the self as narcissistic; it is necessary to understand this apparent narcissism: what drives this desire to tend to the self? The 'looming threat of personal meaningless' (Giddens 1991: 201)? The 'loss of historical continuity' with one's predecessors (1991: 171)? The hunger for 'psychic security' and an elusive 'sense of well being' (ibid.)?

In this context, the Scottish Highland heritage-landscape can be seen as a complex of shrines among which the diasporan tourist may circulate, meditating on their meaning, recognizing their symbolic resonances, finding in each of them a fragment from which to piece together the story of his or her self. But the story goes beyond the individual, and this is perhaps the very point. These are *cultural* narratives, they reinforce communality and continuity, and, in so doing, reintegrate the dislocated self within the body of society: they do indeed represent a kind of homecoming for the 'homeless mind'.

My question – one of them – was whether Rapport and Dawson were correct in their contention that such rooted senses of identity were anachronistic in our contemporary world of movement. In the light of the 'Homecomings' project, I would have to say that it is doubtful. Narratives of identity, of home and homeland clearly interact in complex ways. For some, home is primarily a notional reality and a mobile asset; for others it is also a material reality, a territorial entity fixed by specific historical and geographical co-ordinates. Such diversity of meaning ought to be reflected in our theories. One thing is certain: however it might be defined, *home matters*. The hunt is on, the quarry remains elusive.

Acknowledgements

My thanks to Barbara Bender for her invitation to participate in the 'Contested Landscapes and Landscapes of Movement and Exile' symposium at WAC4 and for her comments on a draft of this chapter. Thanks also to Christopher Tilley and Margot Winer.

References

Barthes, R. 1993. Writers, intellectuals, teachers, in S. Sontag (ed.) *A Roland Barthes Reader.* London: Vintage.

Basso, K.H. 1996. Wisdom sits in places: notes on a western Apache landscape, in S. Feld and K.H. Basso (eds) *Senses of Place.* Santa Fe: School of American Research Press. 53–90.

Basu, P. 1997. Narratives in a landscape: monuments and memories of the Sutherland Clearances, unpublished MSc thesis, University College London.

—— (2000) Sites of memory – sources of identity: landscape-narratives of the Sutherland Clearances, in J. A. Atkinson, I. Banks and G. MacGregor (eds) *Townships to Farmsteads: Rural Settlement Studies in Scotland, England and Wales,* Oxford: BAR British series 293.

Berger, P., Berger, B. and Kellner, H. 1973. *The Homeless Mind.* New York: Random House.

Bourdieu, P. 1985 [1977]. *Outline of a Theory of Practice.* Cambridge: Cambridge University Press.

Casey, E.S. 1996. How to get from space to place in a fairly short stretch of time: phenomenological prolegomena, in S. Feld and K.H. Basso (eds) *Senses of Place,* Santa Fe: School of American Research Press.

Cohen, R. 1997. *Global Diasporas: An Introduction.* London: UCL Press.

Coleman, S. and Elsner, J. 1995. *Pilgrimage: Past and Present.* London: British Museum Press.

Giddens, A. 1991. *Modernity and Self-Identity: Self and Society in the Late Modern Age.* Cambridge: Polity Press.

Graburn, N. 1989. Tourism: the sacred journey, in V. Smith (ed.) *Hosts and Guests: The Anthropology of Tourism.* Philadelphia: University of Pennsylvania Press.

Halbwachs, M. 1971. *La Topographie légendaire des évangiles en Terre Sainte.* Paris: Presses Universitaires de France.

Hutton, P.H. 1993. *History and the Art of Memory.* Hanover: University Press of New England.

Kerby, A.P. 1991. *Narrative and the Self.* Bloomington: Indiana University Press.

Lovell, N. (ed.) 1998. *Locality and Belonging.* London: Routledge.

MacIntyre, A. 1984. *After Virtue: A Study in Moral Theory.* Notre Dame: University of Notre Dame Press.

MacLennan, H. 1961. *Scotsman's Return and other Essays.* London: Heinemann.

McNeil, J. 1997. *Hunting Down Home.* London: Phoenix.

Morinis, A. (ed.) 1992. *Sacred Journeys: The Anthropology of Pilgrimage.* Westport, Connecticut: Greenwood Press.

Nora, P. 1989. Between memory and history: les lieux de mémoire, *Representations* 26.

Olwig, K. Fog and Hastrup, K. 1997. *Siting Culture: The Shifting Anthropological Object.* London and New York: Routledge.

Rapport, N. and Dawson, A. (eds) 1998. *Migrants of Identity: Perceptions of Home in a World of Movement.* Oxford: Berg.

Reader, I. and Walter, T. (eds) 1993. *Pilgrimage in Popular Culture.* London: Macmillan.

Riegl, A. 1982. The modern cult of monuments: its character and its origin. *Oppositions* **25**.

Safran, W. 1991. Diasporas in modern societies: myths of homeland and return. *Diaspora* **1**(1).

Smith, A.D. 1991. *National Identity.* Harmondsworth: Penguin.

Stewart, K. 1996. An occupied place, in S. Feld and K.H. Basso (eds) *Senses of Place.* Santa Fe: School of American Research Press.

Taylor, C. 1989. *Sources of the Self: The Making of the Modern Identity.* Cambridge: Cambridge University Press.

Yates, F. 1966. *The Art of Memory.* Chicago: University of Chicago Press.

Comments on Part II: Far from Home
Nick Shepherd

The second part of the Bender/Winer volume is sub-titled 'Landscapes of Movement and Exile'. The themes of movement, and more especially of exile, impart a special relevance to this part of the work. The United Nations High Commissioner for Refugees (UNHCR) estimates that there are currently around 50 million people worldwide who have been forced to flee their homes, whether as refugees or as internally displaced persons. The estimated number of 'people of concern' to whom the UNHCR administers direct aid stands at 21.5 million, up from 17 million in 1991. The scale and extent of forced mass population movements over the past decade or two far exceeds any other point in our history – barring isolated and spectacular cases. Not only have people been forced to leave home, but they have also returned. Major repatriations since 1990 alone include returns to Afghanistan. Mozambique, Iraq, Eritrea, Somalia, Tajikistan, Myanmar, Cambodia, Rwanda, Angola, Mali, Togo and Liberia.

In fact, the figure of the exile and the wanderer might appropriately stand as the iconic figure of late modernity – not only in the power of its media appeal (the straggling and desperate line of refugees; the night-time border crossing; the arrival in the listless camp or cold northern city), but in the range of critical and dissenting positions which it has opened up. This has most famously been the case in the passionately engaged writings of Edward Said (and the estimated 3.2 million Palestinians worldwide need to be numbered over and above the UNHCR figures[1]), but also in the case of trans-nationals such as Anthony Appiah, who works out of the North American university system but keeps one foot in his native Ghana. The history of South Africa, the country in which many of these chapters were first presented, is no less entwined with the linked themes of dispossession, exile and the longing for home. Estimates vary, but in excess of two million people were internally displaced as a result of apartheid-forced removals. Tens of thousands more fled into exile in the Frontline States, the Soviet Bloc, Europe and North America. Hilda Bernstein has collected some of their stories in a marvelous and poignant work called *The Rift: The Exile Experience of South Africans* (1994). In a section called 'The Wider World' she writes:

> Beyond South Africa, beyond the Frontline States, the exiles scattered throughout Africa, Europe and North America. They set out on unmapped journeys, traveled with the

uncertainty of unknown destinations, found ways to pilot themselves among the confused streets of anonymous cities, mastered difficult, often obscure languages; tasted a variety of cultures, learned to modulate their voices to a European pitch, to adjust their eyes to the foreshortened landscapes, the diminished skies. And knew they would never again be situated in the normal. 'We're always temporary,' said one exile, 'You don't belong.'

In the years following the political transition of 1990 there was a scene which replayed itself at major airports around the country: the flight touching down; the passengers debouching onto the stained tarmac; the returning exile stooping to embrace and kiss the ground. Home. Home and free.

In the late 1980s I briefly faced the prospect of exile myself for a couple of years. In the event, two things happened: the first was the political transformation; and the second was that I stayed on at the University of Cape Town to begin graduate work in archaeology, which is why, in a sense, I am here to write this. I mention this, along with the rest of the detail in this introductory section, for two reasons. The first is to establish the importance of the thematic focus in this second part of the volume, which I believe to be of the first importance – as much for the discipline of archaeology as, more obviously, for anthropology. The second is to establish something of my own position in relation to the theme, and some of the issues which it raises – for it would not be fair if I failed to point out that, in however limited and provisional a way, I have felt a visceral tug around the words 'home' and 'homeland', and know the panic of displacement.

I write from the point of view of an archaeologist and I want, therefore, to make two points in relation to archaeology, both as a discipline and a subject area, before I pass on to a detailed consideration of the chapters. Archaeology stands in an interesting relation to the concept of landscape and to the themes of movement and exile, as well as to the other human and social sciences. In the first place, this is because the methodology of archaeology places the practitioner in a close and immediate relationship not only with the landscape but with the land itself, in all of its particularity. I know of no other discipline which pays such close attention to the details of soil colour and texture, or to the physicality of landforms, features and objects, as a clue to human behaviour and motivation. And the very materiality of this process, the manner in which it moves beyond the processes of thought and intellection to engage the body on all of its surfaces – it seems to me – opens the way to potentially new understandings, and new interpretations of the relationship between people and landscape.

The second point, which has to do more with the history of archaeology and its developments as a practice, concerns the spirit of cautiousness which pervades archaeological affairs. It may be that I write here as a Third World archaeologist at work in a comparative backwater of the discipline, but it seems to me that archaeologists as a group have been cautious to a fault, slow to respond to intellectual change, and scornful of the untried and the new-fangled, most particularly in matters of theory. Almost alone among the social sciences archaeology held on to a radical positivist form of interpretation well into the 1980s. In some of the circles that I move in, post-processual archaeology is still regarded as dangerously *outré*. In fact, archaeology was in danger of missing the post-positivist boat altogether. While other disciplines were grappling with the effects of May 1968, Vietnam and the growing militancy of liberation movements in Angola and Mozambique, we had Lew Binford and David Clarke. This has tended to have two results that I want to mention here. The first is the relative difficulty of cross-disciplinary collaborations in archeology, where these disciplines are drawn from the humanities (cross-disciplinary collaborations with the sciences are a different matter). The second is the relative difficulty of focusing on theory in archaeological discussions, where theory of the sort purveyed by the other disciplines is regarded as abstruse or simply irrelevant.

For these reasons the editors of the volume are to be congratulated. The Landscape Symposium at the fourth World Archaeological Congress achieved a sustained focus over six sessions and three days, in a way that no other symposium that I attended was able to do. Moreover, it attracted contributions from across a range of disciplinary areas, theoretical positions and points of view – and this has translated into the range of contributions in the volume. Together, the editors and contributors expand the boundaries of the possible in archaeology, in ways that are to be applauded and encouraged. That said, the chapters here are a mixed bag, in terms of both quality and approach. Trans-disciplinary research treads a thin line. Life in the borderlands can be exhilarating, but the lack of rootedness, the tendency to eschew disciplinary grounding, can lead to amorphousness, to playing fast and loose with matters of methodology – and my impression is that some of the chapters are the worse for this. Thus my first general comment: much as we enjoy these outriders of the discipline, these riders of the purple sage, the challenge in such situations is to be more controlled, more focused – rather than to hope to dazzle with a couple of rope tricks.

For reasons of space and inclination I have not commented on all of the chapters. In particular, I have not commented directly on an excellent chapter by Orford and Becker (on Owambo women's literature), or on interesting chapters by Basu (on the Scottish diaspora), Harvey (on landscape and commerce in the Southern Peruvian Andes), Selwyn (on bypass roads and mobility regulation in Israel/ Palestine), and Winer (on 'landscapes of fear' on the Eastern Cape frontier) – although my final comment would apply to each of these cases.

My comments begin with Balzani's account of 'kingly walk-about' in the deserts of Rajasthan (in September 1986). Her themes are those of pilgrimage, ritual, physical displacement (and more particularly: walking, experience on foot), and the relation between past and present, or the semi-mythical time of Princes and deities, and the reduced circumstances of drought and political campaign. A crucial piece of contextualizing information is that as a result of the 1971 Deregulation of Princes Act the former rulers of India lost both titles and privy purses. Much of the entertainment is in the detail. I was delighted by the disclosure that H.H. Jodhpur strode at the head of a lengthy retinue which included high-ranking Rajputs, staff, cars, caravans, a video crew and newspaper reporters – and that he would retire to his caravan between strenuous bouts of walking. In 1998 my wife and I completed the *Camino de Santiago*, an ancient pilgrim route which threads its way across the mountains of northern Spain. In six weeks we completed 500 kilometres – sadly, unaccompanied by video crews or an air-conditioned caravan (although my wife was six months pregnant at the time). Balzani invokes Tilley (1994) to introduce a theme which runs across a number of the contributions: namely, the social construction of landscape. She writes: 'The landscape of Rajasthan is here understood as the outcome of centuries of human habitation, wars and coloniza-tion'. In this conception the act of walking and the rituals associated with pilgrimage become attentions paid to the landscape, which are as necessary for its well-being as they are for their human agents.

My single critical comment relates to the framing of the chapter. A central concern is the relation between religion and politics in India, and their expression in terms of landscape – and much of the chapter's interest is given by subsequent events, including the destruction of the Babri Mosque in Ayodhya in 1992, and all that followed from this act. Yet this is dealt with in a single, passing mention. This seems unfortunate, since a fuller account might have been an excellent way of updating events which do, after all, go back fifteen years. Without such contextualiz-ing detail the chapter becomes a historical account whose relation to the funda-mentally changed political landscape of the present can only be inferred.

Bohlin writes of familiar territory, and of landscapes which are important to me – Kalk Bay, South Africa – where I lived for a period in the 1980s, and where I live now. Her interest, rightly, is in memories of the Group Areas removals, a traumatic series of events which reconfigured the city over twenty years, leaving damaged landscapes and damaged lives in their wake. Her interviews turned up interesting material: there are passages here on the sea (and the livelihoods which derive from it), on metaphors of sickness and health, and on the trauma and loss of removal. As with other chapters, there is a conception of landscape as socially produced, but she goes on to make the point that this spatiality is never fixed, but is open to contestation and transformation. Bohlin's central concern is to take issue with the notion of Kalk Bay's exceptionalism – the idea that Kalk Bay escaped the worst ravages of apartheid, or that it somehow presents something different to the communities around it. And while I agree with her substantially, it is on this point that I would like to qualify her account. Yes, it suffered removals; yes, it is a damaged place; but, yes, it remains a special and exceptional place.

I shall base my claim on two grounds. First, on numbers and statistics; and second, on memory – that is to say, on my memory: I remember it as an exceptional place. First the numbers. The scale and extent of forced removals in surrounding communities make their experience qualitatively different to that of Kalk Bay. In the neighbouring Simon's Town, an area in which I did some work in the late 1980s, fully half of the town's residents were forcibly removed as a result of the Group Areas Act. In Kalk Bay some 120 individuals were affected, or around one quarter of the original community. Crucially, partly as a result of the existence of the fishermen's flats, it remained one of the very few racially-mixed residential areas in Cape Town in the 1970s and 1980s – a fact of the foremost significance. Apartheid was nothing if not thorough. It liked clear boundaries – its impatience with the betwixt-and-between was legendary. The bureaucrats who gave us the notions of 'disqualified people' and 'surplus people' also gave us the notion of the 'grey area' – and Kalk Bay remained a grey area *par excellence*. Its mere existence, strung out on an arm of the peninsula, suggested dangerous potentials for mixing and melding, glimpses of an alternative reality – or at least, that is how I remember it to have been.

Now the shops along the main road are given over to antiques. Busloads of French and German tourists clog the parking lot on weekends. My daughter plays in the park that stands on the site of 'die dam'. Like everyone else in this country we are looking to the future, even as we try to come to terms with the damage wrought by the past.

Butler's interest is in the cultural inscription of place – more particularly, in the manner in which Alexandria and Old Heliopolis have been constructed through an overlapping series of narratives as 'an exile of the imagination'. I had the pleasure of hearing Butler present on a related topic at a previous meeting (at the WAC Intercongress in Brac, Croatia, in May 1988) and this chapter does not disappoint. Her strength is her ability to move deftly between competing contexts, and to negotiate multiple literatures and complex readings. Egypt's place in successive traditions is explored, from the colonial imagination (Orientalists, Egyptologists), to the post-colonial imagination (Afrocentrists such as Martin Bernal), to the postmodern imagination (recent Derrida, and an interest in the figure of the 'Egyptian'). She takes on the work of the Personal Landscape Group (most famous member: Lawrence Durrell), and Cheikh Anta Diop.

The chapter's weakness is of a different order. It is bracketed in interesting ways, beginning and ending with passages from Said, who writes, in what amounts to a kind of visceral cry: 'Exile is strangely compelling to think about but terrible to experience. It is the unhealable rift forced between a human being and a native place, between self and its true home: its essential sadness can never be surmounted.' Yet, in the chapter itself, Butler proves strangely reluctant (or unable) to deal with this. I want to suggest that this is, first and foremost, a weakness of method – that her fleetness of attention, her very lightness of touch, makes it difficult to engage in the ways that Said requires. Where identities are 'staged' (or 'enacted'), heritage 'constructed', homelands 'imagined' (or 'imaginary'), subjects 'positioned', what remains of the essential and the true? (and examine Said's language: a 'native place', a 'true home', an 'essential sadness'). Butler writes: 'The gulf between manicured heritage spaces and the desperate experiences of rootlessness, fear, violence, the acts of mass deportations and detentions – 'the perilous territory of non-belonging' . . . is one that, in a global culture, demands the recognition and responsibility of all.' I couldn't agree more. The question remains: How is this done?

Dawson and Johnson's double-hander breaks new ground. Rather than situations of migration and exile *per se*, their interest is in 'situations in which the *imagining* of migration and exile become constitutive parts of the construction and experience of place and landscape' – that is to say, their interest is in 'cognitive movement' and 'vicarious movements' rather than 'actual physical movement'. Their beef, if I have this correctly, is that 'writing on exile continues to authorize a particular group of individuals – the exiled, the migrant, etc. as bearers of a particular kind of existential truth'. They develop their interest via two case-studies, one set in Ashington, North-east England, the other in Hue, Vietnam. The strength of the chapter is to suggest the negotiability of personal identity – the weaknesses, unfortunately, are abundant. Consider this passage by Dawson: 'In essence, while these people face conditions of fixity, like many others, I suspect, they engage cognitively in movement. Furthermore, we may be able to describe fixity and movement as interdependent modalities.' Or this one by Johnson, writing of his female protagonist: 'First of all, having chosen to live in Hue, not desiring to move, not having physically moved, does not mean to say that she experiences no movement.' Well . . .

Dubow takes us back to the Cape of Good Hope, this time in its guise as a British Colony in the nineteenth century. Her interests are in travel-writing and narrative (in the form of the journal) – or, as she has it, in the familiar 'triangulation' of travel, territory and text – but with a difference; for her interests are not so much with consciousness as with embodiment. She writes: 'My aim is to understand the travelling body as a matter of various perceptual and practical competencies: to focus on the drifting mass of the subject's sensory surfaces as well as on the meanings of the physical world that surround it.' With this in mind she produces some marvellous passages: on travel by sea, for example, and on the first sighting of Table Mountain ('an object lesson in optical rhetoricity'). Her analytical eye is as unrestrained as her language – which only occasionally slips out of control; as in this passage on Table Mountain, for example: 'With its play in granite of architectonic horizontals and verticals it stands as the exemplar of the measure and measurable quality'. There is also a thoughtful passage on travel by ox-wagon.

The strength of the chapter is to suggest a means by which we might move beyond a system in which our understandings of spatial perception issue from 'the fashioning of representational systems', to one in which attention is drawn to the body and the individual sensorium ('a body at close range with the ground and cohering with it', as she has it) – which is potentially far more interesting. The weaknesses are twofold. First, in a tendency to overinterpret. Every statement is pounced on, and wrung for meaning; and interesting as the sources are, my impression is that they do not stand up this kind of incessant attention. This tendency runs through a number of chapters in the collection – something to do with lively minds being directed towards an insufficiently adequate object, perhaps? A more serious criticism relates to the scale of her ambitions. In straining after the universal, Dubow draws freely on sources from 1820 to 1890, and from visitors bound for Cape Town to settlers bound for the colony's eastern frontier, 1,000 kilometres away. The point is that the Cape Colony of the 1820s was a very different place to that of the 1890s – socially, politically, economically and spatially. For one thing, the mineral revolution of the 1870s and 1880s had served to upgrade its transport routes, and to change it economic base from an agrarian economy to the mining and industry-based economy – with a proletarianized working class – that it would shortly become. The deeper point is that bodies and sensoria are themselves historically contextualized and geographically situated. To suggest that this chapter might rather have been written as a history of embodied experience would be to begin to grapple with the finer texture of the South African landscape, and the sources which relate to it.

By way of final comment I want to return to the issue of disciplinary grounding. Again, as an archaeologist, the question that I want to put to each of the contributors is this: What would your material look like in relation to archaeology? Or: how might the themes of movement, exile, dispossession, cultural construction and the longing for home he addressed through the collection of methods, techniques and forms of practice which we have come to associate with the discipline of archaeology – in particular, how might they be addressed through excavation? This is a question which most of the chapters pass over (the exceptions are Butler and Winer), but it seems to me worth asking, if only because of the framing of the collection within the broader context of the discipline.

Let me give an example. In 1999, partly in response to the challenge thrown out by the fourth World Archaeological Congress to develop a more contextually, relevant archaeological practice in South Africa, I initiated a public archaeology project focused on school teachers and learners in the Western Cape, under the auspices of the Research Unit for the Archaeology of Cape Town. This is a double-handed project which combines a programme of learner-assisted excavation, with the production of web-based teaching and learning resources for use in Curriculum 2005, the new outcomes-based curriculum which is currently being implemented in South African schools. One of the pleasing symmetries of the project is that it involves teachers and learners in the production and interpretation of archaeological material on a case-study basis, which is then fed back into school curriculum. Our first project was in the small rural town of Genadendal, but our second project – which is the one that I want to talk about – was at Grove Primary School, in the plush suburb of Claremont, just down the road from the University.

Grove School is something of a model in the area, both in terms of its attractive and well laid-out grounds, and in terms of its tolerant and enlightened governing body and racially-mixed student body – still by no means the norm in South African education. Yet, the recent past of the school is intimately tied to a history of dispossession and forced removal. In the late 1960s the area in which the school is situated was declared a white group area. Over the course of the following few years hundreds of coloured families were forcibly removed, and their houses made available to whites at knock-down prices. Grove School underwent a programme of rebuilding in anticipation of the influx of white families. A block of houses adjacent to the school was acquired and the land cleared to make way for a hockey field, which became the latest of the school's impressive facilities.

The point is that when we went to excavate in the school grounds there was no mention of these events in either the official histories or the school's own memory, which was focused on a distant colonial past. In a way which is not unusual in South African life, they formed a buried transcript, an institutionally-repressed fragment of a past which is both painful and unresolved. In this case, the mechanics of excavation – the physical process whereby a group of school learners lifted the sod and recovered a set of artefacts and features dating back thirty years – provided the key which enabled the school community, some of whose families are among those who were forcibly removed, to open discussion around a traumatic series of events.

Ours is a society in which archaeological metaphors abound. Normality is a skin through which the deeds of the past threaten to erupt. We carry the unquiet dead with us, and everybody has his or her story of dispossesion and institutional violence. Landscape, as any number of painters have remarked, is a matter of surfaces. But by dipping beneath the surface, archaeology has the power to subvert the composed and sunlit scene, the green field with its scurrying figures, hockey-sticks raised. My comment to the contributors is that it is by such means, rather than by a kind of forced application of theory, that we drag archaeology into the province of a broader and more interesting set of questions, contexts and disputes.

It becomes a matter, for the ambitious and imaginative practitioner, of remaining both close to the earth and far from home.

References

Bernstein, H. 1994. *The Rift: The Exile Experience of South Africans.* London: Jonathan Cape.

Tilley, C. 1994. *A Phenomenology of Landscape: Places, Paths and Monuments.* Oxford: Berg.

Responses to Nick Shepherd's Comments

Anna Bohlin replies

Places of Longing and Belonging: Memories of the Group Area Proclamation of a South African Fishing Village

I recently gave a talk on the Group Area (GAA) proclamation at a meeting of the Historical Association of Kalk Bay. In the discussion afterwards, a Kalk Bay resident expressed concerns similar to those raised by Shepherd. He urged people to appreciate the fishing community's fight against the proclamation, and to celebrate the highly unusual racially mixed history of Kalk Bay. I certainly do not wish to detract from or deny the validity of such a view. Nevertheless, at the same meeting and after my presentation of the numbers of people affected by the GAA, several people still expressed the view that nobody was forced out of Kalk Bay. The audience on this occasion also comprised former residents who had been forced to move under the GAA. Understandably, they were upset by these remarks, and confronted the speakers by telling them their version of the story. Most of the time, however, when the history of Kalk Bay is spoken about, exhibited or explained to journalists, victims of removal are not present to provide an alternative viewpoint.

Perhaps precisely because of its dramatic position in the landscape, its evocative history and quaint village character, there is a danger that a groundswell of positive memories of Kalk Bay sweeps over the negative ones – the landscape seems to beg a single, unclouded history to match its splendour. Insofar as the experiences of those who were moved are denied, their pain is exacerbated. The challenge seems to be to embrace the tales of both victimization and resistance, as well as the nuanced experiences in between.

Beverly Butler Replies

Egypt: Constructed Exiles of the Imagination

Shepherd's comments correctly identify the two key movements in my chapter. The first, an exploration of the attempts to inscribe memory on place, makes specific reference to the landscapes of Alexandria and Heliopolis as 'exiles of the imagination'. Here, for example, I set against the Western colonial imagination's inscription of Alexandria as 'Capital of Memory' alternative attempts to appropriate and empower. A significant inclusion here, one omitted by Shepherd, is my emphasis on *Egyptian* authors' attempts to 'narrate' nation and the tensions and ambivalences of this project.

The second movement, by way of contrast, shifts its focus to experiences of exile as violent dispossession and to contexts in which attempts at narrativization and inscription are disabled by trauma. I introduce Said's concept of the 'triumphant ideology' as a means to explore the 'gulf' between attempts to 'work through' the symptoms of exile (the successful narrativization of a 'return to Egypt') and the inability of others to appeal to this form of memory work in order to 'reconstitute their broken lives'.

In my conclusion, I recast the 'gulf' between the ability and inability to work through conditions of exile as analogous to the 'gulf' between the 'manicured heritage sites' and 'territory of non-belonging' which, I assert, 'demands the recognition and responsibility of all'. Rather than evincing a 'strange reluctance' or 'inability' to 'engage in the ways Said requires', in solidarity with Said I understand that the response to the question – how is it to be done? – is to be answered by a commitment to assuming a central position in attempts to translate and transform experiences of trauma (as failed memory), pain and silence into narratives of belonging, wholeness, healing and regeneration. What is more, the current increase in demand for heritage, archaeology and landscape as 'resources' for memory work particularizes this responsibility for those engaging in these and related areas.

Jessica Dubow Replies

Rites of Passage: Travel and the Material Body at the Cape of Good Hope

Exercises in interdisciplinarity are always a good way of testing how academics look at their objects and at each other. From his comments, it seems that Nick Shepherd concurs with my general aim to retrieve within a colonial history an analytic of bodily experience: to add sentience to our notions of self and subjectivity, and to understand this realm as properly preceding the orders of representation and epistemology.

Shepherd's criticisms, however, are angled by a methodology somewhat different from my own. For, on the one hand, as he points out, a phenomenological account can be seen to entail a universalism and tempt us to trace, within a perceptual body, the terms of its historical invariance. On the other hand, it is by rejecting all idealisms in order to plunge the body back into experience that phenomenology sees the body as implicitly situated and socialized, as relative to all kinds of conditions and commitments. As such, it is precisely the connection between the space of the body and the time of culture that this chapter has been concerned.

A social history of the kind that Shepherd invokes has valuable things to say about the developments and discretions of political, cultural and economic contexts. Thus, as he says, the Cape Colony of the 1820s and that of the 1890s may afford a very different system of correspondence between modes of action and various sensory fields. However, travellers across this period share not only a common special experience but also common forms of expression. It is this that binds these changing social fields within a broader timescale. Further, it raises the more profound question of the difference between historical sensitivity and a historicist faith in universal experience and its definitive ruptures.

Here too lies the difference between interpretation and indulgent flights of fancy.

Marzia Balzani Replies

Pilgrimage and Politics in the Desert of Rajasthan

My thanks to Nick Shepherd for his careful reading of my chapter on pilgrimage in Rajasthan. I fully agree, in one sense, that more detail on the relation between politics and religion in India would have been a useful way of updating the events that took place fifteen years ago. The main reason for excluding this material was, of course, the 5000-word limit and, in the end, it was not central enough to the pilgrimage itself to warrant inclusion in such a short chapter. The other, more academic reason for the exclusion was based on a sense of trying to do justice to the ethnography and the ethnographic present as it was in the late 1980s and early 1990s (pre-Ayodhya) in Jodhpur. To include this material would have been to rethink the pilgrimage with the benefit of hindsight and a knowledge of events that were not imagined at the time the pilgrimage took place. While this is perfectly acceptable, and is indeed something I have done in the book I have written based on my ethnography, the inclusion of the highly complex local political situation would have made for a very different article indeed. To reduce the level of political complexity and detail in order to include a paragraph or two on the political context post-1986 would have failed to do justice to the situation and risked seriously misrepresenting the events as they unfolded after 1986. I chose, therefore, to write a piece which is very firmly located in its time and the comments in passing about the events which took place years later are included simply to suggest that there is a broader context and that the events of 1986 were a small and local part of a more complex and still unfolding whole.

Mark Johnson Replies

Migration, Exile and Landscapes of the Imagination

Nick Shepherd, as the reviewer, suggests that our chapter highlights the negotiability of personal identity, but seemingly does not appreciate the full political import of our decision to highlight the cognitive and vicarious movements of individuals over and above that of actual physical movement. Why point out that elderly individuals in Ashington or women in Hue, Vietnam, experience cognitive movement and that these imaginings are constitutive of their actual experiences and active constructions of place and landscape? Because in social-science theorizing as in the real world these are precisely the individuals who are daily confronted not only with social and physical constraints on their mobility, but also with discourses which construct them as fixed and docile bodies lacking in both agency and imagination. In the headlong rush to embrace and interrogate 'movement' and 'movers' we cannot ignore the vicarious and imagined movement of individuals who, whether through choice or compulsion, cannot or do not wish to physically move. To do otherwise is simply to reinscribe the same old sedentarist hierarchies within the new idiom of mobility and travel.

Index

aborigines
  Australian, 71–85 *passim,* 189
    relationship to land, 74–5, 83
Acropolis
  see Greece, Acropolis
Afghanistan, 349
Africa
  decolonization, 308
  see Angola, Egypt, Namibia, South Africa
African National Congress, 1
Afrocentrism, 303, 308–11, 353
airports, 9
Alexandria
  see Egypt, Alexandria
Alkalay, Ammiel, 235–6, 237
Amutana, Selma, 294–5
Anafiotika
  see Greece, Anafiotika
Andes
  see Peru, Andes
Angola, 349
anthropology, 350
  approaches to identity, 334–6
  approaches to migration and exile, 320
Apache identity and landscape, 344
apartheid, 296–7, 349, 352–3
  and landscape, 285
Appiah, Anthony, 349
Arafat, Yassar, 234
Arbel, B, 235, 236
  archeological practice, 355–7
  archaeology, 350–1, 355–7, 360
  and colonialism, 170–1
  and historiography, 258–9
  and imperialism, 170–1, 185
  and nationalism, 169–71, 185, 186
  and postmodernism, 166–7, 169, 173–4, 185
  and tourism, 184
  Australian

Ross Factory Archaeology Project, 104–17
  passim
battlefield, 47–9
British, 170, 171
Egypt, 308, 313–14
English, 186
European Neolithic
  domesticity in interpretations of, 171–3,
    185
  impact of contemporary society and
    discourse on, 165–74 *passim,* 185
  importance of agriculture to, 185
  importance of monuments to, 171–2
  importance of ritual and ceremony to,
    171–2
  mobility model, 168–9, 171, 173–4,
    184–5, 186
  recent accounts of, 165–74 *passim,* 184–5,
    185
gendered practice of, 172–3
Greek, 21–32 *passim*
Irish, 88, 95, 149–65 *passim,* 167–74 *passim,*
  185–6, 192
political economy of, 192
relationship to landscape, 350
relationship to movement and exile, 350
architecture, 4
  and social hierarchy, 106
  colonial, in South Africa, 261–7
  vernacular, 261
Aristotle, 241
Ashington
  see England, Ashington
Athens
  see Greece, Athens
Atherstone, William Guybon, 248
Auge, M, 9, 173
Australia, 69–85, 103–17
  aborigines, 71–85 *passim,* 182, 189

relationship to land, 74–5, 83
conservation, 75, 76, 79–84 *passim*
convicts, 103–17 *passim,* 190
  female factory system, 104
  Ross Factory Archaeology Project, 104–17
    passim
  Ross Female Factory, 104–17, 183, 184,
    190
  black market economy, 111–17, 183,
    190
  gender relations within, 107, 109–10
  hierarchy within, 106–11, 117
mining, 71, 77–84 *passim,* 182
Mitchell River Watershed, 72–3, 182,
  189–90
Mitchell River Watershed Catchment
  Management Group, 70–85 *passim,* 182,
  189–90
pastoralism, 71, 75–83 *passim*
Queensland, 69–85
subcultures in Far North Queensland, 70–85
  passim
Tasmania, 103–17
tourism, 72, 75, 81, 83–4, 189

Babri Mosque, 352
Bagenal, Marshall, 97
Bain, Andrew Geddes, 246–7
Barak, Ehud, 234, 235
Barkai, Ron, 235
Barthes, Roland, 334–5
Bartlett, Richard, 91–5, 97, 99
Basso, K. H, 212–13, 344
battlefields
  Scottish, 340
  see also Western Front, battlefields; tourism,
    battlefield
Bedouin, 182–3
  children as cultural brokers, 126–31
  economy, 122–3
  effects of economic change on, 121–31
    passim, 183
  nomadism, 124
  women, 121, 123–6, 130–1
beliefs
  Andean, 198–203 *passim*
  Chinese, 57–8
  Mongolian, 56–66 *passim*

Benjamin, Walter, 242
Bennington, Geoff, 310
Berger, John, 10–11
Bergson, Henri, 341
Bernal, Martin, 353
  Black Athena, 310
Bernstein, Hilda
  *The Rift: The Exile Experience of South
    Africans,* 349–50
Bhabha, Homi, 13
Bharatiya Janata Party (BJP), 212
Biko, Steve, 267
Binford, Lew, 351
boat people, 324
Bourdieu, Pierre, 203–4, 340
Bradley, R, 166
Braudel, F, 258
Brú na Bóinne
  see Ireland, Brú na Bóinne
bypass roads
  see Palestine, Occupied Territories, bypass
    roads

cairns *(oboo)*
  Mongolian, 55–62 *passim,* 66
    Banner (Hushuun) Oboo, 62
Cambodia, 349
Camden, William, 91
Cape of Good Hope
  see South Africa, Cape of Good Hope
Carter, Paul, 242
cartography, 99
  English, in early modern Ireland, 90–5, 99
  see also maps
Cavafy, Constantine, 305, 306
Chalmers, William, 267
Cheah, Pheng, 13
Chetwit, Sami, 237
Childe, Gordon, 185
China
  see Mongolia, Inner
Chinese, in Inner Mongolia
  see Mongolia, Inner, Chinese in
city plans, 26–7
Clarke, David, 351
class relations
  and local identity in Ashington, England,
    321–4 *passim*

Ocongate, Peru, 204
Clifford, James, 8, 9, 13, 14, 242
Cohen, R, 336–7
Coleman, S and Elsner, J, 345
colonialism, 4, 14, 15
  Australia, 76
  Egypt, 303, 305, 353
  Ireland, 88–99, 159, 161
    use of cartography in, 90–5, 99
  Namibia, 289–94 *passim*
  Peru, 200
  South Africa, 241–54 *passim,* 257–68, 275
  Vietnam, 324
conservation
  Australia, 75, 76, 79–84 *passim*
convicts
  see Australia, convicts
crannogs, 88, 95–9
Cultural Revolution, 59, 63

Dayan, Moshe, 232–3
de Certeau, Michel, 242, 247, 253
deconstruction, 303, 310, 311, 313
Delagorgue, Adulphe, 242, 246
Deleuze, Gilles and Guattari, Felix, 8, 243,
  247, 251
Derrida, Jacques, 310, 353
Deutscher, Isaac, 12
diaspora, 8–10, 320, 336–7, 346
  experiential accounts of, 9–10
  Scottish, 333–43 *passim*
    'Homecomings project,' 335–6, 346
Diop, Cheikh Anta, 308–10, 353
direction
  Mongolian ideas of, 65–6
displaced persons, 349
Douglas, Keith, 305, 307
drought, Rajasthan, 211–14 *passim,* 221
Durrell, Lawrence, 305, 306, 314, 353
  Alexandrian Quartet, 307

Eagleton, Terry, 174
economic migrants
  African, 9
  see also gast-arbeiter, Turkish; migrant
    workers
Egypt, 303–15, 353–4, 360
  Alexandria, 304–7, 312, 353, 360

  ancient, 305–6
  modern, 305, 313
  and Black African history, 308–11
  archaeology, 308, 313–14
  association with death, 307
  colonialism, 305, 353
  cultural revivalism, 313–14
  Dahab, Sinai, 121–31
  El-Alamein, 307, 314
  Heliopolis, 307–11, 314, 353, 360
  heritage, 303, 304, 308, 312, 313, 354
  internal conflicts, 313
  literature, 312–13
  modern, 311–13
  nationalism, 312
  negative comparison with Greece, 306–7
  neo-colonialism, 313–14
  Suez Canal, 307
  tourism, 303, 313–14
  see also Bedouin; Personal Landscape Group
empire
  and landscape, 14
England, 133–47, 321–4
  Ashington, 321–4, 354, 362
    conflict over representation of the
      community, 321–4
  Forestry Commission, 134–5, 139–47
    passim
    gender relations in, 146
  New Forest, 133–47, 183–4
    brochures depicting, 140–1
    competing identities in, 135
    competing perceptions of, 144–7
    competing proposals for new conservation
      plan, 141–5
    debates over future use, 133
    history of, 134–5
    images of, 136–7
    maps of, 137–9, 145
    tourism, 133, 136–41
    visual representations of, 136–41
environmentalism
  see Australia, conservation
Eritrea, 349
European Neolithic
  see archaeology, European Neolithic
exile, 303–15 *passim,* 319–30 *passim,* 349–62
  passim

narration of as resistance, 304–7
Exodus, 311

Fedden, Robin, 305, 306
   White Country, 307
Finch, John, 242–3
Forestry Commission
   see England, Forestry Commission
Forster, E. M., 305, 306
Freud, Sigmund, 310–11, 341

Garb, Yakov, 226
gast-arbeiter
   Turkish, 10–11
Gaza Strip
   see Palestine, Gaza Strip
gender
   and archaeology, 172–3
gender relations
   Bedouin, 123–31 *passim*
   in the Forestry Commission, England, 146
geography, symbolic
   Inka, 199–200
Ghosh, Amitav, 235, 236–7
Giddens, A, 344
Gilroy, Paul, 13
Glassie, H, 166
globalization
   and identity, 334
Godlonton, Robert, 241
Golden, D, 231
Graburn, N, 345
Great Wall of China, 57, 58, 60
Greece, 21–32
   Acropolis, 21–32 *passim*
   Anafiotika, 22–32, 183, 184, 191
   celebrations, 30–1
   chapel of St. Symeon, 30
   media representations of, 27
   narratives of, 29–32
      treatment of space in, 30–1
      physical interventions in, 27–9
   Athens, 21, 23, 27, 30
      Plaka, 25, 27
   importance to Personal Landscape Group,
      305–7
   Ministry of Culture, 29
   see also archaeology, Greek

Halbwachs, M, 339
Hamukoshi, Louisa, 295
Handelman, Don and Lea, 231–2
Hegel, G. F., 246
Heidegger, Martin, 244
heritage, 5, 23, 77, 78, 104, 184, 321, 324, 342,
   360
   African, 309
   Australian, 77, 78, 104
   Egyptian, 303, 304, 308, 312, 313, 354
   Irish, 151–61*passim*
   New Forest as English, 135
   Scottish, 339, 344, 346
   Vietnamese, 325–7
   World War I battlefields as, 49
Hishongwa, Ndeutala
   Marrying Apartheid, 296–7
Hiyalwa, Kaleni
   'The baby's baby,' 298
   Meekulu's Children, 300
Hodder, I, 170, 172
holocaust, 229, 230, 311
hooks, bell, 6, 7
Hue
   see Vietnam, Hue
human remains
   see Western Front, treatment of human
      remains
Huntingdon, Samuel, 232
Hussein, Taha
   The Future of Culture in Egypt, 312
Hutton, P. H., 340

identity
   and globalization, 334
   and pilgrimage, 345–6
   and place, 341–4
   anthropological approaches to, 334–6
   Apache, 344
India, 211–22
   Bharatiya Janata Party (BJP), 212
   caste, 212, 219–20
   maharaja, reinvention of the role of, 212
   Muslims, 212, 219–20
   Rajasthan, 211–14, 351–2, 361–2
      climate, 213
      drought, 211–14 *passim*, 221
      famine, 213–14

irrigation, 214
religion and politics in, 352, 361–2
tourism, 212
see also Jodhpur, H. H.; Ramdevji
Inka
see Peru, Inka
International Union of Pre and Protohistoric
Sciences, 1
internationalism, socialist, 322–4 *passim*
Intifada. *see* Palestine, Intifada
Iraq, 349
Ireland, 87–99, 149–62, 174
archaeology, 152, 156–74 *passim*
Brú na Bóinne, 149–62, 168
altering of signposts, 154–6
public disputes over, 153–4
representations of, 152–3
socio-economy of, 152–8
visitor centre, 151–8 *passim*
Céide Fields, 168
Celtic Revival, 87
changing image of, 158–9
colonialism in, 88–99
English perceptions of the Gaelic
settlement, 89–95
use of cartography, 90–5, 99
crannogs, 88, 95–9
destruction of, 95–8
early modern, 88–99
Gaelic pastoralists, 90
Gaelic settlement landscape, 89–95
Great Famine, 87
heritage, 156–60 *passim*
commodification of, 160–2
national identity and landscape, 87–8
neo-traditionalism, 158–60
plantation of, 88–9, 98
post-colonialism, 170
socio-economic changes, 158–60
tourism, 152–9 *passim*
importance to the economy, 159–60
Israel, 225–38 *passim*
memorials, 232
Museum of the Diaspora, Tel Aviv, 231–2
nationalism, 229, 232, 237
landscape and, 226
separation from Palestinian territories,
232–8 *passim*

tourism, 238
war (1948), 232
war (1967), 232
see also Palestine

Jabotinsky, Vladimir, 232
Jews
expulsion from Spain, 229–30, 231
Middle-Eastern (Misrahi), 235–8
passim
Jodhpur, H. H. (Rathor Rajput Maharaja of
Jodhpur), 211–22 *passim*, 352

Kamati, Mekulu Mukwahongo Ester, 299
Kambouroglou, Demetrius, 25
Kattan, Naim, 236
Kavanagh, Patrick, 87
Keane, John B.
The Field, 87
Kedouri, E, 229, 230
Kerby, A. P., 342
Kincaid, Jamaica, 7
Komito, L, 173
Koumanoudis, Stephanos, 25

landholding
Peru, 207–8
landscape
agency of, 198–209 *passim*
and apartheid, 280, 285
and colonization, 14
and commerce, 197–209 *passim*
and empire, 14
and English national identity, 186
and exile, 303–15 *passim*
and history, 4–5
and human identity, 182–4
and identity in South Africa, 276–82
and law, 4
and memory, 4–5, 42, 274–5
and modernity, 7
and nationalism, 226
and ritual, 211
and war, 37–50, 182
approaches to
anthropological, 8
culturalist, 197
phenomenological, 5–8, 9, 133, 361

as historical palimpsest in South Africa,
266–7
as relational structure, 181–3
Bedouin, 121–31
Chinese views of, 55–61 *passim*, 64, 66–7,
181
colonial perception of, 249
commodification of, 190
contested, 3–14, 181–7, 198
definitions of, 3–4, 181–2
discourses of authenticity and, 183–4, 191
Gaelic settlement, 89–95
historicity of, 197
Mongolian views of, 55–67 *passim*, 181
movement through Andean, 206–8
Neolithic, 165–74
of fear in South Africa, 264–6
of movement and exile, 3–15
of separation in Israel/Palestine, 225–38
passim
painting, 40
penal, 103–17 *passim*
politics of, 1–2
prehistoric, in Ireland, 149–62, 165–74, 192
Rajasthani, 213, 352
social construction of, 352
Western understanding of, 197
critiques, 197–8
Levi-Strauss, Claude
Tristes Tropiques, 241–2
Levinas, E, 310
Lewis, Wyndham, 40
Liberia, 349
life stories, 342
liminality, 319–20, 330
literature
Egyptian, 312–13
Owambo women's, 289–300
see also Personal Landscape Group; travel
narratives
Lochnagar Crater
see Western Front, Lochnagar Crater
Lord, John Keats
At Home in the Wilderness, 249
Lord, W. B. and Baines, Thomas
*Shifts and Expedients of Cape Life, Travel
and Exploration,* 251–2
Lovell, N, 334

Lowenthal, David, 186

MacIntyre, Alasdair, 342
MacLennan, Hugh, 343–4
Scotsman's Return (1961), 344
Mali, 349
Mandela, Nelson, 267
Manning, Olivia, 306
maps, 4, 26–7, 40–2
English, of Ireland, 90–5, 99
of New Forest, England, 137–9, 145
trench, 41
World War I
zones rouges, 41, 42
see also cartography
McNeil, Jean
Hunting Down Home, 333–4
Mekulu Mukwahongo Ester Kamati, 299
memorials
Israeli, 232
World War I, 46
memory,
landscape and, 4–5
Mercouri, Melina, 29
Merleau-Ponty, Maurice, 247
migrant workers, 9
and gender, 12
Andean, 202, 204, 207, 209
Egyptian, 124
ethnographies of, 12
from the Cyclades, 22
Indian, 11
Owambo, 290, 294
Palestinian, 233, 238
Peru, 200
Turkish, 10–11
migrants
Caribbean, 13
Jewish, 12
women, 12
migration, 10, 319–30 *passim,* 349–62
passim
mining
in Australia, 71, 77–84 *passim*
modernity, 84, 124, 152, 153, 160, 182,
189–90, 215, 246, 247, 344, 349
landscape and, 7
Mongolia, Inner, 55–67, 181–2

Chinese in, 55–67 *passim*
Chinese military activity in, 58–9, 66–7
   see also Cultural Revolution
monumental sites, 23, 24, 30, 32, 168, 172,
   303, 304, 313
   importance of in interpretations of European
      Neolithic, 171–2
   Inka, 207
   Ireland, 149–62
   Vietnam, 325
   see also Greece, Acropolis
Morinis, A, 345
Moryson, Fynes, 91
movement, global, 8–13
Mozambique, 349
Myanmar, 349

Naipaul, V. S., 13
Namhila, Ellen, 290
   The Price of Freedom, 298–9
Namibia, 289–300
   colonialism, 289–94 *passim*
   ethnography, 290–2
   gender relations, 290, 294
   literature, 293–4
   matrilineal kinship, 291, 298, 300
   migrant workers, 290, 294
   Owambo women's literature, 289–300
      passim
      group songs *(Oudano),* 295–6, 298
      oral, 292, 299
      Song of Chief Iipumbu, 293–4, 296
   women
      marginalization of Owambo, 289–91
narrative, 342–3
   and identity, 335
   see also life stories
Nash, Paul, 40
national identity, 232
   and landscape, 87–8
   and separation, 232
   and space, 24
   Egyptian, 312
   Irish, 169, 170, 171
   modern Greek, 23
nationalism, 229, 230
   and archaeology, 169–71
   English, 170

Israeli, 226, 229–37*passim*
Neolithic
   see archaeology, European Neolithic
Netanyahu, Benyamin, 233
New Forest
   see England, New Forest
nomadism, 168, 320
   and postmodernity, 186
   Bedouin, 124
   Rajasthani, 214
Nomadology, 8
nomads
   Mongolian, 7
   see also Bedouin
Nora, Pierre, 339, 341
   see also sites of memory

O'Flaherty, Liam, 87
Ocongate
   see Peru, Ocongate
Olwig, K and Hastrup, K, 334

Palestine, 225–38 *passim*
   Gaza Strip
      fencing in of, 233
      Intifada, 233, 237
      labour force, 233
      migrant workers, 238
   Occupied Territories
      bypass roads, 225–31*passim,* 237
      El Aroub refugee camp, 227
      permeability of borders, 232–4
      regimes of separation in, 225–6
      regulation of movement in, 226, 232–5
      separation from Israel, 232–5
      uneven development, 232–5, 237–8
      West Bank settlements, 229, 230
   tourism, 226, 238
Palestinians, displaced, 349
Pan-Africanism, 308
Parkin, D, 11
pastoralism
   Bedouin, 124
   Gaelic, 90
   in Australia, 71, 75–83 *passim*
penal colonies
   Australia, 103–17
Personal Landscape Group, 304–7, 353

Egypt compared negatively with Greece,
306–7
importance of Greece to, 305–7
Personal Landscape, 304–5
Peru, 197–209
Andes, 197–209 *passim*
colonialism, 200
Inka, 199, 207
symbolic geography, 199–200
land ownership, 202–3, 207–8
migrant workers, 200–9 *passim*
Ocongate, 200–9 *passim*
class relations, 204
economy, 200–4
ritualized performance of trade, 205
shrine of the Senor de Qoyllorrit'i, 205
women, 207
see also beliefs, Andean; landscape, agency
of; landscape, movement through; ritual,
Andean
photography
aerial, 40–2
battlefield, 40–1
pilgrimages, 352, 361–2
and tourism, 345–6
Andean, 205
of H. H. Jodhpur, 211–22 *passim*
Rajasthani, 7
search for identity as, 345–6
to World War I battlefields, 43–4
place
and national identity, 24, 341–4
approaches to, 21
Irish sense of, 87
see also space
Plaka
see Greece, Athens, Plaka
policing, 4
political economy
and archaeology, 192
post-colonialism, 303, 353
Irish, 170
postmodernism, 303, 313, 335, 339–44 *passim*
and archaeology, 166–7, 169, 173–4, 185
postmodernity, 153, 160

Queensland
see Australia, Queensland

Rabin, Yizhak, 234
Rajasthan
see India, Rajasthan
Ramdevji, 211, 215–19 *passim*
and caste, 219–20
and drought, 218
shrine, 217–18
Rapport, N and Dawson, A, 334, 338, 342, 346
Reader, I and Walter, T, 345
refugees, 10, 320, 349
Jewish, 12
religion, 31–2
renaming, 4
repatriation, 349
ritual
and landscape, 211
Andean, 198–209 *passim*
Rajasthani, 211, 221
roads
and Israeli historiography, 229–31
Roma, 7
Rousseau, Jean-Jacques
Emile, 250–2
Rwanda, 349

Saadawi, Nawal El, 312–13
Said, Edward, 171, 303, 311, 315, 349, 353–4,
360
Saigon
see Vietnam, Saigon
Sammons, William Layton, 245
Sangren, P.S., 174
Scotland
heritage, 339, 344, 346
Highlands, 338–46 *passim*
tourism, 339
see also diaspora, Scottish
separation
and national identity, 232
Sephton, Hezekiah, 260
Serri, Bracha, 236
Shahal, Moshe, 235
Shamena, Magdalena and Erastus
Wir Kinder Namibias, 297–8
Shaw, William, 260
Sheratt, A, 166
Shikongo, Loide, 293–9 *passim*
shrine

of Ravdeji, 217–18
of the Senor de Qoyllorrit'i, 205
shrines
Mongolian, 55
signposts, 4
Singh, Jaswant, 212
sites of memory, 339–42
slavery, African, 311
Smith, A. D., 229
Smith, Harry, 267
Somalia, 349
South Africa, 1–2, 241–54 *passim,* 257–68,
273–85, 349–61 *passim*
apartheid, 280, 285, 296–7, 349, 352–3
archaeology and historiography, 258–9
Cape Colony, 355, 361
Cape Flats, 276–83 *passim*
Cape of Good Hope, 241–54 *passim,* 354,
360–1
narratives of travel to, 241–54 *passim*
Cape Town, 353
District 6, 2, 274
Claremont, 356
Grove Primary School, 356
colonialism, 241–54 *passim,* 257–68 *passim,*
275
architecture, 261–7
British, 257–66 *passim*
Salem Village, 260–6
Dutch, 257, 259, 261
Dutch East India Company (VOC), 259
economies, 259
Great Cattle Killing Movement (1856-57),
267
Hundred Years War (1779-1870), 257
Sixth Frontier War (1834-35), 264–5, 267
cross country travel
by foot, 250–4 *passim*
by ox wagon, 246–8, 254, 355
disease as social metaphor in, 278
displaced persons, 349
Genadendal, 356
Group Areas Act, 273, 352–3, 356, 359
differing perceptions of in Kalk Bay,
282–5
enforcement in Kalk Bay, 282–5
impact on Kalk Bay, 273–6, 280–5
Kalk Bay, 273–85, 352–3, 359

as healthy landscape, 278, 285
churches, 281–2
fisherman's flats, 283–4, 353
identity tied to landscape, 276–82
mosque, 284
wash house *(die dam),* 284–5
landscape and apartheid, 280
post-apartheid, 267
Simon's Town, 353
Table Mountain, 244–5, 253–4, 355
Windermere, 281
Xhosa, 257, 259–67 *passim*
space
and gender relations, 105–6
and national identity, 24
visual representations of, 26–7
Spain, expulsion of Jews from, 229–31 *passim*
Spencer, Bernard, 305
Spenser, Edmund, 91
subcultures, 69–70, 83
in Far North Queensland, 70–85 *passim*
subjectivity,
colonial, 249
Sydney, Sir Henry, 96–7

Tajikistan, 349
Tasmania
see Australia, Tasmania
Taylor, C, 344
Thomas, J, 166, 169
Tiller, Terence, 305
Tilley, C, 217
Togo, 349
tourism, 15, 346
and archaeology, 184
and pilgrimage, 345–6
Australia, 72, 75, 81–4 *passim,* 189
battlefield, 43–6, 182
Egypt, 121–31 *passim,* 303, 313
England, 136–41
India, 212
Ireland, 152–9 *passim*
New Forest, England, 133
Palestine, 226, 238
Scotland, 339
Vietnam, 325–8 *passim*
trade
ritualized performance of, 205

tradition, 31, 198, 200
transport systems, 4, 7
travel guides, 26–7
travel narratives, 241–54 *passim,* 354–5
Trigger, B, 170
Tringham, R, 172
Turner, J. M. W., 243
Turner, Victor, 330, 345
Tyali (Xhosa chief), 267

UNHCR, 349
Upton, Dell, 261

Van Gennep, A, 330
Viet Kieu, 324–9 *passim*
  longing for return, 327–9 *passim*
Vietnam, 324–9
  boat people, 324
  colonialism, 324
  Hue, 325–9, 354, 362
    as authentic Vietnam, 325–9
  Hue Net (internet site), 325
  Saigon, 327, 328
  tourism, 325–8 *passim*
  war, 324
  see also Viet Kieu
Vikelas, Demetrius, 25

walking, 250–1, 253, 351–2
walls
  Chinese in Inner Mongolia, 55–61 *passim,* 67
    see also Great Wall of China; White Wall
war
  Vietnam, 324
  see also Western Front; World War I; World
    War II

Western Front
  archaeology, 47–9
  battlefields, 38–40, 44
    as heritage, 49
    scavenging of, 47–8
  leisure areas, 47
  Lochnagar Crater, 42
  pilgrimages, 43–4, 182
  reconstructions of 1919-39, 42–3
  representations of 1914-18, 40–2
  tourism, 43–6 *passim,* 182
  treatment of human remains, 47–9
  unexploded ordnance, 37, 39, 46–7, 182
  villages détruits, 47
  see also Ypres
White Wall, 58, 59, 60, 61
Whittle, A, 166
women
  Andean, 207
  Bedouin, 121, 123–6, 130–1
World Archeological Congress, 1999, 1–2, 351,
  355
  South African Delegates to, 1
World War I, 37, 38
  memorials, 46
  revival of interest in during the1960s, 45
  see also Western Front, 37–50
World War II, 45
  transformation of British landscape by, 49

Yates, F, 339
Young, Hugo, 170–1
Ypres, 42–7 *passim*

Zionism
  see also nationalism, Israel, 311

Lightning Source UK Ltd.
Milton Keynes UK
16 July 2010

157046UK00001B/28/P